THE EDIFICE COMPLEX

'Essential reading for anyone who cares about the physical world around them' *Independent*

'Ever wondered why totalinarianism and architectural excess go hand in hand? This book details modern architecture's frequent collusion with the bad guys' *Wallpaper*

'A captivating trawl that take in both the politicians that commissioned the buildings and the architects they employed' *Arena*

'Part history, part anecdote, part polemic . . . His acute eye and ear for bombast, dishonesty, boastfulness and the meretricious wherever it appears, results in a brutally honest description of twentieth-century architects and the way in which, almost invariably, their desire to build outweighs most other considerations' *Architectural Review*

'Well written and entertaining' *Financial Times*

'Sudjic knows that architecture is not just a backdrop to our lives. It matters, and he is able to tell us why, clearly and vividly' *Spectator*

'Astonishing . . . The conventional wisdom that despots and their architects inhabit a hermetic milieu, that they are atypical exceptions, is subtly overturned' *The Times*

'One of the best books on architecture of recent years' *Daily Mail*

Journalist and cultural commentator Deyan Sudjic has been fascinated by the relationship between people and buildings for many years. Born in London to Yugoslav parents, he graduated from the University of Edinburgh with a degree in architecture but, in order to save the world from more leaky and mediocre buildings, chose not to practice but to work instead as a writer, editor, curator and critic. He wrote for the *Sunday Times* and the *Guardian* before launching *Blueprint* magazine as its founding editor. Sudjic currently divides his time between London, where he is architecture critic for the *Observer* and a visiting professor at the Royal College of Art, and Milan, where until recently he edited *Domus*, the international magazine of art, architecture and design.

Deyan Sudjic was also Director of the Venice Architecture Biennale in 2002 and spent four years in Glasgow as the Director of its year as the UK City of Architecture and Design (an achievement that earned him an OBE), and has curated exhibitions at the British Museum (on Norman Foster) and at the McLellan Galleries (on architecture and democracy) as well as shows at the ICA and the Royal Academy. He is the author of the much-praised *100-Miles City*, the best-selling *Architecture Park*, and monographs on John Pawson, Ron Arad and Richard Rogers.

DEYAN SUDJIC

The Edifice Complex

*How the Rich and Powerful
Shape the World*

PENGUIN BOOKS

PENGUIN BOOKS

Published by the Penguin Group
Penguin Books Ltd, 80 Strand, London WC2R ORL, England
Penguin Group (USA) Inc., 375 Hudson Street, New York, New York 10014, USA
Penguin Group (Canada), 90 Eglinton Avenue East, Suite 700, Toronto, Ontario, Canada M4P 2Y3
(a division of Pearson Penguin Canada Inc.)
Penguin Ireland, 25 St Stephen's Green, Dublin 2, Ireland
(a division of Penguin Books Ltd)
Penguin Group (Australia), 250 Camberwell Road, Camberwell, Victoria 3124, Australia
(a division of Pearson Australia Group Pty Ltd)
Penguin Books India Pvt Ltd, 11 Community Centre, Panchsheel Park, New Delhi – 110 017, India
Penguin Group (NZ), cnr Airborne and Rosedale Roads, Albany, Auckland 1310, New Zealand
(a division of Pearson New Zealand Ltd)
Penguin Books (South Africa) (Pty) Ltd, 24 Sturdee Avenue, Rosebank, Johannesburg 2196, South Africa

Penguin Books Ltd, Registered Offices: 80 Strand, London WC2R ORL, England

www.penguin.com

First published by Allen Lane 2005
Published in Penguin Books 2006

1

Typeset by Rowland Phototypesetting Ltd, Bury St Edmunds, Suffolk
Printed in England by Clays Ltd, St Ives plc

ISBN-13: 978-0-141-01672-6
ISBN-10: 0-141-01672-8

Contents

Acknowledgements

The author would like to thank, for their varied help, advice and encouragement, Steve Featherstone of Llewelyn-Davies, Peter Murray of Wordsearch, Zhang Xin and Yang Ho Chang, Alex Linklater, Claire Paterson of Janklow and Nesbitt, Charles Jencks, Stefan McGrath and Will Goodlad at Penguin, Jane Ferguson of the *Observer*, and The Research Library, The Getty Research Institute Los Angeles (980060), for permission to quote from the letters of Philip Johnson; and, in their different ways, Sarah Miller and Olivia Sudjic.

I

Why We Build

I used to keep a photograph torn from a tabloid pinned up over my desk. Through the blotchy newsprint you could make out the blurred image of an architectural model the size of a small car, jacked up to eye level. Left to themselves architects use non-committal shades of grey for their models, but this one was painted in glossy lipstick colours, suggesting it was made to impress a client with an attention span shorter than most.

Strips of cardboard and balsa wood stood in for a mosque with a squat dome fenced in by concentric circles of spiky minarets. The gaudy shapes, and the reduction of an intricate decorative tradition to a cartoon, not much different from a hundred other attempts at having it both ways, tried and failed to be simultaneously boldly modern and respectfully rooted in the past. The questionable architectural details weren't what made it such an unsettling image. What really grabbed my attention was the glimpse of the darker aspects of building that the picture captured. None of the uniformed figures clustered respectfully around the model looked like architects, who usually feature conspicuously in this kind of picture; but there wasn't much doubt about the identity of the thickset man with the heavy moustache, looking disorientatingly like a World War Two British army major in his vintage khaki sweater and beret, or the unblinking fascination with which he was gazing so adoringly at his model.

Saddam Hussein, like many authoritarians, was an enthusiastic patron of architecture. Unlike Napoleon III, however, whose fastidious tastes are still clearly visible in the parade-ground tidiness of the boulevards of Paris, or Mussolini with his contradictory passions for modernism and Caesar Augustus, Hussein had no obvious preference for any specific architectural style. He did, however, have an instinctive grasp of how to use architecture to glorify himself and his regime and to intimidate his opponents.

From the moment of its conception, the Mother of all Battles mosque had a very clear purpose: to claim the first Gulf War as a victory for Iraq. Hussein was humiliated in that war. His army was expelled from Kuwait. Its desperate flight home left the highway disfigured by the grotesque train of incinerated Iraqi conscripts, trapped in their burnt-out plundered cars, the roadside strewn with loot. Hussein wanted to build his own reality to try and wipe out that image of defeat – just as the Kuwaitis used their meaningless toy parliament, designed by Jorn Utzon, architect of the Sydney Opera House no less, to suggest that they were a Scandinavian democracy rather than a Gulf oligarchy. Building anything at all while Iraq struggled with the deprivations brought about by Hussein's manipulation of United Nations sanctions was a calculated gesture of defiance. And the mosque itself came loaded with an iconography that made this defiance all the more explicit.

The message of the newspaper picture of Hussein's mosque is unambiguous. Architecture is about power. The powerful build because that is what the powerful do. On the most basic level, building creates jobs that are useful to keep a restless workforce quiet. But it also reflects well on the capability and decisiveness – and the determination – of the powerful. Above all, architecture is the means to tell a story about those who build it.

Architecture is used by political leaders to seduce, to impress, and to intimidate. Certainly those were the underlying reasons for Saddam Hussein's building campaign. His palaces and monuments were tattooed all over Iraq, less indelibly than he would have liked, in an attempt to present the entire country as his personal property both to his external and to his internal foes.

In the south, outside Basra, lines of bronze effigies ten feet tall follow the shoreline: they depict Iraqi officers killed in the meat-grinder war against Iran pointing across the gulf toward the old enemy. An enemy with its own taste for monument-building in the days of the Shah, the product of a failed attempt to construct a pedigree for the Pahlavi dynasty.

In Baghdad itself, the notorious outsize crossed swords span the highway into the city, gripped by giant bronze hands modelled on Hussein's own, but cast in the quintessentially English suburbia of Basingstoke. In Saddam's day, nets filled with shoals of captured Iranian helmets dangled from the two hilts. Such monuments, kitsch as they are, are universal. They date from the victory memorials of the Peloponnesian wars, and the triumphs imperial Rome granted its favoured generals. The same ritual celebration of the defeat of an enemy is reflected in the monumental sculptures cast from captured Napoleonic cannon that adorn the centres of London and Berlin. The idea of the crossed swords was filched without acknowledgement from Mike Gold, an architect based in London who originally proposed it, minus the helmets, as an innocuously whimsical civic landmark for a motorway in Saudi Arabia. In Iraq, its meaning was completely transformed. Versace's inflammatory caricature of sex and money could be worn with a sense of irony in Milan, but not in Milosevic's Belgrade, where the bandit classes took the glitter and leopard-skin look at face value. And in Baghdad, a piece of ironic postmodernism becomes the most literal kind of architectural propaganda. But Hussein had an objective wider than celebrating his questionable victories, and intimidating his enemies. His mosque-building campaign can be seen as an overcompensation for the essentially secular nature of his regime, demonstrating his credentials as a devout defender of the faith despite his taste for whisky and murder.

Yet architectural propaganda is not the exclusive domain of those commissioning a building. As the United States dispatched two more aircraft carriers toward Iraq at the end of 2002, the *New York Times* published a photograph of Saddam Hussein's Mother of All Battles mosque on its front page. Here, four years after the design was first unveiled, was the completed building. Without a hint of scepticism, the paper baldly repeated the conventional media wisdom that the minarets, an outer ring of four and an inner, slightly shorter group of four more, are literal representations, respectively, of Kalashnikov assault rifles and Scud missiles. It's an assertion that existed mainly in the minds of the Western media and their taxi drivers, and which might be a little more convincing if the minarets had tail fins, or were decorated with olive-drab camouflage paint rather than white limestone embellished with blue mosaic. Nor does the outer ring come equipped with gun sights or the distinctive curved magazine and walnut stock of a Kalashnikov. They look much less martial – and much less elegant – than the pencil-slim Ottoman minarets of Istanbul, which certainly do look like rockets. The paper's reporter sounded disappointed after his tour of the mosque: 'Where once visitors were told what seems obvious, how the cylinders of the inner minarets slim to an aerodynamic peak, like a ballistic missile tapering at the nose cone, they are now assured that no such references were ever in the architects' minds.' But by then America already felt itself at war, and such a bombastic interpretation of the mosque was too much of a propaganda gift.

Although the mosque does not use literally militaristic metaphors, its underlying message is hardly reassuring. The image of the exterior is less a howl of defiance than a conventional piece of laboured Gulf hotel glitz, looking more like a police academy in drag than a national monument. More telling was the paper's photograph of the glass showcase at the heart of the mosque with a 650-page transcription of the Koran inside. According to the *New York Times*, the mosque's Imam, Sheik Thahir Ibrahim Shammariu, claimed that the calligrapher used Hussein's own blood, donated over a period of two years at the scarcely believable rate of a pint every fortnight, to fill his pen. Another photograph shows the reflecting pool that encircles the mosque, allegedly shaped like a map of the Arab world. At one end, a blue mosaic plinth juts out of the water to form an island. The paper claimed that this irregular mound took the shape of Hussein's thumbprint. The paper doesn't go into how it could be so sure that it had correctly identified the thumb as distinctively Hussein's own. If true, it carries a message that could not be clearer. The mosque's Imam was disappointingly reluctant to confirm the warlike iconography of the mosque to the *New York Times*, but he was obligingly ready to spell out some of its more occult meanings. The outer minarets are 43 metres high, he pointed out, supposedly for the forty-three days of bombing at the start of the first Gulf War. The four minarets of the inner ring, representing April, the fourth month, are 37 metres high, for the year 1937. The twenty-eight water jets in the pool symbolize the 28th day of the month. Together they spell out 28 April 1937, Hussein's birthday.

In the flesh, the mosque is not a particularly effective way of demonstrating Iraqi defiance; and since Hussein's purpose was to present himself as a devout Muslim, it seems unlikely that he would use the Christian calendar to do it. This emphasis on the power of numbers, if it really is intentional, was uncomfortably echoed in some of the seven plans to rebuild the World Trade Center, revealed in New York in the same week that the story appeared. Richard Meier and Peter Eisenman designed a tower 1,111 feet high, presumably on the basis that a mere 911 feet would have been too short to attract enough attention. Daniel Libeskind famously went for 1,776 feet.

One interpretation of Hussein's enthusiasm for building could be to see him simply as following in the tradition common all over Asia and the Middle East, of employing fashionable Western architects to design prestige projects to demonstrate how up to date he was. Indeed Baghdad had a history of planning gargantuan architectural monuments throughout much of the twentieth century. In 1957 King Faisal II commissioned Frank Lloyd Wright to design an opera house in the manner of Moscow's unbuilt Palace of the Soviets. A colossal thirty-storey-high memorial sculpture of Iraq's greatest Caliph, Haroun al-Rashid, grandson of Baghdad's founder, took Lenin's place as its centrepiece. It would have been a piece of nation-building on an epic scale by an Iraq still emerging from British colonial rule. A commission for Walter Gropius to design a university was actually built. Le Corbusier also secured a commission in Baghdad from Faisal in 1956, designing an arena only completed after his death, when it became known as the Saddam Hussein Sports Centre.

But Saddam Hussein wanted to do more than look modern. He was also attempting to co-opt a much older heritage of monument-making stretching back five thousand years to Ur and the first urban civilizations on the Euphrates. He initiated a series of damaging 'restorations' of Iraq's ancient sites, not flinching from reconstructing the Hanging Gardens of Babylon using materials more commonly found on a suburban housing estate. He had each brick stamped with his own name in the manner of the ancient emperors, to demonstrate that he was their natural successor. He even posted guards in period costume, and equipped with spears, at his version of Ishtar's gate in his Babylonian theme park.

Hussein's determination to use architecture as a propaganda tool to glorify his state and consolidate his hold on it was clear enough. Though it was hardly effective, when measured against his objectives, architecture stands clearly incriminated for the part it played in his brutal regime. But what can you say about those commissioned to execute his ideas? The mosque is certainly a banal piece of architecture, and those who designed it are clearly guilty of a lack of imagination, but does the use to which Hussein has put it necessarily implicate the architect in anything worse?

Architecture has an existence independent of those who pay for it. Simply because the architect of the mosque worked for one of the more brutal of recent leaders, there is no reason to assume that he is himself culpable, as we did of Albert Speer when he was convicted by the Nuremburg war crimes court. The mosque is not itself committing an act of violence; its architectural forms need not in themselves be the embodiment of a dictatorship.

It is still an open question, though one that is often asked, whether architecture can project an inherent meaning at all. Is there, in fact, such a thing as a totalitarian, or a democratic, or a nationalistic building? And if they do exist, what is it that gives architecture such meanings? Can classical columns or glass walls really be described as the signs of fascist or democratic buildings, as some have claimed? Are these fixed and permanent meanings, or can they be changed over time?

If Saddam Hussein had shown the wit, or the cunning, to invite Zaha Hadid, the most celebrated woman architect in the world, and herself born in Baghdad, to design that mosque, we might have been briefly distracted enough to see his regime in a different light. If Hadid had accepted, we would certainly see her differently: at best a political innocent, at worst a naive compromiser. Certainly her chances of getting to build anything in America would have been dramatically diminished. A Hadid mosque would have sent another kind of message, still a glorification of Hussein's state, still an act of defiance, but a claim for the cultural high ground too. It would have suggested a regime more sophisticated than the one that countenanced the cold-blooded murder of Hussein's two sons-in-law and the gassing of thousands of its own citizens. But would Hadid, in the unlikely event that she had been asked, and even more unlikely event that she had accepted, have been seen as playing a part in reasserting a more civilized Iraq? Or would she have been condemned as a pawn in a game of state, prepared to subordinate every other consideration in the pursuit of the chance to build?

It is not only architects who are driven by the overwhelming urge to build at any cost. Saddam Hussein's obsession with building raises a series of questions about the psychology that motivated him. To explore the question of why he, and others like him, invested so much in building, we need to consider whether architecture is an end itself, or a means to an end.

We build for emotional and psychological purposes, as well for ideological and practical reasons. The language of architecture is used by software billionaires endowing a museum in return for naming rights to project power, as much as by sociopathic dictators. Architecture has been shaped by the ego, and by the fear of death, as well as by political and religious impulses. And it in turn serves to give them shape and form. Trying to make sense of the world without acknowledging architecture's psychological impact on it is to miss a fundamental aspect of its nature. To do so would be like ignoring the impact of warfare on the history of technology, and vice versa.

Unlike science and technology, which have conventionally been presented as being free of ideological connotations, architecture is both a practical tool and an expressive language, capable of carrying highly specific messages. Yet the difficulty in establishing the precise political meanings of buildings, and the elusive nature of the political content of architecture, has led today's generation of architects to claim that their work is autonomous, or neutral, or else to believe that if there is such a thing as overtly 'political' architecture, it is confined to an isolated ghetto, no more representative of the concerns of high-culture architecture than a shopping mall or a Las Vegas casino.

It is a flawed assumption. There may be no fixed political meaning to a given architectural language, but that does not mean that architecture lacks the potential to assume a political aspect. Few successful architects can avoid producing buildings with a political dimension at some point in their career, whether they want to or not. And almost all political leaders find themselves using architects for political purposes. It is a relationship that recurs in almost every kind of regime and appeals to egotists of every description. That is why there are photographs of Tony Blair, and François Mitterrand, and Winston Churchill, and countless mayors and archbishops and chief executives and billionaire robber barons each bowed over their own, equally elaborate, architectural models looking just as narcissistically trans-fixed as the beatific Saddam Hussein beaming over his mosque.

This is not to equate George Bush the Elder's presidential library, or Tony Blair's Millennium Dome or his Wembley Stadium, or any Olympic arena that Britain may or may not get around to building for the 2012 games, with Hussein's mosque. To manoeuvre at the court of an elected prime minister to secure the chance to build involves an altogether less corrosive kind of compromise than the potentially lethal survival dance demanded by a dictatorship. But democratic regimes are just as likely to deploy architecture as an instrument of statecraft as totalitarians.

Versailles was built as a court whose architectural splendour and physical location were meant to neutralize the power base of the nobility in the French provinces. Two centuries later, Napoleon III was once more using architecture as an instrument of political power when he engaged Georges-Eugène Haussmann to rebuild Paris on a monumental scale – not so much to curb the power of the Parisian mob as to legitimize his questionable claims to an imperial title. And François Mitterrand saw a Paris adorned by a transformed Louvre, and the Grande Arche at La Défense, as an essential part of his strategy to make the city the undisputed capital of a modern Europe. For all three rulers, how those monuments looked was as much part of the strategy as what they contained. Mitterrand adopted an aggressive architecture of simplified geometric forms in steel and glass to sym-bolize French commitment to modernity, just as the Sun King made Versailles a temple to a royal cult to demonstrate the divine right of kings.

I started to collect images of the rich and powerful leaning over architectural models in a more systematic way after I suddenly found myself in the middle of one. The elder statesman of Japanese architecture, Arata Isozaki, had hired an art gallery in Milan owned by Miuccia Prada for a presentation to an important client. Outside, two black Mercedes saloons full of bodyguards were parked on either side of the entrance, alongside a vanload of *carabinieri*. Inside was another of those room-size models. Isozaki described it as a villa. In fact it's a palace for a Qatari sheik, his country's Minister for Culture. And the palace has to do rather more than accommodate the sheik, his family, his collection of rare-breed animals and his Ferraris, his Bridget Rileys and his Hockney swimming pool, as well as his Richard Serra landscape installation. It is a deliberate effort to inject a sense of cultural depth into a desert sheikdom with little urban tradition. Each piece of the building has been allocated to an individual architect or designer, and Isozaki's assistants are marshalling them for an audience with the sheik to present their projects. The architects wait, and they wait, drinking coffee and eating pastries dispensed by waiters in black tie until the Sheik finally arrives, almost two hours late. Here is the relationship between power and architecture in its most naked form, a relationship of subservience to the mighty as clear as if the architect were a hairdresser or a tailor. The villa was never built. I last heard of the Sheik when the London newspapers reported that he was under house arrest, suspected of abusing the culture ministry's budget.

We are used to discussing architecture in terms of its relationship to art history, or as a reflection of technological change, or as an expression of social anthropology. We know how to categorize buildings by the shapes of their windows, or the decorative detail of their column capitals. We understand them as the products of available materials and skills. What we are not so comfortable with is coming to grips with the wider political dimensions of a building, why they exist in fact, rather than how. It's an omission that is surprising, given the closeness of the relationship between architecture and power. Architecture has always been dependent on the allocation of precious resources and scarce manpower. As such, its execution has always been at the discretion of those with their hands on the levers of power rather than that of architects. Pharaonic Egypt did not devote the surplus from its harvests to the construction of the pyramids, rather than to road building or abolishing slavery, because of any creative urge of the Pharaoh's architects.

Despite a certain amount of pious rhetoric in recent years about architecture's duty to serve the community, to work at all in any culture the architect has to establish a relationship with the rich and the powerful. There is nobody else with the resources to build. And it is the genetically predetermined destiny of the architect to do anything he can to try to build, just as it is the mission of migrating salmon to make one last exhausting upriver trip to spawn before expiring. The architectural profession can be seen, then, not as well meaning, but ready to enter into a Faustian bargain. They have no alternative but to trim and compromise with whatever regime is in power.

Every kind of political culture uses architecture for what can, at heart, be understood as rational, pragmatic purposes, even when it is used to make a symbolic point. But when the line between political calculation and psychopathology breaks down, architecture becomes not just a matter of practical politics, but a fantasy, even a sickness that consumes its victims.

There is a psychological parallel between making a mark on the landscape with a building and the exercise of political power. Both depend on the imposition of will. Seeing their world view confirmed by reducing an entire city to the scale of a doll's house in an architectural model certainly has an inherent appeal for those who regard the individual as being of no account. Even more attractive is the possibility of imposing their will in the physical sense on a city by reshaping it in the way that Haussmann did in Paris. Architecture feeds the egos of the susceptible. They grow more and more dependent on it to the point where architecture becomes an end in itself, seducing its addicts as they build more and more on an ever larger scale. Building is the means by which the egotism of the individual is expressed in its most naked form: the Edifice Complex.

On balance, Haussmann's Paris steered clear of megalomania. Ceauşescu's Bucharest did not. In both these cities, demolition was almost as essential a part of the process of transformation as new building. And destruction and construction can be seen as closely related. Whatever else it was, the assault on the twin towers of the World Trade Center, driven by visceral hatred, was a literal acceptance of the iconic power of architecture, and an attempt to destabilize that power even more forcefully through erasure. The fact that one of the hijackers at the controls of the airliners was himself an architecture graduate only serves to underline the point.

This book is an exploration of what it is that makes individuals and societies build in the way that they do, what their buildings mean, and the uses to which they are put. It looks in some detail at a selection of buildings, architects, billionaires, politicians and dictators, mostly from the twentieth century, in the belief that understanding the nature of their shared obsessions can help us protect ourselves from their more malevolent ambitions. These are buildings that can tell us a great deal about our fears and passions, about the symbols that serve to define a society and about the way that we all live our lives.

2

The Long March to the
Leader's Desk

Adolf Hitler went to Paris only once in his life. He flew there in the
wake of the French Army's collapse as the victorious leader of the
Third Reich he had created, stretching from the Atlantic to the Soviet
frontier in order to wash away Germany's humiliation at Versailles in
1919. He landed at Le Bourget just before dawn on 28 June 1940.
But it was not generals or party leaders who sat closest to him on his
personal plane. Extraordinarily, Hitler chose to savour his greatest
moment of military triumph by sharing it with two architects, Albert
Speer and Herman Giesler, along with Arno Breker, the regime's
sculptor-in-chief. He skipped the obvious political sites. Instead of the
Elysée Palace and the National Assembly he took them to see Charles
Garnier's Opera House. Hitler spent more than an hour testing his
memories of the plans he had studied so obsessively in his days of
poverty in Vienna. He knew the building well enough in his mind to
be able to point out the blocked door that had once led to a room
lost in later alterations with a certain smugness as they toured the
grandiloquent marble corridors.

One of the twentieth century's most unforgettable photographs
was taken on the steps of Les Invalides later that day. It is an image
that is a key to understanding the nature of Hitler's pursuit of power.
Hitler, the former corporal with a lifelong passion for architecture,
had lingered over Napoleon's tomb, and on the way out had entrusted
Giesler with the task of designing something even more impressive,
when the time came. As the group emerge into the sunshine, Hitler of
course is in the centre, wearing a long white overcoat. Everybody else
is dressed from head to foot in black, in an eerie precursor of the
universal taste for Commes des Garçons suits among architects of the

early years of the twenty-first century. Most of them are soldiers, a couple belong to Hitler's political entourage, led by Martin Bormann. But the uniformed man on Hitler's immediate right, pointing into the camera, is Speer. At a respectful distance to his left stand Giesler and Breker, the sculptor, in his Nazi forage cap.

Here is the leader, surrounded by his architectural acolytes. He is a magic figure radiating light, like the Sun King hemmed in by lesser mortals lost in darkness. It is a scene as carefully designed as one of Speer's party rallies, just as pregnant with meaning and, in theory, as astonishing a tableau as if George W. Bush had decided to tour Baghdad in the company of Jeff Koons, Philip Johnson and Frank Gehry. The dictator is demonstrating his priorities and making his intentions manifestly clear: Hitler, the great architect, is ready to redesign the world. And yet, somehow, we never entirely got the message: he wanted to be seen not as a military leader, or a political figure, but as an artist. For so many leaders, architecture represents simply a means to an end. There is the real possibility that for Hitler, at least, it was always an end in itself.

By the time that Emil Hacha finally negotiated the second of the two pairs of outsize bronze gates forming the ceremonial entrance to the Reich Chancellery on Wilhelmstrasse, it was already well after midnight. The Czech President had made the short drive through the empty streets of Berlin from his suite at the Adlon Hotel sitting beside Hitler's foreign minister, Joachim von Ribbentrop. A tiny crowd, no more than fifty people, waited in the rain to see them sweep by on the way to the most difficult three hours of Hacha's life.

This was a brutal time to be embarking on a state visit, but 15 March 1939 was one of the more desperate days in European history. Hitler had reoccupied the Rhineland and annexed Austria without firing a shot. If he could, he was determined to secure full control of Czechoslovakia in the same way. The first and only president of the Second Czechoslovak Republic travelled to Berlin in a despairing and futile attempt to snatch his country back from oblivion. Czechoslovakia had already lost the Sudetenland, with its carefully prepared lines of pillboxes and fortifications on the frontier with Germany, in the betrayal of the Munich conference. Now Hitler wanted to destroy the beleaguered state altogether. Encouraged by Germany, the Hungarians and the Russians were moving to scoop up slices of Czech territory, leaving the rest to Hitler as a protectorate of the Reich. At the same time, the Slovaks prepared to secede to create their own satellite nation, allowing Hitler a free run to attack Poland, his next target in the search for *Lebensraum*.

Hacha had no cards but his dignity left to play. His officials had been telephoning Berlin for the last three days pleading for an audience with the Führer. By the time Hitler finally agreed to a meeting, 200,000 German soldiers were mobilized to move across the frontier. In fact the special train bringing Hacha, accompanied by his daughter, his foreign minister Frantisek Chvalovsky and a small entourage of officials, was more than an hour late arriving in Berlin, delayed by troop transports moving south and east. Hacha's position as a supplicant was made immediately clear. A guard of honour met the President at the Anhalt station, fulfilling diplomatic protocol to the letter; but the reception party numbered only insultingly junior functionaries, and the German bandmaster skipped Czechoslovakia's national anthem. Hacha must have wished that he had stayed in Prague and ordered his troops into action. The negotiating process had started without the Czechs knowing it, and they had already lost the first round. Hacha went to the Adlon Hotel, while his foreign minister, Chvalovsky, called on Ribbentrop at the German foreign office, who then accompanied him to the Adalon. The terms they took to Hacha were so brutal that the Czechs at first refused to leave the hotel. Ribbentrop left them thinking it over for more than an hour while he went to see Hitler alone before finally returning to collect them. According to one account, he passed the time watching a film with the Führer.

Hacha had become president when his predecessor, Eduard Benes, went into exile in 1938 following Neville Chamberlain's refusal to back his stand against Hitler's territorial demands, and his acquiescence to the dismemberment of the First Czechoslovak Republic. Hacha was a respected jurist and the head of the Czechoslovak Supreme Court, but he had little political experience and even less stomach for a fight. Whether his readiness to accommodate Hitler was an attempt to save his own skin or to spare his country from futile bloodshed remains a sharply contested issue. He was to die in disgrace in 1945 in the hospital of the Prague prison where he was held as a collaborator after the Allied liberation of the German protectorate of Bohemia and Moravia. Whatever his intentions, he would have needed real courage to sustain himself as he entered the Chancellery's Court of Honour on that Berlin night six years earlier.

Albert Speer had designed this courtyard, a prelude to the Chancellery itself, as a world within a world, from which there was no way out except on Hitler's terms. Its blank, floodlit walls shut out the city to create a hollow space open to the sky in which Hitler's guards, drilling back and forth, cast giant shadows against the background of its superhuman proportions. The void of the courtyard was filled by shouted orders and the sound of marching boots on stone. Here was a practical demonstration of the expression of political power through building, its symbolic quality put to use for highly specific purposes. Less than a hundred miles away, a well-equipped Czech army with modern artillery, technologically advanced aircraft and Skoda tanks was waiting for Hacha's order to defend their country. In Berlin, however, the President was being made to feel helpless, transfixed by Speer's floodlights on an architectural stage set, meticulously designed to demonstrate to him that he was at the mercy of the most powerful man in the world.

Hacha reviewed his second honour guard of the night, to the musical accompaniment of another military band, and ascended the steps up from the courtyard to the tall, narrow entrance to the Chancellery, flanked by a pair of Arno Breker's 15-foot-high bronzes. They depicted prominently muscled, naked Teutonic giants. The one on Hacha's left held a drawn sword to represent the *Wehrmacht*, while his comrade on the other side, symbolizing the National Socialist Party, grasped a burning torch. Above Hacha's head, set into the German stone of which the whole Chancellery was built, a bronze eagle took wing, gripping a swastika in its claws. Four monolithic columns dominated the steps. Hacha was a short man in his late sixties with thinning, receding hair, prominent eyebrows, and suffering from a weak heart. His ascent – under the gaze of the SS guards in steel helmets and white gloves, bayonets fixed to their rifles – left him out of breath. The steps demonstrated to visitors that ascending to the Führer's higher plane was a privilege, but they also created a windowless ground floor, reflecting the defensive planning of a building linked to three levels of underground bunkers, below and behind the Chancellery. Hacha was white-faced, anxious and dizzy as he made his way across the entrance lobby, completed just eight weeks earlier. He was exactly the kind of visitor that the Chancellery was designed for. If ever architecture had been intended for use as a weapon of war, it was here.

The grandeur of the Chancellery was an essential part of Hitler's campaign to browbeat Hacha into surrender. Beyond the courtyard, itself a kind of summation of the Nazi State, was an elaborate sequence of spaces inside the Chancellery, carefully orchestrated to deliver official visitors to Hitler's presence in a suitably intimidated frame of mind. After a walk a quarter of a mile long, visitors were left in no doubt of the power of the new Germany. This was architecture that was very much a means to an end. 'I have an urgent assignment for you,' Hitler told Speer at the beginning of 1938. 'I shall be holding extremely important conferences in the near future. For these I need grand halls and salons that will make an impression on people, especially on the lesser dignitaries.' Bismarck, of course, was able to orchestrate German unification without the need for any such ego-boosting props. He had worked in the relatively modest surroundings of the old Chancellery, which was swallowed up by Speer's work. But then Bismarck had never wanted to be an architect.

Past the Chancellery guards and out of the way of the floodlights, Ribbentrop ushered Hacha across the porch and into a windowless hall beyond, its walls inlaid with the pagan imagery of mosaic eagles grasping burning torches garlanded with oak leaves, its floors slippery with marble. There was no furniture, nor even a trace of carpet to soften the severity of the hall. A clouded glass ceiling floated over the marble, electrically lit from within to cast a shadowless light, in an inescapably modern, almost art-deco gesture. Even Hitler could not shut out every trace of the contemporary world. This was the space that the sculptor Arno Breker described as 'permeated with the fire of political power'. And it had no other purpose than to impress. Under the hovering glass, and the massive marble walls, the bronze doors at the far end of the hall shimmered and beckoned and threatened. Visitors were propelled down its length as if being whirled through a wind tunnel. As Hacha walked, he was aware of his heart accelerating in rapid fluctuating beats.

Moving through the next set of doors, Ribbentrop led Hacha across the floor of a circular room topped with a dome. Speer designed it in an ineffectual attempt to conceal the fact that even the inexorable march of his triumphal axis toward Hitler's presence still had to adapt itself, for the time being at least, to the random accidents of the geometry of Berlin's street plan and surviving architectural fragments of an earlier state. Beyond this room, Hacha found another echoing marble hall. At 450 feet long, it was twice the length of the hall of mirrors in Versailles. Hitler and Speer never tired of repeating the fact as they reeled off endless lists of the record-breaking architectural statistics to which they laid claim with the Chancellery.

In the far-off distance Hacha could see yet another space, the reception hall, to which Hitler had summoned the Berlin diplomatic corps for the Chancellery's inauguration that January. As he had said then, 'on the long walk from the entrance to the reception hall, they will get a taste of the power and grandeur of the German Reich'. But this was not where Ribbentrop was leading Hacha. The hall that they walked through was 30 feet high. On the left, a parade of windows looked out over Voss Strasse, and on the right were five giant doorways, each 17 feet high. They stopped at the central pair of double doors, guarded by two more SS men in steel helmets. On a bronze scroll above the doorcase were the initials AH. This was Hitler's study, which he called his workroom, though theatre was a more appropriate description. Hacha might perhaps have recognized the eighteenth-century tapestries hanging on either side of the door from his days as a law student on holiday in Vienna. They were taken from the Kunsthistorisches Museum and depicted Alexander the Great's conquest of what was then the known world.

The room boasted a coffered ceiling high overhead. In the far corner stood Adolf Hitler, his desk positioned against one of the five floor-to-ceiling windows. Sprawling over 4,000 square feet, this was hardly just a room. To walk from the door to the desk took a nerve-racking full minute. Hacha may have missed the significance of Alexander's exploits on the tapestry outside, but the marquetry inlay showing Mars with his sword halfway out of its scabbard on the front of Hitler's desk could not have sent a more obvious message on this of all nights. It was a message amplified by the blood-red marble walls, the giant globe on a stand next to the marble table by the window, and the carpet woven with a swastika motif. A bust of Bismarck sat by the desk. Hacha would not have known that this was one of Speer's sleights of hand. The original had been smashed during the building of the Chancellery. Speer had kept what he took to be a bad omen secret and asked Breker to make a copy. 'We gave it some patina by steeping it in tea,' he later claimed.

Far away on the other side of the room, over a fireplace set between twin doors, hung Lembach's portrait of Bismarck. In front of the fire was a sofa as big as a lifeboat, occupied by Goebels and Goering. Air Marshal Goering began to describe the effortless slaughter his Stukas could inflict on Prague. They would start with the destruction of Prague Castle and then move across the city, quadrant by quadrant. In the tension, Hacha suddenly collapsed under the pressure. He rallied, but three-quarters of an hour after his arrival, before the treaty putting the Czechs under German protection could be signed, he fainted again, and Hitler's own doctor was called. 'I had so belaboured the old man that his nerves gave way completely, he was on the point of signing, then he had a heart attack,' Hitler told Speer later. 'In the adjoining room Dr Morell gave him an injection, but in this case it was too effective. Hacha regained too much of his strength, revived, and was no longer prepared to sign.'

It wasn't until 4 a.m. that Hacha's spirit broke, and he finally agreed to put his name to a document that spelled out Czechoslovakia's abject capitulation, declaring that he had entrusted the fate of the Czechs to the hands of Hitler and the Reich. Czechoslovakia had ceased to exist, and Hacha was reduced to the status of a puppet ruler of the German protectorate of Bohemia and Moravia, a humiliation that he had ample time to reflect on during his endless walk back through the marble and mosaic halls of the Chancellery.

Speer's architecture had apparently done all that Hitler had expected of it, dealing a near-fatal blow to the Czech President, and helping Germany overrun an entire country unopposed. Speer had made every piece of stone, every decorative rug, every piece of furniture, every light switch, and each twist and turn in the floor plan, serve to reinforce the message of Germany's inherent superiority.

Speer was passionate about his determination to use real stone, rather than a cosmetic veneer of the material, to create buildings that would have a dignity even as ruins. But in spite of this gesture toward authenticity, at a deeper level his was an architecture of sleight of hand, rather than substance. Germany was not the most powerful state in the world. Hitler was not Caesar Augustus. Speer's buildings pretended that they were. But perhaps all architecture depends on the creation of an illusion of one kind or another.

The Chancellery was a long thin building, much of it just one room and a corridor wide, running the whole quarter-mile length of Voss Strasse. Speer created a symmetrical stone façade for the corridor that faced across the street to address the back of Wertheim's department store. To give this façade a certain palatial quality, he divided it into three, with a set-back central section, and two projecting wings at each end each with their own column-flanked entrance. Taken at face value, the gigantic façade, which implied that a massive palace extended behind it, and the reality, which consisted of just one room plus a hallway, were an absurd mismatch. Official visitors, misled by the expansive grandiloquence of Voss Strasse and arriving at the wrong door, needed to be ushered around the corner, to the sliver of stone that contained the main entrance even though the logic of Speer's architecture suggested it was the palace's back door, for admission. Otherwise, they would miss the whole charade. Skip all those grand entrances, courtyards and halls, and they would be able to stride across the corridor straight to Hitler's desk.

There were actually four levels above ground in the Chancellery, but the façade was designed to make it look as if there were just three, making the proportions so massive that the sills of the lowest windows, supposedly on the ground floor, were 12 feet above the pavement. Pedestrians facing this gigantic stone object found themselves confronted with cold hostility. The message of the architecture could not be made more obvious: this was a place reserved for giants, even if the building served as nothing more than an impressive wrapping for the single most essential element in the design – the triumphal route to Hitler's desk. Hacha experienced it like a potholer, moving from one giant underground cavern to another, never sure exactly where he would find himself, or what he would have to confront next, as an intimidating and bewildering sequence of spaces unfolded in front of him.

Even the process of building the Chancellery was presented as a demonstration of German technical and organizational superiority over other races. Speer and Hitler conspired a little misleadingly to suggest that the whole project took just a year to complete, from start to finish. They announced the scheme to build a new Chancellery only in January 1938, when Speer had already started buying houses on Voss Strasse and was preparing to demolish them to clear the site. Much was made of the thousands of workers brought in from all over the Reich to work on the project, and of the Führer's munificence in accommodating them in Berlin's hotels.

The role of the concentration camp for political prisoners at Flossenburg in Upper Bavaria in supplying the white granite to be used in the building of Hitler's new Berlin was less publicized at the time, but the camps had an intimate connection with Speer's architecture. The SS had established the German Earth and Stone Works company, known as DEST, in 1938 to provide the building materials for the new Germany, forcing their prisoners to work themselves to death, to pay for the system that imprisoned and tortured them. The Flossenburg and Mauthausen camps were carefully sited close to stone quarries so as to serve Speer's needs for his monumental building projects – not just in Berlin, but Nuremberg, Munich and Linz too. The camps and the monuments were part of a single system: each made the other possible. With their stone watchtowers and their turreted walls, the camps themselves represented a certain architectural ambition. Hundreds of Spanish Republican prisoners died building them. Two more camps were established at Oranienburg to supply bricks. Later, when Speer became Hitler's armaments minister, he used them as a threat to intimidate those workers he called 'slackers' and dissuade them from claiming sickness to avoid war work. He was also intending to use slave labour on Berlin's construction sites, guarded by the SS.

Architecture, as Speer practised it, was primarily a means to an end. Aside from its role in supporting the concentration camps, and defining the Nazi State, that end was personal aggrandisement. The

more that he could please his patron the Führer, the greater the rewards. And the more that his work helped to make complete the
victory of Nazi Germany over the world, the greater would be the
resources from which those rewards could be made. The details of
what Speer built were less significant to him than the fact that he was
building what the Führer wanted. Speer studied architecture at Berlin's
Technical University but failed to secure the place that he wanted in
Hans Poelzig's master class – because, said Speer with elaborate and
unconvincing humility, his drawing failed to make the grade. So he
studied under Poelzig's mirror opposite, Heinrich Tessenow, instead.
Poelzig was an expressionist, with a following among left-wing students. Tessenow was an austere classicist, and though never a Nazi
himself, he attracted the right-wing nationalist students who dominated the Technical University. Despite his earlier preferences, Speer
was diligent enough in learning the mannerisms of his master for
Tessenow to employ him as an assistant. Later, Speer was ready to
accommodate Hitler's own far more flamboyant tastes. No doubt if
Hitler had demanded architectural abstraction, Speer would still have
been happy to oblige. But Hitler wanted ancient Rome, and Speer did
his best to provide it.

Speer first succumbed to the sinister glamour of National Socialism when he heard Hitler speak in December 1930. After what he
described as an initial period of softening up by his students, and
watching the Weimar's police force break up a column of brown
shirts, he went to a Nazi student rally in Berlin. He came away
mesmerized. Hitler gave a polished performance, rather than the
harangue that Speer had been expecting. He decided to apply for party
membership in January 1931. It was a move with an immediate impact
on his professional life. Speer's architectural career took off on the
strength of Nazi commissions. He redecorated a villa in the Grunewald
for the party using Bauhaus wallpapers. Then he remodelled a building
on Voss Strasse in the heart of the government district of Berlin that
the Nazis took on in the run-up to the election of 1933. It was a large
and impressive structure in a smart area, near what was to be the site
of the Chancellery, deliberately selected for its confident, respectable
image. Afterwards, Karl Hanke from the party's propaganda department gave Speer the chance to change the course of history when he

showed him the ideas he was working on for the staging of a Nazi festival. 'I saw the sketches on Hanke's desk. The designs outraged both my revolutionary and my architectural feelings.' Speer promptly volunteered his services to produce something rather more glamorous. He choreographed the May Day party rally in 1933 at Tempelhof, and outdid himself at the same event the following year at the Zeppelin field in Nuremberg when he designed its huge flags and its searchlights raking the sky like a Busby Berkeley musical.

Speer was not without competitors. Hitler worked with a whole series of architects and was particularly close to three: Speer, Giesler, and Paul Ludwig Troost from Bavaria, who had specialized in fitting out transatlantic liners and for whom he expressed the most respect. Hitler was introduced to Troost in Munich at the end of the 1920s and displayed a remarkable deference to him, even after the Nazi seizure of power. Troost's architecture demonstrated Munich's place at the centre of the Nazi movement: he built the Brown House, Hitler's headquarters, the party shrine and the House of German Art. Hitler called Troost Germany's greatest architect since Schinkel and asked him to remodel a Berlin mansion for use as the Chancellor's official residence. Only when Troost's health began to fail was Speer appointed as the executive architect, charged with managing the successful completion of the project. During one of Hitler's site tours in 1933 the Führer got talking with Speer and invited the elegant young architect to lunch with a group of senior party figures. Joachim Fest, Speer's collaborator on his memoirs, claims that there was an unacknowledged erotic aspect to Speer and Hitler's relationship. He reads a great deal into the way that Hitler gave a jacketless Speer his own coat, complete with gold party lapel pin, to keep warm on the way to that first lunch.

Troost's early death left the way open for Speer to assume his position as the pre-eminent Nazi architect. But he still had to contend with Herman Giesler, who worked for Hitler in Weimar, Munich and Linz. Such ideologues as Christian Schultze-Naumberg also expected their violent opposition to modernism in general, and the Bauhaus in particular, to be translated into positions of influence. Nonetheless, on the strength of his easy personal relationship with Hitler, Speer began work on a series of other commissions that reflected the aspirations of a new regime attempting to make its mark. He redecorated the German embassy in London. He was asked to add a balcony to the Weimar-era chancellery in Wilhemsplatz, as a suitable setting for Hitler's public harangues. There were a lot more rallies to design, and the Olympics to co-ordinate, and then the vast party rally grounds in Nuremberg to plan.

Hitler treated Nuremberg as a test for Speer, and when he liked what he saw of Speer's reviewing stand, and his confident marshalling of the various elements of the rallying grounds, he appointed him as Germany's Inspector General of Buildings. His principal task was the rebuilding of Berlin. Speer was just 31 years old when Hitler established him in the Arnim-Boitzenburg Palace on the Pariser Platz, next to the Brandenburg Gate, evicting the Prussian Academy of Arts to make way for his protégé. Speer was paid a salary higher than that of the mayor of Berlin, granted a budget to recruit his own staff, and had constant access to the most powerful man in Germany.

The gardens behind the palace had been taken over in the nineteenth century to create an elaborate sequence of exhibition galleries. It was here that Speer kept all the models that rapidly accumulated as the biggest project of his career took shape: the design of Germania, as the new Berlin would be called – the epicentre of Hitler's empire. The office was supplemented by a specially built studio at Berchtesgaden, so that Speer could continue to work when called on to attend Hitler at his mountain retreat. In just five years, he had gone from an obscure teaching assistant to presiding over the transformation of Berlin into the capital of the world.

In his memoirs, Speer painted a picture of his relationship with his most important client that will sound familiar to any architect. He was called to meetings with Hitler by functionaries, simply because the Führer had not seen him for a while. He complained of being forced to cut short his holiday in France to fly back to one meeting with the Führer, only to discover that it had been cancelled on his arrival.

Speer understood the importance of publicity and presentation. He lavished as much care on designing himself as he did on the buildings he produced. He always claimed – in the face of much photographic evidence to the contrary – to prefer not to wear party uniforms.

Matthias Schmidt's book *Albert Speer: The End of a Myth* (published in 1982) shows the lengths to which Speer would go to present his place in history in the most favourable possible light. Even after he emerged from Spandau prison, he was ready to tamper with the Bundesarchiv by substituting a sanitized version of the journal he had kept as Inspector General of Buildings. When his deception was in danger of being exposed, he asked his friend and architectural collaborator Rudolph Wolters to put back a photocopy of the original.

Speer always tried hard to show that he wasn't actually present when Himmler was talking about liquidating the Jews at Posen. There is no question, however, that he played his own personal part in the Final Solution. Speer confiscated 23,765 Jewish homes in Berlin, and expelled upward of 75,000 people who had lived in them from the city. The archives of Speer's buildings inspectorate also contained neatly filed and officially stamped demolition permits authorizing the destruction of scores of synagogues.

Speer was an energetic servant of Hitler. But in the hands of the American Army in 1945, he was quick to try to impress his interrogators, George Ball and John Kenneth Galbraith, by claiming how useful he could be to the Allies. 'He kept presenting himself as an outstanding technician and organizer. He could assume that his enemies would admire a good mind, and a technological talent.'

It wasn't only politically engaged architects like Speer who made buildings with a political significance. Far from it. Politically committed architects of lacklustre ability are rarely as effective at producing politically significant buildings as gifted agnostics. Mies van der Rohe, though the director of the Bauhaus, the radical modernist school of architecture and art, was neither a Marxist, nor a Nazi. Despite such lapses of judgement as signing a call urging Germany to vote for Hitler in the referendum of 1934 that legitimized the Nazi seizure of power, he presented himself as an apolitical figure. But he did manage to build with equal conviction a haunting memorial to the Spartacist revolutionaries Rosa Luxemburg and Karl Liebknecht, murdered in 1919 as they tried to set up a German Soviet – it was eventually destroyed on Hitler's orders – and to produce a design for the new headquarters of the Reichsbank in Berlin that might so easily have been the first landmark of the Nazi regime.

Mies was asked to build the Luxemburg memorial when he mocked the conventional design that the Spartacist party organization had in mind at a dinner and, like Speer in the Nazi Party propaganda office, suggested that he could do better. Mies's design took the form of a stack of unstable brick cubes, restlessly pulling and pushing each other from behind a five-pointed cast bronze star with the hammer and sickle pinned to it. Mies had to hoodwink a foundry owner, reluctant to manufacture such provocative insignia, by commissioning them piece by innocuous piece. The bricks, salvaged from burnt-out demolition sites, were scarred and pockmarked. 'Just a brick wall,' said Mies of the design. 'Like the one they were put up against and shot.'

In later life he gave every impression of not being much concerned whether Luxemburg and Liebknecht had lived or died, which can hardly have endeared him to his client – although perhaps that was an inevitable stance for a newly American Mies, looking to impress the State Department in the hope of an official commission. Even if neither Mies nor the Spartacists supported the objectives of the other, the memorial had brought benefits for both sides. Mies offered Berlin's revolutionary Left the chance to use contemporary architecture as a weapon of cultural propaganda. In the 1960s the Catholic hierarchy used Le Corbusier and Alvar Aalto in much the same way to help them build churches that expressed the continuing cultural relevance of their faith to contemporary life. The French Communist Party asked Oscar Niemeyer to design its headquarters in Paris for similar reasons. As for Mies, he got the chance to ingratiate himself with Germany's progressive elite in the hope of further commissions, albeit of a less provocative kind.

The fact that some modern architects such as Hannes Meyer, Mies's predecessor as Bauhaus director, were socialists, while Hitler loved the classical pantheon, turned architecture into a political argument. For a time, there was a misleadingly literal presumption that abstraction and a free plan were the lapel badges of progressive politics and that classicism was the physical expression of right-wing authoritarianism. In a series of absurd over-simplifications, political ideologues characterized the classical orders as both an unmistak-able symbol of fascist or reactionary politics, and as an expression of the values of the soviet proletariat. Leon Krier, Albert Speer's foremost apologist, suggests that 'Speer's projects continue, not unlike sex for the virgin, to be the object of pseudo-embarrassment for architects.' According to him, 'The inability to deal with the problem today in an intelligent manner reveals nothing about Nationalist Socialist architecture, but tells us a great deal about the moral de-pravity of a profession which, on the one hand, claims against all odds that modernist architecture is better than it looks, and on the other, that Nazi architecture is profoundly bad, however good it may look.' But Krier, a professional iconoclast, never followed the logic of his position to its obvious conclusion by entirely divorcing the form of a building from the values of those who created it, and extended his no doubt polemical admiration of Speer's work to acknowledge Hitler's own architectural talents, which were so important in shaping Speer's buildings.

If classical architecture was, as Krier claims, 'implicitly condemned by Nuremberg to an even heavier sentence than Speer', the flat roof and the white wall and the aesthetics of the machine have more often been presented as the personification of democratic or progressive regimes. Opponents of this architectural language on both the Right and the Left have represented it as the mark of the 'rootless cos-mopolitan' – the code words both Hitler and Stalin used to describe Jews. There is a famous photomontage of Stuttgart's Weissenhof-seidlung, the permanent exhibition of modern housing planned by Mies, depicted as an alien Semitic encampment on German soil to prove the point. But exactly the same signifiers – the flat roof, the bare white wall and the imagery of the machine – were put to very different uses in the service of Mussolini. Indeed, Mies and his great American apologist (and Speer's contemporary and counterpart), Philip Johnson, did their best to persuade Hitler and those close to him that architectural abstraction could be used to glorify the Reich. It was Mies van der Rohe's great good fortune that they did not succeed.

As it happens, Speer and Mies were both ready to work for the most odious national leader of modern times. The difference between them was that Speer devoted himself entirely to realizing the architectural ambitions of his master, while Mies, though he would bend and compromise on political issues, was unyielding about architecture. For Mies, architecture was an end itself, even though he was prepared to allow others to use his work for their own political purposes. Speer, on the other hand, is now as well known for his political life as for his architecture, and indeed for a brief moment he genuinely believed that he could become Hitler's successor. After the war, Speer attempted to detach his work from a political message. He claimed when he became a Nazi cabinet minister that 'The task that I am about to perform is unpolitical. I have felt very good about my work so long as both I and my work were evaluated purely on the basis of my professional performance.' If he could say this about his role building weapons for the Third Reich, he was hardly likely to be any less generous in his own verdict on his architecture.

In the end, Speer never had the creative resources to become an architectural innovator, or even to find his own voice. He would rather have been Poelzig's student, but expediently took on the colour of Tessenow, and then spent most of the rest of his architectural career trying to interpret Hitler's ideas.

How much Hitler himself was against the modern architecture that Mies embraced is not quite so clear cut. Nazi propaganda embraced both the idealized thatch and half-timber of the German peasant cottage – the style used, for example, as a model for the barracks for the troops guarding Berchtesgaden – and, at the other extreme, the simple unadorned steel and glass of the Luftwaffe's building programme. Hitler was always ambivalent about the precise nature of his architectural preferences. In the 1920s, in the Munich beer cellars, he was declaiming that 'a strong Germany must have a great architecture since architecture is a vital index of national power and strength', and that 'out of our new ideology and our political will to power we will create stone documents'. There were certainly some in the Nazi Party, such as Schultze-Naumberg, who hated the success and the prestige of the Bauhaus architects, and who wanted to use the Führer as a battering ram to destroy their rivals. To present them as Marxists, Bolsheviks and Jews was part of the standard rhetoric of the time. 'Tear down the oriental glass palace of the Bauhaus,' demanded the *Anhalter Tage Zeitung* in 1932. In fact, when the Bauhaus became a school for party leaders after the Nazi takeover, a pitched roof was added, presumably in the interests of making it look more German.

In 1932 the *Volkisher Beobachter* raved 'The Bauhaus, that was the cathedral of Marxism, a cathedral however which dammed well looked like a synagogue.' By this time, the school had already moved from Dessau to Berlin, where the apolitical Mies van der Rohe tried to purge it of its reputation as a hotbed of leftist radicalism, to the bitter protests of those students who were members of the Communist Party. Hitler could sound like a Miesian himself: 'To be German means to be logical, and above all to be truthful. Germanness equals clarity.' Mies van der Rohe was ready to take him at his word. He tried to seek an accommodation with Hitler, rather than face exile in 1934. His competition design for the German pavilion at the Brussels World's Fair was clearly related to his famous temple to modernity, the Barcelona pavilion, but with the addition of a swastika on the roof, a gesture that did not keep it from ending up on the floor of Hitler's study with all the other rejects.

The language of architectural debate in Germany had become extraordinarily violent: 'No prison camps parading as workers' housing, subsidized by public funds! Get compensation money from those criminals who enriched themselves with these crimes against national culture!' wrote Bettina Feistl-Rohmeder in *Im Terror des Kunstbolschewismus* (published in Karlsruhe 1938). Yet Mies, Poelzig and Gropius were all invited to take part in the Reichsbank competition – though not Erich Mendelsohn, who was Jewish – which suggested that the Nazi regime had not yet decided that modern architecture was incompatible with National Socialism. It's possible that Philip Johnson, who characterized Mies's work as German, and Bruno Werner, art critic of the *Deutsche Allgemeine Zeitung* who in 1933 wrote that Poelzig and Mies were not Bolshevists, were part of a co-ordinated strategy to appeal to that wing of the Nazi Party lead by Goebbels, who claimed to be interested in modernity. Hitler himself suggested that, 'There is a danger that we might relapse into a senseless and soulless imitation of the past. The architect will not hesitate to use modern building materials.'

Mies could perhaps fight off doubts about the appropriateness of his architecture in a National Socialist state, but he could not afford another question over his political reliability at the same time. While Mies was working on his design for the Reichsbank, the Gestapo raided the factory in the Berlin suburbs that he had leased for the Bauhaus, locking out the students and putting armed guards on the gate. This might have been a deliberate act of cultural terror. However, the closure was more likely to have been the result of low-level spite and petty factional struggles spilling out of Dessau into Berlin than a decision from the highest levels of the leadership. Nevertheless, it was a dangerous development.

Mies showed real courage in confronting the Gestapo in his attempt to have the school reopened. He went to see the culture minister, Albert Rosenberg, to appeal against the closure. He was told that there was no fundamental Nazi objection to the Bauhaus. But Mies's courage may have been tinged with more expedient motives. Perhaps the episode of the Bauhaus was not quite the titanic struggle between ideologies it was represented as being in the 1960s. His decision to go to Rosenberg's office was an act that, as the historian Elaine Hochman suggests, was intimately connected with Mies's own struggle to remain in contention for the Reichsbank competition, the first big architectural project mooted in Berlin after Hitler came to power.

Mies must have seen a possibility of finding a way to continue to work in Germany without having to temper his architectural language to the new regime, by doing just enough politically to avoid being blacklisted, but not so much as to loose his self-respect. This would explain why he was ready to fight to have the closure order on the Bauhaus rescinded, lifting a potentially dangerous black mark on his record as the director of an institution that had been judged subversive. But then he shut it down of his own volition when the conditions for reopening involved the replacement of those faculty members considered racially or politically undesirable by the Gestapo.

The usual view of Hitler's promiscuous inability to present a unified view of what he regarded as Nazi architecture is to suggest that his inconsistencies merely reflected the inherent incoherence of his view of the world. Undoubtedly there was a lack of consistency in a philosophy, if it can be called that, which sought to modernize Germany with autobahns and mass motoring, but which also had followers who believed in the desperate necessity to save the German *Volk* from the evils of the modern city by returning to a pre-industrial past. But there is another explanation for Hitler's inconsistent aesthetic attitudes in the mechanisms of power itself. Hitler's authority, as that of any dictator, depended on retaining control. The classicism favoured by Speer and Hitler had apparently nothing in common with the cottage-style housing built for party followers, or the Miesian modernism of the Reich's aircraft factories, but Hitler was ready to tip from one to the other. Perhaps choosing different styles for different projects was pragmatism, but it also ensured that no one faction could assume an unchallenged hold on the architecture of Germany. All of them had to rely on their relationship with Hitler in their intrigues and jostling for position against their rivals.

Even so, while Hitler was prepared to toy with the rhetoric of modernity, he undoubtedly had a genuine antipathy to the modern movement. The fact that it had been described as the international style can hardly have endeared it to an ideologue who looked for a racial aspect to every cultural form and placed the greatest emphasis on the construction of a powerful national identity for Germany. In the end, his objections to exposed steel, flat roofs and strip windows seem to be rooted as much in personal taste as politics

More than once, Hitler actively considered becoming an architect. After his rejection from the painting course at the Vienna Academy of Art, he thought about applying to the Academy's architecture school, or, failing that, embarking on an architectural apprenticeship. After Troost's death, he was invited to take over the practice by his mentor's widow. The quality of Hitler's surviving architectural drawings, the photographs of him sketching on squared graph paper with a pencil, and the fluency of his plans suggest that this could have been an entirely serious proposition. In his book on Hitler, Heinrich Hoffman recalls asking the man he called his friend why he hadn't become an architect, to be told: 'I decided to become the master builder of the Third Reich.' Hitler's followers were in no doubt that is exactly what happened. At a professional conference in Munich in

1937, Franz Moraller announced: 'Architecture shows everywhere the great hand of our leader. From him come the greatest impulses for the creation of and the search for new ways. In this way, architecture too has a political and cultural role to play.'

Hitler wasn't the only senior Nazi figure with a personal bias toward architecture. Alfred Rosenberg, a Baltic German and editor of the *Volkischer Beobachter*, graduated in architecture from the University of St Petersburg. Perhaps it is a coincidence, and architecture should not be held guilty by association with such figures – architects, after all, come from all ends of the political spectrum (Stalin's loathsome, sadistic secret policeman Lavrenty Beria also trained as an architect). But just as it is as well to keep a careful eye on those political leaders with a taste for writing poetry, such as Stalin himself in his early days, or Radovan Karadzic, the war criminal who presided over the butchery of Bosnia's Muslims, or Daniel Ortega, the dictatorial leader of Nicaragua with the droopy moustache, so an enthusiasm for architecture is a sinister characteristic when present in a certain kind of political figure.

It would be reassuring to believe that Hitler's version of architecture has just as little to do with the real thing as the doggerel of the previously mentioned tyrants has with authentic poetry. The conventional argument that Hitler could not in fact have been a real architect centres on his lack of interest in detail or technique. Yet these are all issues that could just as well be raised against any one of a dozen of the most famous architects practising in the world today. Speer claimed after the war that Hitler would have been a competent if not a brilliant designer – not a view he was in the habit of expressing when the Führer was still alive – and there is no reason to doubt him.

More telling is the criticism that Hitler had no interest in the architectural culture of his times. In Vienna, he seems not to have noticed that this was a city in cultural ferment, in which Adolf Loos, Otto Wagner and Josef Hoffmann were in the process of shaping a revolutionary new direction for architecture, one that was synonymous with modernity. All he could see were the banal gingerbread hulks of the Ringstrasse and the Baroque monuments of the past. This was hardly an appreciation of architecture as a living cultural form. His interest in building was more to do with the attempt to construct his idea of the world, and it was that obsession, as much as his limited talent as a designer, that left him unable to create an authentic work of architecture.

It is significant that Hitler failed to engage with architects of genuine creative ability throughout his life. His relationship with Speer and Giesler would suggest that he looked for the malleable and suggestible to carry out his will and build his vision rather than the truly creatively gifted.

Hitler did not have a sense of what a Nazi building should look like, in terms of how a structure could express a clear ideology, but a tight definition of a coherent architectural ideology is not really the issue. The point of being a dictator is to have the power and authority to be able to say that the architecture of the regime is whatever the leader says it is. An art historian might bring a cool detachment to an examination of the Doric order to define its characteristics. But even a Baroque building is defined as much by interpretation and suggestion than by any single coherent set of signifying features.

Speer designed the Chancellery to do more than intimidate foreigners. It was there to impress Germans too, both by its size and with the mythology that it embodied. Hitler was engaged in the creation of a political system, and he needed a leadership myth to go with it. In his hands, leadership was no longer presented as a bureaucratic and bloodless function of shared responsibilities, cabinet papers, civil service briefs and pragmatic day-to-day politics. In Hitler's fantasies, the Reich was government as it had been in the days of the Roman Empire, in the time of the Germanic chieftains, and of the Prussian kings, transformed into modern dress. In fact he was making things up as he went along, as if he was devising a board game, or refining the rules of a sport. And his buildings were used to test out rules and rituals, ludicrous though many of them were.

The Chancellery was a court, designed to personify and make clear Hitler's assumption of absolute power. Under fascism, Germany's parliament was an irrelevance, and Hitler's cabinet not much less of one. Although Speer's design for the Chancellery included a wood-panelled cabinet room, with a private corridor from the leader's study that would have allowed him to appear and disappear at will, Hitler rarely used the room. Speer records taking ministers on special tours, gazing at the blue leather desk blotters with their names embossed on them in gold letters. All that counted in the state that Hitler built was its supreme leader, and the architecture that represented his position.

Buildings by themselves were not enough. To fill all those rooms, so optimistically named on the architect's drawings as reception halls and cabinet rooms, they needed to be animated by rituals that reflected their role in the running of the state. Mature states have evolved those rituals over generations. Germany in 1939 was anything but a mature state, and Hitler's grasp on power depended not just on force, but on his ability to invent a convincing state choreography. He needed ceremonies, and salutes and protocols and a timetable of daily rituals, just as he needed the uniforms and flags and insignia to which he devoted so much mesmerized care and attention. To try to instil some sense of purpose to the Chancellery in between the irregular performances staged to overawe visiting heads of state, Hitler relied on the ancient idea of the feudal hall and the feast. He created an entourage of personal followers – a chorus that formed the background for his daily routine. Speer recalls a floating court of between forty and fifty people, most of them politically unthreatening party members from the early days in Munich who needed only to telephone the Chancellery's chief steward to secure a place at the Führer's table for lunch, scheduled for two o'clock every afternoon. In Speer's words, hard to take at face value though they are, these were dreary events, to which Hitler was reluctant to admit the army hierarchy for fear of revealing to the *Wehrmacht*'s meritocrats just how unimpressive his inner circle really was. In the evening there were private film screenings, which at least excused participants from the burden of conversation.

Paul Troost had already built a party headquarters in Munich, where one room, furnished with leather-upholstered seats drawn up in a U shape and tapestries, was designated as the party's Senate Hall – conjuring up the idea of the wise old men of the movement meeting to deliberate issues of state. But no such Senate ever existed, and Hitler allocated the space to his deputy, Rudolf Hess, for his office.

Evidently, Hitler himself could tire of some of his games even before he had started them.

Hitler could not stop himself from building, but with every new building he started he had to keep coming up with convincing new uses to fill them. No sooner had Speer completed the Chancellery, with all of its 163,000 square feet, than he was set to work on designing a colossal new palace for Hitler. And Hess was once more earmarked to take over the Führer's cast-offs: he would be expected to move into Voss Strasse after Hitler left. Hitler's palace was to be situated at the heart of the new Berlin, unencumbered by the constraints of existing streets – or budgets. With its gardens, palm houses and courtyards, it sprawled over 2.5 million square feet. Diplomats would have been obliged to trudge half a kilometre from the ceremonial entrance to Hitler's desk. By that time, there would be no more diplomacy, just the rendering of tribute to the supreme leader of the world from his vassals.

Speer's first Chancellery was perhaps the biggest and the most complete of all the ever larger architectural models that Speer made for Hitler's pleasure. It was the diagram for the huge new city that Hitler wanted to build where Berlin had once stood. Architectural models were everywhere in Hitler's world, just as they would figure large in Saddam Hussein's. A huge one, 100 feet long, of Berlin's new north–south axis, was on permanent display in Speer's studio. It came in sections raised up to chest height, so they could be pulled apart to offer Hitler a closer look at the façades, and allow him to explore the effect from pavement level under different lighting conditions. The model was painted to suggest the materials that would have been used, and marching ranks of lead toy soldiers set the mood. Hitler would lead expeditions of dinner guests with flash lights across the garden of the Chancellery – occupied today by Peter Eisenman's holocaust memorial – and through a specially built rear entrance to the studio to see it late at night. There were more detailed models of individual buildings, and much bigger models of Hitler's two personal designs: the triumphal arch and the great hall.

As preparations for building began, life-size replicas of sections of the façades were commissioned by Speer and installed on an outdoor site at Treptow, on the edge of Berlin, to give an idea of what to expect. Hitler was clearly not a man with a liking for unpleasant surprises. He wanted as lifelike a representation of a design as possible, before it was built. Speer even constructed a full-size timber and concrete slice of the gigantic 400,000-seat stadium that he had designed for Nuremberg. Fragments of the foundations on a Bavarian hillside still survive, and are a highlight on the dubious pilgrimage followed by enthusiasts for the architectural relics of the Third Reich.

Like the Chancellery, Germania, as the new Berlin would have been called, was based on a monomaniacal dependence on two primary axes. The north–south axis would have stretched for almost four miles, with a railway station at each end, a primitively obvious restatement of the idea of a city gate. It's surprising only that Speer did not go as far as suggesting the creation of an all-embracing city wall, a move that was left to Walther Ulbricht. The Chancellery's miniature version of the north–south axis bisected the marble hall looking over Voss Strasse, ran through the centre of Hitler's study, sliced the garden at the rear that looked towards the Pariser Platz in half, and finally terminated in Hitler's greenhouse. The city's east–west axis co-opted the Unter den Linden and the Brandenburg Gate, and was reflected in the route running from the ceremonial entrance and the Court of Honour to the Chancellery's reception room. These cross axes can be seen as having their origins in the planning of the Roman cities that so obsessed Hitler, or Louis XIV's bedroom at Versailles, positioned at the crossing point of two of the most important roads in France.

The grand avenue forming Germania's north–south axis would have had a distinct character in different sections, and was studded with monuments, squares and circuses along its length. Hitler's monstrous great hall, like the circular vestibule in the Chancellery, was needed to deal with a change of direction in the axis. It would have acted as a hinge to shift the great boulevard to the west, as it crossed the Spree on its way to its northern pole. Even Speer's paired wall lights, used everywhere in the Chancellery, were closely related to the street lights that he was already beginning to install on Berlin's triumphal new east–west route, from the Lustgarten to the Unter den Linden and the Tiergarten. The parallels between the Chancellery and Berlin itself suggest that Hitler and Speer saw them as being a representation of the same authoritarian ideas about power.

Hitler was one of the most accomplished exponents of the art of corporate identity that the world has ever seen, and he used architecture as a primary tool to manipulate it. His plans for the rebuilding of Germany's cities, and the construction of party and state institutions in Berlin, Munich and Nuremberg, were intended to strengthen the aura of authority and invincibility around the Nazis, just like the black leather greatcoats adopted by the SS but on an infinitely greater scale. Even more significantly, Hitler used architecture to define and make possible his idea of what a totalitarian state should be. Berlin would have been a communal hive for his swarm of uniformed workers and soldiers, with the engorged leader-queen at its centre. The individual counted for less than nothing.

Hitler was using architecture as a means to further his grip on power, but at the same time – as he revealed on the steps of Les Invalides – he clearly understood it to be an end in itself:

Our big cities of today possess no monuments dominating the city picture which might somehow be regarded as the symbols of the whole epoch. This was true in the cities of antiquity, since nearly every one possessed a special monument in which it took pride. The characteristic aspect of the ancient city did not lie in private buildings, but in the communal monuments which seemed made not for the moment but for eternity, because they were intended to reflect not the wealth of the individual owner, but the greatness and wealth of the community.

Only if we compare the dimensions of the ancient state structures with contemporary dwelling houses can we understand the overpowering sweep and force of its emphasis on the principle of giving first place to public works. The few still towering colossuses which we admire in the ruins and wreckage of the ancient world are not former business palaces but temples and state structures, in other words, works whose owner was the community. Even in the splendour of late Rome, first place was not taken by the villas and palaces of individual citizens, but by the temples and baths, the stadiums, circuses, aqueducts, basilicas, etc. of the state and hence of the whole people.

It was exactly these 'community' monuments that Hitler wanted to build in Germany. They were designed to secure the future for the Nazis, and to be a weapon against the democratic present.

'How truly deplorable the relation between state buildings and private buildings has become today!' Hitler wrote:

If the fate of Rome should strike Berlin, future generations would some day admire the department stores of a few Jews as the mightiest works of our era, and the hotels of a few corporations as the characteristic expression of the culture of our times. Just compare the miserable discrepancy prevailing even in a city like Berlin, between the structures of the Reich and those of finance and commerce. Even the sum of money spent on state buildings is usually laughable and inadequate. Works are not built for eternity, but at most for the need of the moment. And in them, there is no dominant higher idea. Our cities of the present lack the outstanding symbol of national community, which, we must therefore not be surprised to find, sees no symbol of itself in the cities. The inevitable result is a desolation, whose practical effect is the total indifference of the big city dweller to the destiny of his city.

As with the Chancellery, Hitler's plans for rebuilding Berlin were driven by a mix of strategic calculation, a morbid fascination with the manipulation of people and places, and the sheer relish of building on a gigantic scale. 'Our enemies will guess it, but our own followers must know it. New buildings are put up to strengthen our new authority,' proclaimed Hitler in his party day speech in 1937.

For Hitler, architecture was a propaganda tool, to be used to inspire his followers and oppress his enemies:

The great building programme is a tonic against the inferiority complex of the German folk. He who would educate a folk must give to it visible grounds for pride. This is not to show off but to give self-confidence to the nation. A nation of 80 million has the right to own such buildings, our enemies and followers must realize that these buildings strengthen our authority.

The sheer scale and size of what Hitler and Speer were planning for Berlin was so vast, and so intimidating, that we understand it now only as a malevolent and feverish fantasy. The gigantic dome that would have dominated Berlin had begun as a sketch that Hitler had carried with him everywhere he went since 1925, along with his dream of a German Arc de Triomphe. It was the starting point for what Speer tried to realize in stone, glass, steel and concrete. The dome would have accommodated 180,000 people, and stood 1,000 feet high. Even today, nothing in Europe would match its scale. 'That a monument's value resides in its size is a belief basic to mankind,' wrote Hitler.

The models have gone. Apparently, an attempt to move some of them out of Berlin in April 1945 failed when a convoy carrying cases of models from the Chancellery was attacked by Russian infantry. The designs now exist only as a series of photographs and sketches, and some carefully delineated large-scale plans housed in the Library of Congress in Washington that chart the streets that had been demolished to make way for Hitler's boulevard. They seem to show a city overwhelmed by an alien sea monster descended from another galaxy sucking the life out of old Berlin. Hitler's monstrous dome is far larger than any other structure in the city, disrupting and perverting its fabric. But this unsettling image, hanging over Berlin like a bad dream, was more than a fantasy. Site investigations had been carried out to see that the load-bearing capabilities of Berlin's soil were sufficient for the dome's weight. Contracts had been signed with Norwegian, Swedish and Italian quarries for the granite to build it. A start had been made on building barracks for the slave labour force that would work on it. Speer had 10,000 Soviet prisoners handed over to his custody to start the Berlin project, and he persuaded Heydrich to provide him another 15,000 Czechs. In return he advised Heydrich on how to realize his plan to rebuild Prague. Speer had also secured the services of the SS to guard his slaves. A date in 1950 had been set for the completion of the new Berlin, to be marked by a World's Fair in the city.

Germania was the work of far more than a solitary fantasist. It represented the efforts of scores of architects, government departments, the armed forces, Germany's largest companies and its universities and hospitals. A relatively modestly scaled capital of four million was to be inflated into a metropolis on the scale of London or Paris, and its population doubled.

Speer's strategy, following ideas already explored by Berlin's planners in the 1920s, was to create a new focus for the city, well to the west of the existing centre. This was not the first time that Berlin had considered such a scheme, but Hitler was certainly the first political leader to treat the project so seriously, and to inject monumental architecture into the mix. He was the first to see the project as a political issue, rather than a technical one. He was determined to ignore the existing Berlin, or rather to subjugate it, to an extent that disturbed even the Nazi mayor of Berlin, Julius Lippert, who attempted to thwart the plan. Germania would have turned its back on the royal palace, the Protestant cathedral, and the Lustgarten, which made up the old centre, and created an entirely new ceremonial, government and business quarter. Germania was notable too for the number of monuments that Hitler wanted it to have. No leader can have devoted so much thought, so far in advance, to planning his victory monuments, not only before the victories had been won, but before he had a country or even an army. To mark his fiftieth birthday Speer had given Hitler a model of the triumphal arch large enough to stand up inside. If built, the real thing would have formed a landmark 386 feet high, more than twice as tall as Napoleon's Arc de Triomphe, close to one end of the Berlin axis. The Great Hall, positioned at the other end of the axis, was another of Hitler's ideas. Less attention appears to have been paid to how the grand boulevard, with three rows of trees on either side and a central green reservation 250 feet across, would have functioned when it wasn't full of ranks of marching soldiers. As a huge, unbridgeable chasm of traffic, it would have cut Berlin in two.

The base of the Great Hall was to be a stone cube, a third of a mile square, with its south face sliced open by a gigantic colonnade, gaping open like a rectangular letter box. The dome oozed out of this base like a monstrously inflated tumour, and was itself topped by a lantern – strictly, a Baroque rather than a Roman motif. Hitler changed his mind several times about the shape of the lantern, as he did about almost everything else, but in the end he opted for a version that was surmounted by a globe that itself carried an eagle, its wings open, its claws bared. From the gigantic Königsplatz hundreds of feet below, the masses could have looked up and, at the right spot, caught a glimpse of Australia and New Zealand rendered in outline in the lower quadrant of the globe. North-western Europe would have been visible only from the skies, or to visitors poring over the model in Speer's offices. Time and again Hitler was photographed with it, his face looming over the model of Berlin, like a distant mountainous landscape overwhelming the city or a rising moon.

The eastern side of the square in front of the hall would have been formed by the old Reichstag. Once a landmark itself, Hitler would have turned it into a toy, dwarfed by the monuments of Nazi Germany arranged in tidy ranks all around it. The army high command and Hitler's new palace would have made up the other two sides, positioned, as it happens, close to the site of the Chancellery built for the newly reunited Germany in the 1990s. The axes would not have been single straight lines, but were to be made up of a series of episodes, hinged around gigantic spaces and vast monumental buildings. Speer and Hitler selected the crossing point between the two axes to position the prodigious new Chancellery, which would have occupied the most privileged site in the whole city. Whether the plan was genuinely an attempt to design a real city, rather than create a parade ground realized on the scale of a city, is open to question. Certainly Speer had no obvious expertise or experience of urban planning before he began the project.

The axis would have spanned the Spree, curving around the dome and the old Reichstag with a new bridge. Beyond that was a vast rectangular artificial lake, three-quarters of a mile long, which would have formed a reflecting pool for the dome and the setting for another group of public buildings: the city hall on one side of the water, designed by German Bestelmeyer from Munich in a manner derived from Stockholm's town hall, the admiralty on the other. It was designed by Paul Bonatz, who, despite securing a number of prominent commissions from the Nazis, considered it expedient to leave Germany for Ankara in 1942. Beyond were the offices of the regional administration, the police headquarters, and, in pride of place, the north station. Behind the regular façades of the waterfront buildings, pierced by a series of picturesquely placed towers, Speer's team drew up studies for a second rank of structures, including barracks for the guards regiments and the War College.

Speer placed Goering's palace, designed on a scale, if it is possible, even more inflated and theatrical than Hitler's, just south of the Chancellery and the Tiergarten.

Hitler's palace was planned around the diplomatic walk. At the heart of Goering's was a great flight of stairs, rising through four floors, whose empty rhetoric was so grandiloquent as to provoke one of Mussolini's architects to exclaim that 'now, they really have taken leave of their senses'. There is something faintly comic about the prospect of Speer shuttling back and forth from Führer to Marshal, planning ever larger, ever more elaborate headquarters for these two sinister arrested adolescents conspiring over the spoils of a future that was not yet theirs, asking their architect for yet more sumptuous interiors as if they were a couple talking to their decorator with a sheaf of cuttings torn from the pages of *Architectural Digest*. Goering was so impressed by the stairs, which switched back and forth, propelling visitors in a zigzag past endless expanses of blank walls, that he commissioned a portrait bust of Speer to stand in the hall that would have served mainly as the most elaborate lift lobby the world had yet seen. 'In tribute to this the greatest staircase in the world, Breker must create a monument to the Inspector General of Buildings. It will be installed here to commemorate forever the man who so magnificently shaped this building,' proclaimed Goering.

A photograph survives of Speer posing for his bust in the studio that he designed for Breker. He is standing looking heroic and gazing into the middle distance, dressed in tweed, with a crew-neck sweater revealing just a patch of tie. Only the party badge on his lapel suggests his political affiliations. Breker, a short man in a smock, is bent reverentially over his chisel, rendering his handsome patron and friend as a creative, but above all decisive, figure.

After he came out of prison, Speer purported to be particularly horrified by his design for Goering's palace. 'This was a decisive step in my personal development away from the neo-classicism I had first espoused and which was perhaps still to be seen in the Chancellery, to a blatant nouveau riche architecture of prestige.' Certainly Goering's palace represented the architecture of excess. All the halls and stairways and salons took up more space than the offices. There was a ballroom, an open-air summer theatre with 240 seats, and a lavish private apartment. The roof was designed to carry a layer of soil 13 feet deep, supposedly as an air defence measure. But it would have been used for a garden dotted with swimming pools, tennis courts, fountains, ponds, colonnades, pergolas and refreshment rooms.

To the south of Goering's building, the axis opened out into a roundabout, where construction was well advanced on the German

House of Tourism, designed by Dierksmeier and Rottcher, at the time of Germany's defeat. To the dismay of Speer enthusiasts, this section, part of the Western sector of the city after the end of the war, was demolished to create West Berlin's culture forum, making way for Mies van der Rohe's New National Gallery and Hans Scharoun's concert hall and library.

As the axis moved southwards, the ministries would have given way to cinemas, shops, and corporate headquarters. 'We had of course recognized that lining the new avenue solely with public buildings would lead to a certain lifelessness and had therefore reserved two-thirds of the length of the street for private buildings,' Speer claimed. 'With Hitler's support, we fended off efforts by various government agencies to displace the business buildings. We had no wish for an avenue consisting solely of ministries.' The axis was too wide ever to have been a genuine street. In this section, cohesion broke down altogether, and Speer's boulevard became an aimless sea of isolated landmarks, as if it were a piece of modernist tabula rasa planning. Among the elements that Speer wanted to include were a Roman bath house, two cinemas, one of them with 5,000 seats, an opera house, a concert hall, and a twenty-one-storey hotel designed by Casar Pinnau, along with a congress centre and law court complex.

Albert Speer was a man who always liked to tell people what he thought they wanted to hear. When he wrote his autobiography, he assumed that his readers, delivered from the nightmare of a world ruled by Adolf Hitler, wanted to be told how dismal the architecture that he and Hitler had planned really was.

Nowadays, when I leaf through the numerous photos of models of our one-time grand boulevard, I see that it would have turned out not only crazy, but also boring. Even these varied parts of the avenue strike me as lifeless and regimented. When, on the morning after my release from imprisonment, I passed one of these buildings on the way to the airport I saw in a few seconds what I had been blind to for years: our plan completely lacked a sense of proportion. We had set aside block units of between 500 and 660 feet. A uniform height limit had been imposed. Skyscrapers were banished from the foreground, thus we deprived ourselves of all the contrasts essential for animating and loosening the pattern. The entire conception was stamped by a monumental rigidity that would have counteracted all our efforts to introduce urban life into this avenue.

The fact that this judgement is mostly accurate does not mean that Speer actually believed it. To judge by the lavishly produced volumes of his buildings and projects he published in 1978, Speer never disowned his work. In front of a sympathetic audience, he was ready to defend his creation rather than to denounce it: 'There were quiet interior courtyards, with colonnades and small luxury shops. Electric signs were to be employed profusely: the whole avenue was conceived by Hitler and me as a continuous sales display of German goods, which would exert a special attraction upon foreigners.'

One of Germany's most famous architects, and several of its most powerful corporations, became involved in this part of the plan. Peter Behrens himself, for whom Le Corbusier, Walter Gropius and Mies van der Rohe had all worked, designed offices for AEG that would have been built just south of the House of Tourism, whilst Nestler designed Agfa's headquarters next to the Allianz insurance giant.

Speer involved as many architects as he could in the project, provided that they were ready to work in what he could broadly describe as a German style. Speer needed the support of the many architects – more mature than he was – who designed the individual buildings. Their experience supplemented his strictly limited repertoire. Wilhelm Kreis, for example, was twice Speer's age, and had been President of the German Architects Guild before the Nazis came to power. As a figure closely connected to the Weimar regime, the Nazis sidelined him, but Gerde Troost spoke up for him and he was commissioned to design some of the most prominent monuments for Berlin. It was Kreis who turned yet another of Hitler's sketches into a design for the Soldiers' Hall, in which it was planned to carve the name of every German soldier killed in battle since 1914 – more than 1,800,000 of them. It would have also housed the railway carriage in which Germany had agreed to the armistice that ended the First World War, once it was captured from the French. That only a fraction of them would have been legible to visitors – or that there might be 10,000 Johannes Schmidts carved indistinguishably one after another – was of no concern to a state in which the individual had ceased to matter.

Speer went ahead and signed contracts with the SS to use white-flecked granite from the Flossenburg concentration camp's quarry to build it.

Speer staged a whole series of architectural competitions for the major individual buildings, but in effect every entry was the same: symmetrical, classical, with a central colonnade, and faced in solid stone. The National Socialists made a fetish of the material, which they represented as a means of binding buildings with the soil from which they emerged. Pinnau tried a couple of times to design sky-scrapers with specifically German characteristics: they ended up as a model for the East Germans when they built Stalin Allee, dominated by domed stone turrets. But the bulk of the new Berlin would have been in uniform blocks, five floors below the cornice, and an attic level above.

At the south end of the axis, Berlin's second station formed the entrance to a plaza more than half a mile long, lined with captured tanks and field guns, culminating in Hitler's own Arc de Triomphe, 386 feet high. You would have seen the dome of the great hall three miles away rising above everything. Speer was particularly proud of the design for the four-level station – bigger, of course, than Grand Central. 'Our happiest concept comparatively speaking,' he suggested. 'Steel ribbing, showing through sheathings of copper and glass, would have handsomely offset the great blocks of stone.' Official visitors would have descended by a large outside staircase; as soon as they stepped out of the station they would be overwhelmed, or rather stunned, by the urban scene, and thus by the power of the Reich.

The east–west axis was, by comparison, more modest. It took up the line of the Unter den Linden, stretching all the way from east of the Museum Island and west through the Tiergarten. Speer moved the nineteenth-century victory column, wrapped with ordnance captured in campaigns against Denmark, Austria and France, from in front of the burnt-out hulk of the Reichstag to the centre of a vast roundabout in the Tiergarten. On the Museum Island, Hitler wanted to build a clutch of new museums. Hans Dustmann, Walter Gropius's former assistant, designed a museum of Ethnology. Wilhelm Kreis worked on a museum of the nineteenth century, a museum of Egyptology and a German museum. This is where Speer planned to create the Mussolini Platz, and where IG Farben was going to build its headquarters.

From 1937 onwards, Speer began widening the east–west axis, reducing the number of intersections and cutting down trees that obstructed the view. Plans were drawn up to relocate the technical university and to demolish the Charité hospital to make way for the Great Hall. Negotiations to build it opened with a consortium made up of a group of Germany's leading construction firms in April 1941. In August of the same year the consortium to build the triumphal arch – 'Bauwerk T' as it was called in Speer's office – was appointed and contracts drawn up to build the Soldiers' Hall. As the war turned against Germany, construction slowed and then stopped, even though 25,000 properties standing in the way of the north–south axis had been demolished, and the railway yards at the Anhalt, Potsdamer and Lehrter stations torn up in preparation for building the Great Hall. Design work continued until 1942.

Instead of a city of possibilities, a place of individual choice, Speer's Berlin would have been capable of just one interpretation. There would have only been one way to understand it: as a celebration of the power that had built it. Hitler spoke of his determination to make a city that would impress 'the farmer from the provinces who travels to the Great Hall and is moved by what he sees'.

Why do we find the idea of Hitler building his own Rome so disturbing? It is perhaps the sense that if he had managed to finish it he would have succeeded in what he really wanted, making his mark on history in a way that would pre-empt judgement or dissent. Destroying his Berlin would have been all but impossible; even if every single building were totally erased, the axis would have left its unmistakable trace. No matter how oppressive or lifeless or maladroit his architecture, the sheer size and scale would have left us, if not convinced by its message, then hard put to explain exactly why we admire the Romans enough to want to preserve every surviving fragment of their cities, and not Hitler's.

To imagine the completion of Germania is to imagine the victory of Adolf Hitler. The one could not have happened without the other. It was an attempt to intimidate the rest of the world, a propaganda campaign on an unprecedented scale designed to glamorize and celebrate the regime, to bind Hitler's followers to his idea of what Germany should be. His architecture expressed his hunger for power and for submission in others. 'If all the documents were to disappear, the historians would still read Hitler's plan to dominate the world in the buildings of the Third Reich,' wrote Speer.

By the time the war ended, Speer's hubris about the ruin value of the Reich's architecture, which he had used to justify the use of such costly 'genuine' materials as granite and marble, looked hollow and empty. Riddled with shell fire and allied bombs, the bronze doors long since stripped away for salvage, the Chancellery's Court of Honour was anything but a noble ruin. It was littered with ammunition boxes and the detritus of a field kitchen, and had seen summary executions and the alcohol-dulled debauched oblivion of the remains of Hitler's court as it waited for the last days. Speer even claimed to have explored the possibility of turning his creation into a weapon against the Führer, with a plan, that may or may not have existed, to poison the air supply to the bunker.

After the German defeat, the allied leaders made pilgrimages to the ruins of the Chancellery to see the death throes of Hitler's regime for themselves, before the Russians finally demolished the remains of the building and used it to quarry stone for their war memorials in Berlin. The eagle from the Court of Honour was shipped back to the Red Army's museum in Moscow. Martin Borman's diary for the early days of February 1945 provides a compelling insight into the surreal nature of the death agonies of the Nazi State. Pounded by American and British bombers mounting daylight raids, much of Berlin was without power or water, while Marshal Konev manoeuvred the Red Army for its crossing of the Oder in readiness for its final attack on the city. 'The Reich Chancellery garden is an amazing sight,' wrote Borman. 'Deep craters, fallen trees and rubble everywhere. Only fragments remain of the winter garden. Voss Strasse is pocked with enormous craters.'

This was the precise moment that Hitler's adjutant contacted Hermann Giesler, the architect who had toured Paris with the Führer in 1940. Giesler, who remained a devout Nazi even after the war, was summoned to Berlin to discuss his plans for remodelling Linz, Hitler's birthplace.

Giesler negotiated the rubble in Voss Strasse to reach the Chancellery on 9 February 1945, bringing with him a new set of plans. Hitler was determined to rebuild Linz to challenge Prague and

Budapest as the Danube's most beautiful city. The architect also brought with him a large model of his project that involved not just a series of new buildings, but also a new industrial suburb to provide the infrastructure to support Hitler's vision for the city.

Giesler's architecture had a lighter touch than Speer's, but his vision of Linz shared the fundamentals of Germania: oppressive scale and an axis from railway station to city centre, along which were ranged a 35,000-seat concert hall and various cultural buildings, including a museum to house the art that Hitler had looted from across Europe. Overlooking the river was a 500-foot bell tower, with Hitler's parents entombed in a crypt at the base, and a carillon playing Bruckner at regular intervals. Hitler's own burial place was to have been a mausoleum with a design based on the Pantheon.

Hitler was utterly absorbed by what he saw, and he spent hours with Giesler discussing his timetable to start work on building the project. Later the next day, an SS general named Kaltenbrunner – born, like Hitler, in Linz – came to the bunker to warn of the imminent collapse of civilian morale in Berlin. Hitler stopped him, and took him to see the model. 'Kaltenbrunner, do you imagine I could talk about my plans for the future if I didn't believe deep down that we are really going to win this war in the end?' Even Hitler's madness and self-delusion had a tactical aspect too.

There is less of Hitler's Germany left than he would have wanted. There are some autobahns and bridges, and Volkswagens. In Berlin, what is now called the Avenue des 17 Juin is wider than it would have been if Hitler had never existed; the victory column is a few metres away from its pre-Nazi location; but all that still marks the idea of Germania are a few lumps of concrete here and there. Munich has the museum that Paul Troost built for Hitler, rescued from destruction when the Americans vetoed plans to dynamite it, though the shrine to the handful of Nazis killed in Hitler's putsch was destroyed. In Nuremburg, there are the unfinished party Kongresshalle and the network of reviewing stands, established for the Nazi rallies. Ludwig Ruff and his son Franz began work in 1935 on the hall, designed to accommodate 60,000 seated spectators in a complex of buildings modelled on the Coliseum and built by forced labour. When Hitler laid the foundation stone, echoing Speer, he claimed that 'even if the voice of National Socialism were ever to be silenced, these masonry witnesses will still arouse astonishment'. He was dismayingly correct.

It was tough enough to survive the war and decades of de-nazification. Total erasure would be to conceal the past. But the plans made by Nuremburg's city council to turn the Coliseum into an innocuous sports centre would have been even more sinister in the post-war years. Finally it was agreed to open a 'documentation centre' dedicated to providing a reminder of what had once happened on the site. The architect for the new museum, the Austrian Günter Domenig, deliberately set out to confront the architecture of the past. Domenig's additions to the original building read unmistakably as a stake nailed into its heart.

The Germany of today is a pacific state that is the least likely aggressor in Europe, and yet these places still have the power to chill the blood. The fragments that Hitler built are stripped of their power to intimidate and threaten. Yet they are still not neutral, for they are both the material and the symbolic expression of Hitler's view of the world. They represented Hitler's objections to the bourgeois individu-alism of the modern city, and his determination to replace it with a communal identity through the shaping effect of National Socialist architecture.

3

Landscapes of Power

Attempting to dignify their taste for monumental marble with some notional deeper purpose in the form of a cultural ideology is a vanity that all the totalitarians have shared. To suggest that there is such a thing as Nazi architecture, or Socialist Realist architecture, in the same way that there was a Greek architecture or a Gothic architecture, is to inflate its status far beyond what the confused reality can justify. For all the rhetoric of Hitler and Stalin's paid ideologues about the principled nature of the architecture of fascism or socialism, its substance amounted to a pathological obsession with size, symmetry and a blatantly literal iconography. Five-pointed stars, hammers, sickles and wheat sheaves for Stalin, swastikas and eagles for Hitler, bundles of sticks and axes for Mussolini, could be used as ground plans, elevations, or decorative detail as required. Sheer size was more important than the way in which the detail of a building or its organization could be understood as representing a state.

We recognize a church as a church because we have seen one before: they have a steeple or a cross. Within the subset of Christian churches, we can recognize an Orthodox church – it has a dome, and has done so for a thousand years. We recognize a minaret as the sign of a mosque, which is also very likely to have a dome. And these archetypes are so familiar that those who design churches or mosques can enjoy a wide latitude in interpreting them while still being understood. We recognize an office building: it stacks up repetitive floors one on top of another. Telling a hotel from a hospital is not so clear cut. Both have a porte cochère, though one is for taxis, the other for ambulances, a difference that provides a useful clue.

It is much more difficult to address the question of what makes us understand a building as fascist, or democratic or Stalinist. The hammer and sickle as an architectural motif removes any doubt, but it is hardly subtle, or capable of expressing many nuances. A genuinely democratic building cannot, one would think, have been built by slaves. But what about buildings built by societies that either owned slaves or profited from the slave trade? By that definition we would have to rule out such otherwise apparently impeccably democratic institutions as the eighteenth-century town hall of Liverpool, a city that depended on Britain's participation in the slave trade with the Americas. Even Periclean Athens was a slave-owning society, though its architecture has come to be understood as the very embodiment of democratic ideals.

Despite the implausibility of defining the nature of a Nazi or a socialist architecture, from the point of view of a dictator any building that they manage to erect is an indisputable fact in support of their cause. Stalin, Hitler and Mussolini all built as much as they could, in the interests of prestige, to demonstrate their energy, and, as in the case of Stalin's transformation of a Moscow insurance company's offices into the headquarters of the KGB, to provide a threatening reminder of their appetite for terror.

Democracies are usually too self-conscious or squeamish for their leaders to be seen intervening quite as directly as the totalitarians in architectural issues. Notable exceptions do exist. There is something oddly reminiscent of Stalin pacing the Moscow river bank in 1931 deciding where to put the Palace of the Soviets in François Mitterrand's order half a century later for the roads around La Défense to be closed one sweltering August weekend to allow the biggest crane in France to be set up to winch a mock-up of the Grande Arche into place: the President wanted to see for himself the impact it would have on the view from the gardens of the Elysée Palace. The dictator was regularly driven around the streets of Moscow late at night to inspect building work in private, fussing over the precise grade of granite to be used on the Moscow underground. Stalin wanted to build the Palace of the Soviets, a structure that would have been taller than the Empire State Building and topped by a colossal representation of Lenin bigger than the Statue of Liberty, to demonstrate his triumph over both the old Bolsheviks and capitalism.

Boris Iofan, architect of the ill-fated project, described Stalin's instructions on the form his design should take as 'comments of genius'. On one occasion, Stalin was observed casually picking up a representation of the onion-domed St Basil's cathedral from a model of the Kremlin to see how the city would look without it.

Totalitarians use architecture as part of their strategy to present themselves as being in a position to control events, and to demonstrate that the application of their will alone is enough to reshape the world. Hitler, Stalin and Saddam Hussein all took a minutely detailed interest in the monumental aspects of the new buildings that marked their regimes. They were forever poring over architectural models, choosing between shades of marble and granite, and being photographed striking dynamic and decisive poses over city plans and architectural models. Just as they had learned from Louis XIV, Napoleon, Catherine the Great and Wilhelm of Prussia, so the dictators of the first half of the twentieth century were themselves to influence another generation of tyrants. In China, Mao followed in Stalin's footsteps, while Saddam Hussein, for better or worse, learnt from both of them. In Romania, Nicolae Ceauşescu's last years were marked by the destruction of large swathes of Bucharest to make way for a crude evocation of Haussmann's Paris that was meant to suggest that Romania had finally escaped from the Balkans. But because it happened in the 1980s, not the 1880s, it looked like a futile and absurdly old-fashioned exercise. In Spain, Franco's Valley of the Fallen outside Madrid presents another version of the same bleak vision of monomania. In every case, there was a reference back to the glory of the distant past, as well as to the example of the more recent buildings of other tyrants. Franco, astute enough to keep out of the Second World War, was still ready to learn from the example of Hitler's Germany in the architectural techniques for glorifying his regime, as well as from the Castilian kings.

While Stalin's criminal policies of forced collectivization, deportations, deliberately induced starvation and mass murder of the peasants, applied with the tragic brutal sadistic cruelty of a Tamburlaine, were killing millions of Soviet citizens, he was busy painting a picture of abundance and success with his plans to rebuild Moscow. Stalin killed the loyal, as well as the disloyal, the honest along with the dishonest.

It was not fear that made his regime so devastating in its effect on its subjects. In building a regime that magnified the chaotic randomness and savagery of life, Stalin overwhelmed and brutalized Russia for three generations. He succeeded in destroying any lingering belief in the redeeming possibilities of reason and justice. Sincere old Bolsheviks were shot in cellars with or without the benefit of a show trial, almost always with a confession. Afterwards, their children were expected to feel honoured to be chosen to present Stalin with bouquets of roses for his birthday. Those Soviet prisoners of war who survived the suffering of German prison camps and were repatriated were promptly rearrested and sent to the gulags. Some of Stalin's closest allies died the most appalling of deaths, hanging from the rafters of their jails impaled through the neck on meat hooks. Meanwhile, Stalin's newspapers were full of images of plans for bold new ministries, meeting halls, radio stations, libraries, hotels and, of course, the metro. For the outside world at least, these images became the reality of his regime. The useful idiots from the West could come and marvel at them and go home to broadcast the blessings of the cult of personality to the world.

The process of building was as important for Stalin's purposes as the finished product. Moscow's shop windows in the 1930s and 1940s could offer little in the way of consumer goods, or sometimes even food. But they were filled with images that depicted the city's planned new buildings in that distinctive dreamlike style in favour during the Stalin years. The dictator had himself portrayed as the fount of all this magnificence, as its creative genius, infantilizing the Soviet Union in the process. The hypnotic images that show the dear leader, decisive, stern, and inspired by the light of genius, pencil in hand, indicating to the rapt members of the Politburo the future shape of the great capital of socialist struggle, were only slightly less ubiquitous than oil paintings depicting a smiling, avuncular Stalin embracing golden-haired Russian children or, depending on the Soviet republic in question, doe-eyed Kazak infants.

One painting shows him in the Kremlin poised over a plan of central Moscow, spread over a carefully modest table, overflowing with books and papers. Stalin is Jesus at the Last Supper, occupying the centre point of the perspective, a position that emphasizes the message of his omniscience. Behind his shoulder, a photograph of John the Baptist in the incarnation of Lenin hangs on the wall, looking down on the scene to bestow his blessing on his rightful heir. The anointed one is surrounded by his disciples. Their heads are bowed. Molotov sits at the table on one side of Stalin, Beria, his secret policeman, is on the other. Lost in wonder at the dazzling insights offered by Stalin, they do not speak as they strain to catch every detail of what is clearly a moment of divine revelation. Even Khrushchev, his eventual successor, looks on with no signs of the doubts that he was later to voice. The dazzling future that Stalin promised his people was rendered in the same style, in a curious blend of innovation and tradition.

Russia's monuments have always had a certain provisional quality. It is their details, which are easier to manipulate, rather than their broader outlines that tell us most about whom they belong to, and what they are celebrating.

The Winter Palace in St Petersburg has reflected the course of political life in Russia for more than 250 years. It was built as an assertion of the imperial status of the country, and in one of its many halls it was decorated with portraits of generals from the tsar's army. They were taken down after the revolution of 1917 and dispersed to signal the triumph of a new order, but are now slowly being replaced as a reflection of a regime that manages to combine the double-headed imperial eagle with Soviet stars as part of its iconography. In the same spirit, Putin has brought back the tune of the old Soviet national anthem, though with new post-communist words to accompany it. The thrones in the audience room of the Winter Palace were removed after the Revolution and replaced by a diamond- and ruby-studded map of the Soviet Union, an image that has itself recently been superseded by a feeble replica of the tsar's throne apparently upholstered in cotton wool.

Moscow still has something of the absolutist quality of an Asian metropolis, a Beijing or a Tokyo, with the heart of power as its empty centre. The Kremlin, like the Forbidden City or the Imperial Palace, is a void in the middle of the urban fabric. By the Kremlin wall, the Stalin-era Hotel Moskva, designed by Alexei Shchusev, who was also responsible for Lenin's tomb, is currently wrapped in a huge plastic hoarding while it goes through its death throes as the demolition men swarm over it. A new hotel will be built inside a replica of the original skin, complete with its curious lopsided façade, one half with large windows, the other half with small ones. The combination is said to be the result of Shchusev presenting a single drawing to Stalin showing two alternatives for the façade. He approved it without understanding that he was being asked to choose between them.

Lenin's tomb in Red Square is a reminder that the Soviet Union was once a place that was interested in cultural innovation. Its open top has a pathos that is far more impressive and yet far smaller than Mao's mausoleum in Beijing. For a few dollars, you can get your photograph taken outside with a surprisingly convincing looking Tsar Nicholas II or, according to taste, with Lenin himself. Both of them come equipped with the appropriate facial hair and head gear.

Walk further down the slope of Red Square towards the river, past what was the GUM department store, now full of La Perla lingerie and Hugo Boss suits, as if it was an airport duty-free shopping mall, and you get a glimpse of yet another monument that tells you Moscow still has its own, very particular way of doing things. Rising high over the water is the black bronze mast of a monument officially dedicated to the establishment of the Russian navy by Peter the Great. It was unveiled in 1998 by Moscow's mayor, Yuri Luzhkov, and occupies most of a small island in the river near the Krymsky Bridge.

It is the work of the feverishly overheated sculptor Zurab Tsereteli. The centrepiece is a giant figure in period costume representing Peter the Great. He stands on the deck of a warship with its sails furled like washing drying on the line. The most disturbing thing about it is the absurdly incongruous scale. Peter's head comes up to the level of the crow's nest, more like a cartoon version of Captain Hook on a gigantically inflated toy yacht than a national hero, even if he has been rendered in millions of dollars worth of bronze at the scale of a twelve-storey block of flats. Stalin did these things better. By the Kremlin wall, a refined equestrian statue of Marshal Zhukov elegantly tramples a dead German eagle under foot.

Emerging from Moscow's Kropotinska metro station, you pass the loafers drinking beer at the café tables, and girls in dresses that stop a yard above the knee strolling in the sun. Across the street is a triple-parked black Audi saloon with tinted windows. A man with no neck emerges from it to move with surprising speed across the pavement to the nearest doorway under the watchful eyes of a younger, leaner man wearing blue-and-grey camouflage fatigues and boots, a machine pistol hanging purposefully from a webbing strap slung over his shoulder. You turn and are confronted by a vision so dazzling that you can hardly see anything else. The five golden domes of the Cathedral of Christ the Saviour hurt the eyes, gleaming in the Moscow sun with a patina that turns a particularly vivid shade of turquoise. Mocking the red stars on the Kremlin's domes, across the Moskva River a chrome and perspex Mercedes star rotates slowly on top of the apartment block that Boris Iofan built for the party elite in 1929. During the purges, faces were missing here most mornings, marched away in the night by the NKVD. The survivors would ask the doormen for the names of the disappeared. Beyond the Mercedes star, a selection of the seven skyscrapers that Stalin's slaves built in the 1950s call to each other over the heads of the city's humbler buildings, waiting for the tower of the Palace of Soviets that never came to redeem its promise to lead them to socialist nirvana.

The basilica is a sacred part of Russia's history. It was a celebration of national deliverance from Napoleon's armies in the war of 1812–14 and paid for by kopeks dropped into collecting boxes by the peasants. A taper lighted at one of its altars was believed to bring good fortune if you could get it home without it blowing out. Easter services attracted thousands of worshippers to the vast white marble structure. A bronze relief frieze of figures runs around the exterior, charting Russian history. Warriors clutch their spears, bearded priests brandish the Word of God, held aloft on metal tablets, like digital cameras raised by supplicant tourists.

The basilica is protected by a grey metal fence, ringed by elaborately swagged cast-iron lamp-posts, lathe-turned stone balustrades, and endlessly bifurcating steps. It sits on a band of slimy, putty-coloured polished granite, with a funereal grey rusticated stone base. Get closer, and you discover that the surface structure conceals a subterranean complex of ramps, roads and underground parking lots that betrays the whole gleaming confection as a faithful hallucination. The real church was dynamited to make way for the building of the Palace of the Soviets in December 1931. The elaboration of the bronze doors, the sculpture and the inscriptions, and the gaudy flower beds, the evocations of the nineteenth-century lamp-posts, the carved stone, are all the work of twentieth-century craftsmen, the kind of thing the people who make hyper-real effigies for Jeff Koons would do if left to themselves. The new church, like the monstrous Peter the Great statue across the river, is the product of Moscow's mayor Luzkhov and Zurab Tsereteli, who was responsible for decorating the interior. Boris Yeltsin himself laid the foundation stone. And the gold leaf, applied by the bucketful to the domes, was paid for by the oligarchs who, with indecent speed, made themselves enormously wealthy during the dissolution of the Soviet Union.

The building of the original nineteenth-century basilica marked one important assertion of Russia's identity; its destruction was an attempt radically to redefine that identity; and its rebuilding is yet a third watershed in the power struggles shaping modern Russia.

Tsar Alexander I commissioned Karl Vitberg in 1817 to design a cathedral of a scale and grandeur to reflect Russia's rank as a mighty and expansive state. With a dome more than 750 feet high erupting from a classical base, it would have been twice the size of St Peter's in Rome. But there were doubts about its feasibility. Then Vitberg was accused of embezzlement and exiled to Siberia. The project was handed over to another architect, Konstantin Ton, who redesigned it in a more traditional Russian style and on a smaller scale, but at 360 feet to the top of the cross on its biggest dome it was still as tall as London's St Paul's Cathedral when it was finally completed in 1883.

The basilica was one of the first of Russia's great monuments to be destroyed in a spasm of iconoclasm that saw even the vast church of St Isaac in St Petersburg converted into a museum of atheism. Stalin set about erasing the landmarks of the past in an attempt to make his conception of the Soviet Union irreversible. Red Square was turned into a giant parade ground, its gates, built in 1680, demolished to make it easier to manoeuvre tanks and missiles in and out. The Sukharev Tower, the tallest structure in Moscow, also from the seventeenth century and used as the city museum, was flattened. So were two miles of the Kitajgorod Wall, with its sequence of towers and gates, along with the church of the Iberian Virgin in the Kremlin and the Kazan Cathedral, built in 1625 by Prince Pozharsky to celebrate Russia's triumph over Poland.

The secret police ensured that the gangs of workmen stripping the gold from the basilica handed over the spoils to the State. It yielded almost half a ton of bullion, despite the anguished protests of those still brave enough to challenge Stalin's determination to destroy every trace of the old order. Several priests who tried to salvage religious relics were summarily shot. Two technicians who refused to take part in dynamiting the remains of the hulk were sent to the gulags. Some of the marble and granite cladding was salvaged for reuse in the building of the Lenin Library. The icons from the altar were sold to Eleanor Roosevelt. But much of the statuary and the glass was deliberately destroyed. Remembering the sacrifices of the Russian people in defeating an invader from Western Europe was off the agenda, until Hitler tried to follow in Napoleon's footsteps.

In place of the basilica, Stalin intended the Palace of the Soviets to be the supreme monument of the new order, a complex of meeting halls for the Communist Party and museums of world revolution, grand enough to demonstrate the final triumph of the proletariat. The process of selecting the design reflected the Soviet Union's transition from its brief moment of cultural pluralism into a despotism, just as the murder, with Stalin's possible connivance, of Sergei Kirov in December 1934 marked the start of the Great Terror.

In 1931, under the supervision of Stalin's close political ally Vyacheslav Molotov, a competition was organized to find a designer for this highly charged project who would produce 'a monumental structure outstanding in its architectural formulation'. Molotov's men looked around the world for suitable candidates. Walter Gropius and Hans Poelzig, competitors for the chance to build Hitler's Reichsbank just two years later, took part alongside Erich Mendelsohn, Auguste Perret, Le Corbusier, and three Soviet architectural teams.

Le Corbusier's design would have been one of the greatest buildings of his career, a pair of fan-shaped auditoria facing each other across a sequence of spaces, signalled by a soaring catenary arch. It did not make the shortlist of three, much to Le Corbusier's fury. His allies in the architectural world made a futile attempt to lobby Stalin to persuade him to change his mind. Not only was it much too late, they also had fundamentally misunderstood the nature of the project. The Soviet Union had moved beyond the idea of presenting itself as the visionary centre of world revolution and was now more interested in consolidating its power over its own people. Like Le Corbusier's, Boris Iofan's design expressed the two main halls of the palace as abstract volumes, but he placed a monumental tower between them, poised between modernity and tradition. Iofan somehow managed to suggest both the Tatlin Tower and a Babylonian ziggurat as his sources. He topped it with a heroic sculpture of a worker that clearly attracted the attention of the Politburo but still remained on a relatively modest scale.

Iofan, not yet 40, was a well-connected architect from the Ukraine who had already constructed a series of landmarks that served to define the new Moscow, and, perhaps unwittingly, the schizophrenic nature of the regime. After studying in Odessa, he had trained as an architect in Rome, where he had clearly picked up some of the more feverish aspects of the Futurists. He redesigned the Soviet embassy in Rome, then went back to Moscow. He built a hospital next to the Lenin Library for the exclusive use of the party hierarchy, as well as the 500-apartment complex on the banks of the Moskva River where they lived in communal luxury while the proletariat they claimed to serve froze for lack of winter fuel.

At this transitional stage, Iofan's design could still be seen as belonging to the radical strand of Soviet architecture. There was a moment when the Soviet Union seemed ready to embrace the architectural avant-garde as the appropriate dress for a revolutionary state. The last decades of the Romanovs had seen Moscow transformed by art-nouveau architecture, while St Petersburg was a base for radical poets and artists, including Malevich and Kandinsky. In the immediate aftermath of the Revolution, Russia became an important centre of contemporary architecture.

There are still traces of that moment in Moscow today. On Miasnit-skaia Ulitsa, you pass a brash expression of Russia's kleptocratic economy, Lukoil's offices, outgrown even before it was finished by the company that grew colossally rich taking over state-owned oil reserves. It later faced bankruptcy from politically motivated tax bills.

Opposite is Le Corbusier's complex of offices, apartments and meeting halls designed as the headquarters for Centrosoyuz, Russia's co-operative movement, in 1928, and now the home of the State Bureau of Statistics. It comes swimming into focus in the summer heat haze, like a ghost from the distant past. Its red basalt stone looks as if it has been scorched and sand-blasted by centuries of use. The cantilevered theatre juts out over the entrance, supported by a forest of fluted Doric columns that seem unlikely to have been built exactly as designed by Le Corbusier. They are protected from traffic by pre-cast concrete flower beds. From the outside, the basic dignity of Le Corbusier's conception remains intact. But inside the door, a militiaman in a bullet-proof vest sits behind a crude wooden counter in a ramshackle coat room, like a squatter in this ravaged but still heroic space. Twin ramps snake back and forth over his head in a manner that is unmistakably Le Corbusier's. The vision of Le Corbusier's extraordinary drawings has faded into an inhabited Pompeian ruin. The marble floor slabs are cracked and broken, tipped up at a 45-degree angle. In some places, all there is to stop you disappearing into Moscow's pungent marshy soil oozing up from below are patches of rotting hardboard. A forest of different-sized columns holds up the roof. Its inelegant complexity suggests that an engineer was asked for a second opinion about the stability of the structure some time after completion. Moscow has a concentration of buildings from the same period that could have made the city a showcase of modernity. Why did Stalin turn away from it? The comforting answer would be to say that the avant-garde was too independent-minded for the controlling nature of the totalitarian state that Stalin was building. There is the possibility that the suicide of his wife tipped the balance of his reason. There is also an undoubtedly nationalist tinge to the choice of Iofan to design the Palace of the Soviets. Stalin had started looking inwards, and backwards, in the 1930s. The past was certainly where his literary tastes lay – with Gorky and Pushkin, rather than with Russia's twentieth-century avant-garde. Stalin understood that Iofan would be prepared to obey his detailed architectural instructions, and Le Corbusier would not.

The idea that the competitors for the Palace of the Soviets could range from Le Corbusier to Boris Iofan seems scarcely credible. They were two architects who hardly seemed to inhabit the same universe – though Iofan did later intercede on Le Corbusier's behalf to get the fees for his work on building the Centrosoyuz headquarters, outstanding for more than six years, finally paid in full. One architect was exploring new ideas about space, unfamiliar ways of supporting structures, and a new architectural language. The other ended up manipulating architectural signs in the crudest, most bullying way. And yet Molotov, the Politburo member supposedly in charge of the selection process, was prepared to look at both.

That divergence between the utopianism of Le Corbusier and the bombast of Iofan's design only widened as the Palace of the Soviets competition's later stages unfolded. Stalin asked the finalists to incorporate 'the best of the past, with modern technology' and, if Iofan's account is to be believed, to make the whole project bigger and more ideologically charged with the imagery of Stalinism. Iofan teamed up with Vladimir Shchuko and Vladimir Gelfreikh and abandoned what avant-garde aspects his first scheme had shown to produce a truly megalomaniacal art-deco tower. This was the original Stalinist wedding cake whose progeny were one day to appear as an unwelcome eruption on skylines everywhere, from Warsaw to Shanghai.

Iofan's tower, or perhaps it should be called Stalin's tower, had seven tiers rising out of a rectangular base and would have been approached across a vast open space stretching all the way to the walls of the Kremlin. Reaching the conference hall would have involved ascending an endless cascade of steps up to an entrance hall fronted by a giant crescent colonnade. Iofan coolly claimed that the old church was 'huge and cumbersome, looking like a cake, or a samovar, it overwhelmed the surrounding houses and the people in them with its official, cold, lifeless architecture, a reflection of the talentless Russian autocracy and the highly placed builders who had created this temple for landowners and merchants. The proletarian revolution is boldly raising its hand against this cumbersome edifice which symbolizes the power and the taste of the lords of old Moscow.'

Having destroyed it, the lords of new Moscow started building its replacement in 1935. Clearing the whole site would have involved jacking up the Pushkin Museum, mounting it on huge rollers and moving it bodily out of the way, which the Politburo were fully prepared to do. Aided by Stalin's genius, Iofan's design eventually reached 1,400 feet, and the symbolic worker had exploded into an effigy of Lenin 333 feet high. The outstretched right arm, pointing Kremlinwards, would have been a major challenge to the laws of gravity, requiring a massive steel cantilever to support it. The tips of his fingers, 20 feet long, would have been lost in cloud much of the year.

Stalin continued to back the project until his death almost twenty years later. During the German attack on Russia, Iofan was evacuated to the Urals with his studio and his models of the palace and continued to work on the design, taking full account of Stalin's comments. 'Why is the podium raised so little above the hall? It must be higher. There must be no chandeliers, the illumination must come from indirect light . . .' Stalin decreed that the architecture of the structure should express the six pledges of the oath that he had taken on his assumption of power after Lenin's death. The main hall, increased to a capacity of 21,000 seats, under a 330-feet-high dome, was ringed by six smaller halls, themed for Stalin's oaths, including the Stalin Constitution Hall and the Hall of the Building of Socialism, as well as a Museum of World Revolution. In the main auditorium, speakers would have addressed the masses from a huge tribune, topped by a cluster of triumphant proletarians carved in marble.

The tower was, symbolically, a tripartite composition: the base was to represent the precursors of socialism, the shaft of the tower Marx and Engels, with the whole crowned of course by the vision of Lenin. From one point of view, at least, the Palace of the Soviets was designed very differently from Speer's Berlin. Rather than having an eye to its quality as a ruin, in the Soviet Union Stalin's sycophants claimed that 'the centuries will not leave their mark on it; we shall build it so that it stands without ageing eternally'.

It eventually transpired that the Soviet Union did not have the skill to build the structure at all, let alone to make it ageless. Accounts of the troubled construction of the original basilica – plagued by flooding caused by a high water table and pressure from the river – were ignored by Stalin's cowed experts. Things seemed to go well at first. The foundations for the Palace had been dug by the end of 1938, and work started on the steel structure. By 1939, the road closures necessary to prepare for moving the Pushkin Museum out of the way had been announced. But the site was getting waterlogged, and nothing that Iofan tried would solve the problem. The retaining walls were tanked with tar and lined with tombstones, but neither stopped the water rising for long.

Many far more powerful men were executed as saboteurs for much less conspicuously embarrassing failures, but Iofan evidently had a special rapport with Stalin that saved him from the gulags. He was left to build the Soviet pavilion at the New York World's Fair in 1939 unhindered, a less aggressive version of his Parisian project, and was treated to admiring coverage in the pages of *Architecture of the USSR*, a magazine that mixed cover portraits of Stalin and Molotov with news of recent projects.

The May 1940 issue devoted twelve pages to Iofan, printing his picture next to the latest version of the Palace of the Soviets, with pages reproduced from his sketchbook showing watercolours of the Pantheon and the Roman amphitheatre at Syracuse. He was described as a master of Soviet architecture, and the piece documented the transformation of the conference hall from its original 1932 design to its final incarnation. In the first version, three concentric drums surround the dome of the hall. Then it sprouted classical wings, with an endless procession of giant Corinthian columns. After that came the tower, and the ever more colossal statue of Lenin. Almost every subsequent issue of the magazine is haunted by the shadowy presence of the Palace. It is there in the background of the artist's impressions of every new scheme designed for central Moscow, a huge rocket blocking out the light, all-seeing and inescapable.

In the end, the German invasion of 1941 stopped work even on Stalin's pet Moscow projects, and the palace's structural steel, by this time reaching as high as the eleventh floor, was dismantled for war use. But the project drifted on, finally abandoned only in 1949. When Khrushchev came to power the excavations were turned into an open-air swimming pool.

If Le Corbusier's version had been commissioned, it would certainly have been easier to build than the ludicrously overblown Iofan project, and it would have given Stalin's regime a very different identity. But it didn't win, and in retrospect it is clear that the choice of Iofan was of a piece with the seven towers positioned at strategic points across the city that Stalin authorized for Moscow in the immediate post-war years. One accommodated the University, another the Foreign Ministry, a third was the Ukrainia Hotel, and others were full of apartments for the *nomenklatura*. They were, it was claimed, national in form, socialist in content, and in this, at least, they certainly differed from anything that the Nazis considered building.

Stalin's tower aside, despite their supposed ideological differences, Nazi Germany and Soviet Russia and its satellites came to resemble each other more and more in their abuse of modern movement architecture, which was expressed in strikingly similar terms. After the war, Karl Liebknecht's nephew, one of the German Democratic Republic's leading architects, declared, 'We are against the Bauhaus, it represents cosmopolitanism and decadence' – words that could have been used by the Nazis. The essential nature of the Nazi and Soviet building programmes was all but indistinguishable, as in the famous architectural confrontation between the two regimes at the Paris World's Fair of 1937, where Speer's pavilion and Iofan's counterpart faced each other. It was only the gigantic rendering of two workers wielding a hammer and sickle on the Soviet side and the eagle and swastika that topped Speer's stone pylon that made it immediately clear which was which.

Huge buildings, triumphal axes, and the use of vast quantities of stone deployed in ways that were designed to intimidate pedestrians characterized all of the totalitarian regimes, Marxist, fascist, or nationalist. In the Soviet Union, the hardening of the political climate against experimentation, and Stalin's manifest preference for a Soviet version of the classicism of St Petersburg, prompted some of the avant-garde to shift towards the tastes of the regime. Rather than not build at all, they were ready to build what the State wanted. The pioneering modernists in the West are to this day characterized as being on the political left, but it is worth remembering that, for Stalin's followers, 'The Bauhaus architects were *déclassé* outsiders, dissatisfied with the existing orders because of lack of commissions from the bourgeoisie.' It's a prejudice that must have been confirmed in 1948 when General Lucius Clay invited Walter Gropius to act as an official architectural adviser to Germany's US-occupied zone. Inevitably, the

GDR immediately turned against the Bauhaus and functionalism and argued for progressive tendencies of national architecture Schinkel style.

The rest of the Warsaw Pact was naturally of the same mind. In 1948, Josef Revai, newly appointed Minister of Education in the People's Republic of Hungary, declared that 'architecture is an ideological and therefore a political question'. He did not have to look far for his answer: 'Any architectural opinion contrary to Soviet architectural opinion is nothing but reaction. Modernist architecture is the only hostile cultural tendency still to be observed in our country.'

To deal with this reactionary tendency, the first national congress of the architects of Hungary declared in 1951 that 'the influence of the architecture and the architectural theory of the imperialist bourgeoisie is hostile both to art and to people, and must be radically liquidated in Hungary'. Asked to indicate a suitably proletarian model for architecture, the Minister pointed to the Moscow metro: 'With its architecture adorned by statues, with, dare I say it, its luxury, it creates a holiday mood for the workers on the way to their jobs.'

Like the socialist realist paintings, Stalin's seven Moscow towers were not hard to understand. Their designers claimed to have liberated Corinthian columns from the bankers and returned them to the people. Under the leadership of Moscow's city architect, they borrowed the battlements from the Kremlin wall, the spires from the admiralty in St Petersburg, and the zigzag motifs of Russia's Orthodox churches and applied them to skyscrapers. They spoke to the masses of a glorious, powerful, respected, glittering Russia, looking back and forwards simultaneously.

The dictators endeavoured to be even more gigantic and even more intimidating than each other. Speer, with characteristic immodesty, suggests that after the Hitler–Stalin pact he was invited to Moscow to offer the Soviets advice on city planning. He reports that he had to reassure Hitler that the Great Hall in Berlin was not going to be overwhelmed by the Palace of the Soviets.

Because he managed to hang on to power rather longer than his contemporaries, Stalin succeeded in rebuilding Moscow on a scale that eclipsed Mussolini's plans for Rome and Hitler's version of Berlin. But all three of them were embarked on what was fundamentally the same course of action. They tried to signal their prestige and their close connections with historical precedent in the marks that they made on their capital cities in brick and stone.

Even Hitler's most devoted sycophants never proposed memorializing his effigy on the scale of the Palace of the Soviets. But Stalin's Moscow is rather more sophisticated in its planning concepts, if not its architecture, than Hitler's ideas for Berlin. The pattern of Moscow, with its radial boulevards and its dispersed regional centres, is not so dissimilar from the slightly later Abercrombie plan for London.

The most difficult question to address is whether a profusion of state-sponsored construction is actually the rational response of a ruler attempting to impose a system of government on a state, or rather a symptom of the monomania that eventually turns all dictators into paranoid delusional sociopaths betraying nothing but vainglory and self-aggrandizing desperation. Grand building programmes could simply be a technique, or may rather be a reflection of the state of mind of those who aspire to dictate to a whole country how it should live. Most regimes in fact seem to exhibit both tendencies at some stage in their development.

All of the first generation of twentieth-century dictators sought to present themselves, despite the cult of personality that accompanied their rule, as governing on the basis of a systematic and fundamentally rational view of the world. They had the vanity to believe that they were presenting a philosophy, a scientific set of beliefs, where possible codified in a manifesto, rather than acknowledging that they depended on brute force and that they ruled by fear. An aspect of this self-delusion was the attempt to develop policies for every aspect of cultural life, including architecture. Lately, Saddam Hussein had the crutch of Ba'athism to lean on, just as North Korea's Kim Il Sung has Juche thought. But neither of these offered much in the way of an insight into architectural philosophy. Saddam's strategy was simply to present himself as the reincarnation of national heroes from the past, and to rebuild the landmarks of their days.

In the new Russia of the twenty-first century, the oligarchs and the semi-criminal businessmen help to fund the reconstruction of pre-revolutionary landmarks, as they roam Moscow demolishing the architectural relics of the Stalin period that are just beginning to attract the concern of conservationists, who now understand them free from their political content and appreciate them both as the vanishing expression of a particularly tortured historical moment, and also for their inherent physical qualities. This suggests that the meanings of architectural expression are always subject to change.

Stalin's embalmed corpse has been banished from Red Square for decades, but postcards of those images of Stalin the architect and Stalin the solicitous father of the nation are on sale everywhere in the Kremlin's souvenir stands. It becomes harder with the passing years to remember that they were ever taken at face value. Did millions really sacrifice themselves for the motherland on the basis of their love for a squalid and brutal dictator who was ready to murder and kill without mercy or reason and chose to have himself represented in the style of the illustrations from an Edwardian children's book? Did they follow without question a man who was so feared by his courtiers that, as he lay stricken by the brain haemorrhage that finally killed him, slumped on the floor, they kept him away from his doctors for hours?

The brutal reality behind the honeyed light of propaganda images is revealed in the photographs that show the people of Budapest risking their lives in 1956 to tear down the massive statue of Stalin that still dominated the centre of their city, three years after the dictator's death. Stalin's graven images had an idolatrous power, and destroying them appeared to exorcise his lingering presence. Bringing down his statue in Budapest was a daunting task that involved considerable firepower, intense street fighting, ropes and ladders, oxyacetylene torches, and many hours of hard physical labour. For days, a fragment of the dictator's head was battered and gouged, that fat sinister smile and the moustache, kicked and defecated on as it lay on the ground.

Saddam Hussein was modelling himself both on Nebuchadnezzar and on Stalin. His borrowings from Stalin's cult of personality can be seen in the huge number of his own images that he erected all over Baghdad, and in the range of their subject matter, depicting him as everything from warrior to father figure and sportsman. At the start of the 1980s, when Hussein really began to get into his stride as a builder, he embarked on his own version of the Palace of the Soviets. The State Mosque, with room for 30,000 worshippers, was meant to be the biggest place of worship in the Islamic world. Seven architectural celebrities, including Robert Venturi, the father of postmodernism were invited to take part in a competition to design it. The jury's decision was never made public, though they did give Saddam Hussein their verdict. Rather than accept it, Hussein convened an international symposium of 300 experts on mosque architecture to look at all the competitors again.

Evidently Hussein, like Stalin, was more interested in having his own way with the design than in allowing an architect the chance to use it as a means of self-expression. Equally evidently, he did not learn many lessons about the eventual fate of dictators from Budapest or Prague, where all that is left of Czechoslovakia's gigantic Stalin monument is a plinth. But by the time of the second Gulf War, America certainly had. It is obvious that George Bush the younger's advisers spent a lot of time looking in great detail at those grainy black-and-white newsreel images of Stalin being dragged down in effigy. They did everything that they could to restage them, frame by frame, in Baghdad, in what they hoped would be a grand finale for their invasion of Iraq.

There is, however, still a difference between image and substance. Hungary's rebels needed no outside help to deal with Stalin's statue, though they might have appreciated NATO intervention to save them from being crushed by the Red Army. In Baghdad it was the American Army's psychological warfare specialists who provided the muscle to bring down Saddam Hussein's bronze effigy rather than a spontaneous act of Iraqi iconoclasm.

4

The World in Stone

By the standards of Hitler and Stalin, Benito Mussolini presided over a relatively benign dictatorship, even if it was one that was still capable of genocidal colonial wars and a brutal contempt for domestic civil liberties. What is not clear is whether it was nothing more than his comparative restraint that saved Mussolini's architects from the same degree of hostility that faced Speer, or Iofan, or the quality of their work. Is it that Marcello Piacentini, or Giuseppe Terragni, or Pagano were better architects, or was it that they worked for a marginally less wicked regime that differentiated the rebuilding of Berlin and Moscow from Rome?

Certainly architecture was as much on Mussolini's mind as it was on Hitler and Stalin's. I have a photograph that shows a group of overweight figures in black-and-white uniforms looming over a model sitting on the floor. In his immaculate double-breasted white suit, finished off with a somewhat unlikely peaked yachting cap, Mussolini is flanked by a group of courtiers. I hadn't realized that the standard blackshirt uniform involved white trousers, never a good look for the paunchy. They stand enthralled by Marcello Piacentini, Mussolini's personal architect, eloquently enthusing about his master plan for Rome's new city, E 42, the culmination of the fascist onslaught on Rome's historic fabric.

Piacentini is poised over the model in that very special moment of animation that every architect knows. They have the client's full attention for a brief second, and know that this is their only chance to convince them that everything they have been dreaming about over months of work should go ahead at last. The fact that this new Rome has already displaced thousands of families from the working-class slums in the historic centre, and has had a profoundly damaging impact on the monuments of Augustus, are issues of which, of course, he is aware. But at that moment, they count for nothing. For an architect, in the instant that he has the undivided attention of a patron with the power to realize his designs, literally nothing else matters: not a fire alarm, not even an earthquake, would distract them; there is simply nothing else to talk about but architecture.

Piacentini himself had no doubt about the political purpose of architecture. It was to be reserved 'exclusively for the great temples of Religion and of the State, to celebrate the virtues of our race, to inflame and move, to glorify and acclaim'. Yet his architecture, but for some of the inscriptions and the iconography of the sculpture, looks nothing like what we conventionally describe as totalitarian. His work is big and intimidating. It is meant to impress, to make the individual feel small and insignificant. But it doesn't project the perverse, claustrophobic sense of wickedness that we can read into the sinister cottage style of some of Hitler's buildings, or his monstrous plans for rebuilding Berlin.

Mussolini, Stalin and Hitler all treated architecture as an indispensable instrument of political propaganda, one which they took an enthusiastic and obvious pleasure in using to maintain their grip on the apparatus of state power. The extraordinarily personal nature of their involvement with construction was a demonstration of their munificence and their omniscience. For the benefit of the newsreel cameras, Mussolini 'let the pick-axe speak', as he swung it up over his head to initiate the destruction of the medieval structures that crowded around the classical monuments along the Tiber. It was an image created to suggest not just his own vigour and potency but to claim that he was the equal of Caesar Augustus and the other emperors who built Rome.

Benito Mussolini had two decades to rebuild Italy, and he seized his opportunity with as much enthusiasm as Hitler. Hardly a city in Italy has been left unmarked by the fascist years. Mussolini's architects built the country's modern infrastructure; its new railway stations and its post offices; its law courts and universities, its factories and sanatoria; and they did their best to identify fascism with progress. Disquietingly for those who doubt that a brutal political system is capable of generating great architecture, Giuseppe Terragni, a long-standing fascist dedicated enough to Mussolini's cause to volunteer to fight on the Russian front, produced one of the great buildings of the twentieth century. His Casa del Fascio in Como is just as ideological in its intentions as anything designed by Speer or Iofan. And yet it is based on a subtle and richly imaginative exploration of space, used to glorify the blackshirt movement without falling back on the obvious visual triggers of size, intimidation or explicit iconography.

Like Troost's Nazi shrine in Munich, the Casa del Fascio exhibited relics of fascist heroes. Terragni put them in a glass cube, rather than a classical temple. Its row of doors were electrically operated to open simultaneously, allowing a blackshirt column to pour out in a body and flood the square outside in overwhelming numbers. The building has a hollowed-out centre, dignifying the various party organizations disposed around it, and is intended to signal the comradeship of fascist volunteers rather than a professional hierarchy in its planning. It's not easy to call it a humane building, but it does not obviously oppress, even if those who built it did.

Fascism was once described as a house of glass, words that contemporary architects would do well to remember before making facile attempts to suggest that transparency – and so, by implication, glass – is inherently democratic. The Casa del Fascio is certainly transparent. But while it doesn't look hostile or out of place under the mountains in the beautiful town of Como, across the way from the neo-classical opera house and the duomo, it certainly speaks of the faith that a generation of Italy's architects had in the fascist revolution. Terragni used architecture to convey an intellectual idea of fascism, and a sense of otherness – a sense that has survived in the building even in its present incarnation as the district headquarters of the Italian tax police.

Terragni was far from alone among Italian architects in eagerly participating in the Fascist regime's building programme. His colleagues designed Mussolini's new towns and built his colonial settlements in Libya, Somalia and Ethiopia. They designed the party headquarters buildings in every Italian city. They designed the propaganda exhibitions that glamorized fascism for the masses. They took part in the competitions for Mussolini's palace in Rome. In fact no prominent architects fled Italy to Britain and America, as they did from Germany. And few careers were cut short by resistance to the regime, although the bravery of Giuseppe Pagano, a former fascist who joined the resistance and died in a concentration camp, and Gian Luigi Banfi, another leading architect who met the same fate, were notable exceptions.

The most complex aspect of Mussolini's view of architecture was in his relationship with Rome. He was simultaneously presenting himself as the inheritor of the empire of the Caesars, a new Augustus, and as a modernizer. That meant demolishing swathes of the city, supposedly with the objective of creating an appropriate setting for such monuments as the mausoleum of Augustus. The mausoleum was preserved, isolated in the middle of a new square, designed in grandiloquent fascist style by Vittorio Ballio Morporgo. The Ara Pacis, the altar built by Augustus to commemorate his victories, was rehoused in a glass and steel box overlooking the Tiber. Sixty years later, it was moved again by a left-wing mayor, who invited Richard Meier to design a new pavilion to accommodate it. Meier promptly fell foul of the Berlusconi government's junior minister for Culture, Vittorio Sgarbi, who attempted to kill the project as much for political as aesthetic reasons.

Mussolini's interventions in the Forum, the Colosseum and the Capitoline did enough damage to Rome's archaeological heritage, but it could have been even worse. He toyed with the idea of creating a palace for his own use, the Palazzo de Littorio, to act as the Fascist Party's headquarters directly opposite the Colosseum. He staged a competition for a design, attracting what in contrast to Hitler's Chancellery were clearly modern schemes. But the language of architectural abstraction was just as capable of creating a sense of intimidation, and the subjugation of the individual to the will of the leader, as Speer's endless classical extrusions.

Mussolini eventually changed his mind and created the Foro Mussolini, to the north of the city. It's a more archaeological-looking version of fascist urbanism. The forum is surrounded by a complex of new buildings modelled on the circuses of ancient Rome. To mark the twentieth anniversary of his seizure of power, Mussolini initiated another architectural showcase on the south side of the city, balancing the forum in the north. Mussolini's new extension to Rome, known as the Exposition Universal Romana, or EUR, was built for an Expo planned for 1942. The original intention was to construct a series of buildings that would be used during Expo year as exhibition and event spaces, before being turned over as the nucleus of Rome's large-scale expansion southwards toward Ostia and the sea. The war intervened and the Expo was abandoned, but enough of the site was developed to leave a powerful taste of what an authoritarian city that used a modernist vocabulary would be like.

The plan was a compromise between Italian architectural modernizers and traditionalists, with the balance of power shifting toward the traditionalists as time went on. It became the focus of the conflict between sharply different visions of what Rome should be and provoked what was to turn out to be the final and fatal break between the regime and Giuseppe Pagano. The loyal fascist who had been involved with the early stages of the planning of EUR denounced Marcello Piacentini, Mussolini's own architect, who took charge. The break did not affect Pagano's devotion to the fascist cause, until he went to fight in Mussolini's army in Albania.

Despite Pagano's doubts, EUR is considerably more sophisticated as a piece of urbanism than Speer's Berlin would have been. The ever competitive Hitler declared the plan 'a meaningless copy without any import'. Piacentini had indeed seen Speer's drawings for Berlin before he set about regularizing those aspects of EUR judged to be too freely expressive or, as the fascists put it, 'Hebrew'. However, EUR is planned on a grid rather than a single monumental axis. A number of landmark structures establish the area in the landscape, the most prominent of which is the Palace of Italian Civilization, the so-called Square Colosseum. The structure is visible all the way from the Villa Borghese in the centre of the city. With its six layers of Roman arches stacked one on top of the other, it sits on top of the hill at the southern edge of EUR. There are 150 steps, untroubled by any sign of a handrail. It looks like a travertine mountain, and feels as daunting to climb as if you were ascending a stepped pyramid in Mexico. At the summit, you will discover that the Palace of Italian Civilization is closed for repairs. Carved in stone across the top of the cube, back and front, is the legend: 'A people of poets and artists, of heroes and saints, of thinkers, scientists, navigators and migrants'. An outer skin stands clear of the inner cube, pierced by arched openings, while an inner one has floor-to-ceiling windows that echo the pattern. The forms could not be simpler: as much a stage set as architecture, and yet the tension between solid and void gives it a real presence.

The Square Colosseum forms the end of one of the grid of avenues running north–south: at the other end is Adalberto Libera's Congress Hall, less obviously classical in its inspiration, with its flattened dome rising over a white stone box. Its entrance is marked by a colonnade of fourteen grey granite columns set in a dazzling snow-white marble screen. The blank front wall has a mysterious floating triangular wedge, designed to carry Francesco Messa's sculpture of a four-horsed chariot, a contemporary version of the quadriga on top of the Brandenburg Gate. The sculpture was never finished or installed. As finally completed, the building was shorn of the elaborate iconographical imagery that would have attempted to root the hall in the Roman tradition. Libera also designed a giant elliptical arch, left unbuilt, that would have been EUR's most visible landmark. It later inspired Eero Saarinen's St Louis arch of 1948, though Saarinen seems not to have been troubled by the fascist connotations of the form.

The grid plan of EUR avoids the monomaniacal quality of Speer's Berlin. It feels more like Milton Keynes, or Orange County. Libera's building and the Palazzo conduct a civilized dialogue with each other. The two most prominent buildings of EUR avoid the central axis, which is marked by an obelisk looted from Egypt, and have a relationship with the third major element that appears on the skyline, the domed church on the southern edge of the complex.

Piacentini's plan subjugated individual buildings to the demands of the overall urban composition. The hollow block next to Libera's Congress Hall forms one side of a square, a street arcade another, and a sweeping urban crescent a third. The arrangement leaves them vulnerable to the problems of conflicting geometry. The terraces that make up most of the city sit on colonnades designed to accommodate shops and cafés. In almost any other Western country they would have been abandoned, revealing the unbridgeable gap between architectural aspirations and commercial realities. But Italy's embrace of the public realm has breathed some life into the streets. Even so, in many parts of EUR the ground floors are all but abandoned, with activity concentrated on the *piano nobile* above, almost as if this were Venice. There is the stench of stale urine in the air as you shelter from the rain in the sweeping colonnades, cut out of the base of each city block. The squalor is poignantly framed by the finest materials that Mussolini's architects could find: turned granite columns, exquisitely laid cobblestones, pale pink plastered vaults, lit by generously proportioned glass globe lampshades. There is white marble around the doors and the windows. In corners there is evidence of tramps sleeping out, sheltering from the worst of the weather. Loudspeakers dangle from cables in the vaults, as if in memory of a long-ago harangue from Il Duce.

Peering in through the de Chirico-like windows and the dust, you see glimpses of abandoned spaces, rooms that have not been used in sixty years, bricked-up openings, and runs of pipe in front of unusable doors. The buildings are embellished with carvings of allegorical classical themes. On the ground floor of what is now an outpost of the Italian Social Security Ministry Icarus floats overhead, and through the door you glimpse a cleaner's trolley with a running shoe stuck over the brushes. Around the corner, flanking the entrance to one of the group of museums in the centre of EUR, five-storey-high mosaic murals depict the glories of Italy's craftsmen and tradesmen. Open its ground-floor door and you find yourself confronted by a wall of sixty steps, a daunting climb to reach the exhibits for even the most determined.

Some of the early buildings are marked by seemingly random outcrops of rough masonry blocks scattered here and there, erupting from the smooth dressed-stone walls, as if to suggest the patina of age and imply that the structure has been built, like the centre of Rome, on ancient foundations, rather than as the instant city that it really is. The banality of later additions from the 1960s that radiate outwards from the edges of EUR have the curious effect of making the original buildings look simultaneously ancient and much more modern than they really are, as if reinforcing Mussolini's original intentions.

The massive blank walls of the Museum of Roman Civilization are more Egyptian than Roman, penetrated only by a deep narrow cut marked on either side by a giant order of granite columns. There is a play between rough and smooth stone, between tufa and travertine, between open and closed. The museum is organized as a series of symmetrically planned pavilions on both sides of a central axis, bridged at intervals by giant porticos, so tall that they don't keep the rain off your head.

On a quiet Saturday morning, EUR has an everyday ordinariness that seems to deny its sinister origins. This was meant to be a glorification of fascism. As it turned out, it has become a neglected if dignified suburb with an unusually urbane character that has effortlessly outlasted the comic-opera regime that gave birth to it. And it has shrugged off its ideology. To live and work here poses no obvious threat to the health of present-day Italian democracy.

At least two of Italy's leading architects in the 1930s, whose work brought them into close contact with Mussolini, and who were themselves convinced fascists, died with particular poignancy in the concentration camp at Mauthausen – the camp originally established as part of the SS's attempt to profit from the supply of building materials for Speer's monumental architecture. Gian Luigi Banfi was a partner in the Milanese practice BBPR, one of whose members was Ernesto Rogers, a cousin of the British architect Richard Rogers. Amongst other projects for Mussolini, Banfi worked on the exhibition celebrating the fascist revolution. The other architect to suffer this fate, Giuseppe Pogatschnig, born in Parenzo in 1896, had been far more deeply committed to fascism. His career would reflect the tortured relationship of architecture with power. Pogatschnig changed his name to Pagano when he joined the Italian Army, fighting in the Austrian campaign in the First World War and later taking part in Gabriele D'Annunzio's seizure of Fiume. He joined the Fascist Party in 1920. Pagano was a convinced believer, dedicated to the cause of Mussolini's revolution, rather than an opportunist. He became a senior member of a group established by Mussolini's nephew that functioned as a political version of a religious sect. Its members described themselves as missionaries dedicated to spreading the Duce's word, and warriors pledged to defend the revolution to the end.

The group was a centre for the manufacture of party ideology. Pagano was responsible for developing a fascist philosophy for the visual arts, as well as being a member of the editorial board of *Doctrine*, the sect's quarterly publication. Pagano's commitment to Mussolini and fascist politics did not compromise the quality of his architectural work. He was a gifted designer and, despite his connections with the regime, an independent-minded polemicist. In Milan he was responsible for the sensitive and entirely modern design of the Bocconi University, a private institution that is Italy's version of the London School of Economics. Pagano was one of the architects responsible for Milano Verde, a radical master plan for modernizing Milan free of the grandiloquence and rhetoric of what is generally described as fascist architecture. He also worked with Gio Ponti on designing Italy's pioneering new electric trains.

In 1933 Pagano moved to Milan, where he edited the magazine *Casabella*, which was more interested in Italian modernism than in fascism. While remaining a committed party member, he became increasingly critical of Mussolini's plans for rebuilding Rome. But that did not stop him from working closely with Mussolini's official architect, Marcello Piacentini, and Pagano helped design the Italian pavilion at the Paris World's Fair that was overshadowed by Albert Speer's German pavilion. In 1941, well into middle age, Pagano volunteered for military service in the Balkans when Mussolini invaded Yugoslavia alongside the Germans. A year later, however, he had lost his faith in fascism and left the party to join the partisans. He was arrested and jailed in Brescia, where he organized a mass breakout: 260 political prisoners escaped. A pen-and-ink self-portrait in beard and glasses survives from his prison days. He was recaptured in September 1944, and died in Mauthausen in the last days of the war, a casualty of totalitarianism whose death was a lesson in the nature of courage to all of us, not least Albert Speer.

Leon Krier, the architect best known for his role in planning Seaside, the outpost of New Urbanism on the Florida panhandle, and the Prince of Wales's village of Poundbury, has been the most active voice in attempting to rehabilitate Speer. Why, he wondered, was it considered necessary to destroy the inoffensive street lights that Hitler's architect had designed for Berlin? Why, Krier asked, did Speer end up as Spandau's penultimate prisoner? Long after Werner von Braun, who devised the highly destructive V2 rockets that were built

using slave labour and which killed so many Londoners, had bypassed
the prisoner-of-war camps and flown to the USA to build the arsenal
of democracy, Speer was still in jail. Could architecture actually be
regarded as a weapon of war like a V2? Perhaps the answer lies in the
way that we tend to blame the architect more than the engineer –
because he envisaged the shape of a totalitarian state.

Speer helped make totalitarianism possible by making it visible.
An architect can conjure a dream of what fascism or Stalinism or
Saddamism might be, even before it exists. He makes an ugly possibility into a terrible reality. And this can make architecture appear as an
instrument of repression. Certainly that is how the Poles understood
Stalin's building of the Palace of Culture in the middle of Warsaw,
and it helped to explain Poland's determination to re-create the historic centre of Warsaw exactly as it had been before the Nazis erased
it. Less clear is how we should react to the physical legacy of vanished
authoritarian regimes. Italy to this day is full of rotting buildings,
many of real quality, that were put up by the Fascists to house their
party organizations. They were confiscated by the post-war government after the collapse of Mussolini's regime, and nobody knows
what to do with them. To demolish them all would be both profligate
and represent a historical whitewash, and yet to restore them could
suggest a rehabilitation of the regime that built them. Sixty years later,
the country is still unable to make up its mind about most of them.

Philip Johnson's career provides another extraordinary example, so
different in its outcome from Giuseppe Pagano, of the search for
power by an architect and the embrace of ideology. He was born
in 1906, just a year after Albert Speer, and, like him, came from a
prosperous provincial middle-class background. Speer's father and
grandfather were architects. Johnson's father was a lawyer.

If, as I did, you feel you really must read Philip Johnson's mail, the
first step is to book an appointment in the special collections section
of the Getty Center's research library in Santa Monica. That way you
don't have to reserve a place in the car park, or wait in line for the
tram to take you up to the top of the hill that the Getty Library shares
with the better-known museum of the same name. The four-minute
journey delivers you to the Getty Plaza, carpeted with travertine

and carefully tended gardens, a democratic cousin of the Square Colosseum. A tidal flow of respectful visitors look mildly awed at the scale of this gigantic bubble of artificial pedestrian life in the land of the freeway. You can see the cars far below, as they push their way through the Santa Monica hills, but you can't hear them. And the air up here is fresh enough to keep the smog at bay.

The library, away to the right of the museum, is a stone doughnut the colour of sour milk. It is the least convincing piece of Richard Meier's monumental complex of galleries, research institutes and libraries housed in a collection of cubes and cylinders scattered across the landscape like toys on a nursery floor. But for all that, it is still suffused with Pacific light and that lush sense of space that is the very particular product of the deep pockets of American cultural philanthropy. Visiting scholars, and the occasional tourist straying off the circuit of the Getty's Old Masters, postcard stands and cafés, find themselves in a gilded world of deference and custom-made furniture.

To reach the special collections you must first produce a driving licence or a passport, then have yourself digitally photographed and complete a registration form. Only after all that are you ushered toward Meier's staircase, spiralling down into the bowels of the library. The door to the special collections is locked, and when you buzz for attention the librarian presses a button to release it. Bags are confiscated, and you are issued with a yellow, lined foolscap pad and a pencil, sharpened to the finest of points. Of course there is no charge. Finally, you reach the archive, a series of outsize envelopes, numbered, catalogued and chronologically sorted. All this feels like an elaborate piece of glossy packaging, deliberately calculated to banish any doubt about the significance and value of the yellowing papers that are about to pass through your hands.

The papers provide an insight into the last era in which prominent architects chose to play a direct and leading political role. Some attempted to use their architectural work in a political sense; others, such as Philip Johnson, decided to abandon the built world for a time in pursuit of direct political power. The Johnson archive doesn't take up that much shelf space. It would have fitted into a couple of suitcases in his attic, if only his glass house in New Canaan had one. It is just a glimpse through a keyhole at a careful selection of Johnson's personal papers. Johnson's involvement with the art world and the Museum of Modern Art, the professional correspondence and the architectural drawings are all documented elsewhere – a fact, needless to say, that is made scrupulously clear in the catalogue.

The selection includes such sentimental souvenirs as a stack of Johnson's cancelled passports from the 1950s and 1960s, collections of photographs, magazine cuttings, brochures and notes for speeches. There is the honourable discharge that Private Johnson, an intelligence observer in the US Army, collected in December 1944, twenty months after he had finally succeeded in joining America's armed forces. In 1941 his application for a commission as a lieutenant in the naval reserve, also here, had been turned down without any explanation. The file that the FBI had opened the previous year on Johnson and his connections with at least one known German agent may have had something to do with his rejection, though it isn't in the archive. In 1942, he tried the navy again but failed his physical examination. When at last he had signed up for the army, he never served overseas.

And then there is the file that contains a sequence of Johnson's letters to his mother. Only one is addressed to both of his parents, suggesting a certain lack of sympathy for his father. Johnson typed them on his portable, two-fingered and closely spaced. They date back to 1926, when he was studying Aristotle and Plato at Harvard, and run through to the end of 1931, to the letters he wrote on the stationery that he had specially printed with his Berlin address: Achenbachstrasse 22 IV.

The letters are funny and clever and disturbing. They reveal a young man dividing his time between philosophy tutorials with the fellow students that he despised – 'they disgust me' – and the Harvard Glee Club. He describes his comic dismay when its performances were described as 'lacking virility' by the *New York Times*. He writes of spending his allowance on pianos and freesias, and reveals his twin obsessions with architecture and fast cars. In fact Johnson sometimes devoted almost as much space to writing about the cars in his life – Packards and Cords mostly – as he did to the buildings he saw. These dual obsessions are encapsulated in one of the Getty's envelopes, which contains a postcard that Johnson sent his mother from Dessau in 1929. On one side is a photograph of Gropius's Bauhaus. On the other is Johnson's message: 'This is one of the most beautiful buildings in the world; you must see it some day.' In the same envelope is a cutting from a German newspaper showing a photograph of a new Cord roadster unveiled at the Paris Motor Show that week. 'How would you like me to call on you in this?' asks a roguish Johnson. 'It's the best car I have seen yet.' Later, he goes on to describe a near-fatal collision with a cyclist in Czechoslovakia.

Johnson was always ready to lapse into purple when writing for effect. In one letter, he describes going to a concert: 'Sokoloff did a wonderful job on a new Bax symphony that some might call cacophony, but I was put out of commission with the gorgeous polyphonic harmonies. It was a gory thing and I saw red blood in my eyes most of the way through. But all the mist and blood of killing was in it, until I had thoroughly convinced myself that I had slaughtered the whole world and that God and I were rejoicing in it. A horrible imagination no doubt but I think it was impossible not to feel that way with it.' These are the words of a young man in his early twenties, trying out alternative identities for size, to see which one fits best, just as he would one day switch his allegiance year by year from Mies van der Rohe to Ledoux to deconstructionism. But Johnson was no longer a young man when a dozen years later he wrote an account of the German invasion of Poland in which he described the burning of Warsaw as 'a stirring sight'. Given that Johnson did indeed suffer a nervous collapse, it is almost as disturbing to read a letter in which he suggests, 'I think I'll have a convenient nervous breakdown next month, and come to Pinehurst where at least the emphasis would not be on trying to think, or trying not to either.'

And then there is the file of newspaper cuttings documenting Johnson's career as a special correspondent for *Social Justice Weekly*. Johnson contributed to the hate-filled propaganda sheet for more than two years. To *Social Justice*, the Klu Klux Klan were natural allies, Roosevelt was the hired hand of the rich, and America was threatened by one communist plot after another. It was published by Father Coughlin, the rabidly anti-Semitic Catholic priest whose radio broadcasts in the 1930s attracted huge audiences. Though not everything that Johnson wrote for the paper is in the Getty archive, there is enough to get the flavour. Here is Johnson writing from the Polish frontier with Germany just a couple of days before the outbreak of the Second World War:

> The Poles are so excited and so worried about the crisis which they feel is at hand that they arrested me at the border, merely for taking pictures. They should have let me go after seeing my American passport, and my American car but the Polish police are in no mood to believe anyone. After eight hours of grilling they let me go.
>
> The whole population of Kepoo where I was incarcerated was out in the fields, 10,000 strong, young and old to dig trenches. Before he would let me go, the chief of police took me out to show me. 'Tell the Germans what you saw, we shall fight them until we die'. Later I told some Germans about the trenches, they roared with laughter, and pointed to their tanks.

This was the same trip on which the respected *New York Times* correspondent William Shirer was forced to share a hotel room with Johnson by the German Ministry of Propaganda. Shirer later described him as 'an American fascist, and a suspected Nazi agent', a suspicion that was evidently shared by the FBI.

Certainly Johnson could have been counted 'an agent of influence' by Germany, as the Soviet Union described its informal allies within the British Establishment in the 1930s and 1940s. They might not have been ready to cross the line to become active spies, but they were certainly prepared to play their part in the propaganda war. Johnson's journalism is neither neutral reporting, nor simple personal prejudice. It reads like part of a sustained campaign, first to suggest that neither Czechoslovakia nor Poland were legitimate states, and so fair game for Germany, and then to stop America from entering the Second World War on the side of Britain and France. It was thus intended to assist Hitler's victory. Johnson, and Hitler's other American apologists, represented the German attack on Poland as no more Britain's business than any of the countless minor colonial wars that Britain had fought in India were Germany's. When that failed to convince, Britain was accused of sacrificing the Poles, who in any case weren't worth fighting for, in its unjustified war against Germany. And by the way, Germany's overwhelming strength meant that it had already won the war, so that any effort to stop Hitler was all much too late.

Johnson's dispatch from Munich in October 1939, by which time the war had started, is in the archive: 'Germany talks peace. It only fails of its object in the British Empire and her crown colony, the US of A. English talk affects us deeply, but leaves all other neutrals cold. Italy goes as far as to answer, "what do you mean when you say Europe is at war, you are not fighting our battle Great Britain, we want peace, and so do Spain, Hungary, Jugoslavia, Holland, Belgium, Denmark, Sweden, Norway and Finland".'

But for some reason Johnson's report from Paris the previous year, in which he wrote as a fact that 'only Jews had a right to free speech in France', is missing. In it, Johnson quoted at length, and with apparent sympathy, a person he described as 'a true born French-woman' lamenting the influx of Austrian, Polish and German Jews, and the way those whom she calls their local cousins were running the country on their behalf. Also absent is the essay that he wrote in *Today's Challenge* in 1939, for the American Fellowship Forum, claiming that 'The USA is committing race suicide.' A picture of a troubled and not very likeable man emerges from his writings. Johnson's anti-Semitism and racism went well beyond the level of casual American country-club prejudice of the time. Writing in *Social Justice*, Johnson describes his trip to Poland: 'I thought I must be in the region of some awful plague. The fields were nothing but stone. There were no trees, mere paths instead of roads. In the towns no shops, no automobiles. There were not even any Poles to be seen in the streets. Only Jews. I visited Lodz, with 680,000 people; it's called the Chicago of Poland. I found it a slum without a city attached to it. The Jews form 35 per cent, dressed in their black robes, their black skull caps, they seem more like 85 per cent.'

He disliked Czechs, or at least the non-German-speaking section of the country's population, whom he appears to consider his racial inferiors. Writing to his mother he describes a visit to the opera in Prague: 'We heard Don Giovanni last night sung in Tschek or Cesk or whatever the damn language is. Just so much spitting as far as we were concerned. At least when you were here everything was in German. And the stupid people with their too broad mouths and blank expressions.' To judge by his article in *Social Justice* describing the nonchalance with which ordinary Germans regarded the outbreak of war, Johnson was prepared to condone prejudice against American blacks too, even if one of his first lovers was black. 'This war can't be worse than our negro occupation after the last one,' he quotes an anonymous German as telling him.

Why would Johnson want to put even a limited selection of these papers into the public domain? Was it an attempt at making a frank disclosure? Johnson's relationship with his own past, which has always been ambiguous, would suggest that the answer is no. There has been a regular series of apologies for his bigotry, including a visit to the Anti-Defamation League in New York in the late 1940s. Johnson's otherwise sympathetic biographer, Franz Schulze, questions the sincerity of this gesture, suggesting that it came only after Edgar Kauffman, his rival at MoMA, commissioned a private detective to probe Johnson's political past and was aimed at damage limitation rather than contrition.

Johnson had long and close relationships with many American Jews. He designed Israel's first nuclear reactor, and built a synagogue for New Canaan free of charge. But in 1993, when Johnson was in Berlin, he made a speech in which he claimed to 'loathe Hitler, but love Friedrich Wilhelm'. He called them 'bad client, good client', summarizing in a way his world view, both in his weakness for the never entirely apposite one-liner, and the sentiments it represents. Much as he would like to have been, Johnson was no Oscar Wilde . He went on to say, 'I spent almost three years in Germany at the end of Weimar. The sex life was new and thrilling. The beer was good and the friendship was better. In my intoxication with Berlin's modern life, I completely missed the underlying political difficulties. I knew no outspoken Communists or Nazis.' This is scarcely a credible claim from a man who had been seduced by the Messianic sight of Hitler in full flow at a Nazi rally in 1931, a man who was well enough informed of Hitler's interests to write a perceptive commentary on architecture in the Third Reich for an American literary magazine. He identified three distinct camps, from Schultze-Naumberg's kitsch, to Schmitthenner's vernacular style, to the Miesian rigour that he hoped would be adopted by the National Socialist modernizers. Unlike most other architects, Johnson devoted six years of his life to a political project that included establishing a right-wing political party, Youth and Nation, for which he devised a flying wedge symbol, and which sometimes called itself the Grey Shirts. He had decided to leave MoMA in 1934 to devote himself to politics. The most informative of the few traces in the archive of this period are a couple of newspaper cuttings. In one of them Charles T. Luccy, the *Toledo News Bee*'s evidently star-struck reporter, describes Johnson the political activist as possessed of 'a kind of priestly fire'. Johnson's political programme was the usual proto-fascist populist brew of the 1930s. 'We oppose communists, but we admire them for their smartness. Reactionaries are our enemies, the ones who have enough, and want to keep it that way.' Johnson promised 'An American solution for American problems. A central bank, a strong air force . . . more emotionalism, less intellectualism.' Decades later. Johnson telescoped all this into a rather less contentious précis: 'I started a radio campaign for higher prices for milk farmers.'

Despite his willingness to explore every form of architectural expression from ziggurats to art deco and to make each of them the starting point of one of his buildings, Johnson preserved an absolute silence on the subject of Speer and his architecture. He was less squeamish about the work of Stalin's architects. In 1994 the director of Vienna's MAK museum, Peter Noever, invited Johnson to open an exhibition on Soviet architecture in the Stalin years. Except for its title, 'The Tyranny of Beauty', the show would have delighted Stalin, with its respectful tone and its glamorous view of authoritarian architecture, depicting a kind of Manhattan on the Moskva. According to Johnson's address at the opening, 'Stalin is today counted as one of history's greatest villains. No doubt he was. This evening however we are asked to look at one small facet of this interesting tyrant, the beautification of Russia, and the glorification of himself.' Even such a determined puncturer of conventional liberal preconceptions as Johnson could not afford to take the same narrow-focus view of Hitler for fear of reopening old questions about his own past. Even an architect who is ready to describe all architects, himself included, as whores.

As a politician, Johnson was hardly convincing. His isolationist, pro-Nazi campaign to keep America from intervening in the Second World War would have been unsuccessful, even without the attack on Pearl Harbor. The various unsavoury right-wingers whom Johnson backed financially to run against FDR got nowhere. His own party failed to attract mass support. Johnson's appeal to the American extreme right was his money, derived from the block of Alcoa shares given him by his father that made him a millionaire, and his status as a public figure thanks to his early career at the Museum of Modern Art, rather than his leadership potential. Even if circumstances had been different, Johnson would never have had the organizing energy to be useful to a Führer in the way that Speer was. But he was able instead to establish himself as a power broker within the world of architecture, and for Johnson that in the end seems to have been enough.

Despite the enthusiasm with which the Nazis and Italy's Fascists were eagerly exploring the use of architecture as a political tool, and his own political activism, Johnson never made a connection between architecture and politics in the 1930s. Quite the reverse: the two always appeared to occupy different compartments of his life. In his political self, Johnson had nothing to say about architecture. He did his best to present architecture as apolitical, perhaps because he found his enthusiasm for Mies van der Rohe to be in conflict with official architectural taste within Hitler's Germany, a society that he otherwise sympathized with. Johnson tried to portray his hero as a German patriot, reflecting Prussian values in the austerity of his work. He tried to paint Mies as the victim of left-wing prejudice, presumably in the hope that this might endear him to the right. 'The Mies home is admittedly luxurious, for this reason Mies is disliked by many architects and critics, especially the communists,' he wrote in 1931 in his critique of the Berlin building exhibition for the *New York Times*. But that does not mean Johnson kept his political prejudices out of his cultural life. He never took to Erich Mendelsohn, one of many German-Jewish architects forced to flee the Nazis. 'Mendelsohn thinks he is God Almighty, and won't give us the photographs. We feel like being nasty and making out his architecture as even worse than it is, in retaliation,' Johnson wrote to his mother while in Berlin collecting material for MoMA's International Style show. He described Hannes Meyer, Walter Gropius's left-wing successor as director of the Bauhaus, as 'a stupid man', and claimed that since Meyer's arrival in Dessau, 'what one learns there is not comparable to what can be got elsewhere'.

While his political campaigns got him nowhere, Johnson's adventures in architectural politics were much more effective. America was introduced to modern architecture in the 1930s by Johnson and Henry-Russell Hitchcock. And by and large she took to it, perhaps because Johnson presented it entirely shorn of any sense of a social programme. Johnson of course succeeded even more effectively in constructing a position for himself at the centre of American architecture, thanks to that sense of his proprietary hold on a successful new movement. Johnson, who failed to build a personal relationship with Le Corbusier, bet heavily on Mies as the greatest of European architects, and was rewarded by Mies's success in America. Johnson's judgement has continued to cast a long shadow over the Museum of Modern Art, an institution that has staged no fewer than eight exhibitions on Mies in its history. Much later on, after he had fallen out with Mies in a late-night bourbon-fuelled argument about the finer points of the design of Johnson's own house, Johnson missed no opportunity to paint Mies as a self-serving and amoral architect ready to do anything to build. Indeed, Johnson's subsequent career after his break with Mies could be seen as the attempted patricide of a long-admired father figure by a spurned young disciple. All that Mies had believed about timelessness, and consistency and rigour, Johnson systematically set out to caricature with an architecture of indulgence and caprice.

'Nazis, schmatzis, Mies would have built for anyone,' the architectural historian Elaine Hochman reports Johnson telling her. It is a remark that can certainly be seen as a case of Johnson projecting his own attitudes on others. It is hard to think of Mies, who was so cool with Jacqueline Kennedy about designing JFK's presidential library that she assumed he didn't want the job, cultivating Donald Trump with the unseemly eagerness adopted by Johnson when he was pursuing the chance of erecting a wall of high-rise apartments for the most lumpen of New York's property developers. Johnson's flattery persuaded Trump to see him as a useful marketing tool, for just long enough to call him 'the greatest architect in the world', but the relationship left Johnson diminished by its transparent opportunism.

Rather than representing an appetite for frankness, the donation of his archive to the Getty may have more to do with Johnson's lifelong search for attention. It's a strategy of titillating disclosure aimed in fact at diverting closer scrutiny, rather than representing genuine candour. Johnson was perhaps the first architect of the twentieth century to understand exactly how much a successful architectural career depends on a mastery of the techniques of publicity. On one level, this was not such a new departure. From Vitruvius to Palladio, Robert Adam to Le Corbusier, publishing handsomely illustrated editions of complete works has been a vital step in successfully establishing a long-lasting architectural reputation. Johnson, however, saw that getting himself on the cover of *Time* magazine was a more useful career move than publishing an architectural monograph that would only be seen by other architects, and decided to do both. He understood the art of the sound bite. He was always careful to remain close to the levers of power through the exercise of patronage. Above all, he was entirely at home with the culture of celebrity.

During the course of an interview with Albert Speer shortly before he died, the art critic Robert Hughes claims to have asked him to suggest a contemporary architect to serve a hypothetical new Führer. 'I hope Philip Johnson will not mind if I mention his name. Johnson understands what the small man thinks of as grandeur. The fine materials, the size of the space.' Hughes wrote that Speer went on to ask him to deliver a copy of a book of his own architecture to Johnson in New York.

Speer carefully opened the book, to the title page, uncapped his heavy gold fountain pen with the floppy nib, and wrote in blue ink in his peculiarly crabby, vertically squished-up hand.

'For Philip Johnson, a fellow architect. With sincere admiration of his most recent designs. Best Regards Albert Speer.'

Hughes says he subsequently met Johnson for lunch at the Four Seasons in New York to hand over the gift. 'You haven't shown this to anyone?' No, Hughes lied, he hadn't. 'Thank heavens for small mercies,' Johnson muttered.

Johnson always courted publicity, both in his overtly political years and as an architect, and he had an unwavering determination to be at the centre of things. *Vanity Fair*, with its tooth-rotting but irresistible

diet of celebrity, middle-class murders and Hollywood politics, celebrated Philip Johnson's 95th birthday in almost exactly the same way
that it celebrated his 90th. It commissioned the fashion photographer
Timothy Greenfield-Sanders to take a picture of American architecture's oldest grand old man, seated in the thick of a dense cloud of
his acolytes in the lobby bar of the Four Seasons, the restaurant that
he designed at the foot of the Seagram Tower. It is inconceivable that
any other architect would have had the same treatment, not even
Frank Gehry, who, with Brad Pitt in and out of his office, is certainly
no stranger to stardom.

The *Vanity Fair* photograph is a tribute not so much to the significance of Johnson's contribution to the history of architecture as a
reminder of his importance to the cult of fame. Frank Gehry sits on
one side of Johnson, alongside Peter Eisenman. Arata Isozaki has
flown in from Tokyo, Rem Koolhaas from Rotterdam and Zaha
Hadid from London. Their presence seems to suggest not just a tribute
to Johnson on their part, but a sense of an acceptance of the old
man's benediction, a laying-on of hands that has certainly helped their
careers over the years. Johnson looks exactly the same each year while
the selection of guests in the *Vanity Fair* photograph gets steadily
younger to demonstrate his continuing grip over architectural life.

Johnson's decision to make his papers part of an academic archive
while he was actively pursuing a professional career could be seen as
an especially calculated form of self-advertisement. Even Frank Lloyd
Wright's correspondence didn't get this kind of treatment when he was
still alive. It is hard to point to a single building that Johnson has
designed in the course of his long career that served to change the course
of American architecture, let alone architecture anywhere else. Even
Johnson's Chippendale skyscraper on Madison Avenue, the granite-
sheathed tower that began life as the AT&T building and now accommodates Sony, presented as ushering in a new age of corporate pomp in
the 1980s through a series of carefully orchestrated photographs on the
cover of *Time* magazine and the *New York Times*, was actually a case
of jumping onto a bandwagon that was already rolling. To treat his
correspondence with this much respect is clearly trying to tell us something more elevated about Johnson, and his historical significance.

Thanks to his endlessly energetic efforts to put himself on show,

Johnson has acquired the status of a national institution. It is a two-way transaction, one that shores up Johnson and which at the same time adds to the reputation of the Getty, which in itself is one of the most remarkable expressions of the determination of an individual to perpetuate their own memory. Getty paid minimal attention to the design of his museum's first building other than to decide that it should take the form of a Pompeian villa rather than replicate Sutton Place, the Tudor mansion that was his English home for years. And he was dead long before the Meier campus opened. He never looked inside many of the packing cases containing the art that his agents acquired in his name before they were shipped off to California. Yet he ensured that his memory would far outlast his financial empire by investing in building a collection of art from all over the world.

Through his seventy-five-year association with the Museum of Modern Art and its department of architecture and design, Johnson has controlled one of the more conspicuous platforms on which architectural reputations have been made in America. He was around in 1932 to champion the international style, and in 1957 to help Phyllis Lambert, heiress to the Seagram distillery fortune, persuade her father that what the family firm needed for its new Manhattan building was a real architect. He suggested Mies, a move that did far more for Johnson's reputation than trying to design it himself. His reward was to be named associated architect for the tower, a necessary arrangement since Mies did not have a licence to practise in New York.

Twenty years later, Johnson was ready and waiting at the moment that corporate America finally decided it was bored with working in buildings shaped by well-bred architectural restraint and wanted to inject a little imperial splendour into its surroundings. Johnson's answer was postmodernism, offering stone façades and classical columns to soothe the fevered corporate brow – a style he adopted ready made from Michael Graves. He used the same trick a decade later when he abandoned the sinking ship of postmodernism in favour of the very next thing, architectural deconstructivism, putting his stamp on an exhibition on the subject at MoMA. It was no mean feat of intellectual agility for a man of any age, let alone an octogenarian.

Johnson had the worldliness to understand that architecture is not a hermetic discipline, no matter how much some of its practitioners persist in behaving as if it were. Johnson's architecture has itself been designed for the maximum generation of publicity. He was the Harley Earl of architecture, constantly looking for taller tail fins and more chrome each season to make buildings that attract attention. It's a hunger for effect that has produced quite a few works that thankfully have never seen the light of day. One of his most grotesque proposals was to put up a life-size replica of the Houses of Parliament on the Thames opposite the Tower of London as a commercial development for the Kuwaiti Investment Office.

London's planning authorities and a weak property market thankfully torpedoed the Westminster replica; but in Dallas, Johnson built an office and condominium development in the form of a giant French château, and in Pittsburgh there is an outsize mirror-glass version of the Tower of London. In Houston, Johnson designed an architecture school in the form of a previously unrealized Ledoux design for a temple. In the ever wilder fluctuations of his enthusiasms, and Johnson's own laboriously public protestations of cynicism, he seemed to be deliberately bent on undermining the very idea of architecture as anything but a personal caprice, stripping it of any other kind of meaning than a craven attempt to pander to jaded tastes. It is as if he were trying deliberately to undermine his more gifted colleagues, and perhaps to satirize the clients whom he flattered to their faces, and abused behind their backs.

While Johnson continually presented architecture as an end in itself, he never offered any real sense of knowing what that end might be. He had every opportunity to build, but did surprisingly little with those opportunities. He had no lasting beliefs, except his determination to go on being relevant. Johnson's career survived his involvement with fascism unscathed, but in the end he became a revolving door, running through architectural history in an apparently random order but at an ever faster pace, to find the source material for his next project.

Of the many architects who worked, or who wanted to work, for the dictators, few were any more coherent about their motivations than Johnson. Some certainly sincerely believed that it was their duty to put their skills at the service of a political cause. Hannes Meyer, the second director of the Bauhaus, who attracted Johnson's contempt, was certainly one of these. For him, the architect had a part to play in constructing socialism to build a society in which the masses were housed in civilized conditions. He wanted decent workplaces, schools, homes and hospitals for the proletariat.

For Meyer and others who thought like him, it was an essential part of that responsibility to be as economical as possible with materials. It was the way to make scarce resources stretch as far as possible. This could even take on a symbolic as well as a functional aspect. Certain materials were designated as bourgeois. Other materials were regarded as honest, or simple, or robust.

It is clear that Le Corbusier regarded his work as ideological too. He, however, was flexible about architecture, and about power. Le Corbusier always situated himself in an ideological sense: Architecture or Revolution? he once asked. But he was prepared to ally himself with almost any political regime in the search for work. In France in the 1930s he flirted with right-wing nationalist politics. In Vichy France he joined the collaborationist regime, and did the same in Algiers. He declined the invitation of the French communists to join the party, even when Picasso had accepted. Whether he had joined or not, Le Corbusier was the subject of a violent campaign that claimed his work was in itself politically subversive. A pamphlet published in 1928 described him as 'the Trojan Horse of Bolshevism', and it was translated in the 1930s and reprinted in German. But Le Corbusier was as ready to work for Stalin as Mussolini, just as Mies van der Rohe worked for Hitler and for the Spartacists.

The conventional critical response to this apparently mutually incompatible range of work is to describe it as hypocrisy. Given the readiness of architects to suggest that their work is somehow the embodiment of an inner 'truth', it is not surprising that when they are taken at their word, they do not come out well. But the legal profession has managed to carve out the space for itself to operate with apparent integrity independently of the merits, or lack of them, of its clients. To suggest that architects cannot do the same, that they cannot simply provide their services, that they have some further ideological responsibility, is to imply that architecture is somehow more important to a society even than the legal system on which it depends. And perhaps it is. It certainly touches on a range of the most fundamental aspects of what it is to be human.

5

The Architect Who Swept the Floor

Yung Ho Chang's studio in Beijing looks much like any other aspiring architect's office anywhere. The walls are white, the floor is bare concrete, and rows of twentysomethings are plugged into computers listening to Dr Dre on their headphones. There are cardboard and foam models everywhere, and an avalanche of magazines in the corner. The difference, as California-educated Yung Ho points out, is that the Beijing of the first years of the twenty-first century isn't like anywhere else.

The studio used to be part of the dormitory for the gardeners who tended the grounds of the Dowager Empress's summer palace. Western soldiers considered destroying the Forbidden City during the Boxer Rebellion, but decided that would be going too far. They confined themselves to burning her palace, as a reprisal for her role in the uprising against foreigners and Christians. They torched it again after she had it rebuilt, but spared Yung Ho Chang's modest grey-brick terrace next door.

Cruise round Beijing's first ring road, the site of the city's medieval walls, laboriously destroyed brick by brick between 1950 and 1962, and you pass the chrome-trimmed glass and granite façade of the Grand Hyatt hotel. On its forecourt the circle of red flags is a fleeting vision of what latter-day capitalist pomp on the Washington Beltway might be reduced to after the revolution. On Chang an Boulevard, Beijing's version of the Las Vegas strip, one block thick, where each grandiloquent institution is protected by its own private car park and gated forecourt, you pass high-rise banks topped with pagoda roofs and golden footballs. They are the confused attempts of a culture emerging from half a century of violent ambivalence, both about banks and the very idea of tradition, to lay claim to some kind of roots in place and time and perhaps to atone for the senseless demolition of Beijing's gates and walls. A brief campaign in the 1990s to create a conspicuously Chinese version of contemporary architecture has left a rash of superfluous tiled roofs and upswept eaves, tacked on to generic functional designs, an uncomfortable tendency typified by the city's bus station.

Every so often you find little encampments of olive-drab army tents, pitched along the pavements as temporary homes for building workers. Construction sites spill out of every gash in the old grey walls that used to define the city. You drive and drive and see no end to the cranes and the clusters of new apartment buildings, interspersed with fields of brick fragments – the remains of recently demolished suburbs. Throughout its history Beijing, like so many capital cities, has been an urban landscape designed to reflect the authority of the regime that controlled the city: one imperial dynasty after another has made it its own. Mao Zedong did the same, and now his ideology-free successors are following in his footsteps.

Chairman Mao's war against the Four Olds – Old Thought, Old Culture, Old Customs and Old Habits – which drove the Red Guards in their brutal and bloody campaign of book burning and persecution of the intellectuals, has been applied to city planning. The rebuilding of Beijing is certainly a cultural revolution of a kind. At pavement level, the city's most ubiquitous new building type is the residential marketing suite: stainless steel boxes and glass blobs, decked with balloons to tempt in customers, who are being sold a concept that reached China only at the very end of the twentieth century: the domestic mortgage. They offer the chance to buy apartments off plan, in a gamble that they will double in price before the builders have finished.

Yung Ho works on what are, by Beijing standards, tiny projects. He has done a few houses, a couple of art galleries, a bookshop, and some offices for a publishing company. In a city in which the basic unit of architectural scale has become the skyscraper, erected a dozen at a time, Yung Ho's buildings are so modest that they threaten to disappear from view altogether. He struggles to make architecture that offers a degree of continuity, as a respite from the relentless pace of change; to maintain something of Beijing's character before it vanishes forever, and at the same time to work as an architect in the Western way. He doesn't say so, but you feel an overwhelming sense of his powerlessness in the face of the turmoil all around him.

Yung Ho designed the Today Gallery as a temporary conversion of an industrial building, spared briefly from the demolition all around. To reach it you must negotiate streets clogged by the traffic of a city that reached gridlock with just 2 million cars for its 14 million people. It used to be the Beijing Beer Factory's boiler house, a utilitarian brick and concrete structure from the 1960s caught in a sweeping bend of the electrified tracks leading into the city's central railway station. But like almost everything else in Beijing, the Today Gallery's future was provisional from the moment it was finished, slated for demolition along with the tens of thousands of traditional courtyard houses, the shops and the power stations and factories, that are being pulled down all over the city.

The main space is a four-storey-high void, a miniature version of Tate Modern's Turbine Hall. It was inaugurated with a group show by a dozen Chinese artists and an opening that was nothing like a private view at the Tate, if only because half the guests looked ready to spend the night on the floor. Beijing, despite the influx of Australian chefs, cigar bars and Big Macs, is still very far removed from a Western city. Just look at the kitchen hands chopping trays of slippery grey poultry entrails on tables set up on the pavement outside the restaurant across the street. Once you negotiated the students guarding Yung Ho's striking steel-mesh entrance ramp dressed in fancy-dress camouflage uniforms and plastic helmets, you were confronted by a screen showing a continuous loop of mute film celebrating the women of the People's Liberation Army storming trenches, marching through the countryside, and repelling the imperialist paper tiger. It was a counterpoint to the evening's main event, a performance by four women artists dressed as night club dancers in colour co-ordinated satin and sequin outfits. Upstairs on the mezzanine level, a twice life-size fibreglass representation of Chairman Mao is sleeping peacefully under a floral print quilt.

'Is this irony?' I ask Zhang Xin, a young property developer.

She'd invited a dozen Asian architects – Yung Ho Chang among them – to build a villa each for a residential development aimed at China's new rich on a privileged site next to the Great Wall, shortly before trying to get her company listed on the New York Stock Exchange. She called it the Great Wall Commune and dressed the staff in fitted black Mao suits with red stars on their breast pockets.

'You know, the Mao years have left a mark on everything,' she answers ambiguously.

Edging past the sleeping Mao, you open a door, and are instantly hit by the acrid tang of cheap confectionery. Song Dong's installation 'Eating the City' is a megalopolis made of cakes and biscuits, organized on two huge tables, lit like a billiard hall. There are wobbly towers of wafer fingers and Swiss rolls, plazas of liquorice and chocolate. Song Dong's cakes could be the closest thing that you will find to a coherent vision of what kind of place Beijing will be in the next decade.

At the point of most rapid change in its history, nobody is entirely clear where the balance of power between the conflicting forces shaping the city rests. The municipal planning commission attempts to use regulations drawn up half a century ago by fraternal party experts based on Eastern Europe's height limits and sunlight angles to direct the growth of the city. Overlaying their efforts is the system of connections and corruption that mysteriously transforms consents for a ten-storey tower into twenty-storey buildings, and randomly dispossesses leaseholders. But there are enough Chinese developers with no preconceptions about how to build to ensure that there is nowhere else in the world where architectural theory can leap into practice with so little time lag.

Within this rapidly mutating city and its apparently chaotic turbulence, there are nevertheless attempts to construct fixed points that will serve to define the focus of power within it, just as there were in Mao's time, and in the dynastic city before that. In the struggle for the power to shape the city's future, the mayor's office and central government can be regarded only as contenders. They must take their place alongside the hard-faced young men hurrying to make as much money as possible before moving to Switzerland. Together they have built a model of tooth-and-claw laissez-faire urbanism that makes Houston look like a social-democratic utopia.

Land is nominally owned by the State, but scores of bankrupt nationalized enterprises that used to control much of the city are frantically engaged in capitalizing on the development value represented by their redundant buildings. They sell 70-year leases that are sometimes parcelled up and sold on several times before a development actually takes shape. What happens when those leases expire is still far from clear, but the uncertainty encourages developers to take their profits quickly and move on. The city insists on residential developers finding the space and the money to build schools. Otherwise just about anything is possible. There is some financial compensation written into most contracts for the dispossessed former occupants of these sites, enough to see them moved out to distant new settlements. But there is no redress for those who do not want to go. Every so often, China's newspapers devote brief paragraphs to accounts of desperate victims of this process setting fire to themselves in Tiananmen Square.

Yung Ho Chang knows about the exercise of power and its connections with architecture in China at first hand. His father, Zhang Kaiji, was also an architect. Zhang Kaiji built some of Mao's villas, as well as the State Guest House in Beijing, inflating its scale at the urging of the party, eager to overawe a visiting Khrushchev sceptical about the achievements of modern China. Mao had recently returned from Moscow's celebration of the fortieth anniversary of the Bolshevik Revolution. His hosts built him a special bathroom in the Kremlin, and he was determined not to give the Russians the chance to patronize him about China's plumbing expertise again. Khrushchev's bathroom was certainly impressive, but he cannot have been reassured to see the architectural embodiment of the Stalinism that he had just begun to denounce at home apparently still flourishing in China.

Zhang Kaiji was responsible for designing the twin museums of the Chinese Revolution and Chinese History in 1958. But his personal relationship with Mao did not save him from a decade spent working as a janitor during the Cultural Revolution. With the Great Hall of the People, the museums form a pair of massive Sino-Stalinist landmarks that serve to define the long sides of Tiananmen Square. They have their contemporary counterparts in two new landmarks that will represent the new China, Rem Koolhaas's headquarters for Central

China Television, and Herzog and de Meuron's Olympic stadium, both due to be completed by 2008.

Ten years in the making, Tiananmen Square is still China's most highly charged and symbolically important urban landscape. It was a very deliberate creation by Mao, initiated for his ceremonial proclamation of the People's Republic of China in October 1949. Tiananmen was both the physical embodiment and a metaphorical representation of a new political order, a theatrical setting for the regime to celebrate its triumphs, to threaten its enemies with its parades of tanks and missiles, to define itself, and to help secure its grip on a vast country. The square was used to mark the shift in power from the Nationalists to the Communists, and to lay claim to the legitimacy of history, as well as to demonstrate the Communists' place in the global order. Mao's Tiananmen was the most ubiquitous image of China, the icon by which the country was recognized all over the world. Not surprisingly, such a charged arena has also been used by those who have challenged the repression with which the Communists have maintained their hold on power. It has become the most contested of spaces, a representation of the authority of Mao and his successors, but also a reminder of the tragic massacre of 1989 and the events leading up to it. And it is now being supplanted as the new urban iconography of Beijing is manufactured with astonishing speed.

Before the Boxer Rebellion, the area in front of Tiananmen was the administrative centre of the imperial city. The emperor's more distant kin lived in this buffer zone between the palace and the merchant city beyond, fringed by shops and narrow lanes, muddy underfoot, dotted with little groves of trees, and still enclosed by walls. Rather like London's Whitehall, another seat of administrative power with its origins in a royal palace, or the Louvre in Paris from which the French Finance Ministry only finally moved in the 1980s, it became a bureaucratic complex by accident. The imperial ministries were concentrated around a courtyard directly facing Tiananmen, among them the Office of Embroidered Robes, as the imperial secret service was known. Foreign legations congregated here after the Opium Wars, determined to extract trading and political concessions from an enfeebled emperor. They became a target during the Boxer Rebellion, and the international struggle to crush it, that caused such serious destruction in Beijing. Tiananmen wasn't yet a formal urban space in its own right, but served as a gateway to the palace. It was the place where supplicants gathered on their way to an audience at court, and where proclamations were posted. China's students rallied here in 1919 to protest at the national humiliation represented by the terms of the Versailles peace treaty. The Japanese proclaimed their hegemony over Asia in the 1930s from Tiananmen.

With Beijing in Japanese hands in the 1930s, Chiang Kai-shek's Nationalists moved their capital to Nanjing. In the aftermath of the People's Liberation Army's military victory in the civil war with the Nationalists, the Communists simultaneously wanted to control the existing symbols of power, but also to wipe out every trace of them. They briefly considered establishing a new capital in the industrialized city of Lanzhou, close to the Soviet border, but in the end opted for Beijing and the legitimacy that assuming the traditions of an ancient capital city would bring with it. To make Beijing their capital and, through it, make China into their state, the Communists knew they had to leave an unmistakable mark on the urban landscape. This would have to go further than replacing the huge image of Chiang Kai-shek painted on flattened oil cans that used to hang from the Gate of Heavenly Peace, first with twin photographs of Mao and his most successful general, and later with a row of four portraits of Stalin, Lenin, Marx and Mao. In fact, Stalin's image remained on show well into the 1980s, perhaps to suggest that China and not the Soviet Union was the true heir of the first communist revolution, or more likely because of the inability of the party to make up its mind on the correct line to take about its past.

When his victorious army rode into Beijing on its American-built trucks and jeeps, Mao shifted the emphasis away from the private world of the palace inside the gate and focused instead on the more public space in front of it. The trees were cut down and the legations expelled in preparation for his proclamation of the new Chinese state, and the simultaneous adoption of the Christian calendar and a new national flag. When Mao declared from a platform on top of the Gate of Heavenly Peace that the Chinese people had stood up, neither Chang An, Beijing's primary east–west boulevard, nor the square itself yet existed.

Mao spent his first night in Beijing sleeping in a pavilion among the lakes and parks of Kublai Khan's pleasure palace, Zhongnanhai, next to the Forbidden City, in a room that his imperial predecessors would have recognized. He chose a selection of Confucian texts for his bedside reading, rather than Lenin or Marx. It is not surprising then that the iconography of the ancient city was so important to Mao's imposition of his authority on Beijing. He wanted to show that he was in command, but also to draw on the legacy of the past to underscore his own position. As if to act out his personal hold on the city, he led a delegation of the party hierarchy precisely 850 feet south along the central axis of the Tiananmen Gate, in a ritual to cut the first sod for the Memorial to the People's Heroes, his first permanent addition to the city.

For some, it was a crudely blasphemous intrusion into the ordered symmetries of Beijing's historic city plan, with its complex layers of overlapping symbolism. The blasphemy culminated in the opening of Mao's Mausoleum, a huge lumpish structure in the centre of the square completed in 1977, which conspicuously blocks the axis that runs right through the city. It was a gesture that François Mitterrand echoed when he commissioned I. M. Pei to build a pyramid in the courtyard of the Louvre aligned on the axis that runs all the way up the Champs Elysée and on to La Défense.

Tiananmen's walls and existing buildings were steadily demolished over a decade to create what has become a 60-acre open square. It's big enough to lose both Moscow's Red Square and St Peter's in Rome, vast enough to absorb one million people. Only Hitler and the Shah of Iran considered creating a public space to match it in size. Big though the buildings around Tiananmen are, they hardly register on the vast emptiness of the square. This would not be a place to linger and feel comfortable sitting on a park bench, even if there were any. The distances are so large that traversing the square on foot becomes an ordeal for even the mildly agoraphobic. Tramping across it in a punishing summer heat, the horizon seems hardly to change as you move from end to end. In winter, the dust storms can make Tiananmen positively hostile. At this scale, it is hardly an urban space in the way that it would be understood in a conventional city. It's so big that any coherent idea of space is negated. With no sense of scale or incident, bigness in the end becomes merely an endless blank flatness. Mao wasn't interested in the idea of townscape or the beautification of the capital. He didn't want a democratic space or a place that would welcome people and allow them to take possession of it. Tiananmen was intended to be the exact opposite – a vast parade ground, its character hinting at what Hitler and Speer would have done to Berlin. This was where thirty years ago the pioneers, children in uniform, pledged allegiance to the party and to liberate humanity from its chains. They were the children who belong to a generation that is now presiding over the most rapid transformation of a society that the world has ever seen.

The regimented ranks of the crowds, uniformly dressed in olive green, bussed in for party and national festivals, the red banners, the trucks rolling through the square with their painted and polished missiles, the faces of the party inner circle on the reviewing stand, these were the architectural elements that defined the square as much as the decorative architectural detail on the façades of the Great Hall of the People. Even in today's China, where Tianamen is a place in which you can find children flying kites and fairground tableaux depicting the scenic highlights of the Chinese landscape in styrofoam, it is only the subways opening into the square from Chang An that seem genuinely to belong to Beijing's people. Here they can linger out of the rain, sipping fluorescent-orange soft drinks and dodging the hawkers handing out flyers advertising unofficial bus services. The square itself belongs unequivocally to the State, and not to its people.

Stalin, a leader who never hesitated to rewrite the past, had pulled down Moscow's Red Gates and the seventeenth-century Sukharev Tower. He had flattened the great cathedral church of Christ the Saviour to make way for the never-completed Palace of the Soviets. And he pushed his satellites to mutilate their capital cities in the same way. The gesture did more to demonstrate their allegiance to Moscow than to impose national party authority on their own countries. Stalin's architects were called on to build a series of 'gifts' from the blood-soaked dictator to his vassal states to underscore the message. Beijing got a Red Babylonian Palace of Exhibitions, just as Warsaw had its Palace of Culture. With technical help and ideological direction from his Soviet allies, Mao was attempting to turn Beijing into the centre of a modern China for the pre-television age, to create an arena in which the nation's fate was to be acted out, in the same way that the priesthood of a Mayan city-state would demonstrate its supernatural powers in the ball courts and plazas of Chichén Itzá. Tiananmen was a puppet theatre, and every performance followed the party's carefully choreographed triumphalist script to the letter. The buildings around the square had their own part to play in that script.

The tenth anniversary of the proclamation of the People's Republic was the trigger for a wholesale remodelling and expansion of Tiananmen. It was the most conspicuous of the ten construction projects Mao initiated to mark the anniversary and impress both his own people and his increasingly disenchanted allies in the Soviet Union. It was both a celebration and a manoeuvre against his rivals in the party and the army. Just at the time when China's peasants began to starve to death in their millions from the famine that was the result of the economic disruption Mao had deliberately wrought on the countryside, the People's Republic was devoting its energies and scarce resources to glorifying state, party and leader.

Paving the enlarged square, and the construction of two vast new buildings on its edges, was completed in just ten months, from November 1958 to September 1959, by a workforce 12,000 strong. They were described as volunteers, working in three shifts for up to sixteen hours a day for the standard daily pay. They lived, ate and slept on the site, so eager were they, claimed Mao, to complete this monument to the revolution. Work carried on throughout the night under floodlights. At the end of 1958, Mao's Soviet advisers had warned him that it would be impossible to finish the project on time. The following June they said it might be done. In September they said, 'China has made a great leap forward', giving Mao a slogan to make his own. The architecture of Tiananmen, indeed the whole concept on which the square was based, slavishly followed the example of Stalin.

Mao was ready to follow Stalin's lead, even after his Soviet counterpart's death, to the extent of asking his architects for an aesthetic approach reflecting Stalin's own taste for monumental forms on a vast scale. Soviet architects held seminars in Moscow to brief fraternal visitors on the most appropriately national form of classicism for a socialist state to use. That China proposed to celebrate its revolution in such a fossilized architectural language at precisely the moment that Mies van der Rohe was completing the Seagram Tower in New York, a time when even Khrushchev was turning to prefabrication, suggested both the cultural isolation of the Chinese communist system and its determination to build a society that looked different from its Western foes, capitalist or communist. By the time that Tiananmen was complete, Khrushchev had already made his secret speech denouncing Stalin. One of the major issues that he focused on was his predecessor's compulsive expenditure on monumental architecture. His visit to China troublingly confronted him with Stalin's Eastern echo.

China in 1949 had not been like Russia in 1919, which with its 300-year experience of Western architecture had created its own indigenous architectural avant-garde. Under the Nationalist Government, China had only just begun to devise an architectural education system. It required the wholesale importation of a profession that hardly existed in China and was led by individuals who had been trained in America and Europe. China's own architectural culture was still based on the principles so powerfully demonstrated by the Forbidden City. Western architecture, of the kind visible in Shanghai or Hong Kong, represented an unwelcome intrusion, a reminder of China's powerlessness in the face of foreigners. It was the last thing that Mao wanted to build. In any case, China simply didn't have the expertise or the resources to build a glass curtain wall, to work with structural steel except in the simplest way, or to build a skyscraper, any more than it could build submarines or private cars.

For Mao's architects, dissent was dangerous. Those few who did criticize the Soviet-inspired remodelling of the city were soon forced to recant. Architects who remained active had limited room for manoeuvre in what they designed. But some looked to introduce a more nuanced interpretation of what Chinese architecture might be than others, and the break with Moscow seemed to offer them an opening.

The Great Hall of the People was designed in 1958 by Zhang Kaiji's contemporary and long-standing rival, Zhang Bo. The two architects were both in their forties when they took on leading roles in the Beijing Institute of Architectural Design and Research, one of the series of state monopolies still in existence today that the party established across the country to reorganize the architectural profession on socialized lines. Zhang Bo, the son of the last governor of the Guangdong and Guangxi provinces in the days of the Qing dynasty, and Zhang Kaiji, a schoolteacher's son, were both graduates of the National Central University in Nanjing, where architecture was taught on the Beaux Arts model.

With its massive Stalinist colonnade and its intimidating bulk, Zhang Bo's Great Hall of the People, an endless and repetitive sequence of assembly halls, one for every province, each decorated with appropriate iconography rendered in the manner of a wall poster, is clearly a descendant of that classically inspired tradition of symmetry and axial compositions where each room leads into the next. There is an auditorium for 10,000 people, the scene of successions of assemblies with no power other than respectfully to applaud their leaders, and a banqueting hall big enough for 5,000 where Nixon and Mao toasted each other. In its sheer square footage, the Great Hall exceeds that of all the palaces of the Forbidden City combined, an attribute that is anything but accidental. Zhang Bo gave the hall the character of an imperial palace rather than a parliament, with its monolithic exterior and generous use of golden yellow, a colour traditionally reserved for royal buildings in China. Zhang Kaiji's Museum of the Revolution and the neighbouring Museum of Chinese History, planned around twin courtyards, stand directly opposite the Great Hall of the People, and respond to it by establishing a deliberate sense of contrast.

The dominant architectural motif of the museum is the loggia, which defines the edge of the square but also welcomes visitors in. Just as Mao was ready to embrace the techniques of emperors in ruling the vast Chinese population, so Yung Ho's father Zhang Kaiji tried, discreetly, to incorporate elements of the architectural language of China's heritage into his buildings. He commissioned painters from the Central Academy of Fine Arts to create murals based on themes from Chinese mythology for a central hall that pays tribute to Marx, Engels, Lenin, Stalin and Mao. Beyond these unassailable party heroes, the faction fights of the Cultural Revolution proved too much for curators, struggling to keep up with the twists and turns of who was in and who was out. The museum remained closed for long periods as they tried to catch up with the party line.

Even when it was first finished, the loggia was a more inviting gesture than the intimidating wall of giant columns across the square. Over time, the museums have sprouted an accretion of cafés and shops spilling out from the podium level that have begun transforming it into an inhabited monument, in the same way that Diocletian's palace in Split shelters fifteenth-century houses and eighteenth-century shops in its massive masonry structure.

These are such vastly scaled buildings that they intimidate pedestrians into insignificance, even as they attempt to suggest a grandeur that reflects the aspirations of the State. They appear to float in the endless wide open spaces of Tiananmen, detached from their setting, like ships at sea. The communist monuments were larger and physically more imposing than those of the emperors, but they still followed the dominant north–south axis. Tiananmen Square was aligned on the Forbidden City, and Beijing's fundamental structure remained unchanged. The risk for Mao in the face of a culture as old and as sophisticated as China's was that the crudeness and the wooden massing of his intrusions in the imperial iconography of the city would be seen as exactly that. By measuring himself against China's traditions, as Saddam Hussein would later co-opt the architecture of ancient Iraq, he could be seen to be failing to live up to them by the country's intellectuals.

Mao's ideologues never took a consistent view as to whether the regime should seek to surpass the past, or else try to wipe it out entirely, as the most decisive statement of power possible. Mao was capable of collecting ancient Chinese calligraphy privately, while at the same time encouraging its destruction in open-air book burnings. Some saw the creation of Tiananmen Square as an onslaught on one of the greatest creations of Chinese civilization, but other leaders wanted to go much further than destroying just the city's walls and its gates, which had been built not so much for defensive purposes but rather as a representation of the Chinese view of the universe. During the Cultural Revolution detailed proposals were drawn up to demolish the Forbidden City altogether, extending Tiananmen Square directly into it, to create a new and supposedly more proletarian government quarter on its ruins. Designs were prepared for new buildings for the Foreign Ministry, offices for the party's Central Committee, a 5,000-seat cinema, a twenty-storey department store and a skyscraper hotel. Indeed tall buildings on this kind of scale would be the only way to make sense of Tiananmen's 60 empty acres.

The Forbidden City survived intact to celebrate the 850th anniversary of Beijing's foundation as an imperial city. For the first 800 years of its existence, it retained essentially the same character: the walled palace-city at its centre, organized on a strict north–south axis, and with concentric rings of walls and gates containing a sea of courtyard houses and narrow lanes, and not much in the way of waterborne sanitation. Tiananmen was a huge hole torn in that fabric, but not yet a fatal wound. Despite the rhetoric of revolutionary change, Mao could see practical advantages in Beijing's traditional layout in controlling a restive urban population.

What appealed about Beijing's ancient structure to an authoritarian regime attempting to consolidate its hold on power was that the city had no democratic urban tradition in the Western sense. Life was lived in the neighbourhoods, while the centre was reserved for the governing class. The party took the traditional Beijing courtyard and used it as the model for the division of the city into self-contained compounds. There was one for each big industrial complex, others for the universities, the army, the hospitals and the embassies – and the regime ensured that there was minimal communication between them and that such potential troublemakers as the university students were isolated by the two-hour walk to the city centre from their newly relocated campuses.

A big factory compound could house 10,000 people, offering them somewhere to sleep, canteens for them to eat in and schools to educate their children, ensuring that they would spend most of their lives within the perimeter wall under the constant surveillance of the party faithful. The masses were dispersed, coming into the centre only for events in Tiananmen that were under the watchful control of the regime. A city like this presents less of a challenge to a ruling autocracy than one in which public space belongs to the people. There was no free, public space in Mao's Beijing; no commercial area, no restaurants, or cafés for the disaffected to gather. After 9 p.m. the city seemed to shut down altogether, reduced as late as the 1990s to medieval darkness.

Beijing no longer goes dark. There are neon lights along most of Chang An now. The city is evolving in ways that its rulers cannot fully control. Private money has, for example, allowed a group of artists to turn a bankrupt engineering factory built by the East Germans near the airport into an enclave of galleries, studios and cafés that coexist with the survivors of the old workforce, bringing a sense of the euphoric cultural freedom of the early days of the collapse of communism in Eastern Europe, temporary paradise syndrome as it might be called. When the SARS epidemic closed the city's cinemas and theatres, informal bars sprang up in the streets. Such liberalizing tendencies have had to contend with equally strong currents pushing in the opposite direction. Immediately west of Tiananmen Square, hundreds of courtyard houses were flattened to build the National Opera House, a huge glass egg designed by Paul Andreu, a French architect specializing in airports. His contribution to Beijing's wide open urban prairie is to put the Opera House in the middle of an artificial lake. It's the perfect contemporary face for a regime that believes in the use of tanks as a modern instrument of crowd control.

To the east of the city, it is the traditions of communism that are being swept away. Zhang Bo and Zhang Kaiji's work in Tiananmen is the core of a handful of untouchable monuments in a city in which nothing is now immune from the threat of destruction. Tiananmen is so central to the foundation of the present state that it could not be any other way. But almost everything else is potentially subject to demolition. And the regime itself is looking to create a new identity for the city that could yet leave Tiananmen marginalized.

Beijing has embarked on the largest building campaign that the world has ever seen. It is the capital of the world's fastest-growing economy, provoking a titanic struggle between a totalitarian political system and the liberalization that is the presumed product of its economic transformation. Half the world's annual production of concrete and a third of its steel output is being consumed by China's construction boom each year. The second ring road that marked the city limits until the 1980s has been followed by the construction of a third, fourth and fifth ring. The sixth is under construction. Cars move sclerotically around unconnected clumps of newly completed towers that threaten to leave the centre as marginalized as Detroit's. The city map looks like a dartboard, with the void of the Forbidden City as its empty bull's-eye. And with the abruptness of a randomly aimed dart, entire new districts appear arbitrarily as if from nowhere. A city that until 1990 had no central business district, and little need of it, now has a cluster of glass towers that look like rejects from Omaha or Singapore. Almost by accident, the area to the east of the city centre has become the focus of a random sprouting of high-rise towers. They are here because this is where the embassies were built when the Communists moved the diplomatic district away from the city centre into what were fields. When China's opening to the outside world came it was the obvious place for hotels to be built, and the commercial towers followed. The government tried to create a counterbalancing financial centre on the western side of the city, demolishing thousands of courtyards to build the Bank of China, but found that it was already too late to challenge the dominance of the east side.

What was the China No. 1 Engineering Enterprise, the largest factory in China and the setting for vain efforts by the Gang of Four to rally support from the proletariat, has been wiped out by a flock of dazzling white skyscrapers designed by the Japanese architect Riken Yamamoto. Construction started in 2001. The 9-million-square-feet project was scheduled to be completed within four years. The first residents of the 4,000 flats had moved in by the end of 2003. Taking me on a tour of the construction site, one of the developers, a young woman still in her thirties, pointed out the fading slogan painted on one of the brick sheds that used to dominate the site: 'Long Live the Party'. It had already been scheduled for demolition.

Not far away, the 10 hectares of the Beijing motor cycle factory, once so dear to loyal party hearts, has been levelled to allow Rem Koolhaas to build the new headquarters of Central China Television. It will be a colossus that takes the form of two leaning towers, seventy floors high, that prop each other up with links at top and bottom to form a gigantic Möbius strip, containing everything from studios to offices. An adjacent hotel block takes the form of an open chest of drawers. This is not just another tower; it has ambitions every bit as explicit as the Great Hall of the People to represent China's place in the world, and its newfound might. In the years since Deng Xiaoping took the first steps toward unleashing China's economic potential, Beijing has built a vast number of new buildings, many of them designed by foreign architects with international reputations. But with the exception of the Fragrant Hills Hotel, I. M. Pei's fruitless attempt to show the land of his birth that modernity did not have to mean the destruction of Beijing's extraordinary urban fabric, few have yet showed any real architectural ambition. China Television, however, was looking for something more than simply another large building.

Koolhaas was invited to take part in a competition that was intended to produce something spectacular, but the competition was organized by people who had no idea what that something might be, even when they saw it. A building emerges from such a process as the product of a whole series of small decisions and accidents, as well as political lobbying, and the manufacture of consensus. Not the least of those accidents was the choice of jurors. Among them was a close friend of Koolhaas's, Charles Jencks, the American son-in-law of the governor of a British colonial bank in Shanghai during the communist victory of 1949, whose book on postmodernism was first translated into Mandarin in 1986. According to Jencks, 'The rhetorical part of the brief was describing the Guggenheim in Bilbao . . . Though height was not mentioned, they clearly wanted a landmark.' Jencks recalls his initial caution. 'I was afraid of being duped, that whatever I said would be used to endorse what might turn out to be a different outcome from the jury's decision.' He was eager to depoliticize what some see as an essentially political process. 'I am here for architecture independent of any other considerations,' he announced at the jury's opening session, heard in silence by a room full of people still reluctant to voice an opinion.

'We were taken to a resort outside Beijing with an artificial lake, it felt like a British country house in a Kansas wheat field. There were lots of fences and gates, and a very prestigious classical gleaming white marble hotel. We were being isolated in a cocoon. It was building the mentality of a team, in a way that some people might find sinister,' says Jencks. Behind the jury sat a whole row of officials, taking notes. 'There was the sense that if CCTV made the wrong decision it would be tough on those who took that decision. It felt a bit like Mandarin times, when people spent a whole lifetime taking a single exam. How could you take a risk when everyone is taking notes?'

The competition had been interpreted by two of the American architects taking part, who between them had designed Shanghai's two tallest buildings, the Jin Mao tower with its tapering supposedly Chinese geometry, and the knitting-needle-shaped Shanghai Financial Centre for the Mori Corporation, as an invitation to build another skyscraper in the same mould. Koolhaas won because he didn't. 'Rem saw at once that in a Central Business District with 300 towers, building the 301st tower was not going to create a landmark.'

Koolhaas's design is not a tower, it's not a slab, it's not even a ziggurat. The design suggests an alien architectural species, an extra-terrestrial life form from another galaxy, gasping to breathe through its fishy gills in the unfamiliar oxygen-rich atmosphere of earth. Cecil Balmond, the engineer working on the design, makes a direct comparison with another high-rise icon: 'Cut the loop, unfold the pieces and you end up with the twin towers of the World Trade Center.' Rather than projecting smooth technocratic efficiency, or nostalgia for the golden days of the Empire State and the Chrysler, the two poles of contemporary high-rise architecture, CCTV has a certain roughness, even a random accidental quality.

Aware that a competition jury's verdict is never enough on its own to secure a project, Jencks set about organizing consent, marshalling arguments in favour of Koolhaas's design that would make its outlandish form seem acceptable to the Chinese hierarchy. He described the design in terms of its evocation of Chinese tradition – issues that Koolhaas himself had never mentioned in his presentation. 'It is a Chinese moon gate, a framed hole, or the heavy shape made in bronze and jade thousands of years ago in China as a symbol of exchange.' But Jencks wanted to cover other positive aspects of the design too, to make sure that he could not be outflanked by those arguing that China at this stage in its development should be looking forward and not back. It would be not just a Chinese icon: it would be understood in any culture. 'It's a pop image, it can be seen as suggesting the Arc de Triomphe, or the Grand Arche in Paris.'

The jury struggled to push a state corporation into spending more money than it had planned to, on a project that would stretch China's engineering and construction capabilities to the limit. Building a leaning tower of this scale in an earthquake zone is without question taking a risk. Koolhaas himself knew that he would have to fight for the project, which was clearly more expensive than both of the other two front runners – Ito's design, and that of the Shanghai Architecture Institute. Koolhaas remade his model to make it easier for CCTV officials to understand, and it was sent off on a tour of the villas of the hierarchy as part of a strenuous lobbying campaign.

How tense this process became is reflected in the more than three months that went by between the jury's decision and a public announcement being made. Even a year after that, the foundation stone still hadn't been laid. Sceptics suggested that the regime still wasn't convinced that it should go ahead with the Koolhaas design. There was more at stake than architecture in the CCTV project. China is still a country that imprisons journalists, persecutes its dissidents, and which is ruled by an autocracy that refuses to loosen its grip on the State despite its lack of interest in ideology. And Koolhaas's building is understood by some critics as playing a part in maintaining that hold.

'What should one make of famous architects competing to build a new HQ for Central China television?' asked the writer Ian Buruma before the result of the competition had been announced. 'Unless one takes the view that all business with China is evil, there is nothing reprehensible about building an opera house in Beijing, or indeed a hotel, a university, or a corporate headquarters. But state television is something else, CCTV is the voice of the party, the centre of state propaganda, the organ which tells a billion people what to think.' China's capitalism is the kind that comes with an absolute prohibition of independent trade unions. It is not a society that believes in consultation, or social welfare. Nor has it developed a legal system yet that will defend its citizens against either state or private enterprise. 'It's hard to imagine a cool European architect in the 1970s building a television station for Pinochet.'

Koolhaas refused to take part in either of New York's Ground Zero design competitions. He said they were an attempt to create a monument to self-pity on a Stalinist scale. Yet at exactly the same moment, he strained every muscle to get his hands on the job of building Beijing's tallest towers, in the service of a state that can hardly be described as less authoritarian than America. When questioned about the ethical implications, his first response was to suggest that China's system is changing so fast that by the time his building is completed, CCTV will have been privatized and China will have given up repression as a political tool. It is unlikely that Mies van der Rohe would have had a very sympathetic hearing if he had won the 1933 competition for Hitler's Reichsbank in Berlin and advanced a similar argument about the bright future promised by the imminent economic transformation of Hitler's Germany, although that is exactly what Philip Johnson was suggesting when he pushed Mies for the job.

When Koolhaas staged a retrospective of his own work in Berlin, in the National Gallery designed by Mies, he splashed the title of the show, 'Content', in simulated spatters of yellow paint across its immaculate bronze-tinted glass walls, as if reproaching the void at the heart of Mies's sublime building. If you ventured inside, you found an effigy of Koolhaas himself. It was a doll, made by the artist Tony Oursler, impaled on a steel rod emerging from the middle of a pile of discarded and broken models. Its miniature black shirt and its grey striped trousers, just like Koolhaas's, were clearly meant to suggest that they came from Prada. A digital projection of the architect's face played over the doll's blank white head. If you listened carefully you could catch snatches of him reading from one of his essays about Junk Space. It could have been a lament for all the dead projects in the show. His abandoned plans for a new film studio for Universal in Hollywood – dropped when Vivendi acquired the company. The megalomaniac scheme to save the Los Angeles County Museum of Art's 20-acre complex by demolishing it. The architectural version of General Westmoreland's strategy for Vietnam – scrapped when it failed to persuade Eli Broad and the trustees to fund it. The Las Vegas Guggenheim – closed for lack of visitors a year after it opened. The scheme to extend the Whitney in New York with a banana-shaped tower bursting out of Marcel Breuer's sober ziggurat – aborted after three years' work at a cost that included the museum director's job.

It's a litany of disappointment that forced Koolhaas to look for work outside America. He couldn't help but find reasons beyond expediency to justify the switch in continents, represented at its sharpest by his fit of bad temper over the Ground Zero competitions. Koolhaas's own autobiography was suddenly turned into the pretext for some sort of historical watershed. He paraded his belief that a vibrant Asia has culturally eclipsed a stagnant, intellectually bankrupt America, after accepting a commission from a glossy magazine publisher in New York to devise teenage magazines. Would he be quite so bitter if Eli Broad and Ian Schrager and the board of the Whitney had not all chosen to dispense with his services in the course of just twelve months? And when Seattle finally opened Koolhaas's Public Library to a universally warm response, Koolhaas himself softened somewhat in his attitude to America.

According to Charles Jencks, Koolhaas was decisively influenced by Andy Warhol's book *From A to B and Back Again*, but Warhol would never have allowed his personal feelings to become so transparent.

To some degree, Koolhaas's career can be seen as a process of deadpan acting out in the blank Warholian manner. At various points he has modelled himself on Skidmore, Owings and Merrill, Le Corbusier and Mies van der Rohe. When Koolhaas and his early mentor Elia Zenghelis established an architectural practice in London they called it the Office of Metropolitan Architecture, an ironical attempt to pitch themselves at the midpoint between North American technocracy and Stalinist centralism, even as they worked from a kitchen table and struggled to pay their photocopying bills. Koolhaas and Zenghelis parted company, leaving Koolhaas in command of the OMA name. He went to Rotterdam, where he created a parody of a big corporate American architectural practice. It was housed in an appropriately bland office slab rather than the usual converted warehouse, but with a bargain basement rent and a workforce consisting entirely of students just out of their teens rather than crew-cut types with bow ties.

But really it is Le Corbusier who obsesses Koolhaas. He has mirrored every stage of his career in his own person. He has Le Corbusier's self-flagellating paranoid belief that the world is against him, even as it presses new commissions on him. He also has Le Corbusier's prodigious appetite for words – no architect has published so many pages as Koolhaas. He has even, after an initial love affair with Manhattan, acquired something of Le Corbusier's contempt for America. And since he has been working in China, he appears to have caught up with Le Corbusier's authoritarian phase. Just as Le Corbusier was associated with right-wing French politics in the 1920s, courted Mussolini in the 1930s, and Marshal Pétain and Vichy France in the 1940s, so Koolhaas has apparently embraced the cult of the strong ruler in his apparent enthusiasm for submitting to political discipline and the search for a father figure.

'What attracts me about China is that there is still a state. There is something that can take initiative on a scale and of a nature that almost no other body that we know of today could ever afford or contemplate,' he says. 'Everywhere else, and particularly in architecture, money is everything now. So that is blatantly not a good situation as it leads to compromises of quality. Money is a less fundamental tenet of their ideology.'

Koolhaas has not always been so dismissive of the power of money. 'I think it's very important to say that we live without complaint, fear or trust under the following regime[s] that you see here: the major currencies of the world, the Yen, the Euro, and the Dollar,' he wrote in the *Harvard Guide to Shopping*. 'They describe a regime that sets our parameters, and those parameters are fairly immutable. But on the other hand, it is also a regime that gives us an almost unbelievable amount of freedom to establish our own trajectories within it.' Of course that was when he was attempting to find a way to demonstrate that it was possible to maintain a critical detachment when working for Prada and a Las Vegas casino, rather than the Chinese Communist Party. Now he is doing both at the same time, searching the streets of Shanghai for a suitable place to build an outlet for Prada, and monumentalizing the new China.

Koolhaas has come to grow increasingly impatient with criticism. 'Participation in China's modernization does not have a guaranteed outcome. The future of China is the most compelling conundrum. Its outcome affects all of us. A position of resistance seems somehow ornamental. On our own, we can at most have good intentions. But we cannot represent the public good, without the larger entity, such as the state. To make matters worse, the more radical, innovative and brotherly our sentiments, the more we architects need a strong sponsor.'

It does not sound like the architect who managed the feat of building a museum in Las Vegas's simulacrum of the Doge's Palace, and who spent $30 million building a clothes shop for Prada in what had once been the downtown branch of the Guggenheim. With much the same combination of enthusiasm, image-building and self-indulgence, the company has poured almost as much money into contemporary architecture as it has put into building gigantic sailing boats for the America's Cup.

For Koolhaas at least, who clearly had no personal interest in accumulating wealth, if not the rest of the stream of architects now being drawn to Beijing, the real attraction of China is the chance to be at the centre of what is clearly the defining urban project of the twenty-first century. He claims that his 700-foot structure is not a traditional tower but is rather a 'continuous loop of horizontal and vertical sections that establish an urban site, rather than point to the sky'. The project is a chance to establish himself as the inventor of a new form of high-rise building that would vindicate his entire career. 'I want to kill the traditional idea of the skyscraper, it has run out of energy,' he told the BBC when he won the Royal Gold Medal for Architecture. While the CCTV design looks wilful and counter-intuitive as a structure, Koolhaas and Balmond claim that it has an underlying logic. The two main towers lean towards each other and are connected at the top with a ten-floor L-shaped wing that juts out into space, and a similar balancing block at ground level. To the non-expert eye, it looks as if the unsupported section of structure spanning the void is increasing the load on the two towers. In fact it allows them to stabilize each other, so reducing the quantity of reinforcing steel needed to build the scheme. Propping is one of the two basic principles on which the structural design is based. The other is what Cecil Balmond calls the skin. Externally, the towers will have a mesh of diagonal bracing in a seemingly random pattern. Rather like the creases on human skin, the greatest concentration of lines occurs at points of maximum stress. 'I knew that there would be some places where you want a lot of bracing, others where you don't,' says Balmond. Together, the skin and the propping allow the interiors of both towers to be free of columns, except for a single row around the lifts, which acts as the backbone of the building. The original idea was to incline the lifts, at 6 degrees, parallel to the slope of the towers, like a particularly steep funicular railway. Every floor would have had the same plan, just shifted by a few metres. But it turned out to be too expensive and too complicated, so the elevators are vertical, skewering the sloping towers like kebabs. The skin belongs to the same family as the exposed diagonal bracing of Chicago's heroic tapering Hancock Tower. The steel box-beams of the CCTV towers will be just as muscular and impressive as Chicago's, wider than a man is tall, and almost as deep by the time they hit the ground.

This is an attempt to push the high-rise building into entirely new territory. To get there, Koolhaas is ready to risk everything. Putting an art gallery in a casino, or a shop in an art gallery, can be presented by a sophist as skilled as Koolhaas as 'critical'. Designing a shop for Prada, or a hotel for Disney, or a Hollywood film studio, still allows him to maintain a nuanced distance from his clients. It is a nuance whose meaning has not escaped the old men of the Central Committee who will be paying for the CCTV project. They did not get there without acquiring a detailed understanding of the realities of power.

For Koolhaas, working in China brings with it the belief that he is moving from mere theory into the making of history. He needs China, but not as much, he believes, as China needs people like him. It is an illusion shared by many architects in their dealings with power. Yung Ho's father had ten years to reflect on it, while sweeping the floor during the Cultural Revolution. Both father and son have confronted the essential dilemma of architecture. Their work has brought them into an intimate relationship with power, but they have remained powerless in the hands of those who wield it.

Architecture defines a regime, but it is never the architect who frames the meaning of the definition. Zhang Kaiji's Maoist patrons wanted to construct Beijing as a city that reflected and enforced their power. His son works within a system that has embraced the market, but in which the architect is even less in command. For CCTV, building a vast skyscraper that looks like nothing else in the world is the architectural equivalent of the Chinese space programme, or the Three Gorges Dam. Koolhaas is trying to move beyond the projection of sheer size as a signal of power. He is offering another message: that CCTV's prestige can be reinforced through cultural innovation rather than by using the more conventional architectural signals.

Koolhaas, at 60, has never attempted to build anything even remotely approaching the size of this project. The fact that the Chinese agreed to hire him was based on the reputation of Arup, the engineers, led by Cecil Balmond, whom he is working with. The successful completion of the building depends entirely on the warmth of Koolhaas's relationship with his engineers. Any cracks in it will open up the possibility of a repeat performance in Beijing of Jorn Utzon's inability to complete the Sydney Opera House. But for China, it offers the prospect finally of moving beyond an attempt to build a representation of a repressive ideology, and constructing instead a new version of the country's national identity.

Switch on CCTV and instead of the clunky propaganda that you might expect, you get MTV-style graphics and, in English at least, a presentation that appears in its style to be from the 1950s. Its respectful, measured coverage of the news is a far more convincing package for the party line than harping on about the Great Helmsman. In the same way, a Koolhaas building is a visible demonstration that the Chinese state is no longer an out-of-touch, culturally backward dinosaur. It may be one of the last nominally communist regimes left in the world, but China has no intention of going the way of North Korea's hermit kingdom.

The focus of demolition in Beijing is shifting from the centre toward the Olympic area north of the city. Officially the site is called a park. But this was a busy residential area once, full of little grey-walled houses, workshops and stores. A huge area has been cleared by bulldozers as effectively as the firestorms caused by American bombing raids gave Tokyo its post-war canvas. For months after the bulldozers had gone, traders brought their donkey carts to pick over the rubble, scavenging for bricks and roof timbers to salvage and sell, before the soil was covered in plastic sheeting to keep down the dust that plagues Beijing in winter, and the site hidden behind corrugated iron walls.

China is using the Games to signal that it has moved beyond the sweatshop economy characterized by low-wage commodity production, bicycles, and social conformity. Stung by criticisms of its murky approach to the allocation of construction contracts, Beijing's municipality has been proclaiming its determination to pursue design excellence and maintain a fairer tendering process. That is why the competition to design the Olympic stadium had an unwieldy thirteen-strong jury. Seven Chinese experts sat alongside Jean Nouvel, Rem Koolhaas, and Dominique Perrault, representing the interests of the flying circus of the perpetually jet-lagged. Submissions came mainly from the usual collection of firms known only by their initials, which have come to dominate international stadium design by turning out an interchangeable series of huge spectator machines that can process crowds quickly and efficiently yet entirely lack personality or charisma. In this context, the appointment of Herzog and de Meuron is certainly a sophisticated choice. It demonstrates that China has reached the stage where it does not need to do the obvious thing. But in an echo of the planning methods of the Mao era, a precise date and time was set to begin construction of the Olympic stadium, even before the architect had been selected.

Jacques Herzog and Pierre de Meuron got the job and duly showed up for the Christmas Eve ceremony in 2003. Their design is both radical and simple. It will be the most distinctive Olympic stadium since the building of Munich's Teflon-coated tents three decades ago. The architects call it a bird's nest. It is formed from an apparently random pattern of structural bands rising out of the ground to create the stadium bowl, like a gigantic piece of papier mâché. The structure is composed of a network of threads of concrete woven together. 'We wanted to get away from the usual technocratic stadiums, with their architecture dominated by structural spans and digital screens. It is simple and almost archaically direct in its spatial impact. The architecture is the crowd, the proportions are intended to shift the spectators and the track and field events into the foreground.' In this it will be a forum that will have a character that is almost exactly the opposite of Tiananmen Square, which was designed to reduce the crowd to passivity, with no sense of itself or its own presence. The stadium, by contrast, will celebrate the crowd.

There is a certain symmetry in the presence of both Rem Koolhaas and Jacques Herzog in Beijing at the same time, working on such significant projects. They like to see themselves as the Picasso and

Braque of contemporary architecture, towering over their peers in the same way that the two cubists once monopolized painting, 'roped together like mountaineers for the final onslaught on the summit', as Braque put it.

Herzog and Koolhaas have indeed set out to collaborate with each other from time to time. There was talk of a joint project to design Tate Modern, before Herzog and de Meuron won the competition to build it on their own. Later they worked on a plan for a hotel in New York for Ian Schrager, torpedoed by Koolhaas's way of breezily antagonizing his client. But in their personalities, and in their architecture, Koolhaas, restless, gifted and erratic, is everything that Herzog, subtle and calm, is not.

Koolhaas at various stages in his career has expressed a lacerating contempt for his fellow professionals, a nihilistic despair at the possibility of making architecture in the contemporary world at all, and a complete lack of interest in the material qualities of building. Herzog and his partner Pierre de Meuron, by contrast, have realized a series of designs that brilliantly demonstrate that these qualities are indeed still profoundly at the root of architecture. Their two projects in Beijing demonstrate precisely this divide. Koolhaas's leaning towers are an ideological statement. Herzog's stadium is an architectural one that nevertheless embraces a humanistic view of the world. And in this sense they could be seen as reflecting precisely the divide between Zhang Bo and Zhang Kaiji on opposite sides of Tiananmen Square.

Both Koolhaas and Herzog have made more headway in Beijing than Albert Speer the younger, who invested considerable energy in lobbying the city's authorities to take up his plan for a 24-kilometre north–south axis for the city, with the Olympic stadium at one end and a huge new railway station at the other linked by a series of tree-lined freeways. Speer is an urbane, spry man approaching 70. If it wasn't for his name, he would be the personification of post-war Germany, the worthy Bonn republic of serious newspapers and liberal politics, where ecology and competently managed car factories are taken for granted. I meet him in his sun-filled Frankfurt office with its blonde wood floor and its atrium full of primary-coloured art. Speer would rather be in Beijing, but in the spring of 2003, the SARS epidemic has made him cautious about travelling to China. He is, however, still busy in Germany, where he worked on Leipzig's unsuccessful bid for the 2012 Olympics, surrealistically in partnership with Peter Eisenman, architect of Berlin's holocaust memorial.

'What I always try to do is to find a politician who will take my plans, look at them, and say, this is my idea, then it works,' says Speer. He is talking about how to turn his plan for the 24-kilometre north–south axis into a reality in time for the Olympics. I feel an overwhelming urge to ask if this strategy is a lesson that he has learnt from his father. I want to snatch the gold chain, the only discordant note in his otherwise impeccably understated outfit of fine cashmere and tweed, from his trouser pocket, grab the watch dangling from it, and see if it is a legacy from his father and check it for incriminating inscriptions. A tiny, paranoid fraction of my mind half suspects that the words 'Von Adolf für Albert' will be engraved on the back in thick Gothic script.

The scale of his scheme eclipses even his father's work for Adolf Hitler and his axis for Berlin. But as an understanding of how the Chinese state works, Speer's strategy is rather less sophisticated than Koolhaas's. There is a certain bathos in Speer's belief in the power of architectural will to impose a sense of order in the chaos of contemporary Beijing. Koolhaas, by contrast, is a connoisseur of chaos.

China is a place where Western architects come in search of work, or to gawp on the edge of the urban abyss of monstrous, uncontrollable growth in much the way that Friedrich Engels and William Morris used to visit nineteenth-century Manchester looking for the same frisson of confronting the unthinkable. What nobody really understands yet is how the inscrutable set of rules that govern Beijing's startling transformations really work, which is what makes Speer, with his neo-Haussmann approach, seem so quaintly irrelevant. Lining up Beijing's museums in neat rows as Speer proposes will not do much to change the lives of the city's displaced victims of development – still less can anyone foresee what will become of the city, with its six ring roads and its diminutive subway system, when it starts to approach Western levels of car ownership. It is already difficult enough to negotiate with one car for every seven inhabitants.

Beijing is a city that is changing so fast that there is even a chance that it may manage to finesse its way out of the grip of a party organization that is no longer communist, but which is still ruthless. If it acquires the street life and the public realm of an authentic city, then it could support a culture more independent of the regime. If that happens, then Koolhaas could be off the hook.

In 1949, a workman painted a stripe across the cobblestones of the Potsdamer Platz to demarcate the line between the British and Russian sectors of Berlin, and so defined the fault line between two warring world orders. The Potsdamer Platz was as battered then as the centre of Sarajevo is today. It was still dominated by the smoke-blackened serpentine façade of Erich Mendelsohn's Columbushaus, a department store and office building from the 1930s that became a base for the Gestapo. The tangle of tramlines and the stone hulks of the buildings whose cliff-like frontages once defined Central Europe's version of Times Square were still visible.

The workers' riots of 1953 turned the Potsdamer Platz into a battle-field. And finally the building of the Berlin Wall caused the entire area to revert to scrub, inhabited only by wild foxes. What had been the centre of one of Europe's greatest cities turned into a wasteland at the edge of two provincial backwaters that no longer spoke to each other.

The stalemate came to an abrupt end with the reunification of the two Germanys. For Berlin, the destruction of the wall was the urban equivalent of the Big Bang. It was like two soap bubbles colliding and turning into one with a rush of air. The scrub briefly became some of the most sought-after development land in Europe. In the euphoria of reunification, definitions of the new shape of Berlin ranged from the utopian dreams of the city's Greens, who talked of turning the line of the old wall into a nature reserve, to those who wanted a clump of skyscrapers to rival lower Manhattan.

The crucial sites, the ones that spanned the wall – the Potsdamer Platz and the Pariser Platz – were acquired within weeks of reunification by a consortium of developers. Despite the attempts of the city's planners to take charge, the building of the new Berlin has essentially been in the hands of a group of multinationals and developers, who staged a succession of architectural competitions to help give legitimacy to their schemes. Sony chose Helmut Jahn, a German-born architect who has worked in Chicago since the 1960s, to build their Plaza. Renzo Piano designed Daimler-Benz's site. There were accusations that the company had used its political connections to buy the site at a knock-down price. An even more acrimonious row accompanied the city's own competition to choose a designer to draw up planning guidelines for the development of the site as whole, to which Piano's design was supposed to conform. The judges fell out, calling each other dilettantes, provincials and philistines.

Unlike China, which has been under the control of a monolithic party regime for the six decades of its existence, Germany in the same period moved from the Third Reich to four-power occupation, to the division between Federal Republic and the Democratic Republic, then to reunification. And each regime has attempted to make its mark on Berlin's urban landscape, to undo the legacy of its predecessors and impose its own identity and authority.

In 1945 the Soviets had rushed to seize as many of the landmarks of power in the city centre as they could. The ministries and the museums, the universities and the opera house, were all occupied by the Red Army before the Western allies could get to Berlin. Only the Reichstag was in Western hands, and with the federal parliament transplanted to Bonn, it had no obvious role left. In 1949 the Russian occupiers took the decision to demolish Hitler's damaged but substantially intact Chancellery, to erase the physical legacy of the old regime. And they used the salvaged stone to build Berlin's huge Soviet War Memorial.

The German Democratic Republic had other targets. Ignoring the protests of his own architects and art historians, Walter Ulbricht decided to demolish Berlin's royal palace begun three hundred years earlier. The ostensible reason was that it was too badly damaged and that it would be too costly for the country to restore it. In fact it can only be seen as an attempt to erase the architectural history of the city in order to construct a new socialist order, following in the footsteps of Stalin's Moscow, and prefiguring Mao's Tiananmen Square. Indeed there was a proposal to bring Karl Marx's remains back from Highgate Cemetery in London and build a tomb at the heart of Marx-Engels Platz, in a conscious echo of Lenin's mausoleum in Red Square.

Ulbricht was later to declare to a party congress: 'The centre of our capital, the Lustgarten and the site of the palace ruins, must become a great demonstration ground where the will of our people to fight and reconstruct can find expression.'

The massive stone palace, with its baroque façades, its corner dome, its two inner courtyards, and its 1,200 rooms, was dynamited in September 1950. 'May it no longer remind us of an inglorious past,' proclaimed a triumphalist party newspaper. It made no comment, however, when Goering's Air Ministry building was transformed into the DDR's House of Ministries by the simple addition of East Germany's hammer and compass insignia to the exterior.

Clearing the rubble from the site of the royal palace to create what was named Marx-Engels Platz took another four months. Ulbricht led the Politburo as it trooped onto a specially built tribune to take the salute at the May Day parade in 1951. The East German architect Edmund Collein worked on a classical high-rise building to take the place of the palace in approved Stalinist style, but it was never built. With Stalin's death, East German architecture went through a sea change.

Part of Khrushchev's denunciation of Stalin's excesses involved a new dispensation on architecture. 'Soviet architecture must be characterized by simplicity, austerity of form and economy of layout. Buildings must be given an attractive appearance, not through the use of contrived expensive decorative ornamentalism, but by an organic connection between the architectural form of the building and its purpose, between good proportions and a proper use of materials, structures and detailing, and through high-quality workmanship.' There is, he said, 'no need to transform a modern apartment block into a church or a museum'. Over the next two decades, Marx-Engels Platz began to fill up with buildings that give a taste of how the Forbidden City in Beijing would have looked if the plan to demolish it had materialized.

The square was originally conceived as a piece of Stalinist urbanism, but its architectural language belonged to another moment. It is a simultaneous expression of two very different messages. The DDR was playing its part in the overthrow of Stalin's cult of personality, loyally following the path set for it by his successors in Moscow, on a site that was originally created as a mark of allegiance to Stalin. At the same time, the DDR was trying to build a convincing capital for a shrunken rump state. Michael Wise, in his account of the rebuilding of Berlin, quotes Joachim Näther, East Berlin's chief architect between 1964 and 1973, describing these developments as driven by 'a raging passion for power, and a raging passion for recognition'. The rebuilding of the centre of Berlin was shaped 'by a desire to send a signal that we are here, we are not going away'.

Immediately after the construction of the Berlin Wall, the Anti-Fascist Rampart as the DDR called it, in itself the most telling architectural symbol of the regime, Ulbricht commissioned Roland Korn and Hans-Erich Bogatzky to build the Council of State building on Karl-Marx Platz. This was where he entertained all those visiting heads of state who were prepared to ignore the Bonn Government's threats to break off diplomatic relations if they recognized the East.

Korn and Bogatzky's building uses granite, sandstone and glass, in a manner that would have suggested modernity in its context, and incorporates the only fragment salvaged from the Hohenzollern Palace, the balcony from which Karl Liebknecht proclaimed the German Soviet in 1919 shortly before being murdered by right-wing militiamen. The balcony forms part of a slice of the baroque building that goes from the ground to the cornice, projecting forward of the main façade. Its richly detailed mouldings, pilasters and cornices make the thin-lipped façade around it look mean and pinched.

The Council of State building was followed by another piece of gratuitous destruction: Schinkel's pioneering Prussian state architecture school was demolished in 1961, to make way for the DDR's Foreign Ministry on the west side of Marx-Engels Platz, a twelve-storey slab faced in white aluminium that crashed through the traditional height limit that gave Berlin its character. Proudly, Erich Honecker tried to demonstrate that the German Democratic Republic was as capable of creating banal modern buildings as anybody else. The television mast on the Alexanderplatz was finished in 1969, with its height – 1,200 feet – and position driven mainly by the determination to make its presence felt in every corner of West Berlin.

Then came the Palast der Republik, with the kind of brash orange mirror-glass façades newly, and briefly, fashionable in America at the time. Finished in 1976, it stands more or less on the site of the old palace courtyard. As a building, the Palast der Republik was an intriguing mixture of the formal and the informal. It housed a parliamentary chamber that, though it sat only occasionally, was the setting for post-communist East Germany's free vote in favour of reunification with the West. But there were also a theatre and concert hall, a bowling alley, and an array of restaurants that actually accepted East German marks, putting them within reach of ordinary East Berliners. The interior was a blizzard of tufted velvet banquettes, swirling op-art patterns on the floor, and cascading crystal chandeliers that seemed to represent the triumph of disco over dialectical materialism. The main façade was adorned with a huge state seal, the same hammer and compass attached to the old Air Ministry, and a tribune for reviewing the May Day parade.

West Berlin's response was to create its own vision of a modern city, albeit one that precious few East Germans would see for another two decades. East Berlin's Stalin Allee was a reflection of Beaux Arts planning. The Kultur Forum, the epitome of modernist urbanism, of objects swimming in space, was the response of Berlin's western suburbs attempting to replace the cultural institutions lost to the East. Hans Scharoun built the Philharmonic Hall at exactly the same time that the East was building the wall. He went on to design West Berlin's new library, while on the other side of the Forum Mies van der Rohe built his last great work, completing the new National Gallery in 1967, two years before he died. Its construction involved demolishing the remains of the German House of Tourism, designed by Dierksmeier and Rottcher as part of a quadrant of stone-fronted blocks that were the only section of Speer's north–south axis for Berlin to have actually been built.

In West Berlin, even the most modest traces of the past were the subject of anxious argument. Should they be eradicated to protect against a recurrence of the malevolence they represent, or should they be retained as a reminder of German guilt and a warning of the horrors that Nazism was capable of? A few even argued that Speer's surviving architectural work should be preserved because of its intrinsic aesthetic merit. Alfred Kerndl, head of the municipal archaeological office in Berlin, argued in terms of historical significance, rather than aesthetic merit, when workmen digging close to the site of the Chancellery discovered the bunker used by the SS guard unit protecting Hitler in the closing days of the Second World War. He wanted to move the crude, racially offensive murals they found inside to the German Historical Museum. Christopher Stolzin, the museum's director, busy transforming the museum from a Prussian arsenal to a modern monument with the inevitable I. M. Pei addition, refused to take them. But Norman Foster did manage to persuade Helmut Kohl to preserve the chalk and paint Cyrillic graffiti left by victorious Russian soldiers on the pockmarked walls of the Reichstag behind glass within his remodelling of the building.

The fiercest argument about rebuilding Berlin has been between those who, like Berlin's city building director Hans Stimman, wanted to restore the city's character of dense urban blocks – soberly designed, with regular window patterns, following as much as possible the old street lines – and to preserve the memory of the events that had shaped the city, and those who wanted to erase them to create an entirely new city.

The new Germany was less prepared to wipe out the traces of Hitler's Berlin than it was to eradicate the traces of the DDR. The Palast der Republik was abandoned when it was found to be riddled with dangerous asbestos. The East German Foreign Ministry was demolished with no regrets in 1996, triggering a campaign to reconstruct Schinkel's building that had stood on the site. For almost a year in the middle of the 1990s, you could have seen a ghostly glimpse of an icon of the lost Berlin, the Prussian city. A businessman from Hamburg called Wilhelm von Boddien paid for a team of art students to paint a *trompe l'oeil* image of the old Hohenzollern royal palace, demolished at Walter Ulbricht's command in 1950, as part of his campaign for its reconstruction. Just as the destruction of the royal palace was used to symbolize the triumph of the communist system, so its reconstruction would demonstrate its final extinction. Working from old photographs and drawings, they created the illusion of the palace's baroque façades on a strip of canvas, following its original outline as closely as they could. But if the project ever comes to fruition, this would not be the re-creation of the city that the Prussian monarchs built. The centre of the new Berlin is the product of a group of developers funded by Sony and Mercedes stumbling to fill the vacuum left by fifty years of uncertainty.

The Federal Republic's Foreign Ministry, meanwhile, was in the process of moving from Bonn into a relic of the Nazi period, the Reichsbank, built to a design selected personally by Hitler, deftly converted for its new role by Hans Kolhoff. And the old Air Ministry commissioned by Goering has been restored a second time, purged of the East German hammer and compass, its Nazi iconography tactfully kept out of sight. A layer of white paint, Eames chairs, and downlighters were considered inoculation enough against the potential danger of contagion from both incarnations of its past. But despite widespread protests in the East against the loss of the Palast der Republik the Bundestag voted to demolish the building and, when funds become available, to authorize the reconstruction of the façades of the old royal palace – at a cost of at least 400 million euros. In the meantime, the deadly asbestos has been painstakingly extracted, and the marble and the lights and the swirling op art stripped out, giving the interior awaiting its fate a new, sparse modernity.

The price of the Federal Republic's decency seemed to be an absolute prohibition on monumental architecture. In 1949, in the same year that Mao claimed his capital, the Federal Republic of Germany was also establishing for itself a new capital in Bonn. It was in many ways the mirror opposite of Beijing – its first parliament building was a former teacher training college. Such humility was a theme that permeated German post-war thinking on design and architecture. The distinguished graphic designer Otl Aicher, for example, a founder of the Ulm school of design, the originator of Lufthansa's modern corporate identity and the man who devised the Rotis typeface, was prepared to follow Adolf Loos and argue that the very use of capital letters meant that German typography had contributed toward making an authoritarian culture possible. And when the British architect and D-Day veteran James Stirling won the competition to design a new building for Stuttgart's Staatsgallerie, a building with a monumental classical plan, he was accused by at least one leading German architect of returning to the forbidden territory of the recent past and producing a Nazi building. Architecture had been such an essential part of the presentation of the Reich, that the post-war period went to the opposite extreme.

What had been one of Europe's leading architectural cultures in the 1920s and 1930s, the home of the Bauhaus and the Ring, has turned into a backwater. So much so that Austria, with 9 million inhabitants, has produced far more architecture of interest than pre-unification Germany with 70 million people.

6

Inventing a Nation

Well before the start of the genocidal wars of succession that tore much of the former country of Yugoslavia into blood-soaked shreds, its two most independent-minded components, Slovenia and Croatia, had already begun to think about the aesthetics as well as the mechanics of making a nation. While they were still part of Yugoslavia's federal government, as significant for their leaderships as planning military action to escape the clutches of Slobodan Milosevic was manufacturing the iconography of their own nationhood. Inevitably, the one was inextricably linked with the other. Creating the imagery of a state and successfully applying it to as large a territory as is plausible can be seen as warfare by other means. And sometimes by the same means. When states or potential states attempt to destroy each other's shrines, parliaments and palaces, extreme acts of violence are involved.

How the Slovenes and the Croats would assert their conception of themselves in a visible sense was an issue that preoccupied both Ljubljana and Zagreb in the winter of 1990. Persuading their own people to risk their lives for an ideal of independence was one thing. Patriotic or tribal sensibilities run deep in this part of the world. Getting oil shippers and arms suppliers, European air traffic control authorities and the International Monetary Fund, to acknowledge their independent statehood was another issue altogether. What would make them accept that Slovenian and Croatian banknotes would be worth more than the paper they were printed on? What would make them recognize the ambassador of an alleged state with no flag or national anthem, let alone an embassy. What would persuade them to provide airliners with landing rights when the airline had no name and no call sign? Most of the answers to these questions, despite the sinister fantasies of the more gullible of nationalists, are technical rather than instinctive. They lie in what might be called the architecture of the state: the official insignias of power and authority that define countries to both internal and external audiences. They are of course artificially created and depend for their success on the confidence – even sleight of hand – with which they are applied. Some countries are better at this than others, even the most cohesive of them. But to suggest that there are technical ways of creating a sense of national identity is to puncture the great myth of nationalism – that it is somehow innate and as inevitable as mother's milk.

State architecture is successful when it is able rapidly to take on the quality of inevitability. Architecture has been important to nation builders even before the time of the Romans and their determination to use the same town plan for every settlement from their frontier forts guarding against the Picts in the north to Libya in the south. In a faint echo of the same strategy, the British left their municipal architecture and their red cast-iron postboxes everywhere they went. Look at the remains of British Shanghai, or the surviving residential compounds of New Delhi, or the post offices of New South Wales, and there is no doubt what the architecture is vainly trying to tell you: this territory is part of a cohesive whole, and its fringes belong to the centre.

Religion and national identity have a way of going hand in hand. In the lead-up to the conflict in Yugoslavia, both the Croats and the Serbs engaged in a bout of competitive church building in order to lay claim to disputed areas. It was immediately visible which side was which. Catholic Croats built demonstratively modern churches, in concrete and glass, whilst the Orthodox Serbs built equally demonstrative Byzantine domed 'traditional' structures in stone and tile. It might simply be that the image of what constituted a church was rather different in the two communities. Or again, it could be that Croatia in 1990 provided a more sympathetic climate for contemporary architecture than Serbia, but in itself that is a phenomenon that might be understood as part of a programme to use culture in a deliberate effort to create a distinctive identity. It's an architectural phenomenon that could be described as a kind of cultural nationalism.

After all, the Marxist states of Europe were taught to place great store on the uses of cultural life, and the need to put it to work to serve the ends of the State.

Once the Balkan wars had started, the obverse side of this policy was the deliberate targeting of the architectural landmarks that defined the identity of the peoples whom the Serb extremists were trying to destroy. And later the other warring parties joined in too. Minarets in Bosnia were blown up. Mostar's iconic medieval bridge was destroyed by Croats. The national library in Sarajevo, with its collection of precious books going back centuries, was obliterated by Bosnian Serbs. Fortunately, the damage inflicted on the ancient city of Dubrovnik by Serb shelling was, by the standards of this grisly war, relatively minor. But in Kosovo, scores of historic Orthodox monasteries and churches were burnt out by ethnic Albanian separatists.

Architecture in its role as nation builder can be understood as a species of military uniform, a powerful way of signalling allegiances and aspirations, of rallying your own side, and intimidating the perceived enemy. Uniforms, like buildings, are ostensibly shaped by practical, functional considerations, but are actually designed to convey some extremely specific emotional messages. Uniforms are designed to make soldiers look intimidating and organized. So in the eighteenth century British redcoats wore shiny black shakos, or bearskins, to make them look taller. But far from subtle analogy, big or tall buildings might be understood to look more impressive than small ones. But for small countries to invest in overblown government buildings is simply to reveal their insecurities rather than to demonstrate self-confidence. Talking softly and carrying a big stick is a more impressive policy.

British prime ministers ran a worldwide empire from a nondescript Georgian town house no different from all the rest of Downing Street. In their eyes it was only insecure dictators who built anything as vulgar as the Berchtesgaden, or needed the reassurance of the Sala di Mappa di Mondo, the vast Renaissance hall in the Palazzo Venezia that Mussolini used as his office in Rome. And yet those sensible, no-nonsense British ministers in their sober worsted wool suits found themselves hypnotized by the stage set that Paul Troost designed for Hitler in Munich, as Britain and France betrayed Czechoslovakia and made the Second World War inevitable.

Colour is an important signal too. Once it was scarlet that was synonymous with martial aggression, blue that represented the Union, and grey the Confederacy, just as various patterns of camouflage on today's field uniforms are much more a signal of warlike intent and organization than genuinely a question of concealment. Buckles and straps and belts and epaulettes were used to create the sense of soldierly purpose. And now uniforms have an excess of pockets and studs and Velcro clips to do the same. All of these have their architectural equivalents: steps and porticoes, and double doors and enfilade plans are all there to provide functional alibis for what are actually ways of signalling the clues that define status or other identity markers.

If you can't rely on your own national symbols, a sense of reflected glory can come from adopting the style of a conspicuously victorious power, synonymous with efficiency, valour and success. Just as America and Japan organized their armies to look like the French troops who had been such models of victorious élan until 1870, so the armies that were established or reorganized after that date modelled themselves on the Prussians. Chile and Bolivia still have dress uniforms that make them all but indistinguishable from the officers of the Kaiser's army. So it was that Attaturk set out to build a new state by importing the architecture of the West for his capital in Ankara, and Pakistan engaged Louis Kahn, and India brought Le Corbusier from Paris to design Chandigarh as the new capital of the Punjab after its partition from Pakistan.

The Yugoslav Army, the last federal institution left before the collapse of the country, wore olive uniforms and forage caps with red stars that made them look exactly like the Soviet Red Army, despite Tito's quarrel with Stalin. The Slovenes and the Croats, of course, were already working on uniforms to make their troops look as much as possible as if they already belonged to NATO. They could see how the television pictures would play even before hostilities started. If one side looked like part of the evil empire, and the other looked like a Western ally, it didn't take the grasp of military strategy of a Clausewitz to see which side was going to get a better press in the USA.

And the banknotes that were on order well before either country had a national bank also reflected national aspirations. The old dinar notes of Yugoslavia were dignified with representations of heroic workers and apple-cheeked peasants. They brandished sickles and gazed proudly over power stations and tractors. They tended blast furnaces and moulded ingots. Naturally the new Balkan states went for images of Baroque composers and Renaissance astronomers rather than an idealized proletariat. They signalled a new and more optimistic future, paradoxically by looking backwards. The Croats had their paper money designed to look as indistinguishable from the Deutschmark as possible, much to the concern of the Bundesbank when the kuna started being passed off on gullible or short-sighted consumers as the real thing, while the Slovenes initially had their talers printed in Britain. Given that a Croatian puppet state had been part of Hitler's strategy for neutralizing Yugoslavia in the Second World War, these were in themselves a stark reflection of two rather different political legacies.

Slovenia was the most determinedly modern of the former Yugoslav states, and the one with enough confidence in its identity to allow it to take the most creative risks with its visual identity. It was prepared to countenance very young architects designing major official buildings as this provided the clearest signal of the distance that the emerging Republic of Slovenia was putting between itself and the bureaucratic climate of the old regime. It also had the most striking banknotes, including one that featured an image of Joze Plecnik, an architect who did as much to define modern Slovenia as anybody.

Plecnik was born in 1872, when Slovenia was still part of the Austro-Hungarian empire, and studied in Vienna. He worked as an assistant to Otto Wagner, architect of the Vienna subway system and the city's striking Post Office Savings Bank with its aluminium sculpture and its glass-vaulted banking hall, before being passed over to succeed to his chair at the Academy of Fine Art because he was not a native-born Austrian. He moved to Prague, where he was responsible for remodelling Prague Castle just before and just after the First World War, working with President Masaryk to turn what had been a monument to the power of the absolutist Habsburgs over their dominions into what he called a democratic castle when, as part of the Versailles settlement, the Czechoslovak Republic emerged from the Austro-Hungarian empire. Finally, Plecnik went back to Slovenia, by then part of the kingdom of Yugoslavia. In the years of the monarchy, Plecnik was responsible for the sensitive development of Slovenia's compact capital Ljubljana, looking for new ways in which to interpret the traditional signals of the country's vernacular tradition, much in the same way that a Czech composer, like Dvořák, say, made Slavonic folk music the starting point for his symphonic work. Plecnik survived the Second World War and continued to speculate about the landmarks of an independent Slovenia, in a discreet way, long into the Tito period, proof of the resistance of post-war Yugoslavia to the monomania of Stalin's architectural tastes.

Plecnik's was the face that Slovenia chose to use to assert itself as a nation for the first time in a thousand years when it used it on its banknotes, suggesting a link with tradition but presenting it in a strikingly contemporary way. Similarly, Slovenia designed its passports to suggest a sense both of modernity and of a distinct identity by using a collage of fragments of the contour map of the country's highest mountain, Triglav, in place of the usual florid engraver's abstractions as security marks on its pages. Plecnik was portrayed in an outsize fedora that cast shadows in curious places on his face, his profile rendered in the manner of an architectural projection drawing. It was a mix of the naturalistic and the abstracted that reappeared in the treatment of the National Library Plecnik designed for Ljubljana, which appeared on the other side of the note.

Architects feature with surprising frequency on banknotes. The Swiss still show the angular features of Le Corbusier on their 10-franc note, despite the fact that he was a French citizen for the greater part of his life. The Finns put Alvar Aalto on their 50-Finmark note until they adopted the euro. Charles Rennie Mackintosh did just as much as Aalto did for Finland or Gaudi for Catalonia to create a sense of a modern, distinctive Scotland, but he never made it onto a British banknote – Mackintosh's equally talented predecessor from Glasgow, Alexander Thompson, was featured on a £20 note.

These are the kind of apparently artificial signals that small anxious nations use to demonstrate who and what they are. But big, confident ones do it too. We all know what America is. Its daily life and its speech patterns are the subject matter of the popular fiction, television and cinema that we all see. It is the stage that the rest of the world watches. In spite of that, America is, like every successful nation, a carefully constructed artefact, an essential part of which is the sense that it is just as natural a phenomenon as the landscape or the weather, that there is nothing artificial about it. It's the flag, it's an accent. It's green money, engraved with representations of whiskered men; it's the White House and the dome of Congress. It's the space shuttle and Boeing. It's skyscrapers and Coke.

Architecture plays a powerful part in the manufacture of national iconography. It creates the landmarks that define national identity, all the way from the skyscrapers of Manhattan to L'Enfant's master plan for Washington. These can become the logos for a country, composed very often for that express purpose.

Of all the countless photographs of Winston Churchill in the role of Britain's war leader, none is more poignant than the image of him picking his way through the rubble of a half-destroyed Westminster on a May morning in 1941. Behind him is the shattered Gothic tracery of the west porch of St Stephen's Church from which fragments of glass still cling in jagged clumps. Churchill's hunched bulk, in homburg and dark overcoat, his face caught in a burst of spring sunshine, is balanced by the equestrian statue of Richard the Lionheart still in the saddle in his chain mail, despite the direct hit scored by a German pilot with an incendiary bomb on the House of Commons the previous night. The crusader king's sword, swung high over his head ready to smite his enemies, is bent and twisted from the heat of the fire that followed. There could be no clearer image of the crisis facing Britain at the most critical moment of the Second World War, and of its continuing defiance.

By 1941, the Palace of Westminster, even though most of it was less than a century old, was synonymous with the identity of the United Kingdom. Germany destroyed this of all possible targets to communicate with unmistakable finality that Britain was finished. Germany only had the opportunity to attack such a pregnant target because Britain had deliberately conceived nineteenth-century Westminster as a national icon. Churchill came out of his Whitehall bunker the morning after the bombing to ensure that another, very different, picture could be taken; one which demonstrated both defiance and reassuring continuity in the face of the destruction.

In fact Britain at war functioned perfectly well, some would say better than it had ever done before. The substance of its democracy survived even without its symbolic home. The House of Commons moved initially into the Lords and then to Church House, seat of the Church of England Synod, just down the road. When the crisis passed, the Commons debated how to reconstruct Westminster. Those few eccentrics who argued for a modern chamber for the House of Commons within the burnt-out Gothic shell were no match for Churchill's rhetoric. 'We shape our buildings, and afterwards, our buildings shape us,' he famously told Parliament. 'We have learned not to alter improvidently the physical structures which have enabled so remarkable an organism to carry on its work of banning dictatorships within this island, and pursuing and beating into ruin all dictators who have molested us from outside.'

Churchill outlined what he saw as the two most crucial physical characteristics of the House of Commons: 'The party system is much favoured by the oblong form of chamber. It is easy for an individual to move through those insensible graduations from left to right, but the act of crossing the Floor is one which requires serious consideration. The second characteristic of a chamber formed on the lines of the House of Commons is that it should not be big enough to contain all its members at once. If the House is big enough to contain all its members at once, nine-tenths of its debates will be conducted in the depressing atmosphere of an almost empty chamber.' This was Churchill as the consummate actor-manager, well aware of both the symbolic aspects of government and the practical stagecraft of state needed to support it.

This was not the first time that the British legislature had burned. Parliament was almost totally destroyed when a careless builder overloaded the furnace in the old House of Lords in 1834 and the resulting blaze got out of hand. But the rambling Palace of Westminster, the product of centuries of building and rebuilding since William Rufus established it as the court of the Norman kings, had never been a self-conscious landmark. It was a ramshackle collection of buildings, constantly extended and altered, much like the terraced house at 10 Downing Street that is the Prime Minister's official residence, rather than a deliberately created national symbol. Would Westminster still have been targeted by Germany in 1941 if it had survived the 1834 fire intact and remained as an anonymous clutter, rather than becoming the best-known landmark in Britain?

Certainly Germany had no equivalent, least of all the Reichstag, which was neither a symbol of unity nor of national identity. It had been built in the closing years of the nineteenth century by the Kaiser to accommodate a tame parliament that never had real power. Its baroque façade, closely modelled on Vanbrugh's Blenheim Palace, had only twice achieved authentic symbolic resonance. The first time was after the Nazi seizure of power when a mentally disturbed Dutch socialist torched it and a billowing smoke cloud erupted from its dome, blotting out the inscription on its pediment. The second was on the day in 1945 when the Red Army was so taken with the heroic figure it cut storming its way up the Reichstag's steps, and then fighting hand to hand through its corridors, that it restaged the onslaught for the benefit of its newsreel unit. The Bulgarian environmental artists Christo and Jeanne-Claude's wrapping of the structure before Norman Foster started work on transforming it into the federal parliament of a reunited Germany was, on some level, a kind of exorcism of those previous images.

How many other parliament buildings have the same instant international recognition as Westminster? After Washington the list runs out very quickly. How many non-Spaniards would recognize Madrid's parliament building instantly, or non-Belgians that of Belgium? But Westminster is another matter. It is a logotype for Britain.

Architects who design genuinely democratic parliaments that aspire to such a powerful identity must tread a cautious path between creating architecture that can express a sense of deep national roots and architecture that says something about its own times. They must avoid seeming too manipulative and give the impression that their work has a sense of authenticity, rather than betraying its essentially artificial nature. Architecture in such circumstances is not just a functional or aesthetic issue; it is nothing less than an arm of statecraft. There can, however, be a wide gap between the objectives of the politicians who commission architects to design buildings to serve their purposes, and the ambitions of those architects.

*

A building can set out to be memorable and distinctive – that is, to be a landmark that can be recognized around the world. It can try to look important, or special or significant. It can be designed to represent in a metaphorical way the aspirations of the State, or its leaders. That is to say, a modern building can be used to suggest that the State that built it is also forward-looking and progressive. The use of traditional architectural languages is an attempt to suggest pedigree and roots, as is the use of specifically national styles.

Such styles very often have their roots in building materials that are the product of the specifics of time and place and the search for economical building techniques. In Amsterdam, the canal houses started off with much the same kind of basic ingredients as contemporary Georgian domestic architecture in England: brick, sash windows and a classical language. But it doesn't take an expert eye to see that the Dutch version is distinctively different. The bricks are narrower, and have different proportions. The windows occupy a larger percentage of the walls. And because Amsterdam's canals encouraged high population densities, those houses have more floors and steeper staircases than their London equivalents. They also need hoists projecting from their distinctive gables to lift furniture and supplies in and out.

These were all technical issues, but when codified into a formula they produced what became a symbolic expression of national identity. Once the Dutch had established their outposts in Indonesia, in the capital that they called Batavia, now known as Jakarta, issues other than the unselfconscious use of convenient raw materials and response to climate came into play. Thousands of miles from home, colonists were reminding themselves of who they were by the shape of the houses that they built. What began as a technical and pragmatic issue became ideological and emotional. And it happened in other Dutch settlements. Walk some of the streets of Cape Town and you can see another re-creation of Holland, built originally to show fearful, homesick colonists that, even here, civilized life was possible. In Greenmarket Square, Cape Town's Old Town House, once the seat of its local government and dating back to 1755, has a clock, a cupola and a balcony that make it look as if it belongs on the other side of the world – and it represented an authority that derived from there too. A century later it was overwhelmed by the building of a new City

Hall made from yellow Bath stone (allegedly shipped all the way from England) in a florid Palladian style that made it look as if it was in Bristol, or Liverpool or Glasgow. It was specifically designed to demonstrate that the colony was now part of the British sphere of influence.

As the balance of power between the constituent peoples of South Africa shifted back and forth, the Afrikaners were ready to assert themselves against the English-speakers. Afrikaner companies in Cape Town signalled their presence with structures such as the Old Mutual Insurance offices, designed by Louw and Louw, in a heavy deco style. The history of the province was carved into the Cape granite frieze on its façade, with its polished bronze doors, its Transvaal granite lobby, and its gold-leaf decorations.

It was a nationalist revival that culminated two decades later in the Voortrekker Monument in Pretoria, the work of Gerard Moerdijk, a Dutch architect who had moved to South Africa in 1935. Only completed in 1949, it is designed to allow the sun to shine through a hole in the vaulted roof, casting a ray of light to illuminate the sarcophagus beneath and asserting the birth of a new Boer republic through sacrifice.

In a colonial society, the manufacture of a new independent identity can depend as much on architecture as on the evolution of a distinct accent. Herbert Baker was an architect who worked in two very different colonial contexts. He arrived as a young man in South Africa when he was just 30. He had an extraordinary relationship with the arch-imperialist Cecil Rhodes, which in its personal closeness, its quasi-erotic intensity and its political consequences seems to prefigure Albert Speer's relationship with Adolf Hitler. Rhodes first encountered Baker at a dinner party shortly after he arrived in Cape Town. He asked him to remodel his newly acquired house, Groote Schuur. Baker developed a style based on the Cape Dutch vernacular, in synthesis with the Arts and Crafts movement of England, as if consciously trying to reconcile the two white settler groups in the colony. Baker went on to define English-speaking white Cape Town, designing the City and Civil Service Club in Queen Victoria street and the Anglican Cathedral of St George, the Lepers' Church on Robben Island, and eventually a wing for the Houses of Parliament when the city became the seat of the legislature for the Union of South Africa.

Rhodes, who had an abiding interest in monument-making, financed his protégé's tour of the classical sites of Europe, from Sicily to Greece, as a preparation for designing a memorial to the dead of the Kimberley campaign. Baker proposed a white marble bath, open to the skies and ringed by Ionic columns, a project that was only stopped when Rhodes's partners at De Beers, worried at the cost, refused to sign the cheques. When Rhodes died in 1902, Rudyard Kipling and Baker between them chose a site for his memorial on Devil's Peak, overlooking the sea above Cape Town. Baker's design was based on the temple of Segesta in Sicily, the colonnades and flights of steps set off with a series of lion sphinxes. Inside is a bust of Rhodes with Kipling's words, 'The immense and brooding spirit still shall order and control. Living he was the land, and dead his soul shall be her soul', carved in the locally quarried stone. If things had been different in South Africa, it would have been part of the foundation myth of a white, Anglo-Saxon state.

Baker returned to Britain ten years after Rhodes's death – though not before he had designed the Union buildings in Pretoria – but his colonial building campaign was not over. He had gone home to work with Edwin Lutyens on the design of India's new capital in Delhi. In the summer of 1912, after King George V laid the foundation stone of his imperial capital, his viceroy unilaterally decided to build it on the other side of Delhi. This act of *lèse-majesté* went by almost unnoticed. Britain was locked in a fierce argument not about exactly where to put this city, but about how it should look.

The foundation of New Delhi, in a city that had seen empires come and go, was almost the last act of Britain's 300-year imperial history in India. It was a strategic move, representing a decision to take the seat of power out of the reach of the increasingly determined Bengali nationalists, angered by the political blunders and administrative reorganizations of the previous viceroy, Lord Curzon. But it was even more an attempt to transform the nature of the British presence in the country. The East India Company had arrived in India as traders and built Calcutta as a European port-city in the image of Britain. New Delhi was to be something far more ambitious. It was attempting to draw on the traditional roots of power in India, to situate British

India in a millennia-old history, and so in some sense to legitimize it. If it was to work as a strategy, it depended on an acceptance by the colonizers that they had been affected by India as much as they had changed it. But New Delhi was shaped by local government officials from London and Liverpool working by remote control, and based on plans brought over on the steamships.

The imperial city's chief architect was the quintessentially English figure of Edwin Lutyens, who was both brilliant and deeply condescending about India. His late father-in-law, Lord Lytton, had been the viceroy, a connection that didn't hurt when Lutyens was angling to design New Delhi. While he was affable enough with his Indian servants, he was shockingly racist about the country to which he owed so much. 'The very low intellect of the natives spoils much. I do not think it possible for Indians and whites to mix freely; mixed marriage is filthy and beastly and they ought to get the sanitary office to interfere,' he remarked in one of his letters home.

But the British had not run an empire for three centuries without acquiring a certain sophistication in how to go about it. And so for several months, a heated debate raged between those who, like the editors of the *Builder* magazine, saw the issue as a crystal-clear case of imperial branding and, on the other hand, those such as George Bernard Shaw and Thomas Hardy who argued for an Indian design and an Indian designer. The *Builder* would have none of it. For them, New Delhi should be made to look as British as possible, in the interests of projecting and maintaining imperial power, not only in India, but across much of the rest of the globe too. 'An empire can nurse no finer ideal than the cohesion of its dominions in cities erected in one style of architecture recognized throughout the world as the expression of its own imperial ideals. The encouragement of such an empire pervading style throughout the colonies, dependencies and protectorates will tend to annihilate distance and conduces to an imperial liberty equality and fraternity.'

Baker, Lutyens's old friend who had joined the New Delhi team, wrote to *The Times* a week after the *Builder*'s outburst about the capital that he and Lutyens were planning. 'First and foremost, it is the spirit of British sovereignty which must be imprisoned in its stone and bronze. To realize this ideal, the architecture of the Roman Empire as embodying the more elemental and universal form, should be used as the basis of the style, while eastern features must be woven into the fabric as concession to Indian sentiment.' Just how little of a concession Baker was prepared to make is made brutally clear from the inscriptions that he incorporated in his design for the Council House, the circular building that now serves as India's parliament building: 'Liberty will not descend to a people; a people must raise themselves to liberty; it is a blessing which must be earned before it can be enjoyed.' It was a far from isolated view. Lord Curzon, speaking of the Victoria Memorial in Calcutta, the relic that he left behind as a reminder of his own period in office as much as a monument to the first and last Queen Empress, believed that: 'In Calcutta, a city of European origin, and construction – where all the main buildings had been erected in a quasi classical or Palladian style, and which possessed no indigenous architectural type of its own, it was impossible to erect a building in any native style. A Mughal building, however appropriate for the mosques and tombs of the Muslim kings, or even for the modern palace of an Indian prince in his own state, would have been quite unsuited for the memorial of a British sovereign. A Hindu fabric would have been profoundly ill adapted for the purpose of an exhibition. It was evident that a structure in some variety of the classical or Renaissance style was essential, and that a European architect must be employed.'

William Emerson, President of the Royal Institute of British Architects at the time, got the job of designing the building. Curzon's only concession was to insist that it used marble from the same quarry that supplied the Taj Mahal. Curzon left India in 1905, and the project was not finished until 1921. Even with its revolving 16-feet-high Angel of Victory on top of the huge dome over a vast chamber occupied only by a bust of Victoria as a young girl, it had already been eclipsed by the new capital rapidly taking shape in Delhi.

Curzon's successor as viceroy was busy trying to damp down the unrest bequeathed him and suggested to Lutyens that his design should 'harmonise externally with the monuments of old Delhi and the traditions of Indian Art'. Sir Swinton Jacob, an expert on the subject, was brought in to advise Lutyens on the details. It would be 'western with an oriental motif'. Lutyens responded by producing the Delhi order – a graft of acanthus leaves and Indian bells.

The plan, aligned on Purana Qila and Jumma Masjid, the focal points of the old city, made a clear claim to the control of the past. But even more, the plan was both the symbol and the instrument of a society that embodied the hierarchical nature of the colonial world, and India's own caste system. British India was organized according to the infinite shades of status conveyed by the Warrant of Precedence, in which, as Philip Davies points out in *Splendours of the Raj*, 'the Civilian Superintendent of Clothing Factories, 44th grade of the warrant, ranked a cut above Deputy Director General of the Indian Medical Services but beneath the Director General of Public Information, all three inferior to the Financial Advisor, Post and Telegraphs.'

Within the grid of New Delhi's suburbs as defined by the master plan, five were allocated according to race, occupational rank, and social status. According to Philip Davies's insightful account of British architecture in India, one was designated for gazetted officers, another for European clerks, a third for indigenous clerks, a fourth for Indian princes and nobility. The princes got a plot of land between 4 and 8 acres, gazetted officers were allocated from 2 to 3.5 acres, while members of the legislature qualified for only ¼ acre. The avenues were allocated to senior ranks, the roads to their juniors. So it wasn't just the size of the house but the address that designated an individual's status. New Delhi was designed to demonstrate its position as a British possession and emphasize the power of the viceroy, whose domed residence occupied the highest part of the city. Flag Staff House, the residence of the commander-in-chief of India's armed forces, didn't get the same prominence as the viceroy's house, a careful reminder that power was exercised through civil rather than military authority. The Council House, a first concession to Indian democracy, was only added to the plan in 1919.

Despite the abundance of imperial symbolism that defines New Delhi, it became the seat of government of a newly independent India just fifteen years after the completion of the city, a reminder that the iconography of power is not the same as its substance.

*

At one end of the grassy mall that forms the spine at the heart of Brasilia, but still in sight of the twin slabs of the Chamber of Deputies, is a curious structure, apparently floating on a reflecting pool. A slender male figure, extending his arm in the direction of the Plaza of the Three Powers, stands on a pencil-slim concrete mast, embraced by a dramatic concrete ribbon. It marks the entrance to the JK Foundation. The initials stand for Juscelino Kubitschek, the Brazilian President who in an apparently throwaway remark during the 1954 election campaign committed himself to implementing a long-ignored provision in the Brazilian constitution to move the national capital out of the colonial port city of Rio de Janeiro and build a new seat of government in the empty heart of the country. It was a deliberate attempt to create a new identity for Brazil, reversing centuries of political and cultural subservience to Europe.

Kubitschek, the Brazilian-born son of Slovak migrants, was to Brazil what John F. Kennedy was to America. Glamorous, dashing, and the subject of a wild popularity cult, his initials are still instantly recognizable to Brazilians even after the JFK magic has faded. You enter the Foundation, designed by Oscar Niemeyer, architect of most of the city's monuments and a lifelong friend of Kubitschek's, by descending a monumental flight of steps that sinks beneath the surface of an artificial lake. Then you find yourself in a re-creation of Kubitchek's study: his books, his pictures, mementos, and his Eames chair are all here. In the next room is his life, recorded in photographs and documents. They show his childhood home in the remote state of Minas Gerais, his diplomas, doctorates and medals. And then there are the theodolites and surveying instruments that were used to set out the city that is Kubitschek's most lasting contribution to his country. You realize that this is no ordinary museum when you find the light level sinking and you emerge into a darkened space, in which you become gradually aware of a polished stainless-steel object floating above a purple neon-lit plinth. It is Kubitschek's tomb, a catafalque irresistibly suggestive of a pharaonic burial site. No wonder hawkers distribute leaflets in the city that claim Brasilia was planned by ancient Egyptian astronauts. After a few moments of contemplation you emerge to find yourself in the sunshine, face to face with a vintage 1975 Cadillac encased in a glass cube. This was the car in which

Kubitschek died after a fatal crash on the road to São Paolo from Rio. The tomb is the embodiment of the architectural representation of power, an essential part of the foundation myth of a city whose very existence is a potent demonstration of the political uses of architecture.

Kemal Attaturk, the soldier turned statesman who created the modern state of Turkey, was the most successful nation builder of the twentieth century. Architecture and urbanism were key parts of his campaign to rescue the Turks from the ruins of the Ottoman Empire. It worked well enough to set an example followed by a whole range of authoritarian nationalists, including the Shah of Iran, Saddam Hussein, and the Marcos family in the Philippines, all of whom faced a similar range of challenges. Attaturk took the decision to set up a new capital in Ankara to replace the Ottoman seat of government in Constantinople partly from military necessity. The old capital on the extreme western edge of the country was still the seat of the Ottoman court until Attaturk finally deposed the last sultan by establishing the Turkish republic in 1923 and the British smuggled him out of the city into exile. Constantinople, or Istanbul as it was to become, was occupied by the British and the French in the closing months of the First World War. Much of the Mediterranean coastline had been seized by the Greek army, with Lloyd George's tacit encouragement. Given these threats to the survival of a state still struggling to be born, Attaturk chose Ankara as a secure base, far inland on the Anatolian plain. But it was also a decision that reflected his view of what modern Turkey should be: a country based on Turkish nationalism in which Turks would be the dominant ethnic group, as the Ottoman Empire had not been. Istanbul's largest structures had been Christian cathedrals before they became mosques. The city had a polyglot diversity of ethnic groups and was hard to define as a specifically Turkish city. Ankara was a chance for the Turks to create a new capital in their own image.

For centuries, the Ottomans had an ambiguous relationship with the Arabs, adopting the Islamic religion and many aspects of their culture, including their alphabet. Their empire had spread across North Africa, into Europe, and eastwards into Asia. It subjects included Christians – Greeks, Slavs and Italians – and Jews, as well as Arab and non-Arab Muslims. And it extended a considerable degree of tolerance to its minorities.

Attaturk's conception of a new state involved a renewed idea of the Turkish national identity, which had ominous implications for the country's Kurds and Armenians. It also reflected a search for the historic roots of Turkish culture for use in the creation of a new and secular state. Ankara, an ancient city with origins that may go back to Hittite times, offered a chance to root the new nation in an ancient and glorious past. But at the same time, Attaturk, who had himself been born in what is now the Greek city of Salonica, wanted to make the new Turkey a significant presence in the European context. He wanted to embrace European modernity.

By the time that Attaturk first saw Ankara, it had withered into a small, dusty town of 20,000 people, albeit one with an impressive ancient citadel. In the decade between Attaturk's proclamation of his new capital and his death in 1938, he took rapid steps to transform the city and its infrastructure to reflect his idea of what Turkey should be: a country clearly rooted in Turkish history and prehistory, but equally clearly a state that was determined to be modern. Turkey built its institutions bit by bit. Stylistically, some of them looked back to the most distant past, in a bid to claim legitimacy. But the most significant architectural projects reflecting the new state were designed by the Austrian Clemens Holzmeister in a sober and contemporary style, a kind of abstracted secessionism.

Holzmeister was initially invited to go to Ankara in 1927 by the Turkish ambassador to Austria to build a new War Office, which turned out to be the first of a dozen more commissions. He would eventually be responsible for the presidential palace, the National Assembly, the High Court, the Central Bank, the General Staff building, and the Ministry of the Interior. It quickly became clear that Ankara needed a master plan to direct the increasingly rapid growth of the city – 3 million people arrived in less than forty years. There was an invited competition for such a plan, won in 1932 by Hermann Jansen, an academic from Berlin. Jansen's plan took a sophisticated, strategic approach, rather than the unsubtle axial formality of Europe's authoritarians. But within his garden city layout, the landmarks of Attaturk's state were given privileged status, and Holzmeister designed almost all of them. Holzmeister's relationship with Turkey deepened over the years. Eventually he was named official state architect, and Attaturk personally selected him, after an international competition, to design the new Turkish parliament building just before his death in 1938, even though it was not in fact completed until 1960.

Holzmeister was educated at the Technical University in Vienna, and by the time that he started to work in Turkey he had become a professor at the Academy of Fine Arts there. His architecture had an austere, sober, rationalist quality to it, without overt decorative detail. By default, it became the language of Turkish modernity, just as Attaturk adopted Western dress – he is still represented on Turkish banknotes in a morning suit and white tie – and banned the fez for Turkish citizens. Holzmeister was just one of a number of refugees from Nazi Germany and Austria who settled in Turkey. They included Bruno Taut, Hans Poelzig and Margarete Schütte-Lihotsky, who helped to give a progressive tinge to Turkey's cultural development. But the relationship between Turkey and Germany was a complex one. Turkey after all was an authoritarian state too, with its own fascist groups and its own racial policies. And some of the aspects of Hitler's architecture were directly applicable to Ankara. Amongst the Germans in Turkey was Paul Bonatz, who had worked on two of the more conspicuous buildings for Speer's Berlin. Holzmeister – though himself an anti-Nazi who had been stripped of his professorship in Vienna after the absorption of Austria by the Reich and who was a permanent resident of Turkey until 1954 – worked on one of his many prominent commissions in Ankara with Josef Thorak, Hitler's favoured sculptor. Adalberto Libera and a number of other Italian fascists took part in the competition to design Attaturk's mausoleum. Even the winning design, by Emin Onat, bore a close resemblance to Paul Troost's martyrs' memorial in Munich.

Ankara can be seen as the physical embodiment of the ideological struggle for the direction that Turkey would take. Its major monuments represent Attaturk himself, and his view of the nature of a secular republic. Its forms were Western, tempered with the memory of Turkey's ancient past, and in their detail they had the effect of scandalizing the more conservative Islamists. Attaturk imported a number of European artists to work on a series of monumental works of representational sculpture that had been taboo for centuries – an even more radical step than abandoning Arabic script and adopting a Latin alphabet over a period of just five months. Despite Attaturk's prestige as the soldier who rescued Turkey from dismemberment in the collapse of the Ottoman Empire, the country's Islamists have since begun to reassert themselves. One recent mayor of Ankara threatened to permit buildings that would have the effect of screening Attaturk's monuments out of sight. But to a remarkable extent, Attaturk's national iconography succeeded in its purpose.

He had explored the pre-Islamic history of the Turks and their forerunners as far back as the Iron Age, to find cultural references that could be revived to shape the national architectural language. He had sponsored archaeological research to produce the necessary historical evidence as legitimization for his view of Turkey. And he had attempted to bypass the authority of the entrenched Islamic clergy by using the memories of those pre-Islamic national glories to construct an alternative patriotic tradition. The Shah of Iran would attempt exactly the same strategy.

As Turkey and Iran began to build a modern infrastructure, they concealed their banks and their post offices and their railway stations behind an architectural skin that was based on cultures thousands of years old. However, Attaturk wanted to replace Ottoman Turkey with a westernized, republican system that in theory would embrace democratic government – not an idea that appealed to either of the Shahs. But they adopted the methods that Attaturk had used to build a secular Turkish state, and in particular his cultural strategy to outflank dissenting Islamists, which depended in equal measure on archaeology and architecture.

Before the Shah finally took the controls of his personal Boeing 707 in 1979 and flew off to exile and an early death in Egypt, allowing Ayatollah Khomeini to take power in an orgy of revolutionary violence and religious intolerance, he had embarked on a building campaign that was even more ambitious, though in the end manifestly less successful, than Attaturk's. He wanted to turn Tehran into the capital of a modern, technocratic nation that would reflect his vision of Iran as one of the world's leading industrial economies. It was a conception that the Shah had inherited from his father, Reza Khan, and it was a project undertaken in the hope that those of his subjects who were not grateful for being transformed from rural peasants living a subsistence existence into prosperous citizens of the modern world would at least be dazzled into silence by the glittering new state taking shape all around them.

The Pahlavi dynasty, if it can be called that with only two crowned monarchs to its credit, both of them deposed, occupied the Peacock Throne that they had appropriated for just over fifty years. The Pahlavis were eager patrons of architecture from the moment the first Shah, a cavalry officer, seized power. His strategy for building a strong state was to adopt the style of an imperial despotism, relying on the iconography of past glories as an essential part of his attempt to silence opposition. He looked for ways to purify the state culturally of Arab and other non-Iranian influences. And he rapidly set about acquiring the requisite trappings: the thrones, the crowns and the uniforms.

The Turkish and Iranian strategies were essentially the same, even if the historical references were different, and Iraq wasn't far behind. For Attaturk, it was the Hittites who had the most appeal; the Shah looked back to Cyrus; and Saddam Hussein, when he wasn't presenting himself as the new Stalin, was suggesting not so subliminally that he was the reincarnation of King Nebuchadnezzar. Which is why Saddam rebuilt the walls of Babylon, and why you can find groups of strange horned beasts on the traffic roundabouts in Ankara's Attaturk Boulevard, enlarged versions of the bronze figures unearthed by archaeologists from Hittite tombs. It's also the reason why the Central Bank in Tehran, built in the time of the first Shah, has an exterior that suggests it belongs to the Persian empire of the Achaemenians (559–330 BC), even though it shelters a conventional modern interior. These strategies, perhaps as an unintended side effect, involved re-creating historical enmities too, which eventually helped fuel Saddam Hussein's appallingly bloody war against Iran.

Unlike Attaturk, the two Shahs had to deal with an existing capital city, rather than construct a new one. Tehran was originally established in the tenth century, and by the fifteenth century had become a substantial walled city, guarded by four gates and 114 towers. The Shahs, like so many authoritarians, were hypnotized by the Paris of Haussmann.

Reza Khan demolished Tehran's walls and drove a grid of tree-lined boulevards through the ancient structure of the city, and beyond, to set the framework for its future growth. In the end, this exercise in strategic traffic management turned out to be of more help to the demonstrators calling for his son's overthrow than it was to the soldiers trying to intimidate them into silence in the closing years of the regime.

The elder Shah's urban strategy extended beyond Tehran, and revealed itself to be as much political as it was concerned with the functional aspects of pragmatic planning. Every town and city throughout Iran had to conform to a standard template. A public space ringed with imperial statues, to be named either Nation Square or Pahlavi Square, was mandatory. Reza Khan was deposed by the British in 1941 when he started to become too close to Hitler's Germany and began trying to play the Allies off against the Axis powers. But his son Mohammed Reza, installed with CIA help after his father abdicated, turned out to be even more interested in building. And, as the country's oil reserves accumulated, he had the money to indulge his passion.

In 1968 the new Shah commissioned Victor Gruen, the inventor of the modern shopping mall, to devise a strategy for Tehran's future growth. Gruen identified an area of vacant land to the north of the city as a future government centre. Lord Llewelyn-Davies won the commission to plan this vast tract of empty land in detail, after an invited competition in 1975. The submissions were presented to the Shah while he was on a skiing holiday. He was said to have come down from a morning on the slopes to see all the competing models, laid out side by side for his inspection. Llewelyn-Davies's vision of a two-mile-wide slice of Manhattan transplanted to Tehran caught his eye.

Llewelyn-Davies, who was apparently somewhat unprepared to take on the design of the largest new capital city in the world, hurriedly recruited a team of American architects and planners to boost the intellectual firepower he could bring to bear on the job. Jaquelin Taylor Robertson brought with him a group of architects and planners, many of whom had been involved with Mayor Lindsay's plans for revitalizing New York. It included a young Harvard graduate who left the project to marry King Hussein of Jordan, and Thierry Despont, who later became a decorator and whose most celebrated commission was Bill Gates's house.

In the mid 1970s, Tehran was a dangerously unstable mix of the medieval and the twentieth century. The Shah's wife invited Peter Brooke to stage avant-garde theatre in the city, the National Gallery of Modern Art was buying up Western art, including a remarkably sexually explicit Francis Bacon triptych. But many women were veiled, and regular visitors to Tehran were keen to avoid making the drive into town from the airport after dark. Packs of wild dogs roaming the highway verges could be a problem if you had a breakdown. There was a de Gaulle Expressway, an Eisenhower Boulevard, and an Elizabeth II Boulevard, as well as an enormous bazaar that looked and smelled as it had done 500 years ago. Parts of the city were home to an elite that had become hugely wealthy very quickly, others still lacked clean drinking water. And the population was growing explosively, rising from 700,000 in 1939 to 4.6 million in 1975. It is now home to 12 million people.

Whether he was aware of it or not, the strategy for the new government centre Llewelyn-Davies was working on closely reflected the underlying realities of Iranian politics. The biggest threat to the Shah was not the Iranian Communist Party but the Islamic priesthood, whose power base in Tehran was to the south of the city, in and around the bazaar. The plan accentuated the divide between a westernized, affluent, northern city and an ancient city of narrow lanes, courtyard houses, mosques and bazaars that was slipping out of the State's control. The relationship between the two took on the nature of an occupation by a colonial power, with a division as sharp as that between European and Algerian sections of Algiers. But what preoccupied Llewelyn-Davies's team was the illusory attempt to devise a plan that could provide what they called a tangible image of the city for the future, one with which the population could identify.

In his submission to the Shah, Llewelyn-Davies ringingly declared: 'A worldwide image must be created where Tehran is known as the finest city of the Middle East.' He conceded, however, that 'We have given as much emphasis to developing an aesthetic and symbolic base for Shahestan Pahlavi, as we have to setting land uses and housing densities.' The core of Llewelyn-Davies's plan was the creation of a gigantic urban square, a landmark that would have given Tehran a public space, to be known as Shah and Nation Square, which would eclipse anything in Europe and would be matched in size only by Tiananmen Square in Beijing. The planners called it a national centre for the twentieth century, and compared its proportions and the arcades that lined it to Isfahahn in the sixteenth century.

Around it would be ranged the key institutions of a modern Iran. The prime minister's office would go on the western side. Kenzo Tange won a competition to build City Hall on the northern side, next to the Ministry for Foreign Affairs, a hotel, and a theatre. Facing them would be the National Museum, the Handicrafts Museum, the Carpet Museum and the Pahlavi Library. Robertson and Llewelyn-Davies believed that this government quarter would give Tehran an alternative centre to the Bazaar, miles to the south, creating a two-centre city – like London, divided between its original square mile, and the Westminster precinct, or New York with Wall Street and Midtown. Tehran's mayor set about implementing the plan. Contracts to build the infrastructure were let. A French company started tunnelling for the metro system. And each of the planned institutions was designed in detail.

One of the biggest architectural competitions of the 1970s was launched to find a design for the library. The ethics of entering were a hotly debated issue among liberal-minded architects. By this time the streets of Western capitals were constantly full of demonstrations by Iranian exiles and dissidents, protesting against what they described as the fascist regime of the Shah and his sinister secret police, the SAVAK. But it did not deter more than seven hundred submissions. Participants could see only the obvious enthusiasm for contemporary design of the Shah's wife, with two years of a Parisian architectural education to her credit before she married. She had already commissioned Hans Hollein and James Stirling to work in Tehran – in those days two of architecture's most radical talents.

The result of the master plan team's work was boiled down to a two-volume privately published book. They are numbered, and came in a maroon slip case. It was written primarily by Jaquelin Robertson, who was to go on to help design Disney's attempt at themed living, the company's own town of Celebration. The title page proclaims that 'this master plan for Shahestan Pahlavi has drawn inspiration from the country, customs and people of Iran, and most particularly from its great building tradition. It is dedicated most respectfully to His Imperial Majesty, the Shahanshah, the guardian of that tradition.' It's a theme that the book warms to: 'No great city has been realised without the support of strong men.'

According to its designers, 'this is not just another large capital city; it has an opportunity for greatness'. It was a pitch that was aimed directly at the vanity of the man who was paying for it all. He is pictured on the title page, in a dapper needle-cord suit and silk tie from Yves St Laurent, standing over a concrete tube onto which a block and tackle has been manoeuvred. Helping the Shah bury the solid gold plaque marking the inauguration of construction on the site is Tehran's last Pahlavi mayor, G. R. Nikpay. He wears a long black robe, embroidered in gold braid around the collar and cuffs, decked in medals, like a hero of the Soviet Union. Within five years, Nikpay would be dead, executed during Khomeini's bloody settling of accounts.

Haussmann's Paris, it was constantly repeated, was the source for the reconstruction of Tehran. Llewelyn-Davies himself claimed, with what in retrospect sounds like a stunningly blinkered understanding of the closing years of the Shah's reign, that 'since Iran is in a period of national resurgence, it is only natural that the capital should become such a monumental expression of national pride. A similar spirit of ascendancy as in time of Napoleon III.' He later suggested that, 'So long as the Shah still ruled, tight central control over the final form was expected and feasible. Baron Haussmann was luckier than we were; Napoleon III survived just long enough to see his city built, but the Shah did not.'

In the event, of course, the Shah had packed his bags for exile, leaving his airports, his armed forces, and his infrastructure to the Ayatollahs. Even before the Islamic Republic of Iran closed the Shah's art galleries and abandoned the plan for the library, the mob had swarmed over the site of the square, ransacking the pavilion in which a huge model of the new city had been on show. It had been flown from London in 1977 on a special Iranian Air Force flight. Tehran's dispossessed destroyed it in moments and went on to try and dig up the gold foundation stone that the Shah had laid four years earlier. Not long after, the Ayatollahs gleefully dynamited Reza Khan's tomb. After the hiatus of the revolutionary years, the Chinese eventually finished the metro system. But the square, the library, and the new city disappeared, swallowed up in the explosive growth of Tehran.

During the kleptocratic rule of her husband, Ferdinand Marcos, the President of the Philippines, Imelda Romualdez Marcos collected buildings with almost as much enthusiasm as she brought to her better-known passion for shoes. From the moment in 1966 when she came to power, until her flight from the presidential palace just ahead of the Manila mob, Imelda Marcos did her best to make her mark as the First Lady by building landmarks that she claimed represented a national resurgence. Almost all of them were designed by a single architect, Leandro V. Locsin, who was ideal for her purposes. He produced a stream of buildings that had the swaggering self-confidence of corporate American modernism, but with just enough of a local twist.

Locsin was an authentic product of the Philippines: a graduate of Manila's Santo Tomás University who had only been briefly in the USA, where he met both Eero Saarinen and Paul Rudolph, the two architects he most admired, before he was declared a 'national artist'. He belonged to one of a group of architects in the Third World who found themselves called on to design the offices, ministries, hotels and theatres that ambitious leaders needed to build to convince themselves that they were in command of dynamic modern states, and at the same time the guardians of national pride. Locsin's formula was to blend a sullen monumentalism that seems to have been borrowed from Gordon Bunshaft at SOM with a strategic dash of national colour, manifested by picturesque roofs and open courtyards. It's a formula that he brought out over and over again, for the Manila Cultural Center's Theater of Performing Arts, for the International Convention Center, the Folk Arts Theater, the National Arts Center, the Center for International Trade and Exhibitions, the Philippines Plaza Hotel, all scattered like giant pieces of sculpture across Manila. With their blank façades, they looked at their best and most striking floodlit at night and seen through the lens of a camera. Locsin used great expanses of water and grass like moats to keep the chaotic city of Greater Manila at bay.

'They were planned to foster national pride in the Philippines Heritage. The arts in the Marcos administration's view are profoundly involved with the spiritual welfare, the soul of the nation; both the creative arts and the performing arts are therefore actively encouraged by government policy to help develop in Filipinos a sense of national consciousness too long dormant under centuries of foreign domination. The edifices commissioned for social civic and scientific projects with which the first lady is equally concerned also reveal the unmistakable features of what is Filipino,' claimed Locsin.

But the symbolism was stultifyingly predictable. For Expo 70 in Osaka, Locsin's Philippine pavilion had one of those over-excitable roofs, sweeping up from the ground, that was intended to express the 'soaring prospects and future orientated outlook of the Philippine people'.

The beginning of the end of the Marcos period was marked by the collapse of scaffolding on the new film theatre, which was being rushed for completion, and by the death of several construction workers, crushed by falling steel. The very buildings being presented as the icons of a bold new republic suddenly seemed to embody the corruption and incompetence of the regime. His patrons fled the country, but Locsin managed to find an even wealthier client in the shape of the Sultan of Brunei, who has managed to remain in power rather longer than the Marcos family.

Architecture has long been a means used by small countries to project their presence on a world stage. The Catalans and the Finns have also both used radical architecture to express a sense of themselves, to define as well as to reflect an identity. The question here is always one of degree: how much is this a self-conscious, 'artificial' creation, and how much is it an authentic reflection of individual traits, of climate, materials and customs?

The greatest difficulty in creating a convincing sense of national identity through architectural means is that it is an essentially artificial process that must mimic supposedly organic characteristics. Climate and locally occurring raw materials suggest certain architectural responses, creating a design language that in time becomes seen as a reflection of a national identity. But the impact of technological change and the globalized trade in building materials, not to mention the migration of people and ideas, makes such signals no longer part of a practical architectural tradition and reduces them to symbolism. The manufacture of identity through architecture is revealed as an entirely self-conscious process.

7

Identity in an Age of Uncertainty

Of all the modern building types, the airport, even more than the skyscraper, has become the focus for national competition, a sign of status as well as a potentially important economic asset. Even as air travel itself has become ever more squalid, airports still fluctuate between the search for economy and prestige. Paris's Charles de Gaulle airport at Roissy dates back to the era of its namesake and so does not qualify as one of the *grands projets* initiated by François Mitterrand. But it might just as well have been. It is a project rooted firmly in the French monumental tradition, not just of doing things on a big and intimidatingly impressive scale but also doing things in a manner deliberately different from anybody else.

The first terminal at Charles de Gaulle, designed by Paul Andreu, is like an image inspired by a set from Fritz Lang's *Metropolis*, a vision of the future that was intended to have a threatening edge and that France has embraced in its determination to become the personification of modernity.

Pressure from Heathrow helped France to take the hugely expensive decision to build a brand new airport at Roissy in 1964. It had become clear that first Le Bourget and then Orly had reached the limits of their capacities. To compete in the European context, the French Government decided that it had to start again. A decade in the making, Charles de Gaulle opened in 1974. In the autocratic French way, traffic was switched from Orly by decree to turn the new airport into the country's main international gateway overnight. When the first terminal filled up, plans were drawn up for a fivefold expansion, around a second, completely different terminal. And with the same clear-sighted, unsentimental ruthlessness that has typified the French way of doing things, they went ahead and built it.

Both terminals at Charles de Gaulle are unlike any other major airport in the world. The second is designed to allow car passengers to be dropped off in terminals that are as close as possible to the aircraft door. It requires passengers to know exactly which gate their flight is departing from, and a great deal of land. But it allowed France to bask in the sleek modernity of the airport's soaring concrete roofs, the great oval windows cut out of them, the dramatic glass piers reaching out to the planes. Or at least it did, until the collapse of a section of the concrete tubes in the summer of 2004, less than a year after Terminal 2D had been completed, marked a tragic setback for Paris's ambitions to become Europe's pre-eminent airport.

But before Mitterrand, there was Jacques Chirac, who on becoming Mayor of Paris killed off the development at Les Halles initiated by the president of the day, Valéry Giscard d'Estaing, and imposed his own solution, announcing that 'L'architect en chef, c'est moi.' It's not the kind of remark that any British prime minister of modern times could conceivably have uttered. But when Tony Blair decided to go ahead with the building of London's Millennium Dome, three months after his overwhelming election victory in 1997, he came close. It was nothing less than a deliberate attempt to create a landmark that would serve as the opening salvo in his campaign for re-election to a second term. He was adopting the style of a French autocrat, even if he did not have the brio to carry it off.

Britain is a country that has had a historic aversion to spending money on large-scale cultural projects. The National Gallery's principal façade overlooking Trafalgar Square was built using recycled Corinthian columns salvaged from a demolition site. The British Museum was funded through a lottery. The commitment of public money to the Dome cut right across that puritanical streak. Until the late 1990s, monument-making had not by and large been an activity that had found much sympathy with the British political elite: quite the contrary. It seemed to go hand in hand with vulgar display, and even carried with it a hint of the corruption that had seen T. Dan Smith, the American-style city boss of Newcastle, jailed for accepting kickbacks during his campaign to rebuild the city in the 1960s.

The assumption of power by the Blair Government, so often described as presidential in its swagger, was accompanied by what was, by British standards, an unparalleled renewal of political interest in the imagery of architecture and design. Suddenly new architecture was no longer an affront in the way that it had been when the Prince of Wales had exhibited such a passionate interest in the subject fifteen years earlier. A crop of eccentrically shaped buildings began to appear all over the country, a plethora of centres and nebulously conceived cultural projects that were high on pious hope, and mostly low on common sense and longevity, opened in quick succession. Many of them did not survive.

Barcelona had used high-profile architecture to awaken from the malign neglect of the Franco years. London, still struggling to remake itself after the collapse of its old industrial and port economy, began to think that it might be able to do the same.

New Labour's buildings were calculated to show the British state in terms of modernity. It was an attitude that coincided with an apparent abandonment of the unstated assumption that it is the duty of British governments to preside over a façade of continuity. Blair invited Oasis to Downing Street, as well as a roomful of architects. There was in this rupture a clear echo of the self-conscious youthfulness of the no longer derided Labour Party administration of Harold Wilson in 1964 with its embrace of technology and popular culture. Tony Blair wasn't after all the first prime minister to bask in the reflected glory of rock stars: at Wilson's behest, the Queen had awarded the Beatles membership of the Order of the British Empire. But Blair was the first to have surreptitiously rechristened his party. Labour had become New Labour when the electorate weren't looking. Where once the British valued the marks of traditional values above all else, a series of financial disasters, from the Lloyd's underwriting fiasco that bankrupted scores of middle-class families to the collapse of the stuffy centuries-old Barings Bank, brought down by a single delinquent – and working-class – trader, suddenly created exactly the opposite assumption. Elderly retainers, doormen in frock coats, and offices lined with ancient wooden panelling had once signalled probity and solid decency. The mess at Lloyd's and then at Barings reversed the signals. The survival of ancient tradition became synonymous with an institution in terminal decline.

The new political class in Britain that took power when Tony Blair was elected in 1997 wanted to move beyond a threadbare, time-expired vision of Britishness rooted in pageantry, the royal family and cricket. They thought that they had learned the lessons of François Mitterrand's Paris and Pasqual Maragall's Barcelona, and the importance of constructing a state based on the idea of modernity. Carefully briefed by the Labour peer Richard Rogers, Britain's politically best-connected architect for half a century, they had made the pilgrimage to see what building could do for an incoming government determined to impress its electorate with a crop of landmarks, and to inject new vigour into run-down city centres. Some of them had even understood what they were looking at. As a result, they embarked on a campaign, as they put it, 'to re-brand Britain' that was both about symbolism and, in theory at least, substance. The representation of the State was an issue, but so was the perceived economic impact of promoting design and architecture.

But the idea of government patronage in architecture was fundamentally alien to British politicians, who schooled themselves to believe in the idea of consensus, partnership, inclusiveness and diversity. The belief in a single vision, which is what a building of intellectual challenge and aesthetic quality must be, simply didn't fit with this world view.

No single building embodied this dilemma as clearly as the Government's plans to commemorate the millennium with a massive structure on the Greenwich peninsula. Formerly 300 acres of toxic Victorian dereliction, the site is now occupied by what was for a while the most highly charged piece of political architecture England had yet seen, and which has now turned into a painful piece of scar tissue for the Government. The Millennium Dome was eagerly adopted by Tony Blair as the apotheosis of New Labour, a propaganda tool to signal a new political dispensation. As revealing as the official rhetoric crowding around the structure were the unintentional meanings it unwittingly highlighted with even greater force.

The Millennium Dome had at its heart a glaring mismatch between ends and means. The Government held its nose and poured £1 billion into the toxic mud of the Greenwich peninsula in the belief that it was embracing modernity. In fact the usually surefooted grasp of political iconography of the Prime Minister's inner circle deserted it. The Dome turned out not to be about the future at all. It was actually a fundamentally nostalgic and even inept return to the 1950s, recycling the Festival of Britain, conflating its two most enduring images – the Dome of Discovery and the Skylon, the needle-shaped landmark supported on steel cables designed for the same event – in Richard Rogers's Teflon-coated tent, with its vivid yellow crown of thorns. Despite the glamorous flourish of the structure itself, it failed to live up to Blair's hopes as a step in his campaign for re-election. Britain was in no mood to make a portentous collective statement about itself. Or even less to be force-fed pious homilies condescendingly sugar-coated with the dubious presentational skills of public-service advertising.

Though the Dome became the very embodiment of New Labour aspirations, it was a project first set in train by the fading Conservative Government of John Major. It was the Conservatives who initiated the National Lottery that was to end up paying for it. And it was the Conservatives who had the idea of celebrating the millennium by allotting one fifth of the yield to the public from the lottery to the Millennium Commission, to be used to build a series of monumental projects across Britain. And it was the Conservative Deputy Prime Minister Michael Heseltine who more than anybody pushed for the idea of a rerun of the Great Exhibition of 1851 and the Festival of Britain of 1951 as the centrepiece of the celebrations for the year 2000. Yet this extraordinarily ambitious enterprise became irrevocably identified with Blairism.

Such inter-party promiscuity was also new for Britain. The Festival of Britain was instigated by an extremely Old Labour government, and begrudgingly opened by a Conservative one that went on to tear down all its physical legacies, save for the Festival Hall, as soon as it decently could. Blair's embrace of the Dome was all the more surprising since it was a scheme that could have been cancelled without the slightest political risk. Blair chose to take it on against the firm opposition of the Chancellor of the Exchequer, Gordon Brown. Indeed it might have been precisely because his great party rival was against the scheme that Blair backed it.

The germ of the idea that led eventually to the Dome had its genesis in a series of conversations among the Millennium Commissioners as they toured the country in 1994, dispensing largesse to such unlikely projects as a scheme to garnish Portsmouth Harbour with a giant water spout, while refusing to fund Zaha Hadid's design for an opera house in Cardiff. Two commissioners in particular, Michael Heseltine and the journalist Simon Jenkins, believed that it was essential to create a single national focus for the millennium.

It was glaringly obvious that such a project could only be built with public money. But the pursuit of the mirage that private investors would build it went as far as the Millennium Commission begging British Airways to take on the risk. The Commission asked Richard Rogers to come up with an architectural strategy for accommodating the exhibition, once the Greenwich site was selected, and his proposal was accepted in 1996. It was a solution born of necessity, its elements dictated by lack of time, and lack of certainty about content. Rather than wrestle with designing a series of individual pavilions to deal with all this, the Rogers team proposed the Dome – actually it was a cable-supported tent. Not only did it look striking, it offered enough flexibility under its capacious shelter for the organizers not to worry about the lack of clarity about what would actually be taking place inside. Instead, construction could safely be started, and detailed consideration of its use could be left until later.

At the very least, this practical approach to creating a structure meant that the show could open in December 1999. As a result, English Partnerships, the Government's regeneration arm, bought the site in February 1997 for £20 million, finally committing taxpayers' money to the project. Then came the election of May 1997 that swept the Conservatives out of power. But even before that, Michael Heseltine had been making representations to Tony Blair about a future Labour administration adopting the Dome. It was, he implied, the most obvious means of celebrating the achievements of a modernizing new government, and this was a new government that was determined to celebrate its achievements.

Which is how the Millennium Dome, the greatest empty gesture of British cultural life, happened. Tony Blair may be as much of an autocrat as Mitterrand, but he lacked the instinctive confidence in his own judgement on architectural issues of the French President. Blair needs to be told what to like, or rather what to say he likes. And despite Richard Rogers's role, there was nobody close enough to Blair whom he could listen to for decisive guidance. Certainly not Peter Mandelson, who spent the best part of a year in charge of the building of the Dome.

Filling the Dome involved some architects of striking ability. But their political patrons had no way of distinguishing them from the hacks who specialized in launching new trucks in flurries of lasers and dry ice, who had been brought in to design large chunks of the Dome's exhibits.

Even before it opened, the Dome became the focus of enormous popular hostility, as sharp questions began to be asked about the precise nature of the message that it would be putting across, and the Prime Minister was forced into mounting a vigorous defence of the project. He could go through the motions of why we should do it. But he had no sense of what the project should actually be, and had to rely on carefully crafted bombast.

Picture the scene. The clock strikes midnight on 31 December 1999. The eyes of the world turn to the spot where the new Millennium begins – the Meridian Line at Greenwich. This is Britain's opportunity to greet the world with a celebration that is so bold, so beautiful, so inspiring that it embodies at once the spirit of confidence and adventure in Britain and the spirit of the future in the world. This is the reason for the Millennium Experience. Not a product of the imagination run wild, but a huge opportunity for Britain. So let us seize the moment and put on something of which we and the world will be proud.

Then we will say to ourselves with pride this is our Dome, Britain's Dome, and believe me, it will be the envy of the world . . .

We are leading the world in creativity, so why not put it on display? Why not shout about it? The Dome will be a celebration of the Best of Britain . . .

The Dome's content will contain a rich texture of feelings: spiritual, emotional, fun. It will combine the best of other attractions in a unique experience. Exhilarating like Disney World – yet different. Educational and interactive, like the Science Museum – yet different. Emotional and uplifting like a West End musical – yet different. It will be shaped by the people. Visitors from all around the world will have the time of their lives.

It was a remarkable performance, but in the end Blair was attempting to justify the unjustifiable, the building at enormous expense of a theme park run by the Government. What on earth made him believe that it was in any way equipped to deliver such a thing, any more than the Government could deliver football champions, or chart-topping musicians? This was a not very exciting, indeed an entirely bloodless version of bread and circuses, and in the light of the condescending, ill-conceived, and vastly over-budget nature of the majority of the Dome's content, for anybody who actually went, Blair's words are impossible to read now without cringing.

To walk to the new world of the Dome from familiar, scruffy, nineteenth-century London you must first negotiate the grimy Victorian streets of Greenwich. They peter out with disconcerting suddenness as you make the transition to the twenty-first century through what feels like an asteroid belt dotted with a few gigantic objects: anonymous sheds, elevated motorways, and an empty landscape of reclaimed spoil heaps and industrial waste. Everyday normality vanishes into the howling urban void that constitutes the margins of most contemporary big cities. In this setting, the Dome has become an anchor in a wilderness, but its meaning is unclear. Is it teetering back into the oblivion of dereliction that the waste tips that once stood on the site represented? Or is it pointing the way to a more optimistic future?

On a summer lunchtime, four humiliating years after the Dome finally closed its doors, the yellow masts towering over the Thames have faded a little, and the huge white Teflon tent looks as if it has begun to sag. The whole place has taken on that desolate, sour sense of emptiness that is the aftertaste, or perhaps the lingering hangover, of most attempts at official grandiloquence, like the rotting glimpses of the future that are still a pungent reminder of the two New York World's Fairs in Queens, or the unfulfilled promises of the Seville Expo.

The weeds are determinedly trying to force their way through the blue mesh fences that ring the Dome's 300-acre site in untidy triffid-like clumps. The red tarmac of the piazza in front of the entrance plaza, and the paving of the concourse linking the Dome to North

Greenwich station, have been set in undulating motion as the mud tries to heave its way back into view, surging up from where it has been banished.

Dandelions are sprouting through the cracked paving slabs. There are fences within fences, and Unit Four security patrols in their high-visibility vests reminding you of the vivid yellow of the Dome's masts as they were before the paint started to fade. The pay booths that were never that busy during the Millennium Experience's sparsely attended run are shuttered and empty. Strange, unidentifiable pieces of electrical equipment sit stacked upside down inside them. The vegetation inside the perimeter is dead, the once carefully tended planting boxes have gone to seed, and their luxuriant green leaves have faded to brown. The security teams still drive around the perimeter aimlessly dodging the tumbleweed in the deserted car parks, scores of them. Only the one nearest the underground station is still in use, filled with commuters from Kent who leave their SUVs and dive down into the Underground as quickly as they can to take the train into town.

The bright showrooms set up by English Partnerships to bring the brittle promise of regeneration to the area – offering businessmen with money to invest all the support they'd need and attempting to persuade potential homeowners that this was the place to bring up a family – are locked and empty now. Through the windows you glimpse the cheap purple sofas of the new tomorrow. They have chairs tipped upside down sitting on top of them. Norman Foster's station is a ghostly shadow of its former self. Big enough to handle huge crowds all day long, it's reduced to a rush-hour trickle. As the commuters emerge they have a chance to look back at the towers of Canary Wharf from the east, a reminder of just how far the Dome still is from the seat of power in London.

The official budget, £758 million, was big enough, a sum so huge in fact that nobody questioned its accuracy, but the true cost was a long way beyond £1,000 million. Of that original figure, £466 million was allocated to building costs, the remainder to operational, market-ing, and contingencies, financed by £150 million in sponsorship, £209 million in commercial revenue and disposals, and £449 million in cash from the Millennium Commission. Laughably, there was a notion that some of that commercial revenue would be paid back to the Government. This sum did not, however, include the cost of site acquisition or decontamination. When this is counted in, the cost of the project would have amounted to £905 million. Both the sponsorship and the ticket receipts fell far short of what was promised, while four years after the millennium the Government had still failed to find a new user and was forced to go on paying maintenance and security bills running into millions. In the end it was reduced to begging an American sports entrepreneur with vague plans for turning the Dome into a stadium and casino complex to take it on.

No British government has been more conscious of the imagery of power than New Labour, or more keenly aware of its impact on the electorate. Thus it can only be because they saw a genuine political advantage from a successful Dome that they chose to invest so much party and personal capital in it. The Dome went through a roller-coaster of different and often conflicting objectives and goals. It began as an attempt to harness the market at the tail end of Thatcherism, and turned into an almost entirely publicly funded symbol of the first Blair term. It was conceived as an attempt to provide a vision of the future, and yet, according to the Dome's one-time creative director, Stephen Bayley, even before he quit, the Dome was fundamentally a 'quaint' idea of an Expo in the nineteenth-century mould.

Hanover's Expo was what the Dome could have been if the Millennium Commission hadn't insisted on reclaiming the toxic waste dumps of Greenwich and had opted instead for Birmingham's proposal to celebrate the dawn of the year 2000 at the National Exhibition Centre. Hanover opted for a makeover of a collection of glum concrete sheds in the middle of nowhere – normally used to show off machine tools and construction equipment – plus a job lot of specially constructed new pavilions of variable quality, rather than a brand new project. At a declared cost of £1 billion, it was at least as expensive as the Dome, and by predicting 40 million visitors in six months, it had a target that the Millennium Commission never dreamed of, even in its most optimistic moments. But because it stuck to the traditional formula of the Expo – acres of brilliantly crafted junk, with the occasional flash of genius – it was less of a disappointment.

We remember successful Expos for the innovation of their architecture and engineering. But the reality of the Crystal Palace was that it was filled with replicas of the Venus de Milo carved in butter. And the same 1889 Paris Expo that built the Eiffel Tower also boasted a replica of the Bastille, stormed every hour on the hour by a troupe of actors got up as sans-culottes. The Dome was neither one thing nor another, not bad enough, but not good enough either. It was too polite to follow in the full-blooded tradition of the great Expos, and its exhibits were too bland and without the redeeming architectural brilliance of the Crystal Palace.

Despite all the morally improving rhetoric about sustainability and new technology, Hanover had a series of pavilions of such baroque kitchness that it was impossible not to warm to them. They at least had the courage of their convictions in a way that very little at the Dome did. You could find a fortress straight out of *Beau Geste* built by the United Arab Emirates, complete with cannon at the main gate, and an Airbusload of authentic desert sand. It was sandwiched between the ski-lift swinging across the site and the Ferris wheel. There was a traditional village from Bhutan embellished with 800 specially commissioned carvings. Croatia's sky-blue box allowed you to walk over a glass-covered beach strewn with archaeological fragments. Monte Carlo constructed a pavilion in praise of tax exile, a dazzling white apartment block with a millionaire's yacht floating in its own tank of water. The Poles couldn't make up their mind whether to go for cutting-edge architectural modernity like their Baltic neighbours, or opt for the ethnic end of the market, exploring the same territory as the Emirates. In the event, they tried to have it both ways, building a plate-glass box into which they inserted a collection of thatched cottages, an effect much like putting a ship in a bottle. But alongside all this, Hanover also had a beautifully chaste pavilion designed by Alvaro Siza for Portugal, as good in its way as any of his permanent buildings. There was an extraordinary Japanese structure built by Shigeru Ban using only paper, and at least one work of real architectural brilliance – the Dutch pavilion designed by the architectural group MVRDV. It will go down as one of the few truly great pieces of Expo architecture, alongside Mies van der

Rohe's Barcelona pavilion and Moshe Safdie's Habitat flats at the Montreal Expo.

And the German pavilions, while none of them were particularly distinguished pieces of architecture, managed to be genuinely engaging. One pavilion the size of a football stadium had nothing in it except a flock of seventy-two self-propelled robots as big as elephants silently circling the giant, darkened interior. Another contained Bach's clavichord, the first car ever built by Benz, a slice of Berlin Wall, and the actual peace treaty Germany signed with France in 1956 to settle the future of Alsace. Rather than build a pavilion, as even the Hungarians and the Yemenis managed, Britain rented an off-the-peg industrial shed from the organizers, customizing it with red, white and blue stickers on the exterior. It purported to celebrate the quality of Britain's architects and designers, but the Government hadn't employed any of them to design it, selecting instead HP:ICM, a previously obscure firm that can hardly be said to have covered itself in glory when it worked on the Body Zone at the Dome with Nigel Coates. On the inside you could find a curious hymn to Blairism subtitled: 'Diversity: It's in Our Nature'. The sum of Britain's contemporary achievements in design was represented by ashtrays from assorted Conran restaurants, alongside the Dyson vacuum cleaner, a wind-up radio, and the somewhat presumptuous suggestion that, based on the birthplace of its designer, Apple's iBook is in some mysterious way an example of British design.

It sat in the shadow of the Dutch pavilion, which was everything that Britain's was not. In the flat and featureless landscape of Hanover, it stood out with the force of a skyscraper in the prairie. It took the form of a layer cake that symbolized the Dutch landscape. There were no exhibits as such, but the architecture was integrated with content. One floor was a greenhouse growing a meadow of daisies under artificial sunlight. Piled on top of that was a forest of oak trees. From the ground you could look up and see the surreal spectacle of the trees sitting on the neon strip-lit ceiling above. The top slice of the cake was a clutch of wind-powered generators and an artificial turf mound. The whole thing had a jangling tension between the natural and the man-made, which is what Holland is all about. It also suggested a national culture with the self-confidence to take a chance on an extremely risky piece of design. Britain's pavilion reflected exactly the opposite, with a condescending ineptness.

For a country of just five million people, Scotland has a remarkably high level of what might be called brand recognition, and not just at the level of caricature. A Scot in rural China or Russia's Far East, or in Brazil, has a far better chance of successfully explaining where he is from than, say, a Norwegian, or a Quebecker, or even an Austrian or a Belgian.

Scotland has a distinctive accent, or rather accents. It has clan tartans – actually a nineteenth-century invention – and the bagpipes that it shares with several other Celtic nations; it has whisky, and shortbread. It has a national poet, its own banknotes and legal system, a national Church and an educational system all of its own. In the hands of a young generation of writers, it has created an energetic and distinctive literary voice.

Scotland and England have shared a head of state for four hundred years since James VI was seduced by the prospect of acquiring the crown of a country so much more prosperous than his own into moving down to London to become James I of England as well. What followed was no conquest, but a gradual merger in which both parties retained their individual identities, formalized in the Act of Union of 1705.

And now, after almost three hundred years, it has its own parliament again, with a new building in Edinburgh that can only be seen as part of a deliberate attempt to use architecture to reinforce that sense of national identity. Designed by Enric Miralles and Benedetta Tagliabue before Miralles's tragically early death, it is a project that demonstrates the engagement of architecture with political life on a variety of levels. Every step of the process has been charged with resonances that go far beyond pragmatic construction issues, from the site eventually selected to the materials used and the nationality of the architects.

Even before the design was addressed, choosing the location provoked endless, mainly politically rooted, arguments. Should the parliament meet in the Scottish capital at all? If it did, should it be on the edge of the city where the land was cheaper, or in the middle? Should this parliament take over the classical landmark earmarked for an earlier failed attempt at setting up a devolved parliament? The latter was rejected ostensibly on grounds of practicalities, but many assumed that it was not considered suitable by Labour politicians because it had become so closely associated with the politics of the Scottish Nationalists. Eventually a former brewery building just off the Royal Mile, adjacent to the Palace of Holyroodhouse, was chosen, a spot that could be seen as locating the new institution within a traditional context, but one free from excess baggage.

The choice of a Catalan architect after a long-drawn-out selection process and the personal involvement of Donald Dewar, Scotland's First Minister, was clearly anything but accidental. The Catalans are the leading role models for ambitious small European nations attempting to assert their own distinctive identities, shorn of any of the darker overtones of nationalism. Scotland, it would seem, wants to be seen in this way: asserting its national identity, but offering an inclusive kind of nationalism, not a narrowly chauvinistic one.

Nobody asked Miralles to use a national style in Edinburgh, and his design is clearly a highly personal one that springs from his own deeply felt architectural sensibility. His original submission touchingly showed as his point of departure a photograph of two upturned turf-covered fishing boats he had found while on a student trip to Britain on a beach that may or may not have been in Scotland. He was suggesting that he wanted to build a parliament that felt like a natural part of the site, rather than an imposition on it. Despite this poetic vision, he had to work with the political ambitions of the Scottish system.

The civil servants leading the project were asked to deliver a building that would accommodate a system of government based on collaboration and consensus in which committee rooms would be the focus of activity as much as the debating chamber. Above all there was a belief among those planning the project that it should not look anything like the Westminster parliamentary model. If it did, it would risk being understood as a deferential offshoot of a metropolitan original. Scotland, or at least the tiny political and administrative elite that claimed to speak for the country, wanted to show that it had left the bad old days of Westminster politics behind. Westminster, so they told themselves, represented the politics of confrontation and obstruction. The very form of Westminster's debating chamber – a rectangle lined by opposed ranks of benches set two sword lengths apart – was, they claimed, calculated to bring out the worst in its members. It is an arrangement that is actually the result of an accident of history. England's Parliament had begun to meet in the choir stalls of the chapel of St Stephen at the Palace of Westminster, and simply took over the existing furniture.

Scotland wanted a supposedly gentler, more constructive layout for its parliament. It looked at the circular model common on mainland Europe, which first saw the light of day in modern times in Dublin, in the Irish House of Commons, now the Bank of Ireland. After a protracted argument, a couple of redesigns, and countless fact-finding missions by the politicians, Miralles ended up giving Edinburgh a gently curved crescent-shaped debating chamber. But it takes rather more than an adjustment to the seating arrangements to instil a sense of collaborative spirit into a fractious legislative assembly, as the members of the Scottish Parliament amply demonstrated in their bad-tempered exchanges in their temporary, circular debating chamber. Nonetheless, this is a case of a political body approaching a major architectural commission aware of more than the pragmatic limits of building.

The old maps of Edinburgh make the Royal Mile, running along the ridge on which the city grew over the centuries, look like an elongated fish spine. The castle, sitting on its rock at the top, is its tail. Holyroodhouse Palace next to the ruins of the abbey at the bottom of the slope is its head. In between, a procession of spiky curved bones mark the wynds and closes of urban Scottish domestic life that open off it on both sides. These narrow lanes and tight courtyards were surrounded by tenements six and eight storeys high. The well-to-do lived on the lower floors, and the poor had the attics. Halfway down the spine, behind its cool, elegant, early nineteenth-century façade, is Scotland's old Parliament House. It was built as a hurried job-creation scheme funded by the city council when Charles I made it clear that the price of a continued legislative presence in Edinburgh, with all the attendant implications for the ongoing employment prospects of fencing masters, wigmakers, tavern keepers, courtesans and claret importers, was the construction, like some sort of seventeenth-century Bilbao Guggenheim, of an impressive new Scottish parliament building. The place was shut down after the Act of Union, finding a new role as Scotland's High Court, but not before the distribution of copious quantities of English gold to persuade wavering members to disband themselves.

The new Scottish Parliament, which began life in a temporary home in 1999 as the guest of the Assembly of the Church of Scotland towards the top end of the Royal Mile, is now housed at the Holyrood end, the gills just below the fish's head. Enric Miralles's remarkable building, a lyrical and complex composition of oak and granite and steel, half buried into a meadow, and wrapped carefully into Edinburgh's medieval fabric, looks the palace straight in the eye. Much, so it is said, to the distaste of the Prince of Wales.

There is always room for a gap to open up between architectural intentions and the message that a building actually transmits. That is certainly the case with Miralles's parliament for Scotland. On one level it is a delicately wrought, romantic poem to the expressive qualities of architecture, and the tactile qualities of wood and stone. On another, and especially in the eyes of Scotland's newspapers, it is a shocking, even scandalous case of the gross mismanagement of public money. A project first budgeted at £50 million ended up costing £431 million. Those first figures didn't include the cost of the land, any professional fees, or tax, but they still reflect a huge increase, and an embarrassment that has at times threatened to overwhelm the parliament, and the message that it was intended to convey. The officials who were charged with getting the project off the ground made educated guesses about costs that were deliberately minimized so that they wouldn't look too frightening. Since they were made, they have come back to haunt Scotland's government. It is true that the parliament building has doubled in size. Queensberry House, a seventeenth-century mansion at the centre of the site, has been rescued from ruin, and the whole site rendered truck-bomb proof. But that's not much compensation for the scale of the cost overrun. Miralles died just after work had started on building the parliament, shortly before the death of Donald Dewar, the new parliament's political sponsor. Their deaths came in 2000, just at the beginning of a series of crises that afflicted the financial aspects of the project.

These are such extremes that they make it very difficult to make sense of the project. If you talk only about the architecture without mentioning the money, you end up sounding like a feeble-minded design victim. Lord Fraser of Carmyle, the thickset former Scottish Lord Advocate, appointed by Scotland's First Minister to conduct a year-long public inquiry into the cost overrun, had an easier time of it. He promised, in a way that makes it sound like a perfectly reasonable proposition, to avoid any consideration of aesthetics in his judgements. But it simply isn't possible to divorce what the parliament looks and feels like in use from what it has cost. It would be as pointless as writing a Michelin guide to a restaurant simply in terms of the cost of the ingredients and their relationship with the bill. How the meal tastes is the object of the exercise.

The figures certainly look bad. If you had set out to build a kitchen for £40,000, and it ended up costing you £400,000, you would need a special kind of stoicism to take much pleasure in the exquisite workmanship of the oak worktops and the Portuguese limestone floor. But a parliament is not a kitchen extension, and the quality of the architecture will last much longer than the burden of the cost. These costs are in any case relatively modest, compared, let's say, to one of those Ministry of Defence procurement contracts for helicopters that can't fly in the rain, or Nimrod AWACS planes that never work at all.

But to say that the building is worth the nightmarish cost escalation is not a view that is very popular in Scotland. The embarrassments of the Holyrood building programme have been an all-consuming obsession for the country for so long that it's going to take time for the parliament to be understood as anything other than a monstrous waste of money. Indeed it is hard to know what Scotland's politicians, newspapers and lawyers would have done without it A country the size of Scotland simply does not have enough serious issues to busy the ranks of all its ambitious self-styled public figures; when they find one, they grab hold of it with an enthusiasm bordering on glee. A really juicy financial scandal, particularly one with the possibility of making regular headlines for any MSP with even a moderate gift for a sound bite, was much more fun than arguing about subsidies for Caledonian MacBrayne ferries and sorting out the problems of the schools examination boards.

Lord Fraser turned himself into a public spectacle on the strength of Holyrood. He set up his own website, hired a spin doctor and commissioned a purple logo. And he took to posing for the cameras in front of the cranes at Holyrood, multiple chins prominent, promising with startling originality to leave no stone unturned. Clearly delighted with his own performance, Lord Fraser conducted the public inquiry with the colossal self-regard of a man who believes he is presiding over a Watergate hearing rolled into the South African Truth and Reconciliation Commission. 'This inquiry should be part of the cleansing process,' he intoned, suggesting that he felt Scotland's pain about spending all that money. 'We have already brought into the public domain much which was unknown, unexplained, or inexplicable. And for that, I can compliment the subtle brilliance of my team.'

From the tone of his pronouncements immediately after he was appointed, Lord Fraser appeared to have already made up his mind that he was going to be digging up serious evidence of wrongdoing. There was a hotline for anonymous whistle-blowers, which by all accounts never even got so much as tepid. And, presumably in an effort to encourage candour in his witnesses, Lord Fraser promised no testimony would be used in criminal proceedings. 'If anyone, or any organization attempts to stop me, I will have no hesitation in naming and shaming them,' he said. 'I am determined that this inquiry will provide the people of Scotland with answers. The people of Scotland expect the truth, they deserve the truth, and I am determined that they will get the truth.'

To give him his due, Lord Fraser's showmanship managed to extract far more courtroom drama from the finer points of quantity surveying, contract law and project management than anybody could have imagined. He discovered a breakdown in communication between Miralles's Barcelona office and his Edinburgh collaborators, RMJM. He may or may not have found that Miralles had no up-to-date professional indemnity cover. The doubts come from the evidence in the transcripts, which is based on the testimony of an official who confesses that he scrutinized a photocopy of a Spanish insurance certificate but didn't have enough Spanish to order a beer.

Fraser managed to skewer a couple of Scottish Executive officials hopelessly out of their depth, and flushed out some of the more self-indulgent of the many grotesques who infest the edges of Scottish political life. Margo MacDonald, the erratic former Scottish Nationalist, who left the party to become an independent MP, claims that the parliament at Holyrood is the greatest catastrophe in Scottish building history. Given that Scotland gave the world the Tay Bridge disaster, that was certainly going it a bit. But Edinburgh politicians tend to talk that way. Lord Fraser also listened politely to David Black's evidence. Black is a conspiracy theorist who has bafflingly attempted to portray Donald Dewar, the politician who initiated the project, as a Richard Nixon figure. He wrote a confused, tortuous and slender book about the project, entitled *All the First Minister's Men*. Yet Black can't make up his mind who is involved in the conspiracy that has caused the parliament disaster. Sometimes it is the Glaswegians who rigged the competition jury to do down Edinburgh. Sometimes it is London, which apparently fixed the parliament to demonstrate how incapable the Scots were of governing themselves, or else to make the institution invisible by fobbing it off with the wrong site.

The Fraser Inquiry scrutinized the tens of thousands of decisions, big and small, that shape any complex building. In the process, two entirely different worlds, architecture and the law, collided but somehow failed entirely to engage with each other. Early in the hearings, Lord Fraser produced Richard Armstrong, a civil servant who had left the project in angry circumstances, of whom he clearly had high hopes. Armstrong was the parliament's project manager until he resigned, or was sacked, when he couldn't get on with the design team. Armstrong produced a memo to his superiors at the Scottish Executive written at the time of the competition. 'I am sorry to say', he wrote, 'that my overall impression is one of disappointment. I find it hard to believe that such an allegedly massive architectural talent cannot produce one approach which is convincing, or acceptable.' He went on to suggest that, if the decision had been his, he would not have shortlisted Miralles. 'With Miralles's other commitments, devoting 21 hours a week to this project was totally inadequate. I scored him

44 out of 70. I would instantly have moved him to number 70 if I had known then that he had no insurance cover.'

Armstrong's reputation for consistency was undermined somewhat by another memo in which he claimed that of all the shortlisted designers, Miralles was one of only two that could seriously be considered. Lord Fraser's counsel probed witnesses with questions that seemed to suggest that he believed Miralles had been placed on the short list improperly because of his alleged friendship with one of the jury and that he wasn't up to the job, presumably with a view to suggesting that this was the root cause of the cost overrun.

Andy McMillan, one-time head of the Mackintosh School of Architecture in Glasgow, was the most forceful architectural member of the competition jury. Disarmingly, he responded to an interrogation that appeared to imply that he was guilty of improperly foisting an architect on Scotland, for no better reason than personal friendship, with his recollection of Enric Miralles talking to Donald Dewar. 'To illustrate his scheme, he produced some leaves and stems which he laid on a plan to show us how the building would sit in the Canongate, but also sit in what he described as the land of Scotland.'

It was the gesture that won Miralles the commission. He was an architect who was much too smart for the obvious metaphors. In particular, he steered well away from that feeble idea about the literal representation of democracy through transparency. Instead, Miralles created a landscape as much as a building. 'The parliament should be able to reflect the land which it represents,' he wrote. 'The land itself will be a material, a physical building material. From the outset we have worked with the intuition that individual identification with land carries collective consciousness and sentiments.' And he maintained the analogy, from that first image of the leaves and stalks that he showed Donald Dewar, all the way through to his idea of a parliamentary chamber that he conceived of as 'an amphitheatre carved out of the rock for gatherings of people sitting on the landscape and identifying with their country'.

These are not concepts that are easily expressed in the charged atmosphere of a judicial inquiry. John Campbell QC skirted past McMillan's enthusiasm and asked him if he had ever stayed at Miralles's house in Berlin. 'I didn't know that he had one,' was the reply. And McMillan went back to architecture. 'Miralles had a poetic idea that there would be a bank of earth which people would sit on, a bit like speakers' corner and discuss things.'

In the transcript of the cross-examination, McMillan pauses, then addresses Campbell directly: 'You may smile; you know what I mean. It is a charming idea. I think he had a passion which came across. One should not really say it, but it is a bit like football matches. We thought we had picked five people all of whom were capable of giving us a world-class building. But on the day of the final presentation, Miralles was clearly better.' On the day, I am sure that is exactly what Miralles was. Better than Richard Meier, better than Raphael Vinoly. Better than Michael Wilford and all the other competitors.

Walk around the foot of the Royal Mile, past the gates of the Palace of Holyroodhouse, and up toward Salisbury Crags – a site of quite exceptional beauty – and there, unwinding in front of you, is Miralles's parliament. It has an elusive sense of settled ease. It belongs to its surroundings.

A parliament, or any other kind of democratic assembly, demands a complex combination of uses that even an opera house or a museum does not have. There is the debating chamber itself, as well as the backstairs aspects – the briefing rooms, the lobbies, the corridors and the committee rooms – that all play their part in creating a political theatre that can make real the ambitions of those who use it. Such chambers are not necessarily the embodiment of elevated ideals. Politics in the raw mostly looks about as interesting as a reading from the telephone directory. There are endless procedural discussions, nit-picking points of order and for most of the day people sit in rooms, shuffle paper, talk on the phone and check their e-mails as if they were in a call centre. The struggle to make something out of this deeply unpromising material is the real story of the design of Miralles's parliament. This is also the story, although one with a very different outcome, of London's new City Hall.

The London Assembly's 500 staff and 26 members could easily have been accommodated in an anonymous office building with no public recognition or iconographic significance. It would have been presented as the financially responsible option. But it would also have left London's government invisible and lacking any sense of authority in its premises.

Ken Livingstone's seat of power is British municipal politics given the Australian cricket treatment. No more fuddy-duddy cricket whites and V-neck sweaters, but floodlights and lime-green pyjamas. Or, in the case of City Hall, purple carpet, yellow walls that look good on television and one of the most conspicuous new buildings in London. On the outside it looks like a giant motorcycle helmet. On the inside, it has been scooped out, to make way for a spiralling ramp of baroque complexity, rising up the whole height of the building. The ramp is there to celebrate the symbolic heart of the building, the debating chamber. But of course it is almost comically overblown. London's councillors meet there just once a month. The rest of the time the chamber sits glorious but unused, unless the Authority rents it out for weddings and dance performances.

The real business is carried out in the offices. The Mayor is up on the top, naturally. Livingstone, who has a finely pitched ear for the meaningless but telling symbolic gesture, asked for an office smaller than the one that he was originally allocated. The elected members are downstairs. They get cellular offices with doors, clustered in the middle of the building – which allows the secretarial staff the windows.

The spiral starts beneath the chamber, wraps around it and then soars above it. Using it to move between floors is of course a possibility. But the ramp is really there to raise the architectural temperature much more than as a practical means of getting from one floor to another: for that there are conventional lifts and staircases.

Fundamentally, City Hall looks the way it does because it is trying to tell us something about itself. It's meant to look special. Miralles's building in Edinburgh achieves so much more. In contrast to Foster's, it breaks down the parliament's bulk into modest individual pieces that merge with the landscape. They open up to the sky to bring sunlight and the landscape into the lobbies and committee rooms, and even the debating chamber. The design uses concrete as a polished sculptural material, with a rich palette of granite, oak and steel. Everywhere you see traces of Miralles's drawings, in the strips that are woven over the windows of the members' offices, in the gashes and gouges in the vaulted ceilings.

What you see from the pavement is not what you experience as you move in and around the building. In fact the parliament is a cluster of buildings. The easiest to grasp is the block that accommodates the members' offices – not that it could conceivably be described as an office block. There is room in it for 129 members and their staff. It is made from granite, some of it from Aberdeenshire in deference to the idea of national pride, and more of it from South Africa in the interests of economy, as well as from oak and sycamore. There has never been an office block like this. Its most characteristic façade looks west, and it works like one of the many wynds that open off the Royal Mile, stepping down the slope from four to six storeys.

Miralles was never prepared to tolerate the bland or the anonymous. For him, work was not simply sitting at a desk. It meant thinking, and contemplation, and noticing that there is a soft rain falling on the slate roofs outside your window, and allowing yourself to be distracted from your computer screen. So the members' offices have vaulted concrete ceilings that make them feel like monastic cells. They have window seats that allow members to climb up into a rounded wooden perch, away from the stresses of jobbing politics, and read or think. Who knows if they will actually do it, or what those offices will look like covered in the detritus of political life, with their electric kettles and their posters and their trophies. But the members and their staff have been offered characterful, individual spaces, where you feel that somebody has actually taken the trouble to make a space that is personal and individual, not the product of a random accident between floor, walls and ceiling.

The west façade is a rock face, pierced by a series of irregular cave-like openings that reflect the shape of the window seat inside the thickness of the wall. It sits at right angles to Queensberry House, originally built in 1667 and mutilated over the years by successive occupiers to the point of being unrecognizable. With nothing left of the interiors, Miralles's strategy in bringing it back into use was to create entirely new spaces within the shell of what survives of the past. It's here that the parliament's presiding officer and his team are based, and it's where Donald Dewar's library has been installed. At ground level, the block is linked to the MSPs' building and the debating chamber, by way of a foyer. And that foyer is roofed with an extraordinary structure that is the physical realization of Miralles's presentation of the drawing and the leaf. Glass roof-lights in wispy patterns create a sort of landscape, inside and out. If Miralles couldn't make members be nice to each other, he could at least give them a ravishingly beautiful space to meet in. His concept of the chamber as a sunlit room with glimpses out to the sheer slopes of Arthur's Seat survived the attempts of the media consultants to turn it into a television studio. Miralles took the theme of the hammer-beam roofs of the old parliament building up the hill and used it as an inspiration for an extraordinarily intricate timber roof.

Miralles's subtlest move was to create a sense of ambiguity about the debating chamber. It is the heart of the building, but it does not instantly reveal itself as such. It takes a careful look at the building to understand where it is, for it is only one among a whole series of sculptural elements that make up the building. The business of this parliament takes place just as much in the six committee rooms, built in a cluster of towers at the back of the debating chamber, or in the television studios in the press tower that sits over the Royal Mile, or in the corridors that link the chamber with the members' offices, and with the administration's offices in Queensberry House.

But this is a parliament that was born in the twentieth century, a moment in history overburdened with the mission to explain, so there is also a sense in which the building has been designed to represent itself. Sweeping planes of concrete and stone erupt from the green meadows of the landscape to define a dramatic entrance. There is a public foyer, on the Salisbury Crags side of the site, where the general public can come for a lesson in Scotland's democracy and wander through exhibition spaces, classrooms and cafés, and it is this that will become the public face of the parliament.

Enric Miralles, when he was alive, never really seemed to lay all his cards on the table. He hinted and he finessed and he imagined, rather than directly described what he was intending to do with the parliament. His evocative drawings and collages were hard to read; they seemed to show an eruption of organic forms from the landscape that didn't quite add up to a building. Only now is it possible to see what he had in mind – and the reality is a powerful confirmation of his talent.

Miralles was an architect of what might be called an old-fashioned kind; his work was full of symbolic and representational qualities. He had a romantic vision that, had he lived, might have encouraged others in an exploration of these issues. When he died, his career cut cruelly short at just 45, he was on the edge of becoming a major figure, but without having yet completed the Edinburgh parliament that would demonstrate that he offered much more than promise.

This is haute-couture architecture: every door, every handle, every window, every light fitting has been designed as if it were a one-off, and it was almost as difficult to build as a Gaudí cathedral. Miralles designed spaces that surprise you as you move from one to another, and where you can suddenly find yourself looking up at the sky, or across another part of the parliament complex to see the landscape beyond.

If Holyrood means anything at all, it is how it will feel in twenty-five years, or in a century, that counts. The parliament will have proved itself architecturally if it can do something to persuade the fractious, the tired and emotional, the exhibitionists, chancers, zealots, and anoraks who make up the mainstream of political life in most democratic systems, as well as the idealists and the self-sacrificing, to think a little bit more about the country that they represent and the essentials of civilized life and to behave in a slightly more measured way. Could it have been built for less? Certainly. Is it value for money? No. But how do you place a value on the view of the green slopes of the hillside outside, or the sense of continuity that comes from installing Donald Dewar's library in the shell of the aristocratic house in which the Act of Union was hidden from the Edinburgh mob?

In the end, the saga of the Edinburgh parliament building tells us that there is no such thing as historical inevitability. Donald Dewar was in many ways the least likely of politicians to indulge in a taste for monumentalism. He was an ascetic and, for a politician, a curiously unworldly lawyer by training. Such people are preternaturally sceptical of aesthetic self-indulgence, and of architects. And yet once he had engaged with the issue, he rapidly understood the parameters of the architectural world, and how to use them to achieve what he saw was required. The result is a building of genuine architectural quality that nevertheless serves the nation-building objectives that Dewar had in mind. Small countries that nurture creative talent wherever it comes from, to produce architecture that is recognizably their own, demonstrate a self-confidence that is more impressive than a more narrowly drawn definition of identity. It's true of any cultural form that is seen to count on a worldwide scale: cinema, art, literature, sport or music. But architecture is the most visible of them all, and the most powerful expression of national identity simply because it can be used to help create a credible national institution.

It is of course not only the most obviously charged buildings, such as parliaments, that come to acquire a complex set of political meanings. Every state building can come to be understood in this way, from an embassy to a court house, a police station or a museum.

Australia marked a century of nationhood when its prime minister, John Howard, opened the new National Museum in Canberra. It's a project that demonstrates just how sophisticated a critique of national identity architecture can offer, even in what was intended to be a celebration of Australianness. While you can find Donald Bradman's cricket bat inside, along with the van that ferried Australia's first mobile television film unit around the outback, the museum is anything but a mindless celebration of the lucky country. It does not shrink from addressing the brutal history of its treatment of the Aboriginals, both in its content and in its very fabric. You can see the pistols and metal clubs that colonists used to murder women and children when Tasmania's first Australians were exterminated. All of this in the name of a celebration of Australia that was paid for by a conservative government.

But nothing on display is more controversial than the architecture itself. The architects, Ashton Raggatt McDougall from Melbourne, put those sections of the museum devoted to the Aborigines into a replica of Daniel Libeskind's museum of Jewish history in Berlin. The scale is slightly reduced and the materials are different. Walls are made from black concrete, puckered to look like rubber, rather than the zinc sheeting that Libeskind used. But the plan is an exact copy of the lightning-flash zigzag that Libeskind created by breaking a five-pointed star of David, except that Howard Raggatt prefers to call it a quotation rather than a copy. Libeskind claimed to be angry, calling it 'shocking, banal and plagiarism'. For Raggatt, however, it is a legitimate strategy, put to work to make a comparison between the plight of the Aborigines whose world was all but destroyed by the settlers' weapons, diseases and alcohol, and the horror of the Holocaust. The message about white Australia's treatment of the Aborigines could not be clearer. It is a comparison that made Ashton Raggatt McDougall far more unpopular with some of the more conservative members of the Australian government than they are with Libeskind. After all, John Howard is the prime minister who has refused to apologize on behalf of white Australia to the Aborigines for their maltreatment.

At another level, the design could be seen as a reflection of a particularly subtle way of white Australia asserting its moral superiority by appearing to be so sophisticatedly downbeat about its history. The museum certainly manages to press a lot of buttons in a way that suggests a rare ability to make architecture matter. For once it's not how the building looks that counts, but what it is saying. With a remarkable site in the heart of Canberra, overlooking Lake Burley Griffin, and aligned directly on the giant flagpole that crowns Parliament House, the museum forms a long ribbon, strung out along the waterfront and turning back on itself in a wide arc to create at its heart a sheltered garden of what the architects call Australian dreams. It's filled with a fragmented map of Australia pockmarked with the names of massacre sites and battlegrounds.

It's not just Libeskind's Jewish museum that provides the architectural source material. The building is a series of fragments, seamlessly and surreally joined one to another with the smoothness of a computer simulacrum. There are enough design quotations threaded together here to suggest that Australia has built a national museum of architecture rather than one dedicated to its social history. One part of the complex is a reworking of Le Corbusier's Villa Savoie, but the smooth, white skin of the original has turned fuzzy black and it has inverted the original façade as a mirror image. In conversation, Raggatt reveals that this is a reference to the sense of cultural inferiority that Australia took so long to shake off. It's a reflection in the architectural sphere of Australia's colonial incarnation as a country in which all culture was imported from a long way off, and which had a habit of getting it slightly, but embarrassingly, wrong. When photographs of the Villa Savoie were first published in an Australian magazine, they were reproduced back to front but, according to Raggatt, nobody noticed. Australians took their cue for what they should be building from the other side of the world, and were too provincial even to be able to get their borrowings the right way round.

Elsewhere on the site a vivid red, flattened, cut-out of the façade of the Australian parliament is used to provide a suitably important-looking home for the Institute for Aboriginal Studies. It looks across a sweep of grass toward the Australian version of Libeskind's museum in Berlin that, in turn, morphs into a central entrance hall in which Raggatt has painstakingly re-created fragments of the brown glass and the window mullions used in the Sydney Opera House. Again, this is a two-edged sampling of an Australian architectural icon. It is a reminder of the crude and unsympathetic glazing that was the work of the Australian architectural team appointed to finish the Opera House after its European designer, Jorn Utzon, was driven out of the country by what have come to be stigmatized as antipodean philis-tines. Also incorporated into the museum is a little souvenir of James Stirling's Staatsgallerie in Stuttgart and an Aldo Rossi building.

It could be a high-culture version of Las Vegas and the themed architecture typified by the casinos, but it isn't. Raggatt has created a building that amounts to a book, even if it is written in a lan-guage that most people will have trouble reading. Ashton Raggatt McDougall don't content themselves with using buildings as meta-phorical words – they have also covered their building with literal words, to provide another, all but incomprehensible layer of meaning. The aluminium skin is pitted with regular patterns of dimples, giant Braille characters used as a form of decoration. It's a language that very few sighted people can make sense of, and which is out of reach of the fingers of those blind visitors who might be able to read it. Raggatt, however, is happy to translate as he leads you around. 'Who are my neighbours?' he asks, pointing at one strip of aluminium on the sculpted skin. 'She'll be right, mate,' he interprets, pointing to another. It doesn't stop there. The colours tell their own story. Frag-ments of the exterior are painted black and red to reflect the Aboriginal flag. Another slice is buff and blue, the colours of the uniforms worn by the convicts in the early Australian penal colonies.

Getting to grips with this museum on its architect's terms isn't easy, even if it is possible to experience it simply as a physical sensation devoid of the intellectual content. There is no Rosetta Stone to unravel all the meanings, just a few broad and not so broad hints. It is an architecture of intelligence and anger, with an ambition not just to redefine Australia's sense of itself, but the role of architecture too. And it is perhaps just a bit too angry to be tolerated by the State as an example of its cultural sophistication. Here are architects who have done all they can to create an autonomous architecture. Official Australia intended this to become part of the country's national iconography, but Ashton Raggatt McDougall's design makes it almost impossible to co-opt. So awkward is the relationship of the museum with the State that the federal government tried to find a way to replace the landscaped courtyard with a more conventional – or, rather, less challenging – view of what an Australian garden should be.

8

The Uses of Marble

For a while, America – or at least those readers of *Time* magazine who still accepted the infallible authority of its judgements about who did and who did not get their picture on its covers – believed that Wallace Harrison was one of the greatest architects of the twentieth century. Certainly he had outmanoeuvred Le Corbusier in the protracted struggle to get his name in the biggest type on the credits for the design of the headquarters of the United Nations headquarters, a project that briefly looked like the most significant piece of architecture of the century. It may have been due more to his capacity for stony silence and pragmatic introspection than to his talent as a designer, but it was an impressive achievement all the same. And he had certainly had every chance to show off his genuine architectural skills on a series of large-scale, highly visible buildings with generous budgets. Harrison helped to shape the New York World's Fair in 1939. At just the moment when Stalin's architects were borrowing New York's skyscraper vernacular to wrap it in the iconography of socialist realism, Harrison was looking at the spatial gymnastics of the constructivists to bring a little radical glamour to the fair's celebration of the triumph of capitalism. Harrison's landmark for Flushing Meadow has a clear debt to Melnikov's drawings from twenty years before. He built New York's first modern airport terminal at La Guardia. He devised the early version of the plans for Battery Park City on landfill on the banks of the Hudson. He also designed such crucial American landmarks as the CIA's headquarters at Langley.

But even more significantly, for almost the whole of his working life Wallace Harrison was court architect to the house of Rockefeller and those bafflingly interchangeable generations of sons, brothers and cousins who all seemed to be called almost the same thing. He was on the team building the Rockefeller Center for John D. Rockefeller Jr. in the 1930s. Twenty-five years later, he co-ordinated the fractious group of architects that designed the Lincoln Center for John D. Rockefeller III. Taken together they added up to two of the three key projects that have served to define the grain of contemporary New York. He rebuilt the Bronx Zoo for Laurance Rockefeller. David Rockefeller called him a friend. But most of all, he was Nelson Rockefeller's architect, a relationship that Victoria Newhouse explores in her biography of Harrison, to which this account is indebted.

Harrison began their working relationship by designing an apartment for him on Fifth Avenue in 1934 – complete with a specially commissioned mural by Fernand Léger. Forty years later he was still working for Rockefeller, by this time Governor of New York State, on the design of the Capitol Mall in Albany, the most ambitious government complex ever attempted in America outside Washington. Albany was a stab at building Brasilia on the Hudson, or even, given its artificial hill-top site and its plaza ringed by pyramid-shaped office towers, a kind of modern-day Mayan city-state, transplanted from the jungles of Yucatan. It was the most conspicuous American example of a phenomenon common to so many politicians: their pursuit of solace and consolation in the process of building.

To Harrison, who was particularly good at cultivating useful friendships, even before he met the Rockefellers, Nelson was someone who could provide, as he said, 'opportunities to work with great people and do beautiful buildings'. He made many other useful friends. There was an executive at RCA he knew who, on the strength of a lunch with Harrison, signed up as an anchor tenant for the Rockefeller Center. And there was Robert Moses, New York's fatally flawed answer to Paris's Baron Georges-Eugène Haussmann, who involved Harrison in planning both of New York's two World's Fairs. William Zeckendorf, Donald Trump's rather more engaging predecessor as the most flamboyant developer in New York, also developed a close relationship with Harrison before I. M. Pei became his in-house architect.

But above all there was Nelson Rockefeller. Fresh from college, the most pharaonic Rockefeller of them all walked into the marketing

THE USES OF MARBLE

suite at the Rockefeller Center one morning and questioned Harrison about every detail of the project his father had initiated, fascinated by the process of building, as much as by its financial and engineering aspects. Despite his patrician style, Harrison had left school to work as an office boy in a local contractor's office. But military service and a spell at the École des Beaux Arts in Paris gave him the air of confident polish that appealed to the younger man. Then came the Rockefeller commissions. 'For an architect, it was like being handed a meringue glacée, it was almost too easy,' Harrison said later.

When Rockefeller started to behave like America's viceroy in Venezuela, where he had acquired huge land holdings, Harrison went with him to build the country's first modern hotel. When Rockefeller went to Washington to run the Coordination Bureau for Inter-American Affairs Harrison went too, as head of the organization's cultural programme, abandoning his practice for several years. Harrison had the use of a Rockefeller-owned apartment in Manhattan. The family made him a present of enough land to build himself a house on the Rockefeller holiday compound in Maine. For a while his ailing daughter was cared for by a Rockefeller trust fund. Harrison became a trustee of at least three of the Rockefellers' cultural fiefdoms, MoMA, Colonial Williamsburg and the Museum of Primitive Art.

Harrison's great moment came when the fledgling United Nations began to look for a site for its headquarters. San Francisco on the west coast and a range of sites in the east were considered. For New York's masters, the chance to make their city world capital was too tempting to miss. Harrison was the essential link between the three men who did most to secure this prize for New York. They had a range of motives. Robert Moses wanted the UN building on the site of his World's Fair at Flushing Meadow to tidy up the project he had initiated two decades earlier. When it became clear that the Secretary-General wasn't going to accept a suburban site, Rockefeller and William Zeckendorf, undoubtedly driven by enlightened self-interest, became involved with putting forward an alternative in Manhattan. As well as all its intangible benefits for civic pride, bringing the UN to the city was certainly going to boost the value of their own land.

Harrison had been working with Zeckendorf on speculative plans for a massive residential and commercial development to replace the old slaughterhouses on the East River, and it was immediately clear that it was a possible location for the UN. Harrison acted as the go-between to make the deal when Nelson Rockefeller persuaded his father to put up the $8.5 million to buy the land from Zeckendorf, and then donate it to the UN.

With that much political and financial clout, there could be little question that when it came to designing the Secretariat and the General Assembly, Harrison was going to get his way sooner or later. But faced with a room full of bad-tempered architects from all over the world appointed to plan the project by the Secretary-General, Oscar Niemeyer and Gordon Bunshaft among them, the process for Harrison wasn't easy. On one occasion, Le Corbusier was moved to such fury that, under the shocked gaze of his collaborators, he started tearing down every drawing except his own from the walls of the studio that the design team shared. But with Rockefeller's gift in the background, Harrison could sit out the tantrums, presenting himself as responsibly responding to the technical and budgetary demands of the UN.

As Harrison grew older, and Nelson Rockefeller became ever more imperious in his unshakeable self-belief, the nature of the relationship between them shifted. Harrison, like Speer and Iofan before him, found himself in the position of interpreting the ideas of his patron. In the words of Max Abramowitz, Harrison's partner: 'The wonderful thing about Wallace was that he could say no to Nelson. But that changed toward the end. Wallace did what Nelson wanted.' In the days when Harrison was in a position to bring major tenants to the Rockefeller Center, or secure Zeckendorf's land holdings for the United Nations project, he had an authority that few architects have ever had. Usually they must rely on their force of personality and their gift for drama in the battle to have their own way. Harrison's connections brought him other, even more persuasive assets that gave him the room to shape buildings. But at Albany, Rockefeller, with a tame government machine in his hands, had not the slightest intention of being diverted by the electorate, and least of all by his notional architect, from his campaign to preside over the transformation of a dim little city on the Hudson into what, at the foundation-laying ceremony, he unblushingly called 'the most beautiful, the most efficient and electrifying capital in the world'.

Nelson Rockefeller might have been an architect himself if his family had let him. When Rockefeller took Harrison up to the family compound in Maine to show him the site for a new country house, Victoria Newhouse describes Rockefeller sinking two wooden posts into the ground with his bare hands to mark out exactly where he wanted the picture window he had in mind to go.

And during his term as governor, Rockefeller insisted that New York State should become a serious patron of architecture, a policy that extended as far as giving Richard Meier his first civic commission, the Bronx Developmental Center. But to judge by Albany, Rockefeller would not have made a particularly skilful architect. Harrison was still in control of the architecture of the Rockefeller house. Albany, in unflattering contrast, is as much a product of Nelson Rockefeller's urge to make his mark as it is of Harrison's gifts for design.

Rockefeller conceived the idea of a monumental new government centre for Albany in 1958, halfway through the first of his four terms as governor. It was a scheme that carried with it an uncomfortable echo of other authoritarians with overweeningly ambitious plans for their capital cities, except in this case with no underlying ideology, bar a slight tinge of Republicanism's liberal wing. It involved rooms full of big models, extensive demolitions and a lingering relish in the taking of the decisions and the making of plans, and a complete lack of interest in the fate of those who would be displaced by them. It was a pattern that Rockefeller's brother David was to follow precisely when he encouraged the construction of the World Trade Center at the cost of the destruction of the small shops and businesses of Radio Row. In this he was aided by Nelson, who as state governor was able to guarantee the viability of the development by leasing space for 1,000 state employees in the twin towers.

When he started out on the rebuilding of Albany, Rockefeller was still intent on becoming President of the United States, and had good reason to believe that he would succeed. Eighteen years and $1 billion later, when Albany was finally finished, Rockefeller's political career was long over. His imperial capital in upstate New York, which had started out as an attempt to establish him as a national figure, had turned into what looked like bereavement therapy. It was compensation of a kind for the political power that he had aspired to, but never managed to achieve. When Nelson Rockefeller left the state capital to serve as vice-president in the lame-duck administration of Gerald Ford, he said goodbye to his own ambitions and didn't even make the ticket for Ford's failed attempt at re-election

Building Albany had been an obsession for Rockefeller, a process that he followed through neurotically down to the selection of every plant pot, light switch, door handle and the approval of every drawing. (It's an obsession he shared with so many imperious businessmen. Michael Eisner was so keen to tell the architects designing Euro Disney exactly what to do that Aldo Rossi resigned. He wrote to Eisner reminding him that the last time an Italian architect worked in Paris it was Bernini for the king of France. Clearly I am not Bernini, he said, but unfortunately you seem to believe you are the king of France.) To assemble the critical mass to make the complex look big enough and impressive enough for his purposes, Rockefeller insisted on rounding up every available state agency, organization and official body that he could bully, intimidate or bribe into moving to the Albany acropolis. The government compound ended up including an unlikely mix of scientific laboratories, an art gallery, convention centre and an auditorium, as well as endless acres of offices. It didn't really matter what they were, so long as they were there and could be used to help bulk the place up.

So determined was Rockefeller to build his monument that he insisted on construction work starting on all the major elements of the project at the same time, to make it impossible for any future occupant of the governor's mansion to stop it. As many as 2,500 workers at a time swarmed over the 100-acre site, creating chaotic conditions, and in the resulting confusion causing serious cost overruns. To provide a plausible alibi for this monomaniacal burst of construction, Rockefeller claimed it was all being done in the name of civic improvement. According to Rockefeller, Albany's centre was in danger of being overwhelmed by a threatening wave of slums that supposedly lapped at the gates of the governor's mansion. In fact, 6,000 people lost their perfectly adequate homes, demolished to make way for the plaza, destroying a stable middle-class community and, if anything, worsening the plight of the city's fragile centre. Rockefeller promised that the redevelopment would include 900 affordable new homes to replace those that had been torn down, as well as an old people's housing complex.

When Harrison's model was unveiled at the end of 1962, the scheme did indeed include a number of low-rise blocks of housing for the elderly, positioned directly south of the mall. The Governor was not impressed by the intrusion. He thought that it would get in the way of the views of his buildings. 'These buildings are too big, don't you think so, Wally?' he asked, disturbed that the purity of his conception of an Olympian government centre was being compromised by its mundane neighbours. According to one eyewitness, Rockefeller was so irritated that he grabbed one of the blocks and tried to slip it off the model before the press were allowed in to see the scheme.

Though the project was funded by the taxpayer, neither the citizens of New York State nor of Albany had any say in the development. If the state had tried to raise the money for the mall, Rockefeller would have needed to put the scheme to a ballot. He didn't, and it was funded instead by a bond issue by the city, which did not have to seek voter approval for such a measure. Albany's mayor then engaged the state to act as its agent in the building process and handed over the money to Rockefeller. From then on, Rockefeller treated the reconstruction of a city as if he were an eighteenth-century English landowner adding a wing to his country seat and supervising the construction of a series of follies in the grounds. It was Rockefeller's idea that Harrison should design an artificial ground level for the mall, creating a megastructure, spanning a shallow valley. The inspiration, bizarrely enough, seems to have been the Dalai Lama's palace in Lhasa. According to Harrison, Rockefeller showed him how 'he wanted to stop the valley with a great wall going north and south. He had seen a something like it on a trip to Tibet. He wanted the feeling of separating the mall into a localized community, up on top of the hill so that he could not only get the vista of the wall, but of the whole capitol adjunct at the top. And that was one of the main things that he kept asking for as the project developed.' As a symbol of democratic government, creating an upper city reserved for bureaucrats, towering over the humble lower city saddled with the burden of supporting them, could hardly be less appropriate. But it seemed to go hand in hand with the official paranoia that was rampant in America, even among liberal Republicans like Rockefeller, during the riots of the 1960s and 1970s. The unrest created a sense that authority was under siege everywhere: in the law courts, in the universities, and in the legislature. It was Rockefeller as governor who ordered the state troopers into the jail at Attica to put down a prison riot in the most brutal way, killing ten hostages and twenty-nine prisoners. And with its walled ramparts, and its insulation from any contamination by the poor, the plaza looked as if it could readily be defended against any future insurrection.

Harrison put a reflecting pool, a not so subliminal reference to the Mall in Washington perhaps, on top of the Albany podium. Ranged along one side is a forty-storey office tower – far taller than anything else in the city – and an auditorium. On the other side of the water is a row of four shorter but still extremely imposing towers. Their distinctive chamfered shape was Rockefeller's idea.

Rockefeller insisted that only marble would be good enough for Albany. Against Harrison's advice, he demanded the use of two particularly unsympathetic shades of white stone for the skin of the buildings: Vermont pearl white, and Georgia Cherokee. They look more like plastic than marble, a collection of what look like objects inflated to the scale of buildings, rather than architecture. The auditorium, known for reasons that are all too obvious as the Egg, is an oval shape hoisted up on stubby legs, with the entrance most inelegantly threaded between them. It was the result of another direct intervention by the Governor. At lunch one day with Harrison, Rockefeller picked up a grapefruit, balanced it on a piece of silverware and demanded, 'Make it something like this.'

It's hard to believe that Rockefeller had not been looking at Oscar Niemeyer's designs for the House of Representatives and the Senate in Brasilia, unveiled two years before the planning for Albany got started. Niemeyer's plan also involved a gigantic platform, like Albany's. It linked two curved forms containing debating chambers and was attached to twin office towers – a layout that equally had echoes of the UN Plaza, on which Niemeyer had also worked. The Brazilian President, Juscelino Kubitschek, did not have as much time as Rockefeller to complete his project. With a constitution that limited him to just one five-year term in office, Kubitschek was even more interested in making a bold start on building than Rockefeller.

The Governor was interested in the overall composition as well as the details. Looking at the model of the mall one day, Rockefeller decided that the mall needed something extra, a bold and abstract geometrical element to balance the original state capital building, built in an ornate French Renaissance style. He suggested a 'freedom arch'. Harrison came up with a flattened ellipse on the same lines as the arch originally proposed for Mussolini's EUR and built by Eero Saarinen at St Louis. In the event, it was never realized as cost overruns escalated.

Harrison was already ageing as the project was built, and seemed to be uncomfortable with anything but the boldly planned simplified volumes of his youth. This nostalgia for the past, coupled with the long-drawn-out building process, spread over three decades, gave the design a dated look long before it was completed. Compared with Brasilia, Albany has a parade-ground stiffness and an awkward formalism that fails to come alive as an urban composition. As a social experiment, it looks even more out of time. In America, the cynical, traumatized 1960s, when the cities were at their lowest ebb, was no time to try and repeat a development with the innocent optimistic faith in the future of the Rockefeller Center. By the time it was finished, Rockefeller's mall had turned into a kind of historical freak, a fossilized throwback that spelt out its self-obsessed origins only too clearly, under the skimpiest veneer of contemporary styling, like a facelifted turbo-prop airliner trying to compete in the jet age. It seems hardly to belong to the real world, let alone a modern city, suggesting instead nothing so much as an adolescent fantasy from a science-fiction magazine.

In the end, nobody quite knew what all the effort was for. New Yorkers hardly identify with their state. Their cities mean much more to them than any wider identity at state level, and a gigantic government mall in Albany was not going to change that. Things in Brasilia were different. As far back as 1891, Brazil's first republican constitution had specified moving the seat of government out of Rio de Janeiro. Juscelino Kubitschek committed himself to building it when he was running for election in 1955 and made the new capital a major objective of his term in office. Despite the reluctance of Brazil's legislators actually to live in their new capital, despite the massive expenditure and the eruption of shanty towns out of sight of the city's monumental centre, Brasilia was widely understood by the country at large as a piece of nation-building on a heroic scale. Moving the capital promised to elevate Brazil to the brink of the First World from its post-colonial torpor. And it did, creating an enormous impact in Brazil, and beyond. But as far as the impact of Rockefeller's monuments on Albany's future was concerned, it was less than twenty-five years before Harrison's convention centre began looking so sadly outmoded that the city embarked on building a replacement on another site to compete with more up-to-date rivals across the country.

Albany was a melancholy finale for Harrison's career, and even more poignant an outcome for Rockefeller himself, a cultured man who had wanted so badly to become an American president. A man who did all that he could to be remembered as a master-builder and a statesman will forever be known as the man whose first contribution to the cultural history of the twentieth century was to order the painter Diego Rivera off his ladder at the Rockefeller Center for including Lenin in the mural that he had commissioned, and whose last was his death of a heart attack while in the arms of his young mistress.

Harrison outlasted Rockefeller and lived long enough to attempt to serve an autocrat even more unabashed in his enthusiasm for architecture as a political tool than Nelson Rockefeller. The Shah of Iran was a ruler who did not even pay lip-service to the notion of democratic government, and who in the end was still more unsuccessful than Rockefeller in his attempts to hang on to power. The last project that Harrison worked on in a sustained way was a competition submission for the Pahlavi Library, intended as much as a huge monument to the Shah as to the secular state that he was trying to build.

Left to himself, Jacques Attali would certainly have wanted to build his fledgling European Bank for Reconstruction and Development from the ground up. Something on the lines of Marcel Breuer's UNESCO building in Paris perhaps – on a site near Les Invalides, with its Noguchi garden, paid for by the Japanese Government, a specially commissioned Calder and a Picasso mural, but bigger and with an even better view. Or, at a pinch, a building with the sculptural quality of the headquarters of the French Communist Party, designed by Oscar Niemeyer, though its location in a working-class Parisian suburb would have counted against it.

Attali would have looked for the most prominent possible site, something like the French Ministry of Finance, which has the presumption actually to dip its feet into the Seine. He certainly wanted the most famous architect he could get – Jean Nouvel, or Dominique Perrault, though this last choice might have been seen as an act of *lèse-majesté*. Perrault was still busy on France's new Biblothèque Nationale for Attali's patron, François Mitterrand, and still stubbornly refusing to yield in his pursuit of Cartesian geometry and all-glass walls, even in the interests of safeguarding some of the most precious books in Europe.

In part, Attali's boundless ambition is a reflection of the relentless sense of entitlement of an *énarque*, a member of the French political elite educated at the École Supérieur des Mines, and the École Nationale d'Administration. Attali, born of a European settler family in Algiers that moved to France from North Africa, still had a great deal to prove. He was moving, or so he hoped, from the political boiler room to the centre of events, and he wanted his new office to signal that shift.

But the search for a high-visibility building for the bank was also the product of Attali's calculation that a new international institution would have to establish itself as rapidly as possible if it were to be taken seriously. And to do that, it has to construct an image of the kind of organization that it aspires to be, long before it has any chance of that aspiration becoming substance. It is an approach that it shares with institutions and organizations of all kinds that use buildings to demonstrate to the world what they are, or what they would like to be.

If you are a Jacques Attali, you believe that if you build the palace, the kingdom will follow. In his pitch with Celebrity Speakers International to sell his services on the conference and after-dinner circuit, Attali unblushingly describes himself as 'a man of action and of reflection'. Supposedly an economist, he was better known as François Mitterrand's resident intellectual, and later as the bag-carrier for some of his less savoury financial transactions, than as a natural leader. But prolonged exposure to his patron's obsession with building gave him a fascination with the architectural trappings of power. Mitterrand had a taste for a peculiarly French architectural language, of perfect cubes, spheres and pyramids, one that connects the new Louvre to the world of the Sun King by way of Ledoux and Boullée and their gargantuan schemes for monuments to Newton. It's an iconography that comes naturally to the country that invented the year zero when it introduced the revolutionary calendar after 1789 and tried to replace Christianity with a synthetic state religion.

France takes it for granted that the architectural landscape is shaped in the most direct way possible by its presidents and mayors and their counsellors, with minimal involvement by the taxpayers whose money actually pays for all these monuments. It is a country in which, following the President's example in Paris, every ambitious provincial mayor from Nîmes to Lille has built themselves either an art gallery in which all the walls and probably the floors too are glass, or a TGV station with a roof like the skeleton of a whale, or a conference centre wrapped in pink corrugated plastic, betraying France's childlike enthusiasm for novelty. To manage the process of building all these political landmarks, Mitterrand's Socialist Party established a special consultancy that allowed it to harvest millions of francs from construction companies eager to secure contracts from Socialist local authorities, money that it then used, illegally, to finance its election campaigns.

Attali was part of Mitterrand's personal entourage for almost twenty years and watched from close quarters as the President poured $2,500 million into eight prestige projects calculated to change the face of Paris, nominally in celebration of the bicentenary of the French Revolution, actually from a mix of political calculation and vanity. And, on top of all that, Mitterrand wanted to live for ever.

Just like Napoleon III, and Napoleon I and Louis XIV before him, Mitterrand was bent on turning Paris into the undisputed capital of Europe, and he needed to create the institutions to match his ambitions. The Louvre was determined to eclipse the British Museum as the most visited museum in the world, just as Charles de Gaulle airport was challenging London and Frankfurt in an attempt to become Europe's busiest air transport hub. In the days before the rise of al-Qaeda, the Institut du Monde Arabe, Jean Nouvel's blade-like structure with a glorious view of Notre Dame, was intended to make Paris the Muslim world's window into Europe, and Europe's into Islam, whilst the Science Centre at La Villette was a vast high-tech complex that tried to redefine the nature of the contemporary museum.

When Mitterrand finally moved into the Elysée Palace in 1981, Attali had the office next door to the President and, so he claimed, the use of a desk that had once belonged to Napoleon. His brother Bernard was appointed to run Air France at the same time, confirming the sense of belonging to the charmed circle around this self-styled socialist with the demeanour of a prince. Jacques Attali was the gate-keeper for Mitterrand, learning at close quarters from his imperial style.

Mitterrand set the tone for his presidency by commissioning Philippe Starck to design the furniture for his private office. The desk was based on the President's initials, its tubular steel legs taking the form of a winged M. It looked fashionable enough to mask the underlying vanity of the gesture. In those days, Starck was a bright young iconoclast, so the desk could be presented as an act of state patronage aimed at showing official France's commitment to the brightest new talents. But it was also a move that seemed to suggest that the President was too grand to work at anybody else's desk, and thus had to have one designed specifically for his own use. The desk, stripped of the traditional signs of status and ostentatious wealth, looked modern. But it was at the same time still an unmistakable signal of Mitterrand's taste for power, which from the point of view of a French autocrat trying to make his mark made it the perfect combination.

Attali contributed a few ideas of his own to Mitterrand's building plans. He claims to have had the idea for a new national library to be packed with high-tech equipment rather than books, a notion that eventually became the four glass towers of the François Mitterrand Library at Tolbiac.

Attali would have loved to have gone through the ritual of a full-scale architectural competition, to find a design for a suitably magnificent home for his empire. He would no doubt have learned from the fiasco of the Opera House at La Bastille, where Mitterrand's judges picked a design they confidently assumed to be by the well-regarded

American architect Richard Meier only to discover, when they opened the envelopes to identify the anonymous drawings they had chosen, that it was the work of the previously unknown Uruguayan Carlos Ott. His design, built on the most sacred site of revolutionary history in France, was not only an inelegant overdevelopment, but failed on a technical level. The computerized hydraulic stage-shifting machinery didn't work as advertised, and the structure suffered for years from falling cladding tiles.

Undoubtedly Attali was involved in Mitterrand's personal intervention in re-shaping the plans for the Louvre and the Musée d'Orsay, where several million francs had been wasted on abortive design work when, on a whim, the President handed over the architecture of the museum spaces to Gae Aulenti. She obliged by creating an interior within the old railway terminus that felt like a tomb. Attali would have seen at first hand the negotiations with the British publisher Robert Maxwell, revealed soon after as a fraudster on an epic scale, over his investment in the pointless gesture of the Grande Arche at La Défense, in the hope of who knows what quid pro quo from the French State.

But the exercise of power, even for the President of France, is still a matter of checks and balances. Mitterrand could persuade the rest of the G7 governments to put up the money needed to set up the European Bank for Reconstruction and Development, even though it was essentially conceived of as a means to extend the French sphere of influence over Eastern Europe. He could even get his bespectacled protégé the job of President of the EBRD. The price, however, was that its headquarters would not be in Paris, but in London, a city that wasn't yet ready for the monumental aspirations of the French political class.

The job of setting up the EBRD gave Attali the chance to pursue his ambitions, if not yet on a scale that matched those of his patron. For Attali, this was not going to be just any bank; it was deliberately designed to be a political centre of power, and hence a personal stepping stone. Its constitution bound the bank to deal only with countries committed to democratic government – a definition that has become increasingly flexible over the years. Ostensibly the intention was to bring the rigour and the freedom of the market to societies emerging from decades of life under a planned economy. Given France's own predilection for dirigiste central planning, and the recent nationalization of large sections of its industries, Mitterrand's inner circle was an unlikely source of expert advice on the subject of privatization.

The headquarters building was originally intended to have been at the heart of a network of branch offices – embassies would have been a better word for what Attali had in mind – spreading across Central Europe to Central Asia in order, as the EBRD puts it, to fill the vacuum left by the collapse of the Soviet Union. But the British Treasury, which was reluctantly footing the bill for the offices at the personal insistence of Mrs Thatcher, who had agreed to the project against her better judgement, wouldn't allow him the option of a new building, or let him get away with the idea of the vice-regal outposts. For once Attali had to accept defeat. By way of a compromise, he briefly explored the idea of taking over an existing building in London with sufficient grandeur to make it a suitable home for what he called 'a central tool in shaping a new political and economic world order'. The classical splendour of Somerset House on the Thames might do perhaps, or a couple of the choicer Baroque wings of Greenwich Palace.

The fact that Mrs Thatcher's civil servants refused to come up with anything he considered suitable provoked a prolonged sulk from Attali, one that was to resurface later when he left London.

He did, however, end up signing the lease for a building in the Broadgate development on the edge of the City of London's financial district. It was a speculatively built office block known as Number One Exchange Place, designed by SOM in a curious neo-Chicago style, a throwback to the early days of skyscrapers, with pinnacles and giant bay windows, and turrets that made it look like a baroque jukebox. It was brand new, ready to move in to, lavishly equipped, and contained some of the most expensive office space in the world. But Attali didn't want an off-the-peg office, no matter how costly. He wanted a building that would be a faithful reflection of the status of the organization that he was trying to establish, and hence of his own importance.

In Attali's mind, generic office buildings clearly equated with blood-less, neutral administrators. How can you persuade the world to take you seriously when you are working from behind a desk in what might as well be the offices of an insurance company? Attali had his court decorators, Jean-Louis Berthet and Yves Pochy, brought in to transform Exchange Place's twelve floors into a stage set for his pet project. That meant going a whole lot further than choosing the colour of the wallpaper for the boardroom.

There were limits on what Berthet and Pochy could do. The land-lords wouldn't let Attali touch the exterior, and the lease specified that whatever he did to the inside would have to be reinstated at the end of the term of the tenancy in 2016. But that didn't stop him from knocking huge holes out of the floors and walls. Attali's first priority was to make the building imposing enough both to impress the bank's own staff and convince its visitors that they were dealing with an authentic seat of power.

Impressive buildings need impressive entrance halls. Attali was convinced that Exchange Place simply couldn't do the job. As far as he was concerned, it wasn't nearly big enough. It could be made to look a bit better by demolishing a couple of the side walls, putting mirrors on the ceiling, tearing out all the travertine and replacing it with snow-white Carrara marble. Better, but still really nothing like enough for Attali's regal pretensions. So he decided to sacrifice the whole of the first floor and make that into a suitably imposing reception area instead, leaving the original entrance underneath as a kind of throat-clearing prelude. Of course if visitors were allowed to use the lifts on the ground floor, they would go shooting past the grand entrance space and miss the effect Attali had planned, so a bank of escalators was installed to bring visitors up once they had got past the 1.5-metre diameter polished steel globe, supposedly a symbol of a world without frontiers. That way, they had no choice but to appreciate the full impact of EBRD's magnificence. To drive home the message that this was no ordinary city office block, a team of Russian artists spent months painting a 200-metre-long mural beside the escalator in the manner of Raphael to celebrate the achievements of European culture.

Given that this is space that costs £52 per square foot, sacrificing most of one floor is certainly a profligate way to spend £500,000 a year. But the conspicuous use of space is a very traditional and highly effective way to delineate status, just like wasting water on golf courses in the desert in Las Vegas. Attali installed his private theatre, a 300-seater set behind the tricksy kind of glass that goes opaque at the touch of switch and complete with a raked floor, that required major structural work to accommodate. It sits next to the bank's own art gallery, where Attali planned to show off the collection that the EBRD started assembling even before it got to see its first customer.

Impressing visitors, which is the primary purpose of a reception area, requires the right mix of deference and sustained anticipation. After all, banks with political aspirations are run by busy people who need to keep their less important visitors waiting a little to make them understand just how privileged they are to be there at all. And for the important visitors, the building needs to be arranged in such a way as to make sure that they can't miss the power and the glory of the organization whose corridors they are being ushered through.

There is a special room just past the reception, in which guests are invited to wait once they have been issued with their visitor badges, with a view across the garden at the foot of the atrium. It means that they themselves aren't left out on show, but they do get to see the scale of the bank while they are waiting. And there are other such spaces scattered throughout the building as holding areas for the more significant directors' offices. A waiting room is a clear signal of the importance of the office that it serves. But for visitors, despite the apparent deference of the manoeuvre, to be shown into one is a signal that they aren't as important as all that. The real elite are met at the front door by the president.

The theatre is not the only ceremonial space injected into the banal structure of Exchange Place. Up on the tenth floor, a large circular hole was cut into the floor slab to allow for the construction of what was officially called the boardroom. It's a double-height space, big enough to take 150 people, with a spectacular view of St Paul's. They sit in a circle, a format that betrays Jacques Attali's vision of this as more of a parliamentary debating chamber than a boardroom in the sense that a commercial organization would understand it.

Why he thought he needed a debating chamber, as well as the theatre downstairs, has never been made clear, but he obviously had a complex series of rituals in mind for the running of the organization, some of which involved addressing an audience in the manner of a schoolmaster from the front, and others in a setting to suggest a gathering of equals sitting in a circle. The specially designed chairs are in white leather and solid sycamore, and Attali commissioned Isidore Gooderis to make a sculpture for the chamber. Using recycled bricks that are set into patinated steel shelves, it is a calculated evocation of the ancient crumbling volumes of an Asian monastery library. But for all the effort that went into the boardroom, the real centre of power is elsewhere in the building.

The president's own office, carefully located on the top floor of course, and positioned immediately next to the press department and his spin doctors, represents the building in microcosm. Office, of course, is not a word that does it justice, The president's office has a casual seating area large enough for eight people to lounge around on sofas, a coffee table stacked with books, a specially made leather and sycamore desk, a separate 12-seat conference room, an assistant's office and a second private office. This opens into a dressing room, a shower room and a private sitting room. It's big enough and expensive enough for Attali to be able to gently patronize visiting heads of state. Imagine the Bulgarian President, say, coming here cap in hand looking for the money to decommission an elderly and incontinent nuclear reactor. Attali, like Fouquet and Wolsey, and every other royal favourite to have faced the wrath of a patron piqued by attempts at grandeur that rivalled their own, certainly must have imagined exactly that.

Berthet and Pochy were house architects to the French Socialist Party, so their work comes wrapped up in a great deal of vacuous political rhetoric about creativity and accessibility. 'As we were planning the building, we had a very strong visual impression in mind, a gigantic tree with a trunk (the eight lifts), branches (the passages) and leaves (the offices).' And of course they make much of their claims about the openness and transparency of the building. 'Only the meeting rooms are equipped with blinds to provide confidentiality,' they claim, somehow managing to ignore all the protective screens around the president's own office.

In the lift lobbies, Berthet had another idea. 'For this new institution, we wanted to express the idea of human creativity, without necessarily using detachable pieces of art. We wanted to work on the marble itself, to demonstrate its transformation from a rough material to smooth, from rough hewn to bush hammered to polished.' All the original travertine was stripped out and Berthet went looking for the whitest, costliest Carrara marble that Tuscany had to offer instead. Finding it was, apparently, not an easy task. The ideal material had, or so say the designers, to be simple and pure. 'We wanted the marble to keep its original aspect, its colours, its mineral oxides, the marks made by wind and rain,' claimed Berthet. 'It had to be cut in several pieces, with lasers, following the structure of each block, then the pieces were fitted together, like a puzzle on the walls of the bank.' The marble ended up costing the bank £800,000, but the polished mirror ceilings make it look as if there is twice as much, presumably as a gesture towards achieving value for money.

Not content with the banks of lifts and the existing staircases, Berthet insisted on installing four more purely decorative sets of stairs, throwing away yet more very costly square feet of office space. All of them use different materials and configurations, for the benefit of those who want to save a couple of minutes walking from the third to the fifth floor, or from the fourth to the seventh, without using the lifts or the escape stairs. One is a solid sycamore spiral. Another is cone-shaped and made from wood and glass. A third is in poured concrete with timber inlay treads.

Then there is the bank's art programme. Along with the faux Raphael in the entrance, there is cartoon Vermeer in the lift lobby, and two sculptures that are supposedly tributes to Leonardo – a winged horse – and Copernicus – a mobile demonstrating the movement of the solar system. To reinforce the sense of a Europe-wide perspective, the meeting rooms are all named after a range of major rivers, from the Danube to the Volga. Even the carpets, crockery, glassware and rugs, and the secretaries' desks have been specially designed and made for the bank.

This is a building that was self-consciously designed to shape the destinies of an entire continent. The question Attali never answered was: did the continent really want itself to be shaped by this particular organization, and if it did, why did it need to be in the lavishly brash style of a Riviera night club?

Perhaps it is not entirely surprising to find that Berthet and Pochy numbered Saddam Hussein amongst their previous clients. Just before the Iraqi dictator attacked Iran in 1984, he presided over the opening of Baghdad's new Saddam Hussein International Airport. Scott Brownrigg and Turner, the architects who built it, were British, and it bears, on the outside at least, an uncanny resemblance to Heathrow's Terminal Four, which they also designed. But the interior is all Berthet and Pochy. The baggage halls were graced by renderings of the gates of Babylon and the spiral ziggurat of Samarra in metal relief 15 feet high. The departure hall has its supposedly Islamic vaults picked out in thousands of twinkling spotlamps, while Hussein's personal terminal, positioned outside the main building for instant access to the runways, has marble floors and mirrored ceilings just like the EBRD.

In London, for all Berthet's rhetoric about openness and democracy, the building is a precise representation of an entirely predictable hierarchy. The staff are in open-plan offices on the lower floors. The directors, who are herded together on floors ten and eleven, get to decorate their 1,000-square-feet private offices as they please, and have the use of the private dining rooms, with their starched linen tablecloths and haute cuisine, something of a contrast to the café for the other ranks on the reception floor.

In all, fitting out the Bank cost £60 million, more than enough in fact to build a completely new office. But Attali wasn't there to enjoy it for long. A sceptical British press, led by the *Financial Times*, started looking beyond the propaganda coming out of the bank about its heart-warming altruism and discovered that, in its first two years, the EBRD had budgeted to spend £1 million on hiring private jets to shuttle Attali back and forth from London to his apartment in Paris. 'I am sorry, but I can't do without them,' said an unrepentant Attali when confronted with the figure. It was personal vanity of course, an assertion of status by a man determined to build an institution that didn't exist, one that Attali wanted to bring into being through sheer will-power.

Attali's project crumbled when his critics began to focus on the absurdity of the gap between the imperial trappings of his court and the poverty of Eastern Europe that he was supposedly attempting to help – and the even more absurd mismatch between the £116 million in loans that Attali had authorized in the first two years of the bank's existence and the £208 million he had spent in the same period on staff, furniture and on rebuilding its premises. He was prized, slowly and painfully, out of office, kicking and screaming at the philistine Anglo-Saxons, a process eased by a £160,000 pay-off.

Without the protection of his patron, François Mitterrand, Attali has had a difficult time of things since leaving the bank. First he was accused of forty-three individual counts of plagiarism in his book *Verbatim*, a record of life with Mitterrand. Then, when France's special investigating magistrates began exploring the seamier aspects of Mitterrand's relationships with unsavoury arms dealers, Attali came under suspicion for the unauthorized use of public funds. He was accused of acting as the conduit for illegal kickbacks to the president involving a French middleman selling Soviet weapons to Angola, charges that were later dropped. The scandal was followed by the affair of the *Economics of the Apocalypse*, a report supposedly produced under the auspices of the United Nations that grossly over-stated the case in an account of plutonium smuggling from the former Soviet Union and which was disowned by the UN Secretary-General, Bhutros Bhutros Ghali. Attali was last heard of trying to conduct the Grenoble Philharmonic Orchestra, to the disgust of its musicians, who threatened to strike in protest at his musical incompetence.

The bank survived Attali, but only just. There have been three presidents since his time, and by 2003 the bank was negotiating with its landlords to leave the building to find somewhere smaller. It chose to stay when it became clear just how much it would have to spend to restore Exchange Place to its original condition.

In the French context, Attali had done nothing less than what was expected of him. He had learnt the lessons of Mitterrand, who had in turn learnt them from Louis XIV and Versailles.

Neither Rockefeller nor Attali achieved their ostensible objectives. Albany will never be a Brasilia, never mind a credible metropolis. And the EBRD will never live up to the ambition of Attali's headquarters. The feeble quality of the architectural response to their ambitions is far less interesting and less telling than the state of mind that drove both of them to such extreme lengths. For them, as for so many other individuals with the chance to do as they did, building – for all their claims to the contrary – was the end not the means.

9

Ego Unchained

Before Gianni Agnelli, Fiat's supremely elegant and charismatic patriarch, was finally interred in the family vault, his body lay in state at the heart of the company's empire in Turin. Thousands of car workers and their families, as well as politicians, bankers and industrialists, filed past the coffin to pay their last respects as if he were a medieval king. This was not in some marble-lined chantry chapel, or in the classical palazzo that you might have expected for the uncrowned prince of Italy. Just a few weeks before his death, Agnelli had presided over the unveiling of his parting gift to his country, a gallery designed by Renzo Piano to house his personal collection of Western culture's greatest hits, a selection of trophy pieces chosen from the last thousand years, acquired during the course of his life and now presented to the nation as a keepsake. Piano's gallery took the form of a steel and aluminium pod, perched as tentatively as a helicopter on the rooftop racetrack of the Lingotto, the cathedral of car factories built by Agnelli's grandfather and converted after production stopped in the 1980s into a glistening post-industrial honey trap of galleries and concert halls. It was never officially described as a mausoleum, but it was here, to the Pinacoteca del Lingotto, that Agnelli's body was brought before burial.

Agnelli's wish was a poignant reminder of the ancient use of architecture as a means of defying mortality, of shaping memory and as a reflection of the psychopathology of power. The apparently fundamental human impulse to leave behind some kind of mark after death, and the unbreakable connection between architecture and the exercise of power, were briefly obscured by the sunnier preoccupations of the 1960s. Architecture for a time was supposedly liberated from the weight of tradition and custom. In the hands of Piano and others like him, it began to be regarded as a means of looking for alternatives to the conventional ways of doing things.

Monumentalism, seen as an excuse for architects to indulge in futile attempts at large-scale sculpture, had got a bad name. Piano's generation tried to reinvent architecture by embracing the everyday world, rather than pandering only to affluent patrons of the kind typified by Gianni Agnelli. Architecture began to be treated as if it were a matter of problem-solving, rather than representation. Piano was as interested in technological solutions as in playing with shapes. As he saw it, architecture should have a light touch; it could be temporary and provisional rather than burdened with the illusory search for permanence. He believed that architecture could serve the poor and the disadvantaged rather than the State or the rich or the Church.

But for all Piano's fascination with the technological possibilities for social change offered by the modern world, for all his enthusiasm for the participatory politics of the 1960s and the 1970s, it is the traditional definition of architecture that has marked his career as precisely as it did that of Alberti or Palladio. Delicately wrought steel, and apparently gravity-defying glass, can carry the same messages as heavy marble or bronze, and serve to define the institutions that society regards as the most important, or the most significant, equally well. Piano's own work in the end has been shaped not by the activists from the inner cities, or by science, but by his relationship with bankers and insurance tycoons. He has built their monuments, galleries and memorials, and he has had to answer to them for it. It's a relationship that he has handled with consummate skill. From Eli Broad to the publishers of the *New York Times* and the followers of the recently canonized Padre Pio, they have made the pilgrimage to one or other of his studios. Perhaps to Paris, where much of the design work is done now, or to the 'research base' that he maintains under UNESCO auspices on a wild cliff overlooking the coastline north of Genoa, where chauffeurs drop their passengers off at the shoreline, leaving them to ascend the rocky slope on a makeshift glass cable car that arrives at the architect's retreat, with its imperial views over the sea. One grilled-fish lunch here, served by Piano's crisply uniformed housekeeper, and they know they have chosen an architect to live up to their aspirations. Even Irvine Sellars, the fashion retailer turned property developer who dressed swinging London in the 1960s in unfeasibly wide trousers, succumbed to Piano's charm and commissioned him to design Europe's tallest building, an office tower above London Bridge station.

Renzo Piano was involved with Agnelli for a quarter of a century. At the beginning there was no clue that the nature of their relationship would shift so much that it would eventually come to include the design of what amounted to a tomb. Agnelli's first commission for Piano and his long-term collaborator, the brilliantly gifted engineer Peter Rice, could not have been more different. They were asked to design a car for Fiat. Agnelli wanted an open-ended speculative exploration of new production and assembly methods rather than a styling exercise. Between that commission and the gallery-cum-mausoleum came the long-drawn-out transformation of the Lingotto itself, once it had outlived its usefulness as a car factory. For Turin, where Fiat was the biggest employer, the old car factory had represented the largest intrusion on the city's landscape since the cathedral was built. It was an enormously important project, both in practical terms and as a symbolic reminder of Fiat's sense of obligation to the city. And it is a two-way transaction. Because Fiat is so closely identified with Turin, its own prestige is diminished if the city is seen to be in trouble and its fabric allowed to atrophy.

Piano is not interested in creating an architectural signature, and that is perhaps what made his work appeal to Agnelli, a man who was interested in being known for acquiring the best rather than the obvious. To ask Piano to design a building for you is to do so in the knowledge that it will not necessarily look like anything that he has ever done before. For some patrons, less sure of their own taste, this would be a handicap. For Agnelli, it was clearly anything but.

It's not hard to see that Piano's genuine fascination with elegant mechanisms and high-performance materials represents a passion that would have aroused a sympathetic response in a tycoon who was equally passionate about speed in the form of fast boats and even faster cars. But however they look and whatever they are made of, as it has turned out, Piano has all along been designing buildings that are in fact responding to the most traditional of all architectural impulses. They speak of power, continuity and memory.

In what must be one of the most unlikely pieces of self-promotion for an architectural practice in the history of public relations, Anthony Browne has posted a dozen images of Hamilton Palace on his website showing the project under construction. He calls it the largest country house built in England since the time of Blenheim but suggests that 'unfortunately it may never be completed. The client, an international financier, was convicted of manslaughter and is serving a ten-year prison sentence.'

Mohammed Raja, a prosperous, slightly sinister businessman with a reputation as a slum landlord, opened the door of his comfortable suburban house on the southern fringes of London one hot July day in 1999 to what looked like a couple of gardeners, dressed in boiler suits and with floppy-brimmed hats that partly hid their faces. His two grandchildren, Rizwan and Waheed, were upstairs when he went to the door. They heard raised voices and shouting, then the sound of a shotgun blast hitting the ceiling. The boys ran downstairs to find their grandfather holding his chest, a spreading patch of wet blood on his shirt. He had been stabbed in the chest five times, but the shot fired at him had missed. Rizwan and Waheed could see two men in the porch; one had a sawn-off shotgun over his knee. Rizwan saw him break it in an attempt to reload.

Rizwan shouted to his brother to call the police. As he did so he could see the gunman in the hallway take aim. He heard his grandfather crying out in pain. He saw that his grandfather had a knife in his hand. The man in the hat and boiler suit pulled the trigger and shot Raja in the face at point-blank range. Both attackers then walked back to the road and escaped in a white Transit van that was later found nearby, burnt out and abandoned.

Three years later Robert Knapp and David Croke stood trial at the Old Bailey for Raja's murder. The jury was told that neighbours had seen two men acting suspiciously on the day and had noticed a white van with the words 'Thunderbirds Two' inscribed on a spoiler above the cab. According to the police, it had been sold three weeks earlier to a man who had given a false address.

The case was relatively straightforward. Blood found on Raja's front door was matched to a sample of saliva taken from Croke after he was arrested. According to the prosecution, DNA testing proved that the chances of its not being Croke's blood were 'one in a billion'. They were found guilty. The trial of the third man in the dock, Nicholas van Hoogstraten, a millionaire property developer, was more problematic. At the time of the murder, van Hoogstraten was driving to Gatwick airport to catch a flight to Nice. The prosecution's case was that Croke and Knapp had carried out the killing on his behalf.

'Although not present, van Hoogstraten was a party to the murder, as it was carried out by the two men at his instigation, for his purposes, and because of the problems and difficulties which had originated between him and Mr Raja,' David Waters, the prosecuting counsel told the jury. Van Hoogstraten was eventually convicted of manslaughter and sentenced to ten years in prison. He was released after just one year when the Appeal Court declared the conviction unsafe. The interests of justice would best be served by a retrial, the three judges decided, but that was not possible as the law stood, so he went free.

With his leather greatcoats and his bouffant hair, van Hoogstraten has the look of a minor rock star from the 1960s. He has a taste for sharp black suits, worn with black tie and black shirt, occasionally set off with an ankle-length white mink coat. Van Hoogstraten is not a man to cross, vengeful in pursuit of debts, delighting in a crudely vulgarized Nietzschean contempt for the polite conventions of bourgeois life. He built a property empire based on buying a chain of cheap flats and houses across the south-east of England, and made a fortune in the process. He is not, by all accounts, a solicitous landlord. Tenants who do not pay their rent are not treated gently, and those that do can still have trouble. A fire in one of his properties killed five tenants.

Van Hoogstraten is clearly aware of the figure that he cuts, revelling in the sense of dark menace that surrounds him. The judge at his arson trial described him as 'a sort of self-imagined devil, who thinks he is an emissary of Beelzebub'. He abuses members of the public who attempt to exercise their right to access the footpaths that cross his land near Uckfield in Sussex in the crudest terms. He calls them scum, defying those who have attempted to enforce the law.

What really makes van Hoogstraten stand out from the run-of-the-mill criminal with a taste for inflicting measured doses of sharp pain on his enemies is his taste for building. No two men could be more different than Agnelli and van Hoogstraten: one is a criminal who has spent years in jail, the other was regarded as a kind of national hero in Italy. But they have this one thing in common. It is as much part of van Hoogstraten's self-dramatization as his wardrobe and his permanent air of barely concealed aggression, which extends as far as making on-air observations to those responsible for jailing him during the interview he gave the BBC on his release from prison. Van Hoogstraten, who seems to have spent at least as much time as Agnelli thinking about death, has gone so far as to commission an actual tomb for himself. He has been building it for almost twenty years, interrupted by his two jail terms – the first for an arson attack on a rabbi in the English seaside town of Brighton who, van Hoogstraten claimed, owed him money – and then by the freezing of his assets by the British courts.

Three generations of wealth made Agnelli look and sound like a patrician, one who at the end of his life was regarded as a statesman by his country, despite the dissipated post-war years that he had spent fuelled by drugs and alcohol in the pursuit of pleasure, mostly in the form of women and fast cars. Van Hoogstraten left school at 16, made his fortune by the time he was 25, albeit not on the scale of an Agnelli, and has been building Hamilton Palace, the house that he says will be his tomb, since 1980. It is a project that is poised uncomfortably on that strange dividing line between the kind of self-belief that can be impressive, despite its transparent vanity, and the semi-comic vulgarity of a criminal with artistic pretensions.

Hamilton Palace, named after the capital of Bermuda, where the young van Hoogstraten took the first steps to making his fortune, is a sprawling neo-classical house tinged with a postmodernism that reveals the era in which it was conceived with pitiless precision. It sits, 600 feet long, incomplete and partly roofless, in a glorious stretch of the Sussex countryside. Van Hoogstraten claims its walls have been designed to last as long as the pyramids of the pharaohs, which seems unlikely given that he also says they are only 3 feet thick. The gallery that forms the most substantial part of the house is intended as a permanent home for what van Hoogstraten claims, but does not substantiate, is a major collection of classical European art. The house is like a merciless parody of the aspirations of the period in which it was conceived. It is an exaggeration of the tastes and fantasies of the generation of supposedly respectable self-made men of the Thatcher and Reagan years which ought to make all of them feel uncomfortable. Van Hoogstraten's house could almost have been conceived as a subversive act of satire, embodying the collision of two worlds: the respectable and the criminal. Neither side comes out of it well. The wonder is that van Hoogstraten didn't take the whole project to its logical conclusion and commission his architect to build a pyramid for him. But in his idea of making the house into his mausoleum, van Hoogstraten has touched on something disturbingly visceral and compelling about the nature of an architectural monument.

Anthony Browne was still an architecture student at Brighton Polytechnic when he first met van Hoogstraten. Browne, who is no Renzo Piano, says that he also had the murdered Raja for a client. He works as a kind of glorified set builder for those who hire him, creating evocations of the worlds that they ask for, rather than offering his own architectural narratives. But his design for Hamilton Palace is far from unsophisticated. It is effectively sited, with a picturesque but dignified silhouette. By the standards of the run-of-the-mill rows of rich men's houses that line the streets of every affluent suburb from Moscow to Bridgehampton, with their fibreglass pediments and porticoes, their carriage drives and their endlessly bifurcating grand staircases and chandeliers, their vast garages and their relentless quest for size, it is positively chaste.

The house is certainly big; Browne claims it sprawls over a scarcely credible 70,000 square feet and had a £35 million budget. It is really just one endless façade, with a central dome and twin wings terminating in pavilions at each end. Browne claims the inspiration is Blenheim, 'and it's not a lot smaller'. Actually, unlike Blenheim, it is more neo-classical than Baroque in style, with paired columns and broken pediments.

Browne's portfolio includes a commission from the late Marquis of Bristol, disgraced heir to a vast and authentic Palladian house, though its hard to understand how an English copy of an Italian original designed two centuries earlier can be considered authentic.

The Marquis, who squandered his fortune on cocaine, asked Browne to design two bathrooms for him: one in baroque style, the other in the Egyptian manner. By these standards, Browne's work for van Hoogstraten is a surprisingly accomplished design. Set off by a boathouse built on the edge of the lake at the centre of the site, it shows his command of an impressive range of effect from the grand manner to a more light-hearted capriccio. But it was Agnelli who felt secure enough to commission Piano to produce a conspicuously contemporary design, while, for all his bravado and aggression, van Hoogstraten has hijacked the most saccharine sweet image of the traditional English country house that he could find to serve as the model for his lair.

Why does Browne think that van Hoogstraten asked him to build Hamilton Palace? 'It's just showing off really, isn't it?' says Browne. 'These sorts of houses make a statement. It's the desire to create a monument, one of those primary artistic urges. Quite often in people's minds, creating something amazing is confused with creating something big, and big means expensive.'

After an endlessly protracted construction process Hamilton Palace is still not finished. Even before van Hoogstraten went to jail, the palace was suffering from the problems that often accompany the building of a house for a – to put it mildly – strong-willed client. The general contractor had walked off the site over a dispute about an unpaid invoice for £407,000. And the architect claims that he had also resigned. 'These projects start off being tremendous fun,' Browne says. 'But then you get on site and have to deal with the builders. Then the client changes his mind. It's somebody else's dream, but it becomes the architect's nightmare.'

During the course of the trial another side of the story emerged. Mark Hylton, described in court as van Hoogstraten's current architect, was asked to recall what had happened when his client discovered that there were major structural problems with the pillars and the floors in the boathouse. 'His response was quite unforgettable really. He went ballistic, very angry, and with very good reason. He said, "Whose fault is this, why has this happened?"' If Browne were to return to Uckfield, it's a fair guess that he would be treated with even less sympathy than the aged Vanbrugh, who was turned away when he appeared at the gates of Blenheim hoping for another glimpse of the masterpiece from which he had been excluded after falling out with his client.

Van Hoogstraten was finally forced to stop work on the house when his funds were frozen by a lawsuit brought by Raja's family, claiming control of assets worth £5 million. At the time, van Hoogstraten was facing fines of £50,000 a week for contempt of court, and yet another action against him for unpaid fees from his former legal advisers.

It's hard to understand what van Hoogstraten imagines that he will be doing in his palace, if he ever gets it finished, in the interlude before it becomes his tomb. His children, born to an assortment of mothers in various countries, are scattered across the world. His friend Robert Mugabe – whose army drove thousands of squatters off van Hoogstraten's estate in Zimbabwe when they slaughtered a herd of his cattle – would be unlikely to be allowed into Britain, so there is not much chance of him entertaining a head of state here.

To use the traditional form of the country house is to suggest that you are the natural successor to the system that it represented, and that you are trying to cloak yourself in its easy confidence to project a sense of how you would wish to be seen. Living up to that way of life is a harder trick to perfect than it might appear. For all van Hoogstraten's studied contempt for the social norms, it demands at least the tacit acknowledgement of a wider community, if for no other reason than to provide an audience to fill up all those grand rooms.

And for van Hoogstraten, the purpose of the palace was exactly the opposite. It offered him the chance to differentiate himself from the rest of the world; to demonstrate that while most of humanity amounts to nothing more than a faceless ant heap, he, Nicholas van Hoogstraten, through the sheer force of his will, has made himself visible on the historic scale of events. He and he alone will be remembered and, as a result, his existence will be given some sort of meaning. From van Hoogstraten's point of view, the project has signally failed in its objective. What he needed was a Renzo Piano to work for him, or a Thierry Despont, the architect turned decorator whom Bill Gates hired to work on the interiors of his gigantic house outside Seattle, and ended up relying on to teach him how to spend his money, how to buy wine, and how to look at pictures.

*

This is a universe in which, however reluctantly, all of us, even the most powerful, must continue to face the unremitting possibility that at any moment we might cease to exist. Not because of the wrath of an angry God, which would at least suggest, flatteringly, that humanity was worthy of His attention, if only briefly. Even a deliberate suicidal act of nuclear self-destruction would imply the possibility of shaping our own destiny. But oblivion could be the product of something as meaningless as the random, arbitrary, emotionless intervention of a wandering asteroid, or a volcanic eruption, or even the emergence of a previously unknown bacillus or species-jumping virus. Against this dismaying background, architecture offers the possibility of a brief interlude of lucidity. Through it, the logical, the ordered and the meaningful is acknowledged as an option, even as the future of world itself is in the hands of the random, the arbitrary and the meaningless, which could wipe out even the cockroaches.

Architecture is a device that allows us the chance to forget the precariousness of our position for a moment, to create at least the illusion of meaning when we measure it against its own internal logic and find some sense of correspondence and predictability. It cannot, of course, impose order on an orderless universe, but within its own terms architecture does offer the possibility of a fleeting respite from the random. Architecture can provide a reference point, against which we can measure our place in the world. Most of the very earliest efforts of humans to make a lasting mark on their surroundings were essentially architectural, and they clearly show traces of the impulse to find a way to connect the transience of flesh and blood with the apparent eternity of the stars. They involved creating platforms of flat earth imposed on the undulating landscape and aligned with the heavens, as if demonstrating the connections between human intelligence and the world beyond its understanding. There could be no clearer sign of a human presence, and the exercise of its intellect, than to show the contrast between order and disorder.

To draw a straight line on the landscape and make it into a permanent form, a human society needs to have developed skills of measurement and observation. And placing that straight line in a natural landscape immediately suggests the presence of intelligent life. But can we really be sure that it is the straight line and the flat plane that represent order and logic, and not the possibly more complex order of the natural world?

Making a mark is an impulse that can take on the aspect of a religious experience. Those early platforms were the starting points for the creation – or, depending on your degree of engagement, the celebration – of sacred sites connected with the supernatural. They produced an architectural language that provided the basis for the monuments of so many different cultures, from the Egyptian pyramids to the Meso-American cities and the classical Greek sites. Architectural intervention in these cases is an attempt to engage and interact with natural phenomena, with the landscape, and with what man can observe of the behaviour of the stars and the seasons. It's like buttonholing God in the street and demanding his attention, as if to make our insignificant activities worthy of notice, or part of some purpose more elevated than the fitful cycles of our own existence.

Attempting to root architecture in this way can be a reflection of a search for spiritual meaning or of scientific research. But equally it can be used as a political tool, in the attempts of one group to control another. Stonehenge makes the sun and the moon appear as if they are aligned in certain ways, on particular days of the year. If there were no monument, and no architecture, then there would be no phenomenon to observe. But when the priesthood is able accurately to predict such phenomena, it can use its knowledge to demonstrate its power to the uninitiated. Even more impressive a demonstration of the priesthood's power is its ability to persuade the uninitiated to build the object that will enforce their subjugation.

To place man-made architectural objects in a relationship with the landscape is one way to try to give them meaning; it is suggesting that they belong to a system. The landscape lasts far longer than mankind. Trying to make our objects part of that timescale offers the consolation of a sense of connectedness with a version of eternity. Architecture searches for meaning at a wide range of scales. Some architects look to the landscape and to the stars as their reference point. Others try to find solace in the idea that naturally occurring forms, such as crystal structures, or skeletal forms or molecular plant cells, can be used as the starting point for architectural form, to allow it to reflect some kind of inner harmony, by achieving maximum strength for the most minimal use of resources for example. In mimicking such forms in their own structures, they evidently believe that their designs will achieve the same sense of balance and order as the naturally occurring world with its patterns and harmonic structure.

Beyond these clues in the natural landscape and the characteristics of organic matter, architects have looked to find ways of creating their own definitions of intellectual meaning that refer to architecture itself, rather than to naturally observable phenomena. They are based on the construction of a set of definitions that provide the clues and signals that determine all of the choices that an architect makes about designing a building. The classical orders of architecture find that determination in a precise set of rules that define the composition of each column, from the nature of the decorative detail around its capital to the proportion of its height to its width. The rules serve also to define the ways in which those columns are grouped, and what happens at each corner of a building, how the building touches the ground, how it meets the sky, and how those columns and their proportions relate to their place in an overall composition. Symmetry is part of the conceptual kit of parts, so is the idea of a sense of harmony and rhythm, which seems to be a metaphor for finding a place in the world.

Other architectural approaches are less explicitly codified than classicism, because they are much more recent and less universally understood. Often they depend on analogy, or the creation of a set of rules that can acquire the sense of a moral force. Such rules, which are perhaps the definition of architecture itself, are the route into a world with a sense of purpose. Perhaps the secret is to use as few materials as possible, which implies a whole set of decisions that will determine what happens when one of these materials meets another. Celebrating the joint by embellishing it allows for less exacting standards of craftsmanship; doing so by leaving it exposed is much more demanding of technical skill. There are those who make their architecture out of the supposed honesty that comes from making each of these positions manifest. Some of these approaches are transparently nothing more than arbitrary and self-imposed. They become the means of defining the angle that a handrail should make with the banisters on a staircase, or how a window is placed in a wall, to demonstrate that each element is part of a larger architectural whole. What the system is matters much less than the fact of its existence.

Objectively, there is no right answer to the question of where to put a window. Or rather there are a lot of right answers depending on the internal logic that the architect has constructed for an architectural system – or even lack of logic or narrative, which is perhaps a more accurate way of putting it. Contemporary architectural narratives begin as personal fantasies, and then through constant repetition become more plausible with the passing of time. As they become more widely accepted, they are taken up by larger and larger groups of designers, before eventually being replaced with another narrative. The idea that architects should design buildings to look as if they were made by machines, rather than the laborious and often messy process of handcraft that is actually involved, was a narrative current for many years and produced something called functionalism.

When Richard Rogers and Renzo Piano designed the Pompidou Centre in such a way that the ducts and pipes servicing the building, as well as the structure holding it up, were made visible – legible, as Rogers put it – they devised a system for design. The system is based on frankness, showing the constituent parts, and again it has an apparent logic, serving to create a fragment of existence in which if you suspend disbelief, and don't ask too many questions, you find yourself in a world in which reason and logic appear to exist. They even came up with a logic for its colour-coded exterior, adopting the standard colours used on engineers' drawings to show electrical circuits. But it is not based on functional necessity. It is actually an aesthetic system, just as the Doric order is. The architect has invented a set of rules that if followed carefully enough produce a coherent building, provided that you accept the fundamental premises of the system.

These systems can appear to be material, or ethereal and spiritual. Architecture spans both these poles in a way that few other disciplines can. Such systems can take many forms, including the belief in the power of numbers, an occult preoccupation that has consumed architects from every period, from the classical to Le Corbusier with his Modulor and his vain pursuit of logic, order and harmony through the hardly comprehensible proportional rules that he devised. And then there is the mysticism of a Christopher Alexander, or the pursuit of an architecture based on ecological imperatives.

Architecture has the ability to modify weather and light. In that, it has power that for once is measurable. Stone and steel last longer than flesh and blood. Over time, architecture takes on the patina and the resonance of the events that have taken place inside it, and of the people who have occupied it. Buildings are historical markers that show the passing of time, and the changes of regimes; no wonder that the totalitarians were so keen to erase those that made them feel uncomfortable or threatened. No wonder that it is architectural imagery that underpins the otherwise banal cult of Freemasonry, with its Great Architect.

No wonder that there has been so much conflict between the architect and the artist over their relative place in the pecking order that serves to define the cultural hierarchy. What an architect can offer an Agnelli, or a van Hoogstraten for that matter, is the sense that they are making a place in which there is some sense of meaning and purpose; a sense of belonging to a wider world, but at the same time celebrating the individual and their place in that world.

The nature of the relationship between the architect and the patron is complex and critical. It has been an act of faith among a certain strand of architects to maintain that great architecture depends on a great client, the strong individual. This is, of course, a somewhat self-serving concept, calculated to flatter the patron, and is fundamentally just as unsatisfactory as the idea that great architecture depends on a single architectural genius.

The counterpoint to the idea of the lost golden age of architectural patronage is the suggestion that the contemporary world forces us to live in a society which is too timid, and too anaemic, to countenance the expression of the individual will, and that the patron has been supplanted by the group, or the committee. The case of Nicholas van Hoogstraten serves to demonstrate how unappetizing that particular version of the concept of the individual will can be. And it is worth exploring for a moment the degree to which the patron is really involved beyond selecting the architect, paying the bills and fending off suggestions from builders that what is proposed is impractical.

There certainly is a kind of individual who commissions an architect and, from vanity or the controlling instinct, sees every decision as being essentially theirs. But it is not the only model for the relationship.

The appeal of construction lies in the special kind of pleasure that is to be had in the process of building, and in the transformation of an idea into a physical reality, sometimes slow and steady, sometimes in large steps. That pleasure is hard to replicate in the daily experience of a completed building. And it may explain why so many individuals, having built once, try to repeat the experience again and again.

But there is more to it than the process of watching a wall rise, or a space take shape. The appeal of architecture to those who aspire to political power lies in the way that it is an expression of will. To design a building, or to have a building designed, is to suggest that this is the world as I want it. This is the perfect room from which to run a state, a business empire, a city, a family. It is the way to create a physical version of an idea, or an emotion. It is the way to construct reality as we wish it to be, rather than it is.

In its scale and its complications, architecture is by far the biggest and most overwhelming of all cultural forms. It literally determines the way that we see the world, and how we interact with each other. For the patron, it is a chance to exert a sense of control over events. And for a certain kind of architect it offers the possibility of control over people. It allows the architect to indulge in the *Gesamtkunstwerk*, the total work of art, so mocked by Adolf Loos in his parable of the poor rich man in which the client has become just another part of an aesthetic composition:

Once it happened that he was celebrating his birthday. His wife and children had given him many presents. He liked their choice immensely and enjoyed it all thoroughly. But soon the architect arrived to set things right, and to take all the decisions in difficult questions. He entered the room. The master greeted him with pleasure, for he had much on his mind. But the architect did not see the man's joy. He had discovered something quite different and grew pale.

'What kind of slippers are these you have got on?' he asked painfully.

The master of the house looked at his embroidered slippers. Then he breathed a sigh of relief. This time he felt quite guiltless. The slippers had been made to the architect's original designs. So he answered in a superior way.

'But Mr Architect, have you already forgotten? You yourself designed them!'

'Of course,' thundered the architect, 'but for the bedroom! They completely disrupt the mood here with these two impossible spots of colour. Can't you see that?'

Some rather similar questions were explored more sympathetically by Ernesto Rogers, the Milanese architect and the cousin of Richard Rogers, in his belief that the values and the aspirations of a culture, when expressed by architecture, could be distilled in such an intense way that it is possible to deduce from the simplest of objects produced by a society, even a spoon, the nature of its largest artefact, the city.

Architecture is intimately concerned with the instinct to control. To order, to categorize, to shape life as it will be lived in a space, to choreograph every activity within every space, demands a certain view of the world, one in which humility is unlikely to figure very large. There is a deep-rooted belief that the architect has succeeded in his task only if he has managed to finesse the client into building not just something that they don't understand, but something that they don't want. It is a view of the world that is the product of an architectural profession that has constructed a sense of itself as constituting a priesthood, defined by its arcane language but also its sense of inferiority about its relative status with other cultural forms.

Architecture of course is about life as well as about death. It shapes the way we live our lives, even if not quite so directly as some architects imagine. It does have a practical purpose, but it is also pursued for its own sake, as a metaphor for something else. It is about control because of the possibility it appears to offer of being entirely in command of our personal environment, and the people that we are sharing it with, if even only for a brief moment. Architecture has the power to frame the world, cancelling out the things that the architect doesn't want you to see, concentrating on those that he does. It directs light, it creates the relationship between where you eat and where you prepare food. Of course any sensible architect makes this a loose fit. You can write in the kitchen, you can eat in the bath, you can sleep in the study. But the architecture has created a grain and a texture that you can go with, and which you can choose to ignore.

It's the mindset demonstrated by the German architect Frei Otto, who named his children in alphabetical order. It's the experience of taking a drive in the back seat of Norman Foster's chauffeur-driven Range Rover, on the way to his private jet, to find that both the seat pockets are filled with pristine sketchbooks, freshly sharpened pencils, and a mobile telephone, just in case something should occur to the great architect in transit and be lost to the world because he is lacking paper and pen to record it before it passes across his field of consciousness, and vanishes for ever.

It's the idea that design can be an instrument for control, as it is for Dieter Rams. So distressing does he find the idea of visual disorder that he used to claim that he took a large paper bag with him on country walks, to collect the rubbish. His own office is a study in neutrality, the Switzerland of the design world, the kind of room in which a single fingerprint on the wall or a paper out of place has the impact of a visual landslide. He designed everything in it, the furniture, the products on the shelves, the clock, the radio, the storage system, and the only colour comes from the orange cigarette packet, permanently in Rams's hands.

Rams devotes enormous effort and patience to designing perfect objects that defeat fashion and cancel out the passing of time by defying visual redundancy. He made the ideal calculator, with the most carefully considered radiused corners, the most perfect buttons, and the clearest sequence of operating functions, only to find this entire category of object had become redundant. He designed the most beautiful, the most functional record player, and the same thing happened. Not only have records all but vanished so have the tapes that replaced them. And the compact discs that replaced *them* are rapidly on their way out too, leaving Rams and his attempts at control and order looking like the hopelessly deluded activities of a Canute, attempting to prevent the tide from washing away the grains of sand on a beach.

Architecture has its roots in the creation of shelter in a physical sense, but it has become an attempt to construct a particular view of the world, whether it is an individual house or a complex of streets and apartments. There is a very different kind of connection between an architect and the mayor who invites him to build a new housing complex in the manner of a Roman amphitheatre, as Ricardo Bofill did in several French towns and cities, and the relationship between that architect and the individuals who will actually live in it.

Despite the efforts of Renzo Piano, and others like him, architecture is still shaped by the powerful, and not the many. But that does not make it any the less significant.

IO

All the Presidents' Libraries

No American president with an instinct for self-preservation would willingly submit to a direct comparison with Thomas Jefferson unless they had a compelling reason to. When George Bush the Elder commandeered the University of Virginia's Rotunda, designed by his distant predecessor, for use in his own presidential library, he certainly thought he had one. Borrowing a little reflected glory to secure what he saw as his rightful place in history as a war hero and all-purpose international statesman must have seemed like the most effective way to wipe out the humiliation of loosing his second-term election. But Jefferson's Rotunda is one of the great landmarks of American architecture, and Bush's version is not. Jefferson was a gifted architect and a discriminating critic. Bush allowed the design of his library to fall into the hands of an architectural-plan factory, best known for churning out a stream of baseball stadia, each new one indistinguishable from the last. Jefferson's university at Charlottesville was one of the defining institutions of the young American republic. Bush's building at College Station, spread over 90 carefully watered acres of what was once Texas Agricultural and Mechanical College – now Texas A&M University – narcissistically limits itself to portraying his own career. It sets out to place the former director of the CIA, America's Ambassador to China, and Ronald Reagan's vice-president, in the heroic tradition.

In much the same way, the eighteenth century portrayed even its least competent leaders as classical heroes, equipped with breastplate and helmet, laurel leaves and toga. But despite its aspirations to grandeur, and an all but complete absence of Dan Quayle, Bush's library is a masterpiece of unintentional architectural frankness. It offers, in spite of itself, an eloquent insight into the emptiness at the heart of Bush's presidency. The rotunda, a form synonymous with civic monuments since at least the time of the Caesars, is deployed in front of the library, like the floodlit sphinx on the Las Vegas strip that sits outside the Luxor casino distracting the traffic. Bush's rotunda is there as a signpost, camouflaging a warehouse filled with racks and racks of grey box files, each marked with the single black dot that identifies it as containing the former President's papers. They are tended by National Archives and Records Administration staff who work, like H. G. Wells's Morlocks from *The Time Machine*, in troglodytic conditions untroubled by sunshine or by more than a handful of visiting scholars in the course of a day.

What the 100,000 or so paying visitors each year come to 1000 George Bush Drive West to see is not the warehouse, or its files. They come for a slick and highly partisan account of Bush's life, full of flaps to lift, levers to pull, buttons to press and fluffy toy dogs for children to pet. The exhibition display was devised by Alexander Cranstoun. He is a designer who, apart from working on Nixon's library and applying a cosmetic facelift to Lyndon Johnson's museum in Austin, was responsible for the trademark Nickelodeon Geyser at the Universal Studios theme park in Florida – a vat of bubbling, squirting, green slime constantly boiling away inside a giant test tube, thirty feet tall.

Eight masts, each flying the Stars and Stripes, stand in a circle in front of the Bush Library's rotunda. They form one side of the pastel-coloured plaza that is at the middle of the George Bush School of Government and Public Service. On the other side is an excessively ample car park. At the centre of the plaza, five horses cast in bronze gallop over an all too literal replica of a smashed segment of the Berlin wall, also rendered in bronze. This is a piece of sculpture by an artist named, improbably but somehow unsurprisingly, Veryl Goodnight. She calls it 'The Day the Wall Came Down' and proclaims it to be a monument to freedom. Like so much else about the library, the intended message of Goodnight's work has to be spelt out in words because its symbolic language, noisy though it may be, is too vague to say anything definite. Goodnight calls herself a Western artist. She says she chose to avoid the art schools of the 1960s, which she saw as dominated by abstraction, and learned bookkeeping instead before being apprenticed to a master in what has become her craft. Now she raises buffalo on the ranch where she built her studio and keeps up a steady output of art based on Western themes. When a second casting of 'The Day the Wall Came Down' was installed in Berlin, Goodnight claims she was awarded the Central Intelligence Agency's Medal of Freedom, perhaps the least-known, and certainly the most two-edged, honour that the world of culture can offer. To judge by her horses, executed in a manner that might owe something to the animators of the *Lord of the Rings* trilogy, Goodnight is backing into territory occupied by Jeff Koons. Her work is no doubt every bit as sincere, even if it is less famous and less knowing than that of the man who put a giant topiary puppy outside the Guggenheim in Bilbao. But her attempt to capture the spirit of a divided country liberated from the Stasi yoke in the form of a pack of horses – roaming through Berlin, pawing at the ground in front of the Brandenburg Gate and getting in the way of the traffic – is just maladroit. Casual observers might conclude that Goodnight's sculpture has been attacked by a gang of anarchic Texan troublemakers wielding spray cans. In fact the graffiti on the rubble beneath the horses is officially sanctioned. It has been carefully transcribed by the artist from the originals in Berlin, as Goodnight's commentary reassuringly points out: 'At President Bush's request, the names of people killed at the Berlin Wall are written on the dove of peace. These names represent over 900 people who were killed trying to escape to the west.'

The source of the figure is not revealed, but it does not match the 82 names recorded as having been killed at the Berlin wall itself during its twenty-eight years of existence. The sheer scale and effort needed to realize the work are presented with more conviction than its content. 'The life-size horses weigh seven tons between them and took three and a half years to complete,' she explains, as if to demonstrate that the achievements of the Bush administration are to be measured quantitatively rather than qualitatively. According to the helpful gloss, there for the benefit of those of us too literal-minded fully to understand the equine allegory, 'President Bush's diplomatic skills enabled the hole in the wall to become so large that all of Eastern Europe was set free from communist rule; the Cold War had ended.'

Rival claims are made by the Ronald Reagan Library in California. Both Reagan and Bush have fragments of the authentic Berlin Wall on show to demonstrate their case for claiming that they personally won the Cold War. Over at the Reagan Library, visitors are invited in semi-biblical language to 'touch a piece of the Berlin wall He sent crashing down, relive the history He made, and look with Him into the limitless future He dared to dream for us'.

For all its celebration of the triumph of America over the evil empire, the Bush Library is set in a landscape glittering with paranoia. Highway billboards proclaim the gospel of permanent vigilance in terms Winston Smith would have recognized from 1984, albeit translated to the Internet. 'Be Afraid or Be Ready; www.ready.gov'. The university website provides continual updates on America's terror alert status, and cautions students planning to travel abroad against wearing bright clothes, or white socks, or allowing their shirt tails out of their jeans in case they are taken for Americans. Except of course, in the countries where only Americans tuck them in, where they should be equally careful to do no such thing. In the long run, if taken seriously, the strategy would start modifying behaviour to the point when the most obviously American thing to do is not to look obviously American. Only an American wouldn't go to McDonald's in Athens. A necklace of the kind of concrete barriers originally devised to deter truck bombers in Beirut guards the entrance to the rotunda. There is a metal detector at the door.

It's not hard to understand why one of the greyer presidents might want to suggest that he had things in common with one of the most talented, the scholar-philosopher who managed to buy Louisiana from Napoleon for a knockdown price. But Bush, or his handlers, also wanted to make the point that though, yes, his was a presidency shaped by America's traditional virtues, the twentieth century did not entirely escape his attention. So despite its classical form, there are no columns on the exterior of the rotunda, and those on the inside have been stripped of acanthus leaves, volutes and entablature, and all the other carefully graded secret signs of the freemasonry of authentic classical architecture. The second half of the 1990s was not the moment for an ex-president to attempt an exact archaeological reconstruction of a Jeffersonian original, or a creative reinterpretation of one. In contemporary America, even a member of Skull and Bones, the elite Yale University society, must reflect the values of popular culture. Princeton University might get away with it, but an overtly classical presidential building would simply have carried too much baggage for Bush to have gone to Robert Stern, or Allan Greenburg, or any of the handful of other architects still interested in and capable of working with this kind of material in a literate way. It would be to suggest an unwholesome level of erudition, and no president, or even ex-president, can afford to be seen as a pointy-headed intellectual. A literal classical building would be equated with the unnecessarily conspicuous display of wealth and, even more dangerously, of learning. Instead, the design is simplified to suggest that it is a modern building, but the library is close enough to a classical model to demonstrate an intimate acquaintance with tradition and the values that implies, especially if you half close your eyes.

Just as Bush himself, for all his homely manner, always let slip just enough details of his education at Phillips Academy and Yale not to be taken for a real cowboy, so the façade of the library is studded with clues hinting at a patrician pedigree. The stone façade has been laid with alternate narrow and thick bands of stone to suggest that this is a descendant of the kind of rusticated wall built by the Romans. It sits on a contrasting coloured stone base. There is a vestigial piece of cornice pinned like a lapel version of the Légion d'Honneur to the front of the porch. It succeeds in looking more like a trophy than a commitment to an architectural language. Above it the rotunda has a line of little square windows incised between more stone bands. Since the top of the drum is all glass, their only purpose is to demonstrate how luxuriously thick the wall is, rather than to let in the already abundant daylight.

The library is faced in stone, the traditional way to signal that a structure is important. But the exposed steel I-beam over the entrance is another badge, implying that this is a building with at least some contemporary aesthetic ambition. Caudill, Rowlett and Scott, the once proud Texan architectural practice that designed it, was swallowed by HOK, a faceless conglomerate, before the library was finished. If you know where to look you can find clues to the bitter disappointments of architectural practice inscribed into the fabric of the building.

Cut into the veneer-thin stone of the neighbouring George Bush School of Government, an inscription claims: 'This final project is a visual tribute to the excellence in design and quality of leadership Caudill Rowlett Scott achieved, as practitioners and mentors to thousands of students of architecture.' Yet it is not their names but HOK's initials that are carved into the sandstone of the library itself. Caudill, Rowlett and Scott still had the grace to understand that it is only good manners to provide a proper entrance to a circular drum. It is not quite such good manners to put up a porte cochère in front of the door with Bush's name on it, as if this was some kind of five-star hotel with a chip on its shoulder. The semi-detached porch that the Roman emperor Hadrian designed for the Pantheon, projecting well forward of his rotunda and topped by a pediment, which Jefferson quoted so skilfully in Charlottesville, has been reduced to a simple box at College Station. The effect is less neo-classical than a piece of late postmodernism, influenced more by Michael Graves's cartoon version of Jefferson than by Jefferson himself.

Hadrian's rotunda, under its sublime dome and its oculus, was the setting for altars to all the Roman gods. Later it became Raphael's tomb, and then the last resting place of the short-lived line of the kings of Italy. Jefferson's University of Virginia had its classrooms and its library where each volume was carefully selected by the former president. Bush's rotunda is empty, but for the donors' names carved, in the serif capital letters first used for the Trajan column 2,000 years ago, into a black and grey granite wall. With all the ingenious inventiveness that American corporate fund-raisers can muster, it spells out exactly how many dollars each benefactor has donated without being quite so vulgar as to lapse into actual numbers. There is one column of names of individuals and organizations, described as patrons, another of benefactors, followed by the founders. Then comes the President's cabinet and finally the President's circle, a group that turned up for the opening ceremony, parking their private jets at the nearby airstrip. They include the Washington Times Foundation (nobody else's newspapers are used in any of the exhibits), the Sultanate of Oman, the Citizens of Kuwait, Al Nahyan and the people of the United Arab Emirates. The Halliburton Foundation, part of an enterprise that went on to cover itself with so much glory in the second

Gulf War and which made Bush the Younger's vice-president an extremely wealthy man, is here of course. So is the Government of the People's Republic of China, listed as mere patrons. It is a list that says as much about the life and times of George Bush – and his son – as the sum of all the thousands of exhibits in his museum, and with considerably more candour. It was of course Harlan Crowe, the library's treasurer, that the *New York Times* revealed as a major funder for the campaign smearing John Kerry's war record in the 2004 election.

There are other presidents who have equally unsavoury names on their walls. In Atlanta, Jimmy Carter includes the Playboy Foundation among his donors. At the Reagan Library, still proudly on display, is the name of Robert Maxwell, the disgraced British tycoon and alleged Mossad spy who fell, or jumped, or was pushed, over the side of his yacht, the *Lady Ghislaine*, into the Mediterranean just before the revelation that he had stolen his employees' pensions became public. And there are certainly more inept ways to design a donor wall. Caudill, Rowlett and Scott knew enough about architecture to avoid the most obvious mistakes.

In the Nixon Library and Birthplace designed by Langdon Wilson, the architects who built the first Getty museum in Malibu in the manner of a Pompeian villa, the donor wall is flanked by twin entrances to the men's and women's restrooms like a giant version of one of those rain or shine doll's house weather forecasters. But then Nixon's is not a federally recognized library and there are in any case precious few signs of any books. As the sign in the entrance proclaims, 'this is the only presidential library that doesn't cost the tax payer a penny'. That's because the Nixon archive, including the tapes, was taken over by the National Archives and Records Administration and is accommodated in a shed in Maryland.

Since designing the Getty villa, Langdon Wilson, whose recent achievements include the Taco Bell building in Irvine, seem to have lost their touch. For Nixon they paraphrased the Getty layout, complete with a reflecting pool, respectfully aligned on the little suburban house in which Nixon was born, standing in the midst of a particularly lurid thicket of yellow and purple flowers. If you want, you can buy a three-foot by five-foot embroidered, 100 per cent acrylic, made in the USA, American flag that has been hoisted up to fly over the Nixon house for a day from the library shop for $40. They throw in a certificate of authenticity, and 'if you want a certain date for that special person just call us'.

Nixon's library is staffed by volunteers in blazers who rather alarmingly call themselves Docents. But they go out of their way to be genuinely nice to every visitor who passes through the doors. They tell you all about the presidential Lincoln parked in one room, and how it was shipped to Moscow so that Nixon and Kissinger could talk without the electronic eavesdroppers that plagued the US embassy when they were negotiating with Brezhnev. 'We had a Russian gentleman here who was involved with security for the KGB at the time, and he told us that they knew they were up to something, but that they couldn't figure it out.' The Docents point out the hall of world leaders at the centre of the library, a group of plaster dummies milling about awkwardly, looking more as if they were trapped in a lift lobby than in the waiting room for eternity. Nixon wrote the guest list himself. De Gaulle with his kepi is the tallest, towering over Churchill in a bowler. Mao stands with his back to Adenauer and Golda Meier, who is clutching a handbag. The Docents eagerly identify the less familiar figures – these days, that's just about all of them – and explain how each one was carved life-size in plaster, dressed in 'actual clothing' and sprayed bronze.

More moving is the case full of keepsakes from American POWs, acquired during their time in Vietnam. There are threadbare prison uniforms, with strange flashes of colour stitched into them that look like the work of an advanced Japanese fashion designer, and cardboard toothpaste boxes and cigarette packets with the Stalinist graphics favoured by the Vietnamese from the Red Cross. The museum goes on to chart Nixon's tortured, even sadomasochistic relationship with the press, culminating in a wall display that shows all fifty-four of the issues of *Time* magazine during the course of his life that put him on the cover. 'More than anyone else', says the caption with not a little trace of pride, despite the humiliating headlines on so many of them. There is a tiny piece of moon rock and a NASA spacesuit. The matching pair of boots look as if they come from the local hardware store and have been sprayed silver, as if for a theatrical production. But the most enlightening exhibit offers a particularly chilling reminder of Nixon's continuing interest in spin. A copy of a memo to H. R. Haldeman outlining the procedures to be adopted by the President in the event of a disaster during the course of the first moon landing hangs behind glass. It includes the script written for the television address that Nixon would have given: 'These brave men, Neil Armstrong and Edwin Aldrin, know that there is no hope for their recovery. But also know there is hope for mankind in their sacrifice.' Prior to the statement, the President would have telephoned each of the widows. 'A clergyman should then adopt the same procedure as a burial at sea, commending their souls to the deepest of the deep, concluding with the Lord's prayer.'

These insights aside, the primary objective of the whole enterprise is to prove that there never was a smoking gun at the Watergate. 'The president knew nothing about the break in, some of his aides became involved in the cover up . . .' is as far as the library will go in conceding that anything went wrong during Nixon's watch. It is, however, only too willing to level charges of rampant vote rigging in Illinois and Texas against the Kennedy campaign in 1960. Nixon lost that election but, as he has it, magnanimously chose not to contest the result in court, to save the country from the agony of endless recounts. The exhibition ends with a black tunnel leading inexorably to the helicopter rising from the White House lawn and that grim 'I have never been a quitter' speech, the one that goes on to suggest that 'the greatness comes when you are really tested'.

Compared to Bush's library, Nixon's is a shrill and slightly down-at-heel shrine for true believers. Bush's by contrast has a slickness that reflects a smoother, more socially secure character, still in command of a ruthless and affluent political machine, that presents the political process in bite-size chunks designed not to test the patience of its audience.

Despite this, back in the Bush rotunda, all there is to see, apart from the donors' names, the shop with its Camp David windcheaters, its presidential-seal mugs, and a cardboard cut-out of George and Barbara positioned at the doors to greet visitors, is a large empty space. It's the perfect metaphor for the president who wasn't there.

The architecture of the rotunda, vestigial though it is, certainly has a more commanding presence than what lies beyond. The bulk of the museum is a high-bay industrial shed, in which the open-web beams and the profiled metal-sheet cladding of the roof are pitilessly revealed, floating above a display fitted out with all the skill and slickness of a casino floor to take visitors on an emotionally manipulative roller-coaster ride through the Bush years. Any sense of architectural space disappears in the face of a zigzag layout designed with the ruthlessness of a Disney attraction, and the same hazy conception of authenticity.

Once past the foyer, visitors turn right around a corner and are ambushed by the sudden revelation of an Avenger torpedo-bomber hanging suspended from the roof steel, frozen in the steep banking turn that is now considered obligatory when displaying military aircraft indoors. This is a warplane of the type in which Bush took off from the deck of the aircraft carrier *San Jacinto* on the day in September 1944 that he was shot down over the Pacific after bombing a Japanese radio station. Not the actual plane of course. Nor is it the parachute that saved his life that day that hangs in a glass case on the wall, but one from the same production run. Bush spent hours in his life jacket alone in the sea, drifting inexorably towards the island he had just attacked. He was snatched from sharks and Japanese patrols by a submarine, the USS *Finback*, a rescue symbolized in the exhibition by a bit of business involving a submarine hatch. 'I had faced death, and God spared me,' Bush recalls in his commentary.

Around another sharp bend comes the next carefully orchestrated incident, a Wurlitzer organ from the late 1940s. It plays a tape loop that features 'Boogie Woogie Bugle Boy' and stands next to a '47 Studebaker of 'exactly the same type that Bush drove across the country on his way to a new life in Texas after Yale'.

Cranstoun, unlike the library architects, was smart enough not to do the obvious thing with the exhibition design. Bush alone among the more recent presidents has avoided the replica Oval Office that has been obligatory since Lyndon Johnson's wife Ladybird forced one on a reluctant Gordon Bunshaft in Austin. Bush serves up the Laurel Office at Camp David instead, in the belief that he was being daringly different in doing so. Bunshaft, who thought that a replica would be tasteless, declined to include it until the library was so well advanced that it was supposedly too late to find the space to make a full-size office. But Mrs Johnson just kept bringing it up. Under pressure, Bunshaft did manage to shoehorn in a slightly scaled down version providing fake Washington windows with a view of genuine Texas sunshine, and curiously detached from the rest of the museum display. The glass incidentally is bulletproof, a precaution specified after a tragic campus sniper incident in the 1960s.

What all the Oval Office simulations have in common is the hushed respect they demand from visitors. They are shrines, preserved behind glass, or at least behind thick red tasselled ropes, to protect them from any act of *lèse-majesté*. Nobody is going to get to sneak behind the replica presidential desk for a snatched photograph. Nobody is going to carve their initials here. The partial exception is in the Kennedy Library, which alongside Jack's Oval Office has an evocation of Bobby Kennedy's office during his time as Attorney General. You can walk around the back of his desk to get a close look at his children's crayon drawings taped to the walls, and the dented white steel helmet worn by one of 300 federal marshals sent into Oxford, Mississippi. There is a moving letter from James Meredith, the black student those marshals protected, celebrating his graduation. This, for once, looks like *the* helmet, and *the* letter.

Oval Offices come and go, as each administration decorates and redecorates. But the President's desk, which puts his back to the window and faces the fireplace at the far end of the oval, dictates the fixed points that go on for ever. They provide a compelling insight into the political uses of furniture. Carter had a pair of sofas positioned back to back across the middle of the room, each flanked by a pair of armchairs. One sofa faces the desk. The other is trained directly at the fireplace. It allows for visitors to get carefully graded privileges depending on their status. The basic visit begins with the dignitary/ supplicant entering. The President rises; handshakes, arm squeezes, body hugs, kisses on the cheek, if considered culturally appropriate; then he waves the dignitary towards the sofa. Both visitor and President have an aide join them in the designated flanking chair. The encounter proceeds to its conclusion. The less privileged visitors then leave. In stage two, useful for bringing troublesome discussions to a positive conclusion or indicating a particular degree of warmth, all rise and move to the second sofa in front of the fire. The President comes from behind his desk to join the visitors and sit side by side with them, in steps as hallowed by custom as a rain-making dance. This is no doubt exactly what happened when, as Carter puts it, 'Deng Xiaoping came to Washington to visit with me'. What does it matter if nobody remembers a word of what was said? What does it matter if you have inadvertently left the impression that America would sit on its hands in the event of a Chinese invasion of Taiwan, when you have gone through a ceremony like that?

In Reagan's day, the layout was more static and offered less in the way of ritual. A pair of three-seater sofas were positioned in the middle of the room on the long axis, allowing the President a direct view of the fireplace from his desk and to meet visitors that included Mother Teresa, Gorbachev, Mrs Thatcher and a selection of Beirut hostages.

Lyndon Johnson clearly wasn't keen on working at his desk. The coffee table with its speakerphone on a pull-out flap, close to the rocking chair with the footstool on the sludge-green carpet, was the seat of power in his day. Kennedy's Oval Office on the other hand, with its ship models and yachting mementos, had a wider role when it became a soothing TV studio for the duration of the Cuban missile crisis. What his audience would not have seen was his secretary Evelyn Lincoln's daybook open for the first week in October 1962. It records an insane schedule of appointments allocated in three-minute segments starting at 5.19 a.m. George Bundy was in twice on this particular morning, the first time at 6.18 a.m. for seven minutes. Then after face time for Dean Rusk and Ted Kennedy, he was back at 6.31 for another three minutes.

Bill Clinton had seen the Kennedy, Carter and Johnson Oval Office replicas and wasn't impressed. He told his architect, James Polshek, that for his library in Little Rock, 'If you can't do it exactly right, don't do it all.' That meant genuine sunshine through actual windows. 'He was adamant about the need for real daylight,' says Polshek. 'The real oval office has a south orientation. Ours has flipped 180 degrees, so the west side is seen as the front, surrounded by borrowed light.' Alone of the libraries, Clinton's Oval has become a real part of the building, rather than a piece of scenery. It stands on the second floor within an oval-shaped column that rises the full height of the building, with the entrance lobby underneath it.

Bush's museum cannot quite make up its mind about tone. Should it reveal Bush as the WASP patrician son of privilege that he was, growing up on a family estate in Kennebunkport, the product of Phillips Academy – motto *Non Sibi* (not for self) – and Yale? Or does it portray him as the self-made Texan that he always claims to be, to demonstrate his populist roots in his adopted state? In the end it opts for the latter. Bush – captain of baseball at Phillips – presents the art of politics and public service as a game for regular folks. 'The adrenaline factor in politics is identical to the adrenaline factor in sports. The extra last throw of a horseshoe is similar to a debate situation or a crisis in the legislature,' he says. And the Studebaker of the type in which he crossed the continent, clearly there to add colour to the display, is accompanied by a claim that 'to celebrate his new life George Bush stopped for lunch outside Abilene, ordered a local beer and chicken fried steak, a dish he had never heard of before, but was to become his favourite meal'. The display offers such precious insights as Bush's words that 'my mother taught me the fundamental things. "Don't brag. Think of the other guy. Be kind to people." The things they have taught me have stood me in good stead.'

The exhibition layout shuffles its way through Bush's career, marking the highlights by constructing a series of landmarks. There is a giant plywood model of the dome of Congress, and a mock-up of the White House. His time in China is signalled by a pagoda that looks much like the kind of thing you might find in an upmarket but somewhat old-fashioned Chinese restaurant. Nixon's library does something similar, not surprising since both were designed by the same firm. There is the bicycle Bush was given when he was America's Ambassador in China, but which shows no signs of ever having been used. Deng Xiaoping is portrayed in tapestry form meeting Bush in 1985. The moment was captured by two artists from the Shanghai Red Star Tapestry Factory, who spent fifty-three days weaving it, kindred spirits of Ms Goodnight and her galloping horses outside. Bush's time as Ambassador to the UN is encapsulated, daringly in the context of the limited world view of the Texas backwoods, by a row of UN flags. There are lots of photographs of Bush in dinner jackets, though none that record the evening in Tokyo when he started throwing up over his hosts.

Visitors also have a chance to sit inside a replica of the President's cabin on Air Force One, and to fasten an actual seat belt; they know all about interactivity here. The first Gulf War is signalled by an hour-glass in which the sands of time are energetically running out. Visitors can reset it as Bush gets ready to draw his line in the sand. There are fashion dummies, dressed in military uniforms and spray-painted silver and white, in carefully non-specific, multi-ethnic, multi-gendered abstraction, an idea that the ubiquitous Cranstoun had already tried out when he gave the LBJ exhibition a makeover in the 1980s. In the Bush Library, he included the chance to get a glimpse of the Kuwaiti desert through night-vision goggles. On the way out is a less than understated cigarette boat that Bush acquired in the 1970s to boost his sporty image, and the offer of a customized letter for each visitor signed by the President and the First Lady.

There is, as in every other presidential library, a selection of state gifts presented by foreign dignitaries. The selection does not suggest that presidential tastes have grown more sophisticated in the eyes of America's allies with the passing of time. Johnson was given a Diego Rivera painting by the Mexicans. Bush got a saddle. Even Nixon collected a Sonia Delaunay from François Mitterrand, although what he thought of it is not recorded. As a finale, Bush has an art gallery for temporary exhibitions. I saw Rick Kelly's show, 'Reflections of Freedom', including his lovingly rendered painting of a flight of Phantoms, entitled with conspicuous insensitivity 'Bad Day for Uncle Ho' to set the tone. It was as kitsch as anything in Saddam Hussein's palaces.

Ronald Reagan's library has no pretensions to patrician values. Reagan had initially wanted to build it on the Palo Alto campus at Stanford. A site was chosen and a design drawn up, but the university rebuffed him, just as Harvard eventually turned its face against accommodating Kennedy's library. Instead Reagan decided to slum it and accepted the gift of a site from a house builder on a ridge at the outer edge of Los Angeles in Simi. In California there is certainly no such thing as a free lunch, and this was one land donation that came with a price. An hour's drive north from Santa Monica, where the suburbs begin to thin out and even the strip malls and the motels are built in what passes for mission style, the streets suddenly begin to take on the names of former presidents. As you wind up Presidential Drive to the library, you pass homes on Roosevelt Drive and Eisenhower Drive, streets so new that they look as if they haven't yet had the shrink wrapping they came in removed. At the top of the hill the land falls away to reveal fresh subdivisions ready for the next explosion of tract houses down in the adjacent valley and the sites being cleared for the bigger, more opulent houses up on the neighbouring hillsides.

On the outside, Reagan's library is a hacienda, all Roman pantiles, chimneys, pink stucco and a loggia built around a handsome open courtyard dotted with folksy benches. On the way in, you encounter a bronze statue of the late president in his denims and cowboy boots. His glossy black Lincoln is parked in a corner of the courtyard. The entrance hall is lined with what looks like plastic wood. The clay tiles on the floor make it feel like a generic Mexican restaurant. Inside the museum gimcrack ceiling tiles and blue carpet tiles crackling with static lovingly evoke the ambience of the convention room of an airport hotel. There are *Bedtime for Bonzo* posters on the wall, and a replica of the diner booth in which Ronnie first met Nancy – with not so much as a photograph of Jane Wyman in sight. The General Electric Theater shows excerpts from the Great Gipper's movie hits.

Reagan's library is much more artless than Bush's, and somehow more engaging too. The copy of the Alzheimer letter that Reagan wrote in 1994 after his diagnosis with the disease silences even the most ferocious of his critics for a moment. The authenticity of Reagan's re-creation of the White House situation room may be thrown into question by the photograph of the real thing included in the caption that highlights the glaring discrepancies between the mock-up and the original. But it is a mismatch that feels almost endearing in its naivety.

The exhibits, many of which look like junk salvaged from the attic, also have a disarmingly homespun quality. You can find Reagan's letter sweater from college days, as well as the one he wore back to the White House from hospital after the attempt on his life, and a bulletproof vest, one of several sent to the White House after the shooting. Alongside it is a copy of an X-ray showing the bullet still lodged in his chest. A cruise missile is casually propped up in a corner behind the TV set on which Reagan talks warmly about Gorbachev. On one table is an array of dummy prototypes made by the Hughes Aircraft Corporation as part of the Shield in the Sky programme, otherwise known as Star Wars. One is a miniature vehicle sensor, the other is an anti-satellite infrared sensor designed for use in the space shuttle. Models of an M1 Abrams tank and a Bradley Fighting Vehicle serve to demonstrate Reagan's enthusiasm for re-equipping America's armed forces on the ground as well. Thankfully, the museum resisted the temptation to accept the full-size versions that their grateful manufacturers would no doubt have been only too eager to donate.

When it was finished, the library had a certain unpretentious architectural charm as well, which benefited from a beautiful setting and a well-chosen site. But encroaching housing, and the decision to extend the library by creating the first mission-style aircraft hanger to accommodate Air Force One, have done much to dissipate that charm. The customized Boeing 707 that flew Reagan and several other presidents around the world is almost as big as the library itself, and its presence makes it feel as if this is the contemporary equivalent of the burial site of a Saxon warrior, entombed with his longship and chariot. And indeed this is Reagan's burial place, just as Dwight Eisenhower built his mausoleum in his presidential library in Kansas.

The short history of the presidential libraries provides a revealing insight into the architectural tastes of the American political class, as well as the uses to which architecture is put and the twists of fashion. Ever since Congress voted to take over the library that Franklin D. Roosevelt designed himself next to his house at Hyde Park in upstate New York, every president has built a presidential library. Hyde Park is the personification of modest domesticity: a U-shaped range of clapboard-covered barn-like structures organized around a garden. It's on two floors but looks lower because of the steep shingled roof. Yet it reflects the extraordinary life of a president who had to deal with the key events of the twentieth century, while confronting polio from the wheelchair in which he was never photographed. Since then, there have been times when it has seemed as if the more lacklustre the president, the larger the library – a phenomenon that culminated with Gerald Ford, who has a building to his name at either end of Michigan. Congress finally moved to limit competitive attempts by ex-presidents to erect ever larger monuments to themselves by passing legislation insisting that they raise funds to pay not just for the building but also for an endowment equal to 20 per cent of the cost before a presidential library is adopted by the Federal Government. There is an extra financial penalty to discourage libraries that are larger than 70,000 square feet. It's a measure that has not been entirely successful. Roosevelt's library is just 30,000 square feet, while Kennedy's is 95,000 and Clinton's 125,000.

Roosevelt notwithstanding, classicism of one kind or another has been the model for almost every presidential library. Jefferson chose the Pantheon, built by the Emperor Hadrian, another leader with a personal talent for architectural design, as the model for the Charlottesville Rotunda. As a result, whether he knew it or not, so did Bush the Elder. But when Gordon Bunshaft, the dominant force in SOM, America's biggest architectural practice in the 1960s, was asked to design Lyndon Johnson's library in Austin, he used a Greek rather than a Roman model. LBJ's library rises over Red River Street like a Texan acropolis as conceived by NASA, a complex of three related, strictly symmetrical structures that step down a hillside by way of a series of ramps overlooking the university lawn. The main library is an all but windowless box, faced inside and out with six bands of travertine, imported from Italy in the teeth of bitter opposition from protectionist American quarry owners. The stone dazzles in the sun against the deep blue Texas sky. A series of reflecting pools leave rippling water patterns on the blank walls, so intensely white that they hurt the eyes even in winter. To one side the LBJ School of Public Affairs is faced in distressed concrete rather than travertine to make it clear that it is paying respectful tribute to the mother ship holy of holies, rather than trying to upstage it. They sit on top of a podium that contains a 1,000-seat auditorium. Its sloping walls look like the ramparts below the Parthenon and are faced in more travertine, in a careful pattern that uses three vertical slabs of stone to each horizontal slab. A deep cornice throws the top of the wall into shadow. Chrome-plated steel discs stud its underside, recalling the triglyph and metope pattern of the Doric order, a detail that might seem calculated to let Bunshaft's fellow architects know that he can navigate his way around classical architecture. But in fact, under the impression that he was a modernist of the most hard-line kind, Bunshaft claimed the arrangement was simply the product of functional necessity rather than history. The concrete roof beams have eight steel cables threaded through them to boost their strength. Each of the cables has a metal disc to cap the anchor point, to which Bunshaft added a ninth in the interests of symmetry. Or at least that's what he said he did.

Look at the library head on and you see that the side walls curve out as they approach the ground, tapering towards the middle, and then flair out again at the top, suggesting a classical column with all the sharp edges chased, not strictly a part of the classical repertoire, but close enough to be a reminder of the idea of entasis. It's not pretty or engaging, but then neither was Lyndon Johnson. Bunshaft recalled his first meeting with the President and driving to the Johnson ranch to look at the cows: 'Johnson was building a prefab on his property, and we went in there and he was proposing to put a window in one wall of a bedroom. I said, if you do that, you won't have any place for a bed. You ought to put it there. He said, "No." I thought to myself, He's trying to figure out whether I'm some pansy decorator, or a real man.'

The library suggests a mausoleum, or the final assembly building for the Saturn rocket programme. In fact Bunshaft's co-architects on the project, Brooks, Graeber and White, in addition to designing Johnson's ranch and his family-owned radio station, had designed the manned spacecraft centre in Houston.

Bunshaft described Johnson as 'an aggressive, big man, who had helped make great social changes into law. You would not think of Lyndon Johnson if you went to Roosevelt's library. It seemed to call for a building of some virility.' Despite its roots in the architecture of Athenian democracy, the LBJ Library feels unmistakably imperial, if only in that it is manifestly more competent in its architecture than the usual run of presidential libraries.

The library's position on one end of the campus's central axis drove Bunshaft to inflate the scale of the project: 'It would have to be massive, even if it were made to hold rubber bands.'

Bunshaft had designed a library before – Yale University's Beinecke Rare Books Library – and he put the lessons he learned there to good use in Austin. Treated mechanically, a library could become simply a storeroom for books. Bunshaft managed to create a space of sullen grandeur at the heart of the building that is undeniably a work of architecture rather than of stagecraft or display. It rises the full eight storeys and accommodates a flowing marble double staircase, rising under a giant carved presidential seal, in a way that cannot fail to impress. 'It's a monumental building, because a presidential library should express the importance of a president and his papers,' felt Bunshaft.

The great hall of the library is dominated by books – one entire wall glows with them, or at least with the scarlet buckram-covered boxes that contain Johnson's papers, behind a regular grid of marble-framed windows, each with an individually spot-lit gold presidential seal. They make it instantly clear what this building is without having to spell it out in words or signs. It makes a lasting impression, one that Jimmy Carter's architect feebly attempted to replicate in Atlanta by offering a perfunctory flash of box files through a glass porthole. It's clear that Bunshaft had no interest in allowing the exhibition that forms the most public part of the library to distract visitors from the magnificence of the space he had created. The exhibits are squashed into a semi-basement apparently as perfunctory afterthoughts.

Though Johnson and Bunshaft clashed over the Oval Office replica, there could have been no architectural practice more appropriate than SOM to design this particular president's library. They represented both the ascendancy and the decline of a certain kind of America. The office established by Louis Skidmore that Bunshaft first joined in 1937 was to expand into the world's largest architectural practice as America itself grew into an unchallenged superpower. It was SOM that created the uniform of modern capitalism in America. In Man-hattan, SOM designed Lever House on Park Avenue, the first glass and steel skyscraper anywhere. It built Chase's headquarters for the Rockefellers, occupying two full downtown blocks, as well as towers for Marine Midland and US Steel. In Chicago, SOM built the Sears and Hancock towers. These swaggering skyscrapers may have owed their aesthetic expression to Mies van der Rohe, but it was SOM that used his vocabulary to create the North American downtown in the 1950s and 1960s. They exported the physical image of America around the world. Everywhere they went, they created a certain kind of steel and marble modernity for governments or corporations struggling to look up to date. They built airports and office towers, convention centres and hotels that had the effect of making every ambitious city in the world look the same. Inside those towers, SOM designed open-plan white-collar factories, equipped with sheep pens and five-wheeled chairs for the clerical classes. For the masters of the universe, they created offices with handcrafted one-off desks, flanked by specially woven tapestries, flattered by downlighters, guarded by Chinese carved figures, and glossy hardwood fittings. The carpets were ankle deep, the leather upholstery was dyed in primary colours, and the chrome-plated furniture came from the Bauhaus. It was a mirage of corporate power that must have impressed the young Jacques Attali.

Their work was entirely lacking in self-doubt; it seemed to represent the faithful and undiluted expression of an America born to rule. And when the Vietnam tragedy, and the burning of the ghettos of the 1960s, and the assassinations, destroyed the self-confidence and unassailability of that America, SOM's confidence evaporated with it. Financially, SOM was battered and bruised by the post-Vietnam economic slump and the oil shock, but its real trauma was philosophical. It was no longer possible to build the way that Bunshaft had done. His generation had invested heavily in the aesthetic of swaggering restraint. It was more than a mannerism: he and his contemporaries had believed in it, regarded it as a moral imperative. When modernism began to be viewed not as a progressive force but as a deeply reactionary tendency, unpopular with both CEOs wanting to make a mark and radical opponents of urban redevelopment, they simply did not know how to respond.

There was a time lag, but just as LBJ decided not to seek re-election in 1968, so SOM at the end of the 1970s set up a series of conversations with the postmodernists to see where to go next. Bunshaft lived long enough to scorn his successors at the firm he once dominated: 'In my book, David Childs [who runs SOM's New York office] isn't an architect at all. He's just a planner who gives everything a pomo [postmodern] skin.'

Bunshaft's LBJ Library was almost the last act of certainty in a career that never considered the possibility of doubt, while the library's exhibits portray an America that has already lost its optimism and certainty and is beginning to understand the need to demonstrate a certain humility. Johnson himself was hardly conspicuously blessed with that quality. But the events of his years in office were so manifestly traumatic for America that the relentlessly positive tone that Bush's library would take was simply not possible in Austin. The Bible that had belonged to Jack Kennedy on which Johnson took the oath of office on the plane taking him back to Washington from Dallas sits in one glass case. In another is a MK-82 500-lb general-purpose bomb of the type dropped in ever larger numbers on North Vietnam in 1964. Almost as chilling are the photographs in the display on civil rights that show the Whites Only Ladies Restroom of a Mississippi courtroom. They could belong to the nineteenth century. But in this setting we are forcibly reminded that they are part of our own times. To his credit, LBJ can display the collection of pens used to sign into law the bills that created his Great Society programme.

At several levels the library reveals a conflict between the taste of the architect – and perhaps even more that of Arthur Drexler, the Museum of Modern Art's director of architecture, who curated the original museum display – and Johnson. The dignified restraint of the original library has been subverted by an attempt to appeal to a different America, energetically abetted by Alexander Cranstoun, the designer of the green gunk fountain, and his ubiquitous silver-sprayed mannequins posing as American soldiers. The stately, if slightly camp, bifurcated staircase at the heart of the library atrium, with its sweeping travertine curves, now has a 1968 stretched Lincoln Continental parked awkwardly underneath it. Not far away is an animatronic figure of Johnson – donated by Nieman Marcus – in a Stetson with one western boot lodged on the hitching-post rail dispensing wit and wisdom at the touch of a button. A pair of Mies van der Rohe's Barcelona chairs, clearly a relic of the previous design regime, have been drawn up as resentful captives in front of this spectacle, as if to suggest the enforced submission of the elite taste of the Volvo-driving classes to the popular will.

Though planning started on the Kennedy Library five years before

Johnson commissioned Bunshaft, I. M. Pei's building did not open until long after Austin had been completed. In fact it was fifteen years, two sites, and three different designs between the announcement of Pei's appointment and the endlessly delayed opening of the library on Columbia Point, a spit of artificial land overlooking the sea south of Boston. Given the tortuously slow rate of progress, it's hardly surprising that it did not turn out to be one of Pei's more impressive designs. But it was to prove a decisive project for him. It consolidated the transformation of a former student of the Bauhaus refugees Marcel Breuer and Walter Gropius from house designer for the piratical New York property developer William Zeckendorf into the preferred architect of presidents with imperial pretensions, from Mitterrand at the Louvre to Helmut Kohl in Berlin's Historical Museum. The Kennedy Library allowed Pei to explore his fascination with the pyramid that he was later to use for Mitterrand for almost a decade. He was to design the only presidential library before Clinton's that militantly rejects the classical model.

The glamour of Kennedy's life and the tragic circumstances of his death made the design of the library as vigorously fought-for an architectural commission in its day as the reconstruction of Ground Zero. The President's widow was introduced to a wide range of architects through an elaborate process of conversations that involved flying Alvar Aalto from Helsinki, Kenzo Tange from Tokyo, Franco Albini from Milan, and even Basil Spence from England to a Boston hotel for a weekend of awkward silences. Were the participants meant to be offering advice and condolences, or to pitch for the job? Spence reported that the whole room was moved to tears when they were read a note from Kennedy instructing an architect in the design of a federal building in which he quoted Pericles: 'Let us not imitate, for we must inspire others.' Jacqueline Kennedy was initially taken with Louis Kahn but, according to Carter Wiseman, Bobby Kennedy wouldn't treat his flights of poetic fancy seriously. Mies van der Rohe was so reserved in their conversations that she didn't believe he really wanted the job. Even Bunshaft was a possibility.

In the end, Jacqueline Kennedy opted for Pei, not yet 50, after a carefully staged-managed interview in his office, specially painted white and emptied of clutter for the occasion. Just before his death,

Kennedy himself had looked at a site for the library on the Charles River that would form part of the Harvard campus. But with Pei appointed, the university offered a second site that avoided the problems involved in clearing the railway freight depot that occupied the original choice. After an excruciating delay, and growing opposition from those who described the project as a Kennedy Disneyland that would flood Harvard with two million visitors a year, the university changed its mind and withdrew its offer. The figures were, of course, utterly fantastic. The most visited presidential library is Johnson's, a fact that is certainly connected with its refusal, unique among the libraries, to charge for admission. Even this never racks up more than 200,000 visitors in a year.

The University of Massachusetts offered an alternative site south of Boston, on an isolated waterfront point overlooking a sewage outlet. Like Bunshaft's work for Johnson, the Kennedy Library uses architectural space, more than exhibits, to engage the visitor. As you arrive, the view out over the water is hidden from sight, to be revealed only as you enter the vast, empty, ten-storey glass extrusion that is at the centre of the complex. Chopin plays tastefully over the speakers, and from the entrance terrace with its black granite floor there is a view to the sea across a soaring space with its huge American flag hanging like a waterfall from the steel-truss roof. In the distance you can see the skyscrapers of Boston, and the jets on their way down into Logan. This is a memorial as well as a library, 'dedicated to the memory of John F. Kennedy, 35th president of the USA and to all those who through the art of politics seek a better world'.

By the time it was finished, Pei's design had lost its initial clarity. Worse, by 1979 it looked simply dated. The balance between architecture and content had shifted decisively. Bunshaft could batter his way through all opposition and build a presidential library that really was a library. Pei, working with the designer Ivan Chermayeff, a contemporary of Kennedy's at Harvard, had to incorporate the narrative storytelling aspects of a presidential library. And in this way, the JFK Library has set the pattern for all the subsequent presidential libraries. On the way to the cinema that begins the tour, visitors get a glimpse through grey-tinted glass of the 26-foot sloop that was given to Kennedy by his parents for a fifteenth birthday present. The library is less than thirty years old but seems far older. Not as ancient as Pei's pharaonic geometry with its black glass prism, white cube and cylinder would imply. But its restless shapes and its position against the sky somehow recall those heroic black-and-white photographs of the landmarks of the modern movement.

On the December Saturday that I am here, forty years to the day after the assassination, the boat is stored on Cape Cod, its regular winter home. Three signal flags spelling out JFK barely move in the biting cold as geese fly overhead. There are just a handful of visitors inside the library itself. Outside, a Somali taxi driver sits listening to his radio, blaring about the lockdown by the air cavalry of an Iraqi town on the Syrian border .

The world this building evokes seems impossibly remote. Its television sets show blurred images of the 1960 presidential campaign, when politicians still made speeches that were worth listening to, when Frank Sinatra sang 'Everybody's Voting for Jack'. It was a time when the Kennedy brothers wore silk top hats for the presidential inauguration. And the matter-of-fact documents displayed on the wall carried bulletins from a world on the edge of being vaporized. The words 'Eyes Only, Reproduction Prohibited Unless Declassified' are stamped across a series of pieces of paper displayed on the wall of one of the exhibition rooms. I look at one, and am jolted to find myself reading a letter from Khrushchev that has been written apparently from the heart:

Just imagine, Mr President, that we had presented you with the conditions of an ultimatum which you have presented us by your action . . . You, Mr President, have flung a challenge at us. Who asked you to do this? By what right do you do this? . . . You are no longer appealing to reason, but wish to intimidate us.

No, Mr President, I cannot agree to this and I think in your own head you recognize that I am correct . . . We will not simply be bystanders with regard to piratical acts by American ships on the high seas. We will then be forced on our part to take the measures we consider necessary and adequate in order to protect our rights. We have everything necessary to do so.

In the same case, dated just six days later, a second document reproduces the verbatim text of the translation of another more despairing message from Khrushchev to Kennedy, relayed via the US embassy in Moscow. Declassified by the CIA, only in 1968, it begins: 'I think you will understand that if you are really concerned about the welfare of the world everyone needs peace. Both capitalists, if they have not lost their reason, and still more we communists, people who know how to value not only their own lives, but more than anyone the lives of their people. I see, Mr President, that you are not devoid of a sense of anxiety for the fate of the world. I have participated in two wars and know that war ends only when it has rolled through cities and villages everywhere sowing death and destruction.'

The exhibition ends as it can only end, with the black walls of a room marked November 22 1963 that shows images of the funeral, but not the assassination. You exit, past the photographs of de Gaulle and Harold Macmillan in black, past the image of the memorial stone at Runnymede witnessing the gift of an acre of England to the United States of America. Finally you emerge from the black room into a ten-storey void looking at the sky, the water and the Boston skyline, a process that feels like the moment of release after a funeral service. You turn to see words from Kennedy's inaugural address: 'All this will not be finished in the first 100 days, nor will it be finished in the first 1,000 days, nor in the lifetime of this administration nor even perhaps in our lifetime on this planet. But let us begin.'

To mark the twentieth anniversary of Philip Johnson picking up the first Henry Moore trophy and cheque that come with the Pritzker Prize for Architecture, the Pritzker family prevailed upon the White House to host the ceremony. Bill Clinton made the presentation to Renzo Piano. It has certainly done Piano's subsequent career in the USA no harm.

As it happened, architecture was very much on the President's mind that year. With the end of his second term in sight he was beginning to think about life after the Oval Office, and in particular about his presidential library. He had been one of the guests at the opening ceremony of the Bush Library. Deeply unimpressed by its architecture, he left vowing to do something very different when his turn came.

'I want', said Clinton a few months later, 'something that is welcoming, but has a sense of grandeur.' Two Pritzker winners had already designed a presidential library. Gordon Bunshaft, who died in 1990 was no longer available. The other was I. M. Pei.

Clinton had of course seen both buildings. He thought that the best modern building in Washington was Pei's addition to the National Gallery, and that the best presidential library was the Kennedy. But to hire the same architect as Jackie Kennedy would have seemed perhaps too much like self-aggrandisement. He looked at the other Pritzker winners as possible architects for his library. The non-American winners were clearly not an option for such a symbolically charged project, and by all accounts none of the other American recipients – Robert Venturi, Philip Johnson, Richard Meier, even Frank Gehry – managed to hit it off with Clinton. What, the president was in the habit of asking, do you think of that museum in Balboa? And how do you think that titanium will look in twenty years? There was a certain amount of lobbying. Steven Spielberg had recently had a house designed for him in the Hamptons by Charles Gwathmey, and he suggested that he might be just the architect for the job. Disney's Michael Eisner – who had transformed the Mouse Kingdom with buildings by Michael Graves, Frank Gehry, Robert Stern, Antoine Predock and Arata Isozaki – offered some names. But in the end it was the Clinton's decorator who suggested that they talk to James Polshek, an architect who had recently completed New York's Museum of Natural History and who had no known Republican sympathies. Clinton had definite ideas about what he wanted. He was looking to use his library, as Jimmy Carter had done, as the springboard for the next step in his career as a freelance international elder statesman.

As a piece of planning, the Carter Library does much better than Bush's, but its architecture is glum to the point of catatonia. It occupies a suburban site in a leafy residential neighbourhood full of big comfortable houses with landscaped grounds where middle-class soccer moms take the dog for a walk on a Saturday. It's very close to Atlanta's downtown, not far from the World of Coke and the Martin Luther King historic site. Landscaping took a higher priority than architecture. Car parking is screened out of site, and visitors walk to the entrance through the formal symmetry of a garden arranged around a series of pools, flanked on both sides by white park benches and pergolas, like the country retreat of a retired Caesar. The illusion is somewhat undermined by the sign warning visitors that a shirt and shoes are required. But behind this dignified approach, the design breaks down into a banal series of circular pavilions that betray the faintest of faint echoes of Frank Lloyd Wright's style, no more than the cosmic hum left after the Big Bang. The two large pavilions on the left are the library and the museum. On the right are five smaller interlinked circles that house Carter's offices. Straight ahead, a series of landscaped gardens and lakes look out over Atlanta's skyscrapers in the distance. But inside, the layout is inept and the exhibits unfortunate. Access is through one of two 250-seater cinemas, placed back to back and designed to show the introductory film continuously, an inflated provision that is the product of euphoric over-optimism about visitor numbers. On the wall that proclaims the former president to be a peacemaker and protector of human rights, Carter invites the non-existent crowds 'to consider some of these decisions that I had to make, and as you visit with us today, to ask yourself what importance they have and then to come to the town meeting to discuss them with me'. The town meeting turns out to be a dismal space under a rotunda less convincing even than Bush's, with five people sitting on the benches, and Carter's blotchy orange image playing to the camera on a flickering TV screen.

There are no mannequins dressed as soldiers here and no rock music playing over the PA system. Just a reminder of the Nobel Peace Prize awarded to Carter in Oslo in 2002 in the form of a particularly hideous painting on velvet by Vald Jensen and a lunch table laid for Deng's state visit in 1979. Well actually only half of it: a mirror in the middle does the rest. In another corner is a hefty automatic voting machine of the hanging chad era. It's configured for the Carter–Reagan election. There are places on the ballot for endless state and county offices, for the Libertarian Party, and for Angela Davis. With perhaps unnecessary frankness, it seems to have been set by someone who was not planning to vote for Carter.

Clinton wanted the same combination of library and offices. It's hard to imagine him entirely turning his back on his base in Harlem for Little Rock, the city that came up with $17 million to persuade him to set up there. But he has ended up with a piece of architecture as impressive as that of any of the presidents, one of the few that addresses an urban context, and which plays its part in the renewal of a run-down area of the city. It takes the form of a glass bridge cantilevered out over the river with a spectacular view over the city.

'We were invited to the White House in 1999,' says Polshek. 'We got 90 minutes in the Oval Office. We took an associate partner from Little Rock with us and they got on right away. Clinton said, "Will you do one of those napkin sketches, you architects do?"' Polshek told him they are apocryphal. 'But we do them sometimes, Mr President.'

Polshek wasn't going to risk letting the job slip out of his hands by limiting himself to just one sketch. He and his partner worked on three different designs, drew them up, and built three detailed models to explain them to an audience unfamiliar with architectural drawings. 'We presented on the night of the Columbine massacre. He was late, which was unusual. He came in very agitated and red eyed. His first words; "Here as we speak, they are killing our children." He gave us 45 minutes in the map room.'

Polshek advised against the greenfield site the city had offered. It was too obvious and too easy. 'We ended up on brownfield railroad land that could act as a catalyst for development.' It's a site littered with industrial history: the Union Pacific and the Rock Island lines both crossed the river here. And the 100-year-old Choctaw Bridge across the Arkansas River, now disused, provides a handsome fragment of industrial archaeology. It also turned out to be immediately next to the local newspaper, the *Arkansas Democratic Gazette*, which was violently opposed to the building of the library. Polshek offered Clinton three conceptual strategies for the library. Did the president see it as a villa in a park, a campus, or a single major building? Then there was the question of how to realize the strategy. The first version was to align the library along the Arkansas River frontage, but that didn't seem to be making the most of the site. 'We had a joint epiphany, when we realized that if we made the building perpendicular to the river, its principal views would be to the west and downtown. You could look up and down, see six bridges, and so become fully aware of the city.'

As well as the museum, the building includes a big meeting hall and a suite of offices for the Clinton Foundation. The form of the building, a glass cantilevered structure, came from the bridges. It can be read as a contextual gesture, but also as a metaphor that Clinton could identify with. As the detailed design evolved, Clinton kept coming back to the idea of the glass bridge. 'In a political way, and for reasons that have never been explicitly stated, he is very concerned about openness, which is why he wanted there to be so much daylight,' says Polshek. 'The National Archives and Records Administration expected a blank box for the library, but Clinton was clear that the staff shouldn't live like moles. So we put the people up in light in a pavilion on the roof, and the books in the vault.'

Despite their painfully obvious limitations, the presidential libraries belong to a long line of would-be architectural monuments stretching all the way back to the Library of Alexandria and beyond. In their gestures towards making an enduring mark, they can be understood as being driven by the same impulses that motivated Imhotep and Augustus, Louis XIV and Napoleon III, to say nothing of François Mitterrand. All of them have attempted to put architecture to work to defy the inevitability of death, to dignify their own lives, to shape a city and to find the consolation of a sense of meaning in an orderless world. The Bush and Reagan libraries are perhaps more limited in ambition than their predecessors, but they are still as much political as architectural statements.

With their display cases of tributes accumulated over the decades, their accounts of valour in battle and public service, and the celebration of a leader's triumph over the enemies of the State, they have uncomfortable parallels with the practices of those later Roman emperors who had themselves deified. If there were ever going to be a cult of president worship, the libraries are where it would start. But unlike their predecessors, the presidential libraries belong to a period that is agnostic about the possibility of making a lasting mark. Perhaps we have simply seen too much history and too many ruins to believe in architecture as a manifestation of a state religion anymore. Despite their ambitions, the libraries – Bunshaft's acropolis in Austin excepted – mostly seem flimsy enough to blow away at any moment, leaving nothing behind. Most are simply not up to the architectural part that they are intended to play.

In France they do things differently. François Mitterrand, the most imperial of recent French presidents, was much more prepared to take a personal interest in his library than Bush the Elder. On a December morning at the very end of 1995, Mitterrand rose from his sickbed. His veins were flooded with morphine to dull the excruciating pain of the pancreatic cancer that would finally kill him three weeks later, and he was dressed, slowly, in a suit that had now become too big for him. After his puffy face had been powdered for the television cameras, he was driven to Tolbiac, in working-class eastern Paris, to preside over the opening of the French National Library. Never mind that it was the opening of a library with no books – of the 10 million volumes that the 39 kilometres of shelves had been designed to handle, just 180,000 were in place. Never mind that it would be another two years before all the staff moved in. This was a building that Mitterrand himself had conceived, and he imposed it on the country in the teeth of the bitter hostility of France's scholars.

Death had been much on his mind in the last years of his presidency. The philosophers he used to invite to dinner at the Elysée would find themselves drawn into long mediations with the President on the meaning of mortality. Books, readers or librarians were not the issue. For Mitterrand, seeing his personal monument finished was all that counted. He had chosen the untested Dominique Perrault as the architect himself. And in the knowledge that he was nearing the end, he found the $500 million needed to force construction to move at breakneck speed expressly so that he could experience a glimpse of immortality in the glassy splendour of the world's most modern library – a library that would bear his name.

Mitterrand always had a taste for Euclidian geometry. The pyramid at the Louvre and the open cube at La Défense were both products of his personal preferences. Now he had the library with its four, wildly impractical eighteen-storey towers looming over the Seine, marking the corners of a huge sunken garden. Short of installing his tomb here, the comparison with Napoleon's last resting place at Les Invalides could not be clearer. The architect's original idea of putting the books in the towers and the readers in the base had to be inverted to ensure that precious first editions did not fry inside the glass towers, or risk being soaked by the Seine if it burst its banks. Perrault's design no longer made sense as anything other than a mausoleum. But there was no time for him to change the library's shape if the President's timetable was to be met. Mitterrand insisted that it was to be met, even at the expense of his architect's reputation.

A Tomb at the Drive-In

Given that it has a best-seats-in-the-house view of the Orange County freeway, Richard Meier's new visitor centre for the Crystal Cathedral is finished in a particularly appropriate shade of BMW dealership silver. On the second floor a piece of construction debris has been left behind by the contractors and is still waiting to be tidied away. It is only after a second or even a third look that you notice that the shrivelled and blistered strip of tarmac, the bitumen-patched, tar paper damp-proofing, and the rough-sawn timber joists supporting them have all been lovingly laid to rest on a cube of polished travertine, signalling that they are to be understood as sacred relics and not garbage. And on this tarmac in ancient time those feet did indeed walk. This is, as the peeling paper caption tells you, an original section of the roof from the now demolished snack bar at the Orange County Drive-in Theater on which the Reverend Robert Schuller took up his stand one Sunday in March 1955, to conduct what he describes as his very first worship service.

For musical accompaniment, Schuller and his wife had bought a church organ on easy terms. They towed it to the drive-in behind their station wagon that morning. He preached to a congregation of fifty, attracted by his advertisements in the local paper. Sitting in their Plymouths and their Buick coupés with the tops down, they listened respectfully to his sunny message of blithe can-do optimism crackling out on the public address system over the fan-shaped parking lot. Next to the marble cube is a perspex box sitting on a plinth. It contains a collecting plate, piled up with $83.75 in 1955 vintage quarters, pennies and dollars, and the occasional five-dollar bill, the exact sum raised by that first collection.

In a small way, Schuller has done for architecture what Oprah Winfrey did for American literature, and he provides a compelling reminder of just how much religions of all kinds depend on architecture to convey their message, motivate their followers and put themselves ahead of their rivals. There are still people who listen to the Revd Robert Schuller's Sunday sermons in their cars. But his ministry has expanded enormously, thanks in part to his weakness for collecting famous architects and exploiting them for their publicity potential. Ten years after that sermon, Schuller moved up the road from the Orange Theater to Garden Grove, where, with Richard Neutra as his designer, he built what he called the world's first walk-in/drive-in church. Schuller's congregation went on growing, to the point that, after a series of additions to the first building, he decided that he needed a second church on an adjacent site. This was what became the Crystal Cathedral, as Philip Johnson's gigantic glass iceberg, completed at the end of the 1970s, is known. And now Richard Meier has added his steel drum to the acres of gardens that constitute Schuller's personal version of the Vatican City, to offer visitors something to do when services are over.

The gardeners and the maintenance men tending the Crystal Cathedral's grounds in the summer heat murmur quietly to each other in Spanish, even though the improving, upbeat biblical messages scattered everywhere are all in determinedly monoglot English. At the entrance to the cathedral is a Holy Family group, equipped with donkey, and carved with such startling, lifeless banality that it is hard to understand how it can share the same universe as Johnson's svelte and knowing architecture. But it is just one of scores of art works of equally numbing mindlessness distributed all over the site. Under the bell tower in a special circular chamber lined with a stockade of multi-coloured marble columns and equipped with a glass door is a rotating Christ, easily mistaken for a hologram, but actually hollowed out of a clear perspex cube. How is it possible that the same man who took such a sophisticated approach to commissioning architecture and used it as an effective propaganda weapon for his church could believe that this was art? These are not questions that seem to have occurred to the Revd Robert Schuller. He is a cleric untroubled by false humility. Indeed at every stage in his career he has taken a special pride in coaxing his congregations to reach deeper and deeper into their pockets to build churches that are bigger and more ambitious than the barns that were expected of him and his kind. 'I am an Iowa farm boy. Where did my passion for great art and architecture come from?' he asks himself with cloying immodesty in his autobiography. 'I cannot build just anything, It has to glorify God, so qualifying as a thing of beauty that will be a joy for ever.'

But Schuller does confess to having been deeply hurt when he read the parable that the Reverend Wendell Karsen, a missionary in Hong Kong, wrote about his church in the *Church Herald*. Karsen, as Schuller tells it, imagined the wretched of the earth converging on Garden Grove for a glimpse of the Crystal Cathedral, only to see their reflections in the mirror glass and reeling back, shocked at the image of their misery. 'One of them picks up a rock, and throws it at his own image. Others follow suit, until the cathedral is reduced to rubble, then ransacked by the starving in search of food and raw materials to ease their suffering.'

Schuller consoled himself with the thought that he had been misunderstood. All the money apparently spent on the building had actually gone to a good cause, feeding the families of its builders, and he seems to have shrugged off the hurt easily enough. 'For whatever reason, critics such as the Reverend Karsen failed to see the role played by great monuments throughout the history of the church. The cathedrals at Chartres and Notre Dame, along with Westminster Abbey and St Peter's in Rome continue to inspire us centuries after the last workers set the last stone in place, and inlaid the last stained glass window.' This is true, though it is a somewhat self-regarding comparison to the warped space-frame structure and its liver-coloured marble podium that he commissioned from Philip Johnson.

Sitting in Richard Meier's snowdrift-white office in Manhattan, where the draftsmen are corralled in little cattle pens to make space for an exhibition of his work, I ask him if he ever discussed art with Schuller.

'No,' he smiles a little weakly. 'No.'

So how did he get to meet his client?

'I was elected to the American Academy of Achievement, for their Man of the Year Award. When I went to the dinner in Jackson Hole, he was there. And we talked. People are put off by his exuberance and passion. But I like him.'

Schuller is a Christian, but his theology is concentrated, as he puts it, on individual responsibility and self-improvement. There is a lot more focus on his homilies, inscribed in foot-high, chrome-plated steel letters pinned to Meier's walls, than there is on Christ's suffering. Rather than being offered more challenging spiritual insights, visitors are promised 'Inch by inch, and everything is a cinch', and 'Tough times never last, but tough people do'.

Meier is not a Christian, and the Visitor Center is not, so he says, a religious building. Its purpose is to provide a public space that offers visitors somewhere to spend time before and after services, filling the spiritual void between the car park and the pews. There is a chapel on the top floor – a sunlit white space without an altar, but equipped with some uplifting paragraphs from Philippians inscribed on the wall, a few dozen office chairs arranged in a horseshoe, and a view of the cemetery. It hardly registers against the far more dramatic spaces below it that serve to define the building's purpose.

Meier's architecture exudes a sense of light-filled elegance that sits uncomfortably with some of the things it contains. Even his soberly tasteful carpets seem to be shrinking away in alarm from the burden of sickly sentiment that they are expected to carry. In the exhibition space, next to the fragment of the snack bar roof, is a dismaying procession of larger than life-size bronze representations of a selection of the preachers who have visited Garden Grove over the years. They show a wildly ecumenical taste in their costumes. Billy Graham is in a western suit and stacked heels. Bishop Fulton J. Sheen, the first television evangelist, is resplendent in full cardinal's get-up, complete with cap, cape and ring, alongside a somewhat alarming statue of Schuller himself, suggesting that the eventual purpose of the Visitor Center might also be to provide a tomb for its founder. There is a jarring mismatch between the objects and their museum-like context. Look at the objects in isolation, and you see them as overwhelmingly kitsch. Against the background of the white walls, and the subdued palette of materials, your preconceptions try to wrench your brain into understanding them in a different way. Two Americas that very seldom meet have come face to uncomprehending face here.

Schuller is not so certain that this isn't at some level a religious building. It is, he says several times, a 'museum that motivates'. Every visitor is handed a leaflet that tells them, 'You are standing in the middle of a sermon that has been lived.' To the agnostic eye, this could be the standard off-the-shelf Richard Meier museum atrium, as seen in Atlanta, Frankfurt, Barcelona, and half a dozen other cities: a soaring space, shaped by heroic architectural gestures and a Corbusian-inspired geometry. We have become so accustomed to museums that take on the role of the sacred spaces of the modern world that it should be no surprise to see a semi-religious space attempting, not entirely convincingly, to look like a museum. The east wall is a great sail of glass that forms the backdrop against which a white steel ramp zigzags back and forth on its journey to the roof. There are inevitably a lot of external staircases and elaborately cantilevered balconies etched against the sky, the kind of things that Meier has perfected over the years and can now build in his sleep.

The doors at the entrance slide out of sight to open up most of the ground floor to the sunshine and the gardens. But instead of the predictable black leather and tubular steel Le Corbusier armchairs that you would expect to find in such a space, it is furnished with the kind of reproduction antique furniture and generic sofas that you can see over tea and cucumber sandwiches in the lobby of the Kuala Lumpur Shangri-La Hotel. The cut flowers on the low tables are 'lovingly donated by the Sterling family'. Instead of the installations by Boltansky, the canvases by Clemente, and the inevitable Serra sculpture that are the conventional background to Meier's architecture, there is only a portrait of Robert H. Schuller, a gift of Lyt and Venita Harris. Schuller is depicted as a luxuriantly silver-haired, red-faced patriarch in his pastor's robes, which would look as if they had been borrowed from one of America's more conservative university deans were it not for the two-tone purple and violet colour scheme. His gown, worn over a conventional collar and tie, is exactly the same as the outfits adopted by the rest of his priesthood, but for the two additional patches of imperial purple on the collar.

There are other elements familiar from the contemporary museum in this space, but all of them have been subtly distorted. There is a museum café of course, except that here it is designated as the food court – called the Miracle Café: 'We serve Starbucks with pride'. And there is a shop, but rather than the usual collection of impressionist postcards and miniature versions of iconic modern movement furniture, it sells God's Health Plan ('adds years to your life'), blue and pink velour Crystal Cathedral leisure suits, Crystal Cathedral mints in tins inscribed 'God loves you, and so do I', and glassware designed by Richard Meier. A red-jacketed guide sets off with a group of visitors every half-hour on a tour of the art collection in the grounds and the architectural highlights of the cathedral campus. There is a ticket counter too, where you can make reservations for the services at the Crystal Cathedral just across the plaza. And of course there is a donor wall, just like the one in every museum in America. Except that for once there is no coyness about naming names. Next to the shop is a white granite wall on which the names of 'the pillars of this construction project' have been etched. According to the inscription, which radiates a degree of social insecurity that seems curious in an organization that is otherwise so sure of itself and its faith, 'The founders of this international center for possibility thinking', as the Visitor Center is called by everybody except its architect, 'are the first people to step forward and embrace the dream of this world class structure. Each committed a gift of $1000 or more to provide funds to retain one of the greatest world recognised architects of the 21st century, Richard Meier, commissioning him to capture the dream and design a timeless physical frame for this ministry to see the home site of the crystal cathedral.' It does seem uncomfortably important to the Revd Schuller to suggest that the eyes of the world, as well as God's, are on Garden Grove.

For those pillars of the church who weren't quite so quick off the mark with their chequebooks, beyond the wall there is still the promise of the incomplete transparent crystal-brick wall glowing with light tinged the palest of pink. Visitors are invited to 'gaze at its glistening majesty, each name engraved for the ages, by a donor who made a $500 gift possible to help construct this magnificent structure. Add your name here.' As another of those stainless-steel sentences distributed throughout the building blithely proclaims: 'There is never a money problem, only an idea problem'. But to judge by the exposed raw roof trusses, and the air-conditioning ducts visible in the exhibition space, there is still room for a few more donations yet to finish off the museum that motivates.

Overhead, at the top of the atrium, three huge light collectors are intended perhaps to convey the only subliminal religious message contained in the entire structure: they may, or may not, be hinting at the concept of the Trinity. For Meier, light is the acceptable face of the sacred. But everything else in the way of a religious message in the building has been reduced to the blindingly obvious by his client. For almost two thousand years even the simplest and the humblest Christian churches have been loaded with iconography and an imagery explicit enough to allow the faithful to read a religious message in their architecture and the art that they contain. But they have been capable of being interpreted on a variety of different levels, from overt symbolism to more occult readings, through orientation, plan and detail. Schuller has built a church for the age of large-print books for the visually impaired. It leaves no room for doubt or personal interpretation, or subtlety. It reduces the consolations of religion to an Esperanto cartoon, a subtitle, or an advertising jingle.

'If you can dream it, you can do it.' Visitors are handed a leaflet from Dr Robert H. Schuller inviting them to experience what he calls a structure with a sermon. 'Every structure makes a statement, but this exciting new building is the first structure ever designed to preach a life-affirming, dream-building, possibility-thinking sermon. Check them off as you go. First of all, the sermon starts with a BIBLE VERSE. In the glorious Grand Lobby of this elegant new Richard Meier structure, stand in the center of the lobby and look up at the glistening stainless steel letters to read the timeless words of Jesus Christ.'

And when the self-guided tour, sprinkled with an abundance of capital letters and exclamation marks and glistening adjectives, is over, the leaflet suggests that, as they do after every good sermon, people like to go and have something to eat, and maybe go shopping. And that's all on hand, in the shape of the food court and the store.

Schuller was born into a Dutch Reform Church family in rural America, with the conservative prejudices of his kind. He felt his calling as a young man and set out to take religion from the farm to the godless suburbs. His ministry began in Chicago, and for a time he broke with the National Council of Churches for being too soft on Communism. The Soviet Union repaid the compliment by featuring him in Leningrad's Cathedral, after it was converted into the Museum of Atheism, as a wicked exploiter of the gullibility of the masses by soaking them of their savings to pay for his churches. He evolved into a freeway evangelist with a sunnier disposition, taking a more ecumenical view than most of his peers. He dropped the paranoia and started meeting popes and rabbis and communists. There is even an image of a bemused Mikhail Gorbachev at the Crystal Cathedral. Schuller was ready to hire Philip Johnson, an unabashed homosexual, and Richard Meier, who is a Jew.

'Don't call yourself a Dutch Reform, or a Methodist Church,' he once advised tyro pastors and ministers planning their first move into the exploding and churchless new suburbs of southern California. 'Drop the labels, and call yourself a community church.' It's a formula that has certainly been successful. Every Sunday, Schuller's congregation comes from all over the Los Angeles sprawl, pouring into Garden Grove and crowding the car pool lane. They fill the seats of the Crystal Cathedral for a service, or perhaps performance is a better word, that is broadcast around the world as the *Hour of Power* on Christian cable channels and seen, Schuller claims, by twenty million people every week.

The Crystal Cathedral delivers an audience that Americans on the stump with a political axe to grind, or a book to sell, have been almost as eager to cultivate as Oprah Winfrey's. The *Hour of Power* has featured Gerald Ford and Dan Quayle, Charlton Heston and Ray Kroc, Norman Schwarzkopf, and even Philip Johnson, who brazenly claimed divine inspiration for his design for the cathedral.

The campus has grown continually over the years, relentlessly swallowing up orange groves and walnut trees and the tract houses that used to surround it, in plots ten acres at a time. In its hunger for more land, it has even taken on the local shopping centre and outbid it. To record the scale of the giving that has made it all possible, Garden Grove's pavements are embossed with the names of donors, each one set in a framed border shaped like the Crystal Cathedral's floor plan. The effect is very much like the Walk of the Stars on the pavement outside Grumman's Chinese Theater in Hollywood.

On Easter Sunday, such is the demand for seats for the Glory of Easter, a service that promises live animals, flying angels and professional actors, that there are no fewer than eight performances through the day. Big for Schuller is better. Larger and larger congregations are the way to reach ever more people, by creating the sense of a shared civic occasion that only religion and sport can now offer in the suburbs. And they provide a bigger pool of donors to build bigger churches. The Crystal Cathedral is the church that says it has the fifth-largest organ in the world and claims to have the biggest cross and the longest stone wall in architectural history – unaccountably, the well-travelled pastor who could teach Donald Trump a thing or two about self-promotion seems not yet to have encountered the Great Wall of China.

The view of the cathedral from the freeway is a critical part of Schuller's strategy for attracting the larger and larger congregations that are needed to fill his steadily increasing numbers of seats and parking places. As you drive through Orange County, the ivy-decked noise barriers that edge both sides of the road hide most of the landscape, rendering any building without a tower invisible. All you see are the very tops of things. Bits of shopping centres, inspired at considerable distance by Daniel Libeskind and Frank Gehry, bob up and down in the aimless flotsam of multiplexes and malls that come swimming into view as you head south. Then there is a Sheraton Hotel, disguised as a Disney castle, to be followed soon after by the 'real' thing: Disney's towers picked out in a palette of pastel colours that warn you that you are getting closer to Schuller's Vatican. Gliding past Anaheim you glimpse fragments of the Mouse Kingdom's helter-skelters. The freeways themselves are developing their own version of white-knuckle rides, terrifying linguini-thin concrete viaducts exploding in starbursts above the clover-leaf intersections. Then on the left you can see the Angel Stadium, fronted by a pair of giant orange baseball caps. And on the right, the Crystal Cathedral comes into view. Slightly detached from the main building, Johnson's chrome-plated paraphrase of a campanile marks out the presence of the complex on the Orange County flatlands, just like the turrets of Disneyland a mile away. There is no danger of actually hearing the bells from the freeway, but Schuller wanted the tower anyway. It's both a signpost and an advertising hoarding. The diffuse scale of Los Angeles makes the tower an essential response to its context, providing an updated version of a very traditional element on the urban skyline. The Crystal Cathedral faces the Tower of Hope, a stubby cream-coloured block designed by Richard Neutra that contains Schuller's offices and which is topped by a chapel and the outsize cross. The most recent addition to the complex, Meier's drum-shaped Visitor Center, floats midway between Neutra and Johnson.

When Schuller first began building up his church, he realized instinctively that he needed something to make him stand out from the competition. The Orange Drive-in was all very well as a base for the early days of the movement, but the area was rapidly turning into a new type of city rather than a suburb and Schuller wanted to build a church with the appropriate civic presence to match his maturing audience.

Just like the Mormons, who defined themselves with their massive complex of temples in Salt Lake City, or the Seventh-Day Adventists, whose sub Frank Lloyd Wright style churches span the globe like gas stations, or for that matter the Cistercians, who had defined the distinctive form of their churches and monasteries eight hundred years ago, Schuller needed an architect to help him get his message across in the most memorable way possible. His permanent church was meant to embody the open-air origins of his ministry; that meant lots of glass, and creating the sense of the outdoors, even when the congregation was indoors. And an expanding new congregation could use the reassuring endorsement of hiring a big-name architect to design its church, just as America's small-town banks have always tried to strike a balance between looking imposing enough to suggest that your money was secure, but not so over-endowed with marble and Corinthian columns as to look as if it was being squandered.

Richard Neutra's picture had recently been on the cover of *Time* magazine, talking about his interest in nature and the outdoors, a combination of celebrity and hokey philosophizing that was enough to arouse the clergyman's interest. Schuller drove up to his office to see him, with his own sketch for the 'walk-in, drive-in cathedral'. As Schuller tells it, his opening gambit was to ask Neutra why he should work with him. Schuller was duly impressed by the Austrian-born

Neutra's immediate reply: 'Hire me, and your buildings will never go out of style.'

Over the years, Neutra ended up working on four projects at Garden Grove. There is the glass-walled church itself, a meeting room, a bell frame, and finally the office tower with its huge cross on the roof. These were not Neutra's best works – he was reaching the end of his creative life when he worked on them. But, in their context, they have a certain dignity that is still apparent. Certainly they were the nearest thing to architectural high culture in Orange County at the time.

Schuller insists on claiming at least part of the credit for designing them. According to the exhibition in the Meier building, Schuller 'was acquainted with Richard Neutra, one of the great architects of the time, whose philosophy was called biorealism. The two men are a team, and bring to the world a new and different kind of church building, marrying the outside with the inside.' That the church has no stained glass was the result of Neutra successfully persuading Schuller that he should keep the lines of the church 'clean, sharp and vertical'. This was not how Schuller had envisaged his church would look. But when it was finished he made it part of his identity, and the Johnson church ended up with no stained glass either.

With rubble stone walls laid in vertical bands, and the surrealistic tricks that Neutra plays with cut-outs at the foot of the masonry to make it look as if it is floating, this is a highly mannered form of church architecture. Schuller was unconcerned by Neutra's lack of commitment to his religion. He was happy enough with his architect's enthusiastic embrace of sunshine and nature, and his fame. It was to supply the leitmotif for all Schuller's buildings. He kept coming back to the idea of preaching in the open air, just as he had done on the roof of that snack bar at the original drive-in site, and he asked his architects to interpret that spirit in their buildings.

It was certainly the basis of Philip Johnson's work at Garden Grove. According to the exhibition's commentary, the brief for the design was the product of Schuller's prayers: 'Lord, if we must build a new sanctuary, let it have glass walls and a glass roof. Let me see again the blue skies and the trees.' The white-painted structural steel of the Crystal Cathedral, invisible from the outside, makes you feel as if you are in the middle of a cloud when you go inside. Johnson was a shrewd choice on the part of Schuller in the 1970s. He was at just the point in his career when he would start to achieve his highest visibility. And Schuller knew how to get what he needed out of him. Johnson's first design was a relatively conventional church. Schuller's response was lukewarm. What he needed was something spectacular, and Johnson got the message. The cathedral turned out to be one of his most photogenic projects, an advertisement for both Johnson's architecture and Schuller's church that was constantly being photographed and published. And the association with as established a figure as Johnson helped shift the church away from the perception that it was a marginalized sect.

When Schuller first appeared in Johnson's office with his sketches and his tales of working with Neutra, Johnson was apparently under the impression that Schuller was himself an architect looking for a job. He told Johnson what he really wanted. There had to be seating for a congregation of 3,000, and the building must blend and not compete with the Neutra tower, bell frame or sanctuary. Then he explained that there was no money to build it – the Lord would obviously provide. In the meantime, Schuller took out a bank loan to pay Johnson his fee. Shortly after, at the church's twentieth anniversary, Schuller set about the process of raising the cash. He stood before an audience of 7,000 people to talk about the future and elevated the host, or rather he held up a little model of Johnson's building, high over his head. 'I believe that this project will be validated by a $1m gift, soon,' Schuller declared. The money duly materialized on time. Building the church, however, was more expensive, and more technically demanding, than he had expected. Schuller wanted an all-glass structure in an earthquake zone and, to complicate things still further, California was just beginning to think about enforcing energy-saving building codes. But he managed it, raising the money and dealing with the complex nature of the construction process. And at one bound the Crystal Cathedral leapfrogged Schuller over the heads of his rivals in the increasingly competitive world of television evangelism. The zigzag space frames left exposed inside the building, and the elegantly fabricated glass exterior, made Schuller's congregation look like the confident face of the future – 'a world class building', as Schuller would and does say, over and over again, not a dim provincial has-been. The low-rent preachers, the Swaggerts and the Bakkers, were in trouble already, but the Crystal Cathedral left them for dead. Johnson had given Schuller's ministry a draw that made even Neutra's buildings, with their rubble stone walls and their tapering exposed steel joists, look a little flat.

The Garden Grove Vatican has grown and grown, just like a museum. Except that here, the decisions are all taken by the Reverend Schuller, in consultation with the Almighty, rather than a boardroom of quarrelsome trustees. It's easy to scoff at the Crystal Cathedral mints, the copies of the God Diet piled high in the bookstore, at the little shopping bags with a silver-embossed representation of the Crystal Cathedral, just like something from Bloomingdale's, and the message on the Cathedral's director of communication's answering machine that assures you, out of the blue, that 'God loves you'. But the buildings are something else. As Richard Meier says, without architecture, what would there be at Garden Grove?

On the surface, the Crystal Cathedral has the charisma and the confidence to make you think that it represents religion in a form to be reckoned with. But even the most cursory trip around Los Angeles' recently built Cathedral of our Lady of the Angels shows just how far any newly established denomination has to go to catch up with the Bishop of Rome. Los Angeles' new cathedral, a replacement for the earthquake-damaged nineteenth-century structure of St Vibiana, over-looks the freeways, just across the street from Frank Gehry's Disney Concert Hall, but it feels as if it has all the weight and authority and wealth of a 2,000-year-old organization behind every detail. It was designed by Rafael Moneo, an architect who began his career with Jorn Utzon working on the design of the Sydney Opera House, and it says a lot about the continuing role of architecture in religion. It is an attempt at creating an example of one of the oldest urban institutions in the centre of a very new kind of ultra-decentralized city. It hints at the increasingly Hispanic character of Los Angeles, but in Rupert Murdoch's financial support for the project it also reflects the contemporary restlessness of power in the city. And like the Crystal Cathedral, it has attracted bitter criticism from those who see it as money squandered on vanity and self-promotion, rather than put to work by the Church in serving the pressing needs of the poor.

This is a cathedral designed by a European architect in a manner that struggles to reconcile a traditional idea of what a cathedral should be with the realities of life in California. It sits on top of four levels of parking: the faithful make their way here by taking the lift. Moneo has given the cathedral a pedestrian square, but it is marooned and isolated from the streets around it, hanging over the edge of the Hollywood freeway. Moneo optimistically describes its twelve lanes of melting asphalt as the contemporary equivalent of a river but, as if unconvinced by the metaphor, has tried to screen and protect the cathedral from its impact as much as possible. The effect is closer to a walled monastery, with a sense of enclosure and retreat from the world outside, than a cathedral as the focus for a religion engaged with the city around it.

Like Schuller's church, Our Lady of the Angels can seat 3,000 people. It is part of a complex that includes a rectory for the Archbishop and his resident priests. There is a businesslike conference centre, and offices planned around a cloister garden. The two-level plaza is overshadowed by the 150-feet-high campanile.

Moneo deliberately avoided making an entrance opening directly from the street. Instead pedestrians enter at the lower level of the walled plaza and move up a grand staircase to the upper plaza. From there they are pulled up and into the church, towards pews and the altar. It is a route that is designed to give worshippers the sense of the spiritual journey of the individual, moving gradually from the profane to the sacred, a journey that takes them upward into the light as their feet tread the Spanish limestone floor.

The liturgical content of the church is a mix of the comfortably familiar and the safely innovative. Rather than entering from the west end, directly facing the altar, the church is designed with two ambulatories, one that takes visitors past a series of side chapels, the other that provides access to the crypt.

Moneo veers between evoking the massive masonry structures of Gothic Europe and responding to the context of California and its own complex traditions. The massive yellow-ochre concrete walls of the structure refer to the mission architecture of the earliest Spanish colonial settlements in Los Angeles. But the result is flabby and puffy, rather than the highly crafted piece of architectural sculpture that

Moneo had clearly intended it to be. The interior, with its zigzag route to the body of the church, is clearly intended to orchestrate a mounting sense of expectation. The main entrance is to one side of the altar, and forms the beginning of a processional route upward that requires a sharp turn. Once negotiated, it reveals the altar – picked out in sunlight that has been carefully filtered through veined alabaster – only when visitors have had time to adjust to the solemnity of their surroundings. From the north ambulatory, a staircase provides access down into the crypt, embellished by stained-glass windows made in Germany in the 1920s and salvaged from the old cathedral of St Vibiana that Moneo's building replaces. Niches and tombs here are marketed like apartments in a new condominium tower. A few well-placed leaks about who has been looking over them for space, and the bookings just come flooding in. The emotional resonances of the routine religious art in Moneo's cathedral are no more convincing than the banality of the work at the Crystal Cathedral.

There are parallels between the design of a place of worship and a theatre. In a traditional nave, with rows of parallel pews arranged on either side of an aisle and facing directly towards a pulpit, the awareness of the congregation of its own presence is limited. A series of tiers facing each other, as in a theatre in the round, does more to make the members of a congregation aware of each other's presence. And like the abolition of the proscenium arch in the theatre, the arrangement makes a congregation feel more like an active participant in a religious ceremony, rather than a passive spectator. But there are limits to the architect's role in achieving this. Too much design, and it is not just those traditionalists who put a premium on maintaining forms sanctioned by precedent who begin to feel as if they are being consciously manipulated, and that their faith is being invoked by artificial or synthetic means.

Religious art may have declined into the mindless production of the routine and the lifeless, characterized by crucifixes turned out on an industrial scale, lacking in aesthetic ambition or conviction. But familiar banality can still seem less threatening than objects that have been touched by a genuinely creative, but potentially disturbing vision. The vacuity of so much contemporary religious art is an issue that has seriously exercised Christian intellectuals for at least a century. Father Marie-Alain Couturier, the French Dominican priest who initiated a renaissance in sacred art in the 1940s, believed that part of the responsibility for the decline of the Church's appeal in the second half of the twentieth century lay in its loss of a link with the creative arts. The sculpture associated with the Church, and religious art in general, had become a hermetic category lacking in any freshness or conviction. More cautious Catholics could see this but were worried by the risks the Church would be taking by commissioning contemporary art. Couturier tried to overcome their anxiety by setting an example, showing what was possible with a series of demonstrations. He was responsible for Henri Matisse being commissioned by the Church to decorate the interior of the chapel of St Paul de Vence and to design the vestments for its priests, setting a precedent that was followed around the world. And it was Couturier who put forward Le Corbusier's name for the two great religious commissions of his career: the pilgrimage church of Ronchamp in south-eastern France, and the Dominican monastery of La Tourette. Together, they served to set a new model for contemporary religious architecture, with strongly sculptural forms and a sense of sanctuary and enclosure, as well as an appropriation of natural light to reveal and conceal architectural forms, creating a sense of dematerialization, and mystery.

Couturier's commissions encouraged Catholic dioceses around the world to experiment with more challenging architects. And the Catholic Church has shown continuing interest in attempting to present itself as part of the contemporary world in architectural terms. It's an impulse that can be seen in the Vatican's celebration of the second millennium with Richard Meier's Dio Padre Misericordioso jubilee church in suburban Rome, after an international competition in which other architects, including Frank Gehry and Peter Eisenman, were also asked to compete, or in the monks of Novy Dvur in the Czech Republic, who commissioned John Pawson to build Eastern Europe's first new monastery in a century.

'Light is the means by which we are able to experience what we call sacred,' says Meier, with a telling use of the word as a euphemism for the spiritual. The three shells of Meier's church create an enveloping atmosphere, in which the light from the skylights above creates what he calls 'a luminous spatial experience' and in which 'rays of sunlight serve as a mystic metamorphosis of the presence of God'. For Meier, 'The jubilee church will show the true modernity of the Catholic Church's efforts to adapt to the revolutionary time we live in.' But he found the process of designing the church in Rome was much more opaque than working with Schuller in Garden Grove. 'Schuller's participation was very evident at the beginning and the end of the design process. He might change his mind, but you know where you are. With the Vatican it's never so clear.' Meier says that his only argument in Rome was about the cross over the altar. 'I wanted simple geometry. The church insisted on a representation of Christ on the Cross. So I said I am sure we can find something from the 16th century in the Vatican's basements. Well we ended up with a 19th century cross that turned out to be papier mâché.'

Religion has continually used architecture as a propaganda vehicle and to create a shared sense of identity. A religious building is devised to make the individual worshipper feel a sense of belonging to the larger body of the faithful, and in some sense to play a part in revealing sacred truths – thus the particular concern with orientation common to the major religions. Every mosque must face in the same direction. For Christian churches there is a presumption in favour of placing the altar at the east end, facing towards Jerusalem and the rising sun. The cruciform plan was inspired by the body of Christ on the Cross.

In the mosque, the representation of the human figure is unacceptable. Christian attitudes have fluctuated on the issue. At various times iconoclastic sects and assorted species of puritans have decried the depiction of the human figure in religious art as idolatrous, or blasphemous. Equally, certain architectural languages have become associated with certain religious movements. In the nineteenth century some reformers equated the Gothic, pointed style with truly Christian architecture, and found the pagan associations of classical architecture with the temples of the Greeks and Romans distasteful.

In many religions there is a recurring need to replicate a founding church or temple. The Sikh and Hindu migrants to Western Europe, for example, have made literal re-creations of temples that follow their originals precisely in form and detail, and have in some cases imported specialist craftsmen from the subcontinent with the high levels of skill needed to build them. The orientation of religious buildings and their interaction with natural phenomena – especially daylight but also the stars – reflect the earliest attempts of sacred architecture to frame the heavens, to position themselves, to provide memories and to produce recognizable building types that carry in their fabric the imprinted message of the sacred.

But there is also a level on which architecture is used to define a mood: to create a sense of space and expectation, of reverence, that serves to make individuals feel that they have been transported out of the everyday world and are for a moment open to the sacred. It cannot be seen as stagecraft, because to do so is to reveal the mechanism by which the atmosphere has been created, and this is to open the possibility that the experience is a conscious manipulation, a piece of theatrical stagecraft that is somehow not 'real'. Religious faith cannot be seen to be reduced to a conjuring trick if it is to retain credibility.

Looking up at light is a symbolic call to consider the heavens; it puts the individual at a physical disadvantage, it turns an intellectual understanding into a visceral physical experience. For an architect to be able consciously to set out to create the atmosphere of sanctity is to reveal the underpinnings of the process to unsympathetic scrutiny. Hence the importance of tradition over innovation in church architecture. And yet the mechanical repetition of traditional patterns in the end becomes deadening and ineffective.

Size can be a reflection of importance, as can location: churches, mosques, synagogues, temples have this in common when they are built on prominent sites and have imposing proportions. But the sacred can also be extremely concentrated when signified by special materials and techniques. The Gothic cathedrals depended on special skills possessed by only a few, as well as the most costly stone, the gold leaf on the altar, the bronze doors, the mosaic embellishments. The conscious, self-denying orders – the Shakers, the Quakers, the Cistercians – conversely tried to create a sense of identity through restraint, and through simplicity.

All architecture has its origins in sacred building. Its techniques, intellectual as well as material, have shaped architecture's contemporary role and given us our understanding of an architectural language, with temporal as well as a spiritual content.

12

The Uses of Culture

The Guggenheim in New York sold 320,000 tickets for its exhibition celebrating the architecture of Frank Gehry, more than for any other show in its fifty-year history. It called it a retrospective but the reality, stretching all the way up the sea-sickness-inducing spiral at the heart of the museum, was nothing less than Gehry's coronation by Thomas Krens, the Guggenheim's director, as 'the most important architect of our time'. With an uneasy mixture of the folksy and the self-regarding, Krens simultaneously compared Gehry to Michael Jordan and Frank Lloyd Wright – a comparison which was perhaps calculated to say as much about Krens as it did about Gehry. If Gehry really was the most important architect in the world, then that would clearly make Krens its most important architectural patron.

In thirteen years at the Guggenheim, Krens had turned a modestly scaled museum with an endowment and a collection a fraction the size of much less well-known institutions into a global art circus, positioned conceptually somewhere between the Bellagio casino in Las Vegas and Louis Vuitton, thanks in large part to the drawing power of Gehry's sensationalist architecture. Krens had made Gehry a star and, in return, Gehry made Krens the most talked-about museum director in the world. For better or worse, no institution had come to embody the role of culture in the contemporary economy, and the uses to which it could be put, more than the Guggenheim Museum.

Krens had behind him the startlingly successful establishment of the Guggenheim's colony in Bilbao, and the launch of outposts, albeit not quite so impressively, in Berlin and New York. Oblivious to the implosion of the dot-com bubble, he had presided over the $20 million launch of Guggenheim.com earlier in the year. With *Martha Stewart Living*'s former homes editor to help, it was a commercial website that was meant to make the museum rich. The synchronized opening of two more Guggenheims in a Las Vegas casino, representing a collision between high and popular culture beyond parody, was imminent. And Krens was already talking about building yet more franchises in Tokyo and Taiwan, Rio and Salzburg, and St Petersburg and Edinburgh.

But Krens's ability to defy the laws of gravity would never be quite the same after the Gehry show. Within a year, the chairman of the Guggenheim's trustees was publicly threatening to sack Krens if he couldn't balance the books. The budget was slashed, a hundred jobs were lost, and exhibitions were cancelled or postponed. The Las Vegas Guggenheim, in its Rem Koolhaas-designed rusty red steel box in the bowels of the Venetian casino, had shut after a humiliatingly short life. The Soho Guggenheim had been swallowed up by a new Prada store, and Guggenheim.com had vanished in a flash of very expensive pixels. The huge new Gehry-designed Guggenheim on the East River was put on hold, and then definitively cancelled. And Bilbao saw a collapse in its visitor numbers that prompted British Airways to cancel its direct flight from London.

The usual explanation for this catastrophic sequence of reverses is to suggest that the Guggenheim was somehow just another victim of the tragic aftermath of the attacks on the twin towers, which took place just ten days after the Gehry show closed. But the museum was already in deep trouble without any help from al-Qaeda. All the signs were there in the Gehry exhibition. In its hubris, and its narcissistic self-obsession, the show revealed an institution in the grip of an ego-fuelled thirst for glory. Its director and his trustees were bringing out the bombastic worst in each other, distracting the Guggenheim from pursuing its self-proclaimed cultural purpose.

Like an aggressive young fashion designer brought in to rescue a fading couture house, Krens's first move as director had been to purge the Guggenheim's product line of the dated and the mumsy, in favour of the up to the minute. He sold Chagall and Modigliani and bought Panza di Buma's collection of conceptual art. And he signed up a new architect to make a big splash with his flagship boutiques.

Gehry makes an unlikely Frank Lloyd Wright. He has a self-deprecating irony of a kind not usually associated with American architects. Nor does he show much interest in the opaque language that plagues so much of what passes for contemporary architectural discourse. Gehry is apparently at his happiest messing around in a workshop with a soft black pencil and some yellow drafting paper. But not very far below his amused affability is a more complex personality, offering material that Gehry has mined for some of his most interesting work.

Gehry was born Frank Owen Goldberg in Toronto in 1929. Like many architects, he changed his name. But it wasn't a suggestion from a mother-in-law that transformed Charles-Edouard Jeanneret into Le Corbusier, or Ludwig Mies into Mies van der Rohe. Gehry has since said that it was a decision that he regrets, but it is too late to reverse. He did however accept the invitation of Jean Chrétien, Canada's prime minister – issued, so Gehry says, in the middle of a long-distance telephone conversation about ice hockey – to take up Canadian citizenship again.

Like that of Louis Kahn or I. M. Pei, Gehry's early architectural career gave few clues of what was to come. In between designing apartment buildings, jewellery stores and shopping centres for Victor Gruen, in what can only be called a commercial vernacular, Gehry started experimenting with cardboard furniture. His obsession with fish imagery in the 1980s, which included building a restaurant in Japan in the shape of a giant carp and creating a fish out of a cloud of steel mesh on the Barcelona waterfront, seemed to suggest that something Jungian and out of the ordinary was about to emerge. But it wasn't until he reached 50 that he built anything of real power. He developed an artist's wariness of offering too many apologies for his work. Why make a building look like a fish? 'Oh I don't know, I just kind of liked it.' But at other times he would talk about his childhood memories and of playing with the live carp that his mother would bring home each week for Friday night supper.

Los Angeles itself was Gehry's other important source. With its seemingly random urban landscape of colliding shapes and odd juxtapositions, Gehry's architecture reflects the context in which it was born. When you are surrounded by freeways, giant advertising signs and drive-in restaurants in the shape of giant bowler hats or hot dogs, there is not much point trying to create chaste, well-mannered buildings. And this was the direction that Gehry began to explore. It was too much for many of his potential clients in Los Angeles, who still felt more comfortable with safely established architects and a less challenging approach. Only much later did the city's power brokers begin to see a Gehry house as a more conspicuous measure of success than the usual art collection or charitable foundation could ever be. In LA, a Gehry house has come to rank so far ahead in the infinitely competitive game of social status that a Warhol portrait, even with a certificate of authenticity, hardly registers. A Gehry house is much cheaper than a Lear jet but is way ahead not just on rarity grounds, but also because of the time and effort and respect that it implies. The tycoon who already has everything and still needs reassurance can console himself with the thought that here was a man spoken of in the same breath as Frank Lloyd Wright by no less an authority than the Director of the Guggenheim, who was ready to spend his precious time planning *my* bathroom, and manipulating the spatial relationship of *my* swimming pool with *my* living room.

Despite the commissions to design houses that started to come thicker and faster, it clearly rankled with Gehry that it had taken him so long to win a major civic project in his home city and that so few others followed. Arata Isozaki designed MoCA, and Gehry regrets that he even entered the competition that he wasn't meant to win. The Getty went to Richard Meier. And when Gehry finally did get a serious project in his home town – the Disney Concert Hall – construction stopped almost as soon as the foundations had been dug when the trustees ran out of money. Gehry was beaten in the competition to design the Our Lady of the Angels cathedral by Rafael Moneo. He was overlooked again when the LA County Museum of Art went looking for an architect. By this time he was claiming that he didn't do competitions. More of a problem was the fact that any architect LACMA's director Andrea Rich appointed was going to have Eli Broad as their real client, a billionaire with whom Gehry had already had a series of unhappy experiences.

The Bilbao Guggenheim catapulted Gehry into an orbit far beyond the limits of Los Angeles. His design was a sensation because it looked nothing like an art gallery, nor, for that matter, much like a piece of architecture as architecture had previously been understood. With its puckered titanium-skinned roof, swooping and soaring through the bridges and embankments that line Bilbao's river, the Guggenheim was more like a train crash than a building, a home-made mutant version of the Sydney Opera House.

Its biggest achievement was seen as its part in the transformation of Bilbao from a grimy and run-down industrial backwater plagued by terrorism, with just a couple of international flights a day, into the sort of place where affluent Americans might spend a weekend, and which could figure in the opening sequences of a Bond movie – not, it has to be said, universally regarded as the essential measure of urban civilization. It stripped away a lot of the alibis for building museums, revealing the egotism and showmanship beneath the rhetoric of self-improvement and scholarship. Form was no longer following function, it was following image.

Bilbao is hardly the first place to use a collection of objects to transform its economic fortunes. It's a practice that goes back to the trade in holy relics by all faiths, from Shias to Catholics, that saw cities snatching sacred bones away from each other, and the construction of elaborate shrines to accommodate them in order to encourage a lucrative pilgrimage trade. When Germany's Finance Minister Count Lutz Schwerin von Krosigk attempted to hold down spending on the rebuilding of Berlin in the 1930s, Hitler told Albert Speer to ignore him: 'If the finance minister could realize what a source of income to the state my buildings will be in 50 years. Remember what happened with Ludwig II. Everyone said he was mad because of the cost of his palaces. But today most tourists go to upper Bavaria solely to see them. The entrance fees alone have long since paid for the building costs. The whole world will come to Berlin to see our buildings. All we need do is tell the Americans how much the Great Hall cost. Maybe we'll exaggerate a bit and say a billion and a half instead of a billion. Then they'll be wild to see the most expensive building in the world.' Evidently, the Führer has a claim to having invented the Bilbao effect.

What made the Gehry show at the Guggenheim so revealing was the way that you could pick away below the surface and find traces of just about all of the preoccupations of a particularly gaudy decade congealed within it, just as the landscape which had brought them into being was about to be transformed for ever. The show appeared to be about architecture, but it was really about the excess, egotism and greed of the 1990s. Here was a selection of the urban icons pursued with quixotic abandon by ambitious cities all over the world. Here were the trophy houses of the egotistical robber barons of the new economy. And here was the awkward relationship between architecture and art at its most raw and painfully exposed. No wonder that Richard Serra was getting so uncomfortable about the way that Gehry, his former friend and collaborator, was being talked about as much as an artist as an architect. 'We are in a time now when the architect kind of rules,' he said at the time on TV. 'I draw better in my sculpture than Frank Gehry draws in his architecture. Frank is parading right now, and so are all those mouthpiece critics that, you know, support him as an artist. Hogwash.'

Architecture has a curious position in the cultural landscape. It is the most visible expression of cultural and civic values. It has a history of being at the very heart of statecraft. And yet for most of the second half of the last century its discussion has been marginalized in the context of a primarily literary and musical domination of high culture – not least because the architectural elite withdrew into an ever smaller ghetto, erecting barriers of incomprehensibility against the world.

Not only were people getting more interested in art galleries than in art, Gehry was an architect who could build a gallery and pack in an audience as well, without the need to fill it with art. What was that going to do to the prices of Gehry's architectural models?

What was not immediately visible in the Guggenheim was the fragility of the bubble on which all this architectural exhibitionism was based. In a distillation of the Zeitgeist that was almost too neat to be true, the major sponsor for the Gehry show was Enron, indulging in a last gesture of cultural largesse just before it went down in history as one of the greatest corporate fraudsters of all time. Enron's President and CEO, Jeff Skilling, wrote in all his pomp, months before the company imploded, an introduction to the catalogue so embarrassing that you would have expected the Guggenheim to pulp every surviving copy. 'Enron shares Mr Gehry's ongoing search for the moment of truth, the moment when the functional approach to a problem becomes infused with the artistry that produces a truly innovative solution. This is the search Enron embarks on every day, by questioning the conventional to change business paradigms and create new markets that will shape the New Economy. It is this shared sense of challenge that we admire most in Frank Gehry. We hope it will bring you as much inspiration as it has brought us.' Skilling, along with several of his executives, eventually faced his own prolonged moment of truth when he surrendered to justice in Houston, having destroyed the jobs of thousands of employees and robbed countless shareholders of their savings.

Dominating the show was Gehry's bravura plan for yet another new Guggenheim museum; this time it was a huge 572,000-square-feet structure designed to sit on stilts over the East River at the end of Wall Street. Mayor Giuliani had just offered Krens the land as a gift, and promised some cash to go with it, suggesting that the project was about to take on the solidity that marks the turning point between a speculative fantasy and a serious possibility. At the most banal and obvious level, the whole exhibition could be seen as a fund-raising event for the new building. Krens was boosting his architect by presenting his most glamorous project as a museum piece in its own right, even before it had been built. But the downtown Guggenheim was not the only one of the procession of models beneath the cascade of perforated metal ribbons that Gehry had dangled over visitors' heads with revealing things to say about the nature of contemporary architectural culture and its incestuous relationship with power. These were not the icily perfect white models of an architect attempting to impose his own sense of order on a reluctant world. They had the purposeful roughness of the cardboard furniture that Gehry was making in the 1960s when he was first involved with Claes Oldenburg and Richard Serra, and it moved them imperceptibly away from the status of working tools, or sales aides, toward the expressive quality of objects infused with artistic ambition.

The model for what the catalogue called the Lewis Residence – 'house' was much too modest a word for it – included a shiny blue plastic fish, a pointed Moorish dome, folds of red cloth, and strips of metal foil, that had been collaged together. This particular project began as an invitation to remodel an existing house in Lyndhurst, Ohio, and was eventually abandoned, ten years later, after the design had ballooned into an all-new fantasy palace sprawling over no less than 42,000 square feet. The unbuilt house gets twelve pages in the catalogue, second only to the Guggenheim in Bilbao with fourteen. Gehry tactfully suggests that the Lewis project allowed him to explore the themes that have shaped his work ever since.

People who commission Frank Gehry to design houses for them are a group unlike any other. Among their characteristics, self-doubt is conspicuous by its absence. The client for the Lewis house, Peter Benjamin Lewis, became chairman of the Guggenheim's board of trustees in 1998 and is a man who personally contributed $77 million to the museum, before he acrimoniously resigned in 2005. When Lewis became the chairman of the board of trustees, Thomas Krens announced: 'As the Guggenheim has grown to become one of the world's great cultural institutions, Peter is certain to provide the kind of inspired vision the Guggenheim will require to flourish in the 21st century.' He is certainly a flamboyant figure. He has a 255-foot boat, named the *Lone Ranger*, big enough for an on-board swimming pool and a crew of eighteen. He has made no secret of his taste for marijuana, a predilection which brought him a night in a New Zealand jail when the sniffer dogs at Auckland airport got excited about the contents of his briefcase. He even suggested to his employees at Progressive Insurance that he would go on working until what he called 'the Rockefeller event', as he described Nelson Rockefeller's fatal *in flagrante* heart attack. After his left leg was amputated below the knee as the result of a vascular disease, he developed a habit of removing his prosthetic limb during interviews and clasping it to his lap. But all these eccentricities could perhaps be seen as following in the example set by the museum's founders: Solomon Guggenheim, and his German baroness Hilla Rebay, with her unshakeable belief that drastic dentistry was the gateway to spiritual health.

Lewis made his money – $1.4 billion of it, according to *Forbes* magazine – by turning the car insurance business started by his father from a company with 100 employees and revenues of $6 million in 1965 into a giant with 14,000 employees and revenues of $4.8 billion in 2003. According to the catalogue, 'the plan to renovate the original house was quickly abandoned in the face of mounting needs that overwhelmed the structure'. It's an interesting use of the word 'needs', suggesting that a team of dour engineers had been wrestling with a series of sober, functional imperatives driving the design as if they were the inexorable laws of physics.

Gehry is much less guarded about the story of architectural obsession that the Lewis house represents: 'Peter kept adding to the programme.' Lewis asked for a ten-car garage, and Gehry designed it. Then he said he needed storage for his art collection, and the design changed again. Then he needed a private museum. Later that expanded when Lewis said he needed space for a director for the museum, and space for a curator, and for a library. And of course for a state-of-the-art security system, including panic rooms and an escape tunnel, and somewhere for a collection of Persian rugs, and still the programme kept changing.

Gehry was dealing with that very special form of indecision associated with an excess of wealth, the kind that makes a grown man unable to make up his mind whether he needs one guest house or two. Or whether he would rather keep the garage out of sight of his front door than get wet walking to the house from his car after parking – and all the other vanities and neuroses and insecurities that even a great architect cannot always keep from looking absurd.

In Lewis's eyes, at least part of the point of the house was to get his own back at what he regarded as the Cleveland establishment. Lewis wanted to put a 75-feet-high Claes Oldenburg golf bag in his garden that would have been clearly visible from the grounds of the neighbouring Mayfield Country Club, an institution which he felt had humiliated him as a 12-year-old half a century earlier. 'I was taken for a swim there by a school friend who told me the following day that he had been taken to task for being kind to a Jew.' It is perhaps fortunate that Lewis had never encountered Philip Johnson, brought up in Cleveland himself, whom he asked to design a guest house for him, in his earlier, Grey Shirt years.

Presentations turned into circus performances. 'Every time I went to see him he'd have a film crew in tow. On one of his birthdays he flew back the model and he invited the Governor of Ohio and many other guests to a big party,' says Gehry. 'I had to make a presentation of his house to this party.' Gehry responded by making a model the size of a playpen.

The project kept being cancelled when Lewis took fright at the cost. Then he would go back to Gehry to try to convince him that he was serious about getting the house built, and that the most important thing in his life was to get his architect to go back to work. The budget kept rising from $5 million, to $20 million, to $65 million, and even to $80 million. Then Lewis's son got involved: 'He spent three weeks working in our office, and he decided that we were skimming him.'

Lewis is divorced, and his children are all adults. It's hard to imagine how all of those rooms would have been used simultaneously and the sheer effort and choreography that would have been needed to make them come alive as anything but museum pieces. America's obesity epidemic had evidently hit its domestic architecture as well as its waistline. The film crew did, however, manage to complete their film on the non-building of the Lewis house. Jeremy Irons contributed a reverential voice-over.

Taking another turn around the Guggenheim's spiral, past Paul Allen, Bill Gates's one-time partner at Microsoft, who indulged his passion for Jimi Hendrix by having Gehry design the $240 million Experience Music Project in Seattle, you found a model of the Peter B. Lewis Weatherhead School of Management at the Case Western Reserve University in Cleveland. This is the one Gehry design for Lewis which did get built.

It's not as colourful or as expensive as the house would have been, but it is still explosive enough in its disdain for orthogonal geometry. It carries Lewis's name because he contributed $36.9 million to the cost. It was not, apparently, an entirely happy experience for him. Lewis's original contribution was to have been $15 million, but he was persuaded to more than double his donation after building costs escalated from $25 million to $61.7 million, a cost overrun that apparently he did not begrudge Gehry, but which caused a violent falling out between Lewis and the university. He told the *Cleveland Plain Dealer*, just after the Guggenheim's exhibition closed, that Case Western was 'a diseased university that is collapsing and sucking

Cleveland into a hole with it'. He demanded that the university trustees restructure their board and cut their numbers in half. Until they did, he would be boycotting every charity in Cleveland.

But then Lewis isn't very keen on Cleveland anyway. As his view of the golf club would suggest, Lewis has long had an uneasy relationship with the city. In the 1980s he wanted Gehry to build a fifty-storey tower for his company. He unveiled a model of the design, curiously missing from the Guggenheim show, in his apartment in the city. Donald Judd, Richard Serra and Claes Oldenburg were involved with the design – one version looked as if the skyscraper was reading a giant version of the local newspaper. It never got built, at least in part, Lewis suggests, because he felt so insulted by what he took as a personally slighting remark made by one of the guests at the unveiling. 'I have felt marginalized, disdained, excluded, laughed at,' he said, and took his building away. Years later Lewis told a journalist that he was so angry that he wanted to throw the man, whose offence had apparently been not to have recognized him, down the stairs.

As chairman of the Guggenheim's trustees, Lewis's primary task should have been to find a way to deal with the fact that the Guggenheim's economic model of constant growth simply didn't work. Krens had gambled that a worldwide network of museums would allow him to spread exhibition costs across his (increasingly restive) colonial subjects in Berlin and Bilbao, and wherever else he planted the Guggenheim flag. But touring the kind of blockbuster shows needed to pack in the crowds and balance the budgets does not work that way. A museum is not the same as a publisher packaging international co-editions to boost print runs and bring down costs. Lenders don't like lengthy tours, and the savings from shared costs turned out to be far smaller than Krens had assumed. Despite all its frenetic activity, the Guggenheim could not generate enough revenue to stabilize its budget. It was forced into a constant search for new sources of cash. At one point Krens came close to renaming the museum the Lefrak Guggenheim, in exchange for a few million dollars from a family of property developers. The outcry embarrassed the Lefraks enough for them to alter the conditions of their gift. But the $15 million that Krens extracted from Giorgio Armani in exchange for his use of the rotunda for an exhibition of his clothes, and the sponsorship money from BMW for using the same space for a display of its motorcycles, were widely seen as surrendering the museum's dignity. These windfalls did no more than stave off the prospect of financial disaster temporarily. Opening the Bilbao Guggenheim netted the museum a $20 million fee from the Basque government, which in addition took care of the salaries, the running costs and the acquisitions budget. But the Guggenheim was forced to dip into its endowment to meet its New York running costs in 2001 and 2002. In the two previous years it had sold $14 million-worth of its art holdings to pay its bills, and it was relying on Ron Perelman, president of the Guggenheim, for a further cash injection of $20 million. Las Vegas didn't bring in the profits or the visitors that Krens had predicted. The Guggenheim.com flop cost the museum's backers $20 million. The curators couldn't afford to mount their exhibitions programme as planned, but all that Krens could focus on was how to find the money to pay for the next big architectural model to ship to the Far East to tempt a new partner into yet another new Guggenheim, like Ludwig of Bavaria madly stripping his Treasury to build castle after castle. He was, it seems, perfectly ready to countenance selling seats on the board to the highest bidder. Lewis replaced Perelman as the chairman of the trustees, as he puts it, by more than doubling his pledged contribution to the museum. 'I bought myself the job,' said Lewis. After clinging on with grim determination to the wreckage of his relentless expansion plans, and continuing to talk up increasingly fantastic schemes for new outposts for the Guggenheim, Krens finally ran out of road. Enough is enough, Lewis declared: 'There was a mess about how finances had been managed. It had first used yesterday's reserves and then used tomorrow's optimism. I stopped cajoling and started threatening.' Lewis saw the proposed budget for 2003 and issued Krens with an ultimatum: 'Either you go away and come back with a real plan, or we will have to talk about your leaving,' is how he explained his position. Lewis's threats persuaded Krens to cut the 2003 budget for the Guggenheim by 13 per cent on the previous year. Lewis sweetened the pill by giving the Guggenheim yet another $12 million to clear its outstanding debts, but tried to make it clear that the price was no more fancy architecture: 'If Frank Gehry designs a public-service building', as Lewis was by now calling the proposed new museum, 'that gets built in downtown New York, I am willing to contribute the last 25 per cent. But there are conditions. No energy is to be diverted from the museum to new building.'

The message seems to have been lost on Krens, perhaps because, as he claims, 'it's easier to raise money for a building than a show. A building is permanent. The people who give money have a sense of confidence about the worth of a building.' His thoughts were echoed by Frank Stella, who believes that architecture appeals to donors because 'They know they are not being cheated. They don't want to spend $60 million on a van Gogh because, secretly, they think the real estate is worth it, and the painting is not.'

Even after the Downtown Guggenheim was finally abandoned, Krens was still hopelessly addicted to airports, architects, models and contracts with ambitious mayors. He signed one in Rio for a Brazilian Guggenheim museum designed by Jean Nouvel that would be mainly underwater – Gehry couldn't agree a fee with Krens to work on the project. It was budgeted at $250 million, and Krens hinted unwisely in public that it would make the Guggenheim $40 million in fees. But the project quickly got bogged down in recriminations in Rio about the morality of spending so much public money in a city ringed by *favelas*, and one that, unlike Bilbao, already had an architecturally distinguished Museum of Modern Art and a thriving tourist industry. The Rio courts ruled the deal illegal, and the Guggenheim trustees voted to drop the project. A similar deal with Taiwan, involving a building designed by Zaha Hadid, was under consideration. It would have been built in Taichung, supposedly to attract more tourists, but the city's airport had no international flights, and the council refused to back the scheme. Despite Krens's relentless optimism, the Guggenheim was under severe financial strain, raising the possibility either that the cash crunch was so bad that Krens had no choice other than to roam the world in pursuit of more quick-fix financial deals to keep the creditors at bay, or that he simply couldn't help but keep playing at architecture to distract himself from impending disaster. Lewis himself was so hooked on building that he was never going to succeed in reigning in a director who shared his obsessions. Either way, the Guggenheim's critics were starting to ask difficult questions about what would happen if the museum defaulted on its bond issues. Was the collection itself ultimately at risk? The question became more acute when Lewis lost a bid to discipline Krens, and resigned as chairman in 2005.

Unlike Lewis, Eli Broad has actually built a house designed by Frank Gehry. It's on a 3-acre hillside site in Bel Air. Like Lewis, Broad has a taste for conspicuous art. In place of the 75-foot golf bag that Lewis wanted, Broad had a 60-ton Richard Serra piece called 'No Problem' fabricated on the East Coast and shipped to California on flatbed trucks, to sit in his garden. But Broad's house wasn't in the Guggenheim show because Gehry found his client's micro-management style intolerable. If there is ever a Gehry Foundation established to rule on the provenance of his surviving work in the manner of the Warhol Foundation, the Broad house would be the most problematic case that it could face.

Broad, the richest man in Los Angeles, made his money by carpeting three states with tract houses designed down to the last nail and screw to be as cheap to build as possible. He knew exactly what he wanted in his own house, except of course that he couldn't design it for himself. But he wouldn't wait for Gehry to complete the working drawings either. Gehry disowned the project when his client went ahead anyway and built the house without him. That didn't stop Broad from preening for photographers in his new house. 'Most large American companies are run by managers who preside over the status quo,' he boasted. 'They are apt to live in traditional homes and be interested in art from previous eras. But if one is an aggressive entrepreneur, he's drawn to new thoughts. And probably to contemporary art and architecture. It's innovative and energetic.'

Broad is much richer than Lewis. *Forbes* estimates his fortune at $3.4 billion, the result of two distinct business successes: the first was in house building with the KB Home Corporation, the second was SunAmerica Inc., a pension company. Others put his wealth at $5 billion. Broad now describes himself as a venture philanthropist – that is to say, he uses his money and his friendship with Los Angeles' former mayor Richard Riordan to bend the city to his will. He backed the successful campaign to persuade the voters of the Los Angeles Unified School District to approve a bond issue to build the first new schools in the city for three decades. He was involved in the construction of the Museum of Contemporary Art, where he survived the resignation of a major fund-raiser from the board, and his lawsuit against the museum for the return of his $1 million donation when his fellow trustees refused to fire Arata Isozaki, the architect he had appointed in the first place. Broad was instrumental in attracting Pontus Hulten as the museum's director, and also implicated in his rapid departure. Now he wants to make Grand Avenue into the Champs Elysée of Los Angeles.

If Lewis is the type that wealth leaves paralysed with the kind of indecision demonstrated by the saga of the house that was never built, Broad knows exactly what he wants. And what Broad wants to do is to put his name on buildings. There is already an Eli Broad College of Business and Graduate School of Management at Michigan State. There is a Broad Art Center at UCLA. Cal Arts has the Edythe and Eli Broad Center and Broad Hall, and there is also a Broad Center for Biological Sciences. The Broad Art Foundation, as yet, has no permanent gallery of its own for its holdings of more than seven hundred works by a hundred contemporary artists, with Koons, Basquiat, Warhol, Sherman, Holzer and Salle particularly well represented. And he is using that collection to command the attention of the world's museums, a process which he is clearly enjoying hugely. According to the Broad Foundation's own website, '*Art News* recognised the Broads as among the top ten collectors of art world wide.' But it is Broad's money, rather than his eye for art, that drives the collection. The *LA Times* waspishly described his policy of accumulating work by artists who already have substantial reputations as 'shopping not collecting'. He has been involved with the boards of MoMA, the Whitney, the Hammer and the High museums, and most recently with LACMA. Each time, Broad flirted with the idea of construction, looking for the chance to make a landmark in his own image, decided that he wasn't going to get his way, and moved on.

Even without the house, Broad was a behind-the-scenes presence at the Guggenheim's Gehry show because of his impact on one of its major exhibits, the Walt Disney Hall. Though Broad was involved with fund-raising for the hall, he provoked another confrontation when he attempted to take command of the construction process out of Gehry's hands and the architect threatened to quit if he lost control of the design. It's hard not to see Broad's loan of part of his collection directly to the Guggenheim in Bilbao for a temporary exhibition without going through New York as a deliberate twisting of Krens's tail. Shows in Bilbao that originate in New York allow Krens to charge a fee; those that don't, earn him nothing. Broad flew to Bilbao accompanied by ex-Mayor Riordan and another wealthy friend with a Gehry-designed house in Los Angeles, Rockwell Schnabel, America's former Ambassador to the European Union.

Certainly it was Eli Broad's attention above everybody else's in the room that Rem Koolhaas was attempting to engage on the day at the end of 2001 when he made his presentation to the board of the Los Angeles County Museum of Art, longing to resolve the burden of a sprawling and unsatisfactory collection of disparate galleries. Koolhaas knows how to make a memorable presentation. This time it was punctuated by a series of words, flashed up one at a time. DISOBEY, to suggest that he was not following the carefully drawn up brief. LACMAX, to encapsulate his conception of demolishing all LACMA's existing buildings and replacing them with a single new structure.

This, Koolhaas said with a straight face, would be the most economical solution to the museum's problems. It was of course just the kind of bold gesture calculated to appeal to a man like Broad, approaching 70 and determined to build a landmark before it was too late for him to be able to enjoy the pleasure of walking around it. But after a year of negotiations, LACMA dispensed with Koolhaas's services. Even Broad's arm-twisting abilities were not enough to unlock the donations needed to build it, and, wealthy though he was, he would not put up all the cash needed himself. Broad donated $1.2 million pump-priming money and loaned LACMA $1 million to put a ballot measure to the city's voters that would have raised $98 million for the Koolhaas design under the pretext of earthquake and fire safety improvements. Three donors, a couple of foundations and the state's money would add up to $250 million, enough, he calculated, to get the project underway. But the bond issue was defeated, there was no cash from the taxpayers, and Broad started talking to Renzo Piano about adding a Broad Pavilion to the LACMA campus. What really killed the Koolhaas design was that it had transgressed one of the fundamental rules of museum building. All those existing LACMA pavilions, some of them no more than twenty years old, that Koolhaas wanted to demolish had each had their own benefactors, with their names inscribed over the door. Koolhaas was providing a brutal reminder to every potential donor of the transience of all things, even money and museums.

Broad celebrated his seventieth birthday by announcing a $60 million gift to LACMA. There would be $50 million to build a free-standing new building designed by Renzo Piano, and another $10 million towards acquiring new works. Broad is clearly more adept at having his way with recalcitrant museum directors than Peter Lewis. The Guggenheim spends money on what Thomas Krens sees fit. Broad had LACMA's director, Andrea Rich, in a corner, especially after she had invested so much personal prestige in the abortive Koolhaas project. Broad is too coy to promise his collection to LACMA, or even to make a long-term financial commitment. Though the new building will be called the Broad Contemporary Art Museum at LACMA – presumably on the basis that a museum has a better chance of survival than a mere gallery – the running costs will be the responsibility of LACMA. Renzo Piano has become the favoured architect of rich people seeking immortality. Before Broad, he worked for Dominique de Menil in Houston, and for Ray Nasher on his private museum in Dallas. And before that, there was Gianni Agnelli.

Broad has demonstrated with brutal clarity the essential nature of the balance of power between rich men and museums in a way that seems to be repeated every couple of decades. He is following the example of the Lehman family, which as part of the price of making a donation of their collection to New York's Metropolitan Museum insisted on the reconstruction of their living room within the museum, as if following the funeral rites of the ancient Egyptians. They also stipulated that there would never be loans made from the collection and nothing but Lehman works could be shown in the gallery without the approval of their own set of trustees.

The roots of the modern museum, for all its espousal of liberal values, lie in two of the most fundamental of human impulses: to defy death, and to glorify power. The museum is the synthesis of the shrine and the monument. But from the very beginning loot has also had a key role to play in its evolution. Napoleon determined to make Paris's position as the capital of Europe clear by systematically relieving his conquered subjects of their art treasures and putting them on show in the Louvre. His attempt to take the Rosetta Stone to France from Alexandria failed when it fell into British hands. But he did have the bronze horses of St Mark's Square removed from Venice and paraded around Paris in the victory celebrations for his Italian campaign. With Napoleon's exile, the horses eventually went back to Venice, which of course never even considered passing them back to their former owners in Constantinople – from where, in the midst of an orgy of rape and pillage that passed for a crusade at the start of the thirteenth century, La Serenissima had grabbed them in the first place. But Byzantium was not the original owner either. Some scholars suggest the horses may have been brought from Chios, others think that they came from Rome. Should they be returned once again, along with all the other classical sculpture that adorns Venice, and the lions that sit outside its Arsenale?

The horses at least went back to Italy; not all of the flood of art seized by Napoleon made it back home across the Alps. There is of course something genuinely shocking about the brutal simplicity of Napoleon's version of connoisseurship; acquiring the national treasures of others by force is an uncomfortable throwback to barbarism, even if it did lead to the creation of one of Europe's greatest museums. It's a reminder of the days when victorious generals got the chance to drag captured enemies behind their chariots, or when Mussolini stole a collection of obelisks during his Abyssinian campaign, or Hitler's plans for a gigantic art museum in Linz, to be filled with loot from all over Europe and designed for him by Herman Giesler, an architect who regarded Speer as a Judas. We have come to understand the museum as the repository of disinterested scholarship and civilized values. But the museum has always had a highly political role. And its rise has been fuelled by a potent blend of vanity and economic and national policy. The fate of the Parthenon Marbles is a clear case in point.

You don't have to work very hard to understand what the Greek Government was trying to tell the world about itself when it appointed Bernard Tschumi as the architect for a new museum to house the

Marbles in Athens. Never mind for a moment what Bernard Tschumi's new Acropolis Museum would look like. From the point of view of Greece's socialist government of the time, he was the ideal architect to design it. Not only was Tschumi not Greek, and could therefore be presumed to be neutral in the struggle for the Marbles, but he is also moderately fashionable. So his appointment could be presented as a confident, open-minded gesture of cultural maturity rather than the more predictable selection of a favoured local son. He may not quite have lived up to the dazzling promise of his first major built commission – the pioneering urban park at La Villette in Paris – but the Marbles demand to be treated with extreme politeness rather than be subjected to an aggressive architectural statement.

That is why Tschumi, both politically and aesthetically acceptable, won the second competition to design the museum in ten years, after the first collapsed in chaos. He brought credibility to the whole process. Small wonder, then, that the Greek Culture Minister invited Tschumi to accompany him on his charm offensive to London in an attempt to embarrass the Marbles out of Britain in the run-up to the Athens Olympics. Hiring a fashionable Swiss-American to build a glass-walled museum is not just Greece's way of reminding us of its claim to the Marbles; it's also trying to say that it is a sophisticated modern state. One Athens newspaper went so far as to contrast Tschumi's light-filled design, allegedly typifying the new Greece, with what it called 'the grim and depressing British Museum'. But it's the unconscious message that is more interesting. Creating a half-empty museum to house sculptures it is never likely to obtain suggests a gesture of impotent anger rather than confidence.

Tschumi's plans showed how the Marbles could be reunited with the monument from which they parted company almost two centuries ago. Not that they would actually go back on Ictinus' frieze, where there would be nothing to protect them from the corrosive atmosphere of modern Athens. Tschumi's strategy was to create a museum at the foot of the Acropolis overlooking the Makriyanni excavations and partly extending over them. Visitors enter through a solid base and wind their way gradually up through a series of double-height galleries displaying the museum's collections in chronological order, telling the story of the site from the archaic period and moving through to the

Roman Empire. Along the way, they encounter the inevitable shops and restaurants. Finally, in a theatrical climax to the careful sequence of displays, visitors come blinking up into the sunshine, climbing into a giant glass box to see the Marbles against the backdrop of the temple itself, attached to a set of internal walls aligned precisely on the Parthenon. Tschumi maintained that the glass walls could be designed to protect both sculptures and visitors from the climate, but it's hard to believe that the furnace-like heat of the Athenian summer can be handled without a daunting amount of air-conditioning, sunshades and tinting that would have the effect of shutting out the views and the light that were the object of the exercise in the first place.

Britain said no to the return of the Marbles, not for architectural reasons, but because the British Museum resolutely refuses to contemplate existence without them. But there are serious questions – more than simply its glass walls – that could be asked about Tschumi's design. It suffers from being the product of a brief which, like his appointment, is as political as it is cultural.

Much of the logic of the Greek case for the return of the Marbles rests on establishing a visual link between them and the temple. But to achieve it, Tschumi was pushed into building on a site that Greek archaeologists fear has been irreparably damaged by the disturbance of the construction process. There were protests against the preliminary site works, which have, it is claimed, destroyed Christian and classical remains. The socialist government ignored them and continued to maintain it was committed to opening at least part of the museum in time for the Olympics, lest it be left looking weak and incompetent. In fact construction had only just started at the time of the Greek elections in February 2004 that saw the Socialists ejected from power. A new Culture Minister briefly threatened to cancel the project once and for all, and to pursue his predecessor in the courts for ignoring legal rulings against the project and the archaeological damage it would do.

In fact the building of the museum could be seen as the continuation of the transformation of the physical remains of the Parthenon into a monument to a very particular view of Greek identity that has been going on for almost two centuries, a process that presents the Acropolis today as an isolated, ethnically pure moment of history – cleansed of all the later additions that were in themselves of enormous historic interest. A mosque, a Venetian fortress and a series of Roman and Renaissance remains have all been excised to create the iconic view that Athens now projects to lay its claim to the most glorious moments of Classical Greece. In the same way, Tschumi's Parthenon Museum is alleged to have destroyed layers of priceless archaeology metres deep in the interests of making a political gesture. In the event, there was nothing to see of the museum during Greece's moment of Olympic glory.

Every country uses its museums as part of a repertoire of instruments with which to define itself. In Britain, at the same time that Tschumi was trying to construct an idea of Greece, both the Tate Gallery and the Victoria and Albert Museum were reshuffling themselves and the images and objects that have served to construct a notion of Britishness ever since they opened in the nineteenth century. Both institutions share an ambiguity towards those objects. It's an ambiguity that can be read as the deconstruction of an identity as much as a celebration of it. Both the newly unveiled galleries at Tate Britain and the V&A's British Galleries are bigger than the Parthenon Museum would have been. But they are invisible to the outside world. Britain prefers to express itself in transformations of old buildings rather than in showy new ones. Tate Britain has become the nation's mantelpiece. A sequence of drawings by Blake share a wall with a portrait of the poet Chatterton on his deathbed, while Turner's curious image of a forlorn, vanquished Bonaparte hangs opposite. It's still an art gallery, but it is also a repository of the nation's favourite keepsakes and souvenirs. At the V&A's British Galleries you get to see the mantelpiece as well as what is on it. You move from the state bed from Melville House in gorgeous crimson Genoa velvet, through the music room from Chicksands Priory, past gilded carriages and an oak bookcase as big as a house. There are magnificent marble fireplaces under Adam ceilings, Thomas Hope's wilful, bloody-minded furniture, and a cabinet that appears to have been designed by William Burges while under the influence of laudanum. Here is the refined delicacy of pre-modern design by Godwin and Christopher Dresser and the chair that Charles Rennie Mackintosh had made for his own Glasgow flat. This is the story of Britain's ambivalent reaction to the avalanche of things that industrialization made possible. You can find the first sketch for the Crystal Palace that Joseph Paxton made on a blotter. And next to it is wallpaper by William Morris.

The other tradition from which the museum springs is best represented by Peter Eisenman's prodigious City of Culture taking shape on the outskirts of the Galician city of Santiago de Compostela. An opera house, a library, a museum and a complex of academic buildings are being built in one huge gesture, in the form of a hillside. Its purpose is ostensibly to provide a new economic resource for the city that once prospered on the pilgrims drawn by the saintly relics that the Galicians had managed to acquire. It is also there to immortalize the memory of Manuel Fraga, the veteran politician who began his career in the Franco era, who commissioned the City of Culture in his late seventies, and is clinging to power to see it finished. Santiago de Compostela depends on huge subsidies from Madrid and Brussels, and a grandiloquent refusal to face up to the practical problems of running an opera house in a city with no tradition of opera.

Not long after the collapse of Koolhaas's LACMAX project, a previously obscure body known as the East of England Development Agency launched what it called, with almost comic bathos, an international competition to find a 'visionary plan for a landmark, or series of landmarks'. The agency said it was looking for 'an icon that will foster a sense of identity for the region as a whole'. It was part of its strategy to present the East of England as 'a region of ideas', and a measure of how far the mania for exhibitionistic architecture had spread. No site was specified, nor had any money been committed, which hardly inspired confidence, but one board member claimed that this piece of wishful thinking was 'a fantastic opportunity for us to come together as a region and decide how to present ourselves to the rest of the world'. Setting aside the wounding likelihood that the rest of the world would continue to treat eastern England with the same indifference that it had adopted ever since the decline of the wool trade in the fifteenth century, it's not hard to guess the kind of thing that they had in mind: the opera house with the titanium fish scales designed by Frank Gehry as a free-form blob, or a gratuitously eccentric footbridge by Santiago Calatrava. Competitions such as this have become ubiquitous, leading all but inevitably to the kind of architecture that looks designed to form the backdrop for car commercials, or one of those Eiffel Tower in a Snow Storm paperweights. The search for the architectural icon has become the most ubiquitous theme of contemporary design. If it is to stand out from an endless procession of decaying industrial backwaters, rural slums and development areas that are equally star-struck, and equally determined to build their own icon that will bring the world beating a path to their doors, then it must come up with something really attention-grabbing. One Bilbao can shock its way into the headlines, but repeating the trick is the way to an architecture of diminishing returns in which every sensational new building must attempt to eclipse the last one. It leads to a kind of hyperinflation, the architectural equivalent of the Weimar Republic's debauching of its currency.

Everybody wants an icon now. They want an architect to do for them what Gehry's Guggenheim did for Bilbao and Jorn Utzon's Opera House did for Sydney. When the Walt Disney Hall finally opened in Los Angeles, most of the speeches at the opening ceremony talked more about what this new concert hall was going to do for the city's image than about its acoustics.

This is by no means a foolproof way to achieve architecture of discretion and tact, or even of quality. The effect of all this image building is just as damaging to the architects as to the cities that commission them. There can never have been a moment when quite so much high-visibility architecture has been designed by so few people. Sometimes it seems as if there are just thirty architects in the world, the flying circus of the perpetually jet-lagged consisting of the twenty who take each other seriously enough to acknowledge the presence of another member of the magic circle when they meet in the first-class lounge at Heathrow and another ten running on empty, who have been rumbled by their peers but who for the time being can still pull in the clients on the strength of past glories. Taken together, they make up the group that provides the names that come up again and again when yet another sadly deluded city finds itself labouring under the mistaken impression that it is going to trump the Bilbao Guggenheim with an art gallery that looks like a train crash, or a flying saucer, or a hotel in the form of a twenty-storey-high meteorite. You see them in New York and in Tokyo, and they are, with just two exceptions, all men; they are on the plane to Guadalajara and Seattle, in Amsterdam, and all over Barcelona of course. And now they are all converging on Beijing. They cross and re-cross each other's paths, taking part in the same invited competitions, appear on the platform at the Pritzker Prize ceremonies, and on the juries that select the victors in the design competitions that they do not enter themselves. Why has this happened? Partly because architecture has managed to make its mark on a wider culture in a way that it has never done before: buildings get noticed. The trouble is that given the sheer weirdness of so much contemporary architecture, how can their clients tell that their particular train crash, meteorite or flying saucer is going to turn out to be the landmark they are looking for, rather than the pile of junk that they half suspect it might be?

The answer is that they can't. So they rely on that list of thirty names drawn from the ranks of those architects who have done it before. They are the ones licensed to be weird. Commission one of them and you can be confident that nobody is going to laugh at you. Just like buying a suit with the right label when you know nothing about fashion. But it's a self-defeating process. The more that those few names hoover up all the high-profile projects, the fewer there are to choose from the next time around. This has the effect of turning architecture into a brutally divided business, caught between famine and glut. Architects either have too much work to concentrate on any of it properly and thereby destroy their reputations by parodying themselves, or so little that a kitchen extension can turn into a life's work, and they starve. It doesn't do the apparent beneficiaries of the process much good. All the relentless attention and hype has a worrying effect on some of the more suggestible members of the flying circus. They start believing it all. They can't help that little hint of amused disdain for any architect outside the charmed circle who isn't actually in the room at the time. But there is also the constant anxiety not to be upstaged for fear that their membership will prove only temporary. It is the natural outcome of the bizarre quest for the icon that has swept architecture.

Santiago Calatrava, the kitsch dark side to Gehry's playful, free invention, still calls himself an architect. In fact he has given up designing buildings to concentrate on producing icons. There is the mass transit station at Ground Zero, with its soaring glass wings pointing skyward, and its steel beak touching the ground with an uncomfortably close resemblance to the American Airlines logo. His Opera House in Valencia looks like the bleached skeleton of a long-dead sea creature, inflated to giant scale. Calatrava is constantly unveiling new footbridges to add to a collection that already includes specimens in Bilbao, Barcelona, Merida, Manchester and Venice. Touchingly, he continues to cling to a functional alibi. Closely examine one his drawings and, though it might look like a proposal to inflate a lobster to the scale of a skyscraper and construct it out of reinforced concrete, you will find a helpful, descriptive label: for instance, 'opera house'. Or in the case of the whale's tail that he has actually built in Milwaukee, it says with equally surreal economy of means: 'art gallery'. Of course there is hardly any gallery space inside the Calatrava addition: it's there simply to attract attention, to remind the world that the gallery exists. It was seven months late in opening, and cost so much to build that the museum replaced the director and cut the staff. You could see Calatrava either as the greatest beneficiary or the primary victim of the sudden mania for icon building. He began his career designing beautifully crafted structures with great economy of means. But his ever more eager clients have condemned him to keep repeating himself, with ever noisier special effects to distract us. Calatrava designed what is called a concert hall in Santa Cruz, a city of 250,000 people on Tenerife. Officially the white concrete shells are described as resembling a wave breaking over the seafront. The less sympathetic would interpret it as a gigantic representation of a nun's veil, or even something of a steal from far-off Sydney. Either way it is the classic 'iconic' project: a cultural building, designed with a heavy subsidy from public funds, with the express purpose of getting previously obscure cities into the pages of inflight magazines. Calatrava is a one-off, and famously trained as both an architect and an engineer. It's a combination that has allowed him to create the suggestion of a sense of inner logic around his work, providing an alibi for what could otherwise be seen as blatant exhibitionism. Calatrava has about him a whiff of the otherworldly vision that lingers around those who profess to find a hidden order in blades of grass, snowflakes and rock crystals. From it he has concocted a kind of genetically modified

Gothic that is now the main theme of his work. Or perhaps it is prefabricated Gaudí squeezed by the metre like toothpaste from a tube. Its bravura visual quality is enough of a diversion to prevent his patrons asking why exactly his extension to Milwaukee's art gallery should look like a whale's tail, or his Valencia opera house should have a structure reminiscent of a mollusc, or from having to justify them in terms of functional performance. Or why his roof for the Athens Olympic stadium was so complex that it was completed only days before the opening ceremony for the games.

The museum has been the most vulnerable building type to fall to this tendency, because it's the easiest to play with. Architects can manipulate it, but the real problem comes when people try to do the same thing for a public library, or a housing scheme. The more clients continue to ask for icons, the less inclined is a new generation of architects to oblige. Shallow, garish, show-off buildings suffer from the law of diminishing returns. The smart response from younger architects taking a strategic view, such as Foreign Office Architects, is to design buildings, like their ferry terminal in Yokohama, that can't be reduced to logos. And the most successful new museum to open in America is an old cardboard box factory on the Hudson river, completely free of self-conscious monumentalism. Perhaps, like art nouveau, which flourished briefly at the end of the nineteenth century, the icon has become ubiquitous just as it is about to vanish.

13

High-Rise Syndrome

There is a strange and moving photograph of Minoru Yamasaki looking as vulnerable as a child, standing tentatively in front of the World Trade Center holding a tiny model of the twin towers in the palm of his hand like a toy. He was no longer young when the picture was taken, but he is still a slight, diminutive and, above all, a touchingly sad-looking figure. If you didn't know that he was the architect of the two gigantic obelisks soaring skyward behind him, he could be Charlie Chaplin, trapped in the machinery of Modern Times, or a simple-minded clown trying to hold back the Great Dictator's army with a water pistol. Or he could be conducting some obscure magic rite, with a propitiatory offering in his hand.

The strangest thing about the picture is that there is no sense of triumph, or even of achievement in Yamasaki's downcast eyes. This Nisei child, born in poverty to Japanese immigrants in America, appears to take no pride in the immensity of the mark that he has made on the swaggering skyline of the richest city in the world.

You can't help but try to scour the image for clues to find some kind of meaning beneath the surface, to see if there is any precognition in it of the appalling events of 11 September 2001. It's an idle exercise. Maybe Yamasaki had a hangover on the day that the picture was taken, maybe the photographer was annoying him, or maybe he was worried about the troubled state of his marriage – any or all of which would have been likely possibilities. Maybe he was weighed down by the hostile response of his peers to the design of the towers. They were described as pieces of minimal sculpture, inflated to an absurdly monstrous scale. They were said to be dehumanizing, because they reduced the individual to visual insignificance. They gave no clue as to the kind of activities that took place inside them. The very idea of ultra-tall buildings was seen by some as a primitive throwback.

In his palpable anxiety, Yamasaki does not look like a man who is comfortable about having designed the tallest building in the world. It's an impression strengthened by the passage in his architectural autobiography in which he explains why all but a handful of the tens of thousands of windows in the twin towers were just 22 inches wide: 'These windows are narrower than one's shoulders. I have often gone to a high floor, and comfortably placed my nose against the glass to view the plaza below. I can't do this in a building with floor to ceiling glass and mullions, say five feet apart, because, experienced as I am in high rise buildings, I still have a strong feeling of acrophobia.' Yet the picture also seems to suggest some of the reasons for the continuing grip that very tall buildings have had on the imagination of the world.

For Minoru Yamasaki, who in his own person represented a link between the lost golden age of New York's skyscrapers from the 1930s and the modern world, to be prepared to admit that he is scared of heights is like hearing the Pope confess his doubts about the existence of original sin. Before he set up on his own in Michigan, Yamasaki had worked for the two architectural offices that between them did more to define the American skyscraper in the 1930s than any one else. For six years he was with Shreve, Lamb and Harmon, the firm that built the Empire State. Then he moved to Harrison, Fouilhoux and Abramovitz, the architects who led the consortium responsible for designing the Rockefeller Center.

The World Trade Center was always meant to be big and imposing, but Yamasaki suggested transforming the concept of a complex of new buildings into the tallest structure in the world with a design that finally overtook the Empire State when it topped out in 1972. And it was Yamasaki who had the idea of concentrating almost all the office space proposed for the site into just two identical towers – a pattern that he used again in the twin triangular towers of Century City in Los Angeles. Yet when Yamasaki died in 1986 he was well on the way to professional obscurity. He was all but forgotten in America, where his early promise seemed to have been irretrievably eclipsed by the notorious demolition of his huge Pruitt-Igoe housing project in St Louis. Yamasaki's AIA Award for the apartments did not save

Pruitt-Igoe from poor construction standards, or absolve it from the near-total absence of a maintenance budget and a concentration of desperately poor occupants. The sad history of that project was transformed from a local disaster into an emblematic event signifying a wider malaise, not only in America's public housing policies, but also in its cultural life. The photograph that caught the moment when dynamite charges exploded across the front of the stricken hulk of the apartment blocks, which collapsed into a cloud of dust, was endlessly reprinted as a symbol of the vanishing confidence of a generation of architects who no longer believed that they could construct a more civilized version of the world as they found it.

It certainly wasn't the first architectural project that failed to live up to the promises of its designers and builders. But it was clearly a traumatic experience for Yamasaki. To have one such episode is to achieve the kind of notoriety that would overshadow almost any career. Yamasaki had two of them – the second, posthumous disaster immeasurably worse than the first.

Yamasaki was a difficult man, with apparently no gift for guile or self-preservation. Like many architects, he lived only for architecture. He was anxious enough about his reputation to expunge any image of the Pruitt-Igoe project from his autobiography. But he could not help himself from including a questionable watercolour landscape that he had made shortly after starting his own office that was, as he proudly proclaims, used by a client as a Christmas card. He tells you more about his marriages – there were four, the first and the last to the same woman – than is comfortable in a conventional professional monograph. He was brought up in the kind of poverty that made him determined to escape from it. But when Yamasaki, sitting in his provincial Michigan office, opened the letter from the Port Authority inviting him to New York to discuss the idea of designing a major office complex in Manhattan, budgeted at $280,000,000, his immediate response was to suggest that there was an accidental zero too many. If there wasn't, he said, then his office was too inexperienced to handle the job.

During Yamasaki's lifetime, the World Trade Center was bitterly criticized for its anti-urban qualities. The 5-acre public space at its centre, which the architect fondly compared to Siena's Campo and

St Mark's Square in Venice, was regarded by many as a poor substitute for the scruffy vitality of the fourteen blocks, with their radio stores and tailors and bars, that were demolished to build it. The sheer bulk of the twin towers seemed to run entirely counter to the porcelain-like decorative delicacy of those projects that made him talked about, for a while, in the same breath as Eero Saarinen and Philip Johnson. Yamasaki's office was busy until his death, but for an architect to build commercial projects in unfashionable parts of the world in their later years, as he did, has never been a good move for those interested in building a lasting critical reputation.

The catastrophic destruction of the towers just at the moment when the critical view of them was beginning to become more positive transformed the meaning of Yamasaki's professional life.

Yamasaki not only had a link with the early days of the skyscraper, he also seemed to have a direct connection with its nemesis. A persistent legend linked the construction firm that Osama bin Laden's father owned with the two projects that Yamasaki built in Saudi Arabia – the airport terminal at Dhahran whose arcades joltingly recall the World Trade Center, and the Saudi Arabian Monetary Authority building in Riyadh, practically the last project of Yamasaki's career. Anwar Ali, governor of the Saudi Arabian Monetary Authority, had called Yamasaki in 1970 to ask him to design his new headquarters in Riyadh. Yamasaki replied that he was too busy with the twin towers to take it on. As he tells it, Ali told him that he didn't mind waiting, and called him back three years later when the World Trade Center was finished. Was it because Ali appreciated the sensitivity of Yamaski's concrete vaults at Dhahran airport, with their delicate synthesis of Arab traditions and modern materials, or was it because he was determined to use the architect of what was the biggest tower in the world at the time to build his own office?

There have been specious suggestions that the World Trade Center was designed as a conscious evocation of the centre of Mecca. In fact the arrangement of T-shaped low blocks forming a perimeter around a plaza that Yamasaki devised for the World Trade Center is an almost exact replica of what he had done in Seattle, his native city, for the Federal Science Pavilion at the 1962 World's Fair. It was the project that had attracted the New York and New Jersey Port

Authority to him in the first place. His Gothic pavilions are still intact, marching through Seattle's biggest park like Martian monsters on the loose from *The War of the Worlds*. They are a ghostly echo of the twin towers' two ground floors, rendered in concrete, and grouped around stagnant ponds, under the shadow of the panting, wheezing lift that clatters up and down the shaft of the space needle, topped by a giant frisbee that is Seattle's most famous landmark. The difference in Seattle was that the pavilions were designed to be an oasis from the crowds that swarmed around the competing attractions of the fair. In New York the sheer bulk of the towers had an overwhelming physical and psychological impact on the plaza and its less than inspired arrangement of circular pool and second-rate sculpture.

Yamasaki had the conventional attitudes to the city of an architect of his time. He thought it fortunate that there was not a single building worth saving on the fourteen tiny irregular blocks that made up the World Trade Center site, which he regarded as time-expired and inconvenient: 'The tremendous number of intersections make it impossible to walk or drive. This area was planned for horse and carriage days.' But Yamasaki had enough insight to realize that it would only be a matter of time before another building was declared the tallest in the world, and that his design needed to do more than break records. He had also considered the objections to the enormous bulk of the towers and the way that they presented sheer cliff-like walls towards the city rising straight up through all 110 floors. He had spent a lot of time walking around the Empire State Building trying to get a sense of what his towers would be like, and he convinced himself that they would be beautiful. 'There was no diminution of the soul,' he claimed. 'No ant-like feelings in the face of such a large object. Man had made it, and he could comprehend it. I am happy I was able to design these very buildings with the proper scale relationship so necessary to man. They are intended to give him a soaring feeling, imparting pride and a sense of nobility in his environment.'

Apart from its impact on the skyline of Manhattan, the most memorable physical aspect of the World Trade Center was the sheer weight of all those storeys pressing down on you as you tried to negotiate the plaza between the two towers. To do it required a measure of determination. Standing up on the World Trade Center's Plaza, you could feel the pressure of two sheer towers rising up into the sky on either side of you. To move across it was like passing through a narrow gap in the thickness of a monolithic wall. Their mute mass was enough to put the air between them into compression, and to force your muscles to push back against them. As you moved towards the entrance of the North Tower you could feel the pressure build up as you came closer and closer. The weight above you grew more and more intense, even as the building itself appeared to become more transparent as your point of view shifted to look head-on at the shining aluminium fins rising the height of the towers. Negotiating the threshold required the greatest psychological effort of all. The door seemed to carry the weight of the entire building. It trapped you for a moment as you summoned up your courage. Then you were through, and there was a sense of release into the soaring space of the double height lobby, for a moment denying the presence of the 110 floors stacked up over your head. After that came the experience of the lift: the air pressure build-up made your ears pop, pressing your feet to the floor in the ride to the top. Emerging out into the rarefied atmosphere 1,302 feet above the ground brought with it an uncomfortable sensation of anxiety as you waited to see if the tower really did sway in the wind as you had always heard it would. It did, but not that much. The shock absorbers – needed to restrain a building with nothing heavier than an aluminium skin to hold it down – kept the sway to just 8 inches in 100-mile-per-hour winds.

We have tamed ultra-tall buildings and made them part of the invisible background to daily life by denying their extraordinary qualities. Once the skin is in place, a high-rise building is no longer the preserve of nonchalant steel-riggers taking their lunch on huge I-beams jutting into the void. It becomes a banal cocoon for water-coolers, dress-down Fridays and leaving parties. But Yamasaki was still ready to confess to the possibility of fear of what he had created.

San Francisco's Golden Gate Bridge exerts such a powerful pull on would-be suicides that there are documented cases of the desperate driving across the Oakland Bridge, ignoring the many and varied possibilities it offered for putting an end to themselves, just in order to reach it. The Golden Gate is a lightning rod, one that seems to create the weightlessness that triggers feelings of vertigo, as if there is nothing to hold you down anymore, nothing to stop you floating upwards, no reason not to let go and fall. It is something to do with the investment of all the energy needed to span such a long distance, and to move so high over water to do it. And perhaps with the sense that a big bridge has had the effect of making the placeless into somewhere unique, signalling the presence of the ambition of making a mark on the earth, the most fundamental impulse of mankind. Very tall buildings can induce similar feelings. They exert a real physical impact on us. They shape the landscape.

By the time that I made it up to the Windows on the World, the World Trade Center was no longer the tallest building in the world. The Sears Tower in Chicago, designed by SOM, eclipsed it in 1975, and yet this was still a complex of extraordinary force. The twin towers erupted from the midst of a cluster of lower towers, and somehow managed to impose a sense of order and discipline on them. They created a skyline that was instantly recognizable from any angle as New York, unlike the anonymous silhouette of so many cities that use the same vertical elements without managing to achieve a sense of identity. How many people can immediately tell from a photograph whether a cluster of towers is Atlanta, or Los Angeles, or Seattle? The World Trade Center had a personality, and it was what gave the towers their impact, as much as their height.

The towers were interpreted as a signal of power and authority by those who wanted to challenge America's hold on the world. They were, it was insinuated, the personification of the evils of capitalism. The idea of building them was first put forward by David Rockefeller, as part of an urban renewal proposal that would have the effect of safeguarding his investment in the area. His brother Nelson, from his Albany citadel, ensured its financial viability when, as Governor of New York State, he leased space in them for 1,000 civil servants. But they were actually built by a group of public officials in a bid to revitalize the local economy of the city, badly damaged by the loss of traditional employers as shipping operations in Manhattan vanished in the 1950s. And the buildings were filled not by the heartless masters of the universe, but mainly by clerks and cleaners and civil servants.

The World Trade Center was conceived as a demonstration of confidence in New York, a city that was experiencing a loss of direction and facing worsening budgetary crises. It was a gigantic urban life-support machine, an iron lung intended to engineer the resuscitation of the city, an unmistakable and extraordinarily visible signal that New York was still a force to be reckoned with. Outside America, of course, the nuances of one city jockeying with another became blurred. The World Trade Center came to be seen as an American icon, rather than a reflection of New York's nervousness about the jobs it was losing to the suburbs and the sunbelt.

Its architecture had a terrible drubbing from Yamasaki's peers, especially from the generation that saw themselves as young radicals at the time that it was finished, and who turned out to be just the people who were in the running to rebuild it when it was destroyed. But the generation that came after them had a different perspective, rediscovering the grandeur of its heroic proportions, and coming to an understanding of the extent to which the twin towers had become part of New York's popular identity.

There is no doubt that there were problems with the World Trade Center. The raised plaza was a particular *bête noire* of planners: it was seen as driving out life and urbanity, creating an isolated and forbidding enclave, while the shopping space was driven underground into labyrinthine malls. Yamasaki's one moment of brilliance in the design was its duality. He established the idea of twin towers as an element in the typology of high-rise building.

The attack on New York came precisely at a moment when, after decades of scepticism about building high, the world had embarked on a particularly feverish bout of skyscraper building. In London, Norman Foster had just finished building his second tower for the Hong Kong and Shanghai Bank, this time at Canary Wharf, and was starting work on the unmistakable cone-shaped Swiss Re tower. Renzo Piano had secured the commission to design a tower for the *New York Times* and got involved with a quixotic project to put the tallest building in Europe on top of London Bridge station. Jean Nouvel was planning a tower just as phallic as Foster's Swiss Re for Barcelona. In Asia every burgeoning metropolis was looking to establish its presence with a crop of ever taller structures. There were clusters of towers underway in Vienna and Milan. Melbourne and Sydney were competing to build the tallest apartment tower in the world. Dubai was trying to establish itself as a resort centre with what it claimed was the tallest hotel in the world, even though Shanghai had built much higher hotel rooms by putting a hotel on top of fifty storeys of offices.

It had all been so different just a couple of years earlier. After the revolt against the lumpish high-rises of the 1970s, it was taken for granted in most European cities that nothing else should be allowed to break through a strict but unstated height limit. Then, equally suddenly, the received wisdom was turned on its head. Building tall became an obsession for architects, not just in Asia and America, but in Europe too.

When Asia's cities are building towers as fast as they can in a deliberate effort to modernize themselves, those Western cities that don't follow suit begin to look somehow quaintly old-fashioned and fossilized. At their best, high-rise towers are elegant, technologically sophisticated and represent the future of the city. Yet they get built as the by-product of a primitive, unsubtle battle of egos. Politicians became fascinated by the image of the high-rise city, whether it is the Mori Corporation's transformation of Shanghai or Ken Livingstone's London. As its mayor, Livingstone has been doing his best to bring new towers to London. This is ostensibly because it is what the multinationals want to stop them moving to Frankfurt, or New York, but the reality owes more to the unsubtle symbolism of being the biggest or the tallest, and so the most important.

The timing of the attacks on the twin towers certainly made it seem as if the terrorists had been listening to the debate and had got the message about the symbolic significance of high-rise architecture. One of the hijackers who led the 11 September attacks, Mohammed Atta, was himself a graduate of Cairo's school of architecture, and a postgraduate urban planning student in Hamburg. If he had been a lawyer or an engineer, or a software designer, it would simply have suggested that this was another disaffected middle-class radical. But the architectural connection seemed to suggest something else. It was as if he had recognized that the opposite side of the will to build is the attempt to delete.

Mohammed Atta was born in 1968 into a middle-class Egyptian family. He had enrolled at Cairo University in 1985 in the engineering faculty, whose four-year architecture course has a syllabus that allowed him to explore the history of architecture in both the Arab and the European worlds. It taught him to draw, and how to analyse a design problem. It taught him to think about how buildings worked, what made them stand up, and how they were made.

During a period of rapid change, in a traditional society contemporary architecture represents a particularly sharp cultural confrontation. The Middle East has been importing it from the West for decades. It appeals to wealthy regimes because they are interested in representing themselves as part of the modern world, just as they would go shopping at Boeing or Airbus to equip a national airline, or an air force. But the transformation of a city with new buildings that seem like insensitive transplants from another world with different values can be seen not just as a sign of change, but its direct cause. It is a painful and continuing reminder of the tension between modernity and tradition. For those who study architecture in the Arab world, it is not hard to see the acquisition of these apparently alien skills as a humiliating acknowledgment of technical and cultural weakness. It does not need to be understood in this way. Atta studied at the oldest architecture school in the Arab world – Hassan Fathy, Egypt's most distinguished architect, was its most famous student. Fathy pioneered the rediscovery of Egypt's vernacular building techniques and devised a sensitive architecture attuned to the particularities of climate and indigenous skills, and an awareness of the fundamental cultural traditions that shape the way that buildings are used. With his concept of an architecture of the poor, Fathy focused on the needs of the country's dispossessed, rather than Egypt's Westernized elite. If Atta's concerns had genuinely been to use his professional training to effect social change, this would have been an inspiring model for him. Instead Atta left the country for Europe.

The Technical University of Hamburg-Harburg, known by its initials as TUHH, is one of Germany's newest universities, established only in 1982. It has a suburban campus close to the River Elbe. It sits in a complex of mainly new buildings that have at their heart an agora stepped into semi-circular tiers for Socratic dialogue, a reflection of the belief of the town planning department's dean, Professor Dittmar Machule, in the virtues of traditional urban forms. Machule received a grant from the German Vibrant Cities Foundation to conduct a research programme to determine what makes a city centre lively. But it was more likely that it was Machule's work in Aleppo, the 5,000-year-old Syrian city, funded by the German Government's technical assistance programme for conservation and rehabilitation, that attracted Atta to Hamburg in 1992. Atta's time in Germany seems not to have been entirely financed by Osama bin Laden. He earned money working for a couple of years as a draftsman for Plankontor, a planning consultancy in Hamburg. He enrolled in the postgraduate planning course and, after spending time in Syria, wrote a thesis that explored the conflicts between traditional Islamic urbanism and modernity. His examiners found a dedication on the flyleaf of words taken from the Koran: 'My sacrifice and my life and my death are all for Allah the lord of the world.' Machule gave him the highest marks for the thesis.

Watching those monstrous television images of the twin towers of the World Trade Center collapsing, many architects found themselves speculating not so much about the unknowable question of why this horrific event was unfolding unstoppably in front of them, but how; and then, almost immediately afterwards, asking themselves what it would mean for them as professionals. It's a response that could be seen as the ultimate in self-absorption. Face an architect with an unwatchable tragedy and all he or she can think about is how the welding on the steel structure was done or what it is going to mean for city planning. But to focus on the technical is to find some sort of psychological comfort in the midst of seemingly limitless anxieties.

The 16-acre hole in the ground that had been the World Trade Center rapidly acquired a viewing platform, poised like a diving board over the edge of hell. To deal with the three-hour queues that built up on the opening day, you had to get a ticket, just like you do at the London Eye. And, not far away, the Max Protetch Gallery opened an exhibition of speculations – proposals would be too strong a word – from architects on how best to rebuild the twin towers. For once, architects were not talking merely to themselves: they had the whole of New York looking over their shoulder. But was the viewing platform a sensitive response to a public need or a piece of disaster tourism? Even Liz Diller, the architect who made the platform, wasn't sure: 'If we'd known just how many people were going to use it, I'm not sure that we would have done it.' And for architects, deciding whether or not to take part in the Protetch show wasn't easy either. Zaha Hadid and Will Alsop both said yes, but Peter Eisenman, the New York architect who designed Berlin's monument to the Jewish victims of the Nazis, declined. So did Richard Meier. It was too soon; it was going to look like tacky self-promotion; it was plain ghoulish. And, in any case, it was all going to be pointless. It was obvious to anybody who thought about it for a moment that the future of the site was going to be shaped not by the imaginations of the dozens of architects who did take part in the show, but by the roomful of developers, insurance loss-adjusters and politicians carving up the area between themselves. Yet that is not to say that the exercise was not worth trying. It forced architects to grapple simultaneously with both the everyday and the horrifying. How, on the one hand, did you deal with a relic of an approach to planning seen as hopelessly outmoded, one that created a monoculture of office space, cut off from the surrounding streets by elevated pedestrian plazas, and, on the other, address the fact that this site is a mass grave?

Part of the dilemma is the timescale that architects must try to deal with. Ground Zero's meaning has changed already. One day it will be a place where people go to meet their accountants, have keys cut, pick up their dry-cleaning and sit on park benches. The emotional charge will still be there, especially for those who have lost children or partners, but it won't be there all the time. It will be an everyday slice of the city again. The creation of a memorial of more or less power is not the real issue. It's about exploring how to make a city. And not just any city. New York is *the* city, the product of a ruthless confrontation of a grid plan with geography and money. We have almost talked ourselves into believing that cities should be fluffy little village-like backdrops to Frank Capra movies; but the World Trade Center proved, with unanswerable force, how beautiful and majestic the brutal clarity of logic can be.

The idea of asking a single firm of architects to produce no fewer than six different ways of rebuilding the World Trade Center, then whittling them down to three preferred options, and finally incorporating their least unpopular features into a single master plan, could have come straight from the White House staff's modus operandi for explaining plans to effect a regime change in Baghdad to a president with a short attention span. As a strategy, it's bad enough applied to global realpolitik. As an instrument of urban planning for one of the most highly charged sites in the world, it was nothing short of a disaster. Things started badly enough when the Lower Manhattan Development Corporation held a competition to find an architect for the job – not on the basis of their ideas, but on a credentials pitch.

They picked Beyer Blinder Belle, a firm best known for its restoration of such nineteenth-century New York landmarks as Grand Central Station but without much of a track record in new thinking. They were paid $3 million and were expected to come up with six different ways of dealing with Ground Zero in a matter of weeks. It is a task that would have defeated a Le Corbusier, never mind a businesslike but uncharismatic professional office. The results were not, claimed the Development Corporation, meant to be taken literally as architectural designs. Rather, Beyer Blinder Belle's diagrams were intended to show where new towers might be built, and what could be left as open space. Even if this was the right way forward, the presentation did nothing to make the case. The architect's leaden drawings were taken literally and universally condemned as not being up to the job. Their renderings seemed to show generic provincial cities, not the skyline of the most dynamic metropolis in the world.

Like glib salesmen, Beyer Blinder Belle brought out their sample case to offer passers-by any kind of memorial they liked. One was a memorial 'plaza', another a memorial 'square'. There was also a memorial triangle, a memorial garden, a memorial park, and even a memorial promenade. As if the sense of loss could be dealt with by a banal multiple-choice test. The reaction came down to two mutually irreconcilable views. On one side, a sense that none of the proposals matched the massively impressive quality of Yamasaki's lost towers, and that if the city is to heal it must build something to match the impact of what has been destroyed. On the other side there is a sense that this is a mass grave, and should be treated as such. Just four weeks after unveiling Beyer Blinder Belle's six schemes, the project went back to the drawing board. Admitting none of the options put forward was right, the LMDC announced 'a worldwide development competition' to pick another architect, and asked them for a design with a bit more 'excitement, creativity and energy'. But the confused issue of who actually gets to decide what happens was never addressed. The New York and New Jersey Port Authority owns the site and the destroyed buildings. The Mayor of New York has some responsibilities, but the State Governor has more power. Silverstein Properties, the developer that acquired the lease on the offices in the towers shortly before they were destroyed, and which was in line for the insurance pay-out, quickly emerged as the player who had the last word.

Larry Silverstein was clearly preparing to ignore the competition altogether. Confusingly, SOM took part in it but withdrew after they had made their presentation. Despite the initial belief that the attacks on the World Trade Center represented the end of the skyscraper as a viable building type, anxiety about them evaporated surprisingly quickly. In the immediate aftermath of their tragic destruction, David Childs began designing a structure that, while it would have stood as tall as the twin towers, only had occupied space on its first sixty floors. It was, he believed, the maximum number of floors that New Yorkers would be comfortable with. Quite why he and his client Larry Silverstein hit on sixty rather than fifty-eight or sixty-seven as the reassuring number, he never managed to explain. But that is the model that he developed six months before the Lower Manhattan Development Corporation launched its chaotic competition to re-build Ground Zero. Childs and Silverstein were convinced that the structure should be at least as tall as the lost towers, for no other reason than as a symbolic gesture. When Daniel Libeskind first unveiled his plans to rebuild the World Trade Center, he was regarded as a serious-minded architectural intellectual, locked into the most arcane kind of private professional discourse, understood only by its initiates. But from the moment he began to talk about his designs live on CNN, it became immediately apparent that he was about to turn into something entirely different.

'Like so many others, I arrived by ship in New York harbour as a teenager and as an immigrant,' he began, looking and sounding like a turbocharged Woody Allen. 'The Statue of Liberty and the Manhattan skyline made an unforgettable impression, and this scheme is all about that.' For an architect to talk like this might have sounded hollow at any other time or place. It certainly sounds hollow after all the jockeying for position and the lawsuits that followed Libeskind's pyrrhic victory in the competition. But in the glass-vaulted winter garden of the World Financial Center, from which the open wound in the rock and mud that was all that was left of the twin towers was clearly visible, the impact of his words, as Libeskind obviously knew, could not be anything but electric. He drew a round of applause as he finished speaking, ringingly declaring that rebuilding was an assertion of life in the face of tragedy.

For a moment he had stopped being an architect altogether. Libeskind was offering an emotional response to a collective tragedy. He had become a charismatic public figure, as if this particular issue was too much for architecture by itself to handle. For the cynics, and their numbers swelled rapidly as Libeskind's design developed, he was becoming a therapist as much as an architect. But for Libeskind it was a highly personal and completely uncalculated response. He had put everything into the project, suspending the scepticism that many architects felt about the flawed competition process. Frank Gehry won few friends by refusing to take part, suggesting that the $40,000 fee for participants was demeaning.

'I know people say that the competition was window dressing, and that the real decisions are being taken somewhere else. But I couldn't feel cynical,' says Libeskind. 'At one level you have a civic responsibility, you are not just an architect, you are also a member of the public.' By the summer of 2004, Libeskind's lawyers were looking for $1 million from Larry Silverstein. They settled for less.

Of all the architects taking part, Libeskind was the only one not afraid of using the 'I' word. Strangely enough for a profession that cannot be anything but egotistical, the first person singular personal pronoun is almost always finessed away. Its always 'we' did this, when an architect means 'I'. But not Libeskind. 'I went to look at the site', he said, 'to see and feel what it is like to be standing in it, to see people, to feel its power, and to listen to its voices, and this is what I heard, felt and saw.' His competitors took a very different tone. Even though Stephen Holl, a prominent member of one team, actually saw the destruction as it happened from his office windows, and Norman

Foster was in a New York hotel on 11 September, they used a more distanced, neutral voice, creating a sense of professional objectivity.

Liebeskind designed a ring of boldly sculpted blocks to deal with the 11 million square feet of office space that has to be accommodated on the site and gave them hints of an architectural language that those who have seen his Berlin Jewish Museum will recognize as distinctively his own. But what really counted were the multiple layers of symbolic meaning he tried to give the project. He identified the bedrock 70 feet below ground on which the towers once stood as their most moving memorial. 'The great slurry walls are an engineering wonder, designed to hold back the Hudson River. They withstood the unimaginable trauma of the destruction, and stand as eloquent as the constitution itself, asserting the durability of democracy, and the value of individual life.' Libeskind's original design left this raw wall as a silent monument. As things turned out, Libeskind won a competition staged by a public body that had neither the money to rebuild the towers, nor control of the land on which they stood.

The eventual result of the competition was nominal victory for Daniel Libeskind, but SOM designed the key building, a process that has damaged the way Libeskind is seen by his peers. There are two utterly different Libeskinds. One is a deeply serious architectural intellectual. His drawings are ink-and-pencil explosions that look more like an obscure form of musical notation than conventional architectural images. They came spattered with fragments of concrete poetry, and Dadaist texts. He is an architect who would rather not build at all than not build things his way. And there is the opportunist Libeskind who is prepared to do anything that it takes to get the job – and that includes simultaneously hiring two different public relations firms in New York with a brief to get him on *Larry King Live* and discussing the finer points of his cowboy boots and his spectacles in the style section of the *New York Times*. He was certainly the first candidate for Dean of Columbia University's School of Architecture ever to have appeared on the *Oprah Winfrey Show*. More troubling to some in New York was the enthusiasm with which he played the patriotic card in the race to secure the World Trade Center commission. He took to wearing a Stars and Stripes pin in his lapel. He wouldn't stop talking about that first glimpse of the Statue of Liberty from the ship that brought him to the land of the free as a teenage immigrant. And even though he hadn't actually lived in the city for twenty years, he told every interviewer: 'I am a New Yorker, and an American.'

It was probably the schizophrenic combination of both these Daniel Libeskinds – the intellectually credible populist and the super salesman – that was anointed by Mayor Bloomberg and Governor Pataki as the architect of the reconstruction of the World Trade Center. The political skills of Libeskind's wife Nina, a Canadian whose niece is, she tells you, Naomi 'No Logo' Klein, were certainly also a major factor. No wonder that some observers have been more than a little confused about the emergence of this new Libeskind, whose existence they previously never suspected. The *New York Times*'s architecture critic at the time, Herbert Muschamp, was particularly confused. From having greeted Libeskind's shortlisting as inspiring, and his initial submission as 'marvellous', Muschamp suddenly decided that it was in fact 'manipulative kitsch'. When the competition came down to a straight fight between Libeskind and his Argentine rival Rafael Vinoly, he wrote that Libeskind's scheme and all its emotional symbolism – the tower 1,776 feet high, conspicuously echoing the Statue of Liberty's torch, the 'wedge of light' that every 11 September would not in fact ensure that there are no shadows cast on the site between 8.46 a.m. and 10.28 a.m. as Libeskind promised, the Park of Heroes, tracing in the ground the paths taken by New York's firemen as they rushed into the twin towers, and above all Libeskind's idea of leaving the massive rock wall open in a deep pit – was the embodiment of Cold War propaganda.

The Libeskind camp was predictably outraged. Libeskind's executive assistant started an e-mail campaign urging sympathizers to write to the *New York Times* demanding that it sack Muschamp. The hapless assistant quickly issued a shamefaced apology, saying that it was done 'without the approval or the knowledge of Daniel or Nina Libeskind'. Rather more effective a riposte was the torpedoing of the chances of Muschamp's favourite, Rafael Vinoly, by a report in the *Wall Street Journal* on the eve of the closely run race that, contrary to Vinoly's claims that he had left Argentina as a political exile fleeing persecution by the military dictatorship, he had actually built his career untroubled by the junta and its generals. Despite his intensity about architecture, Libeskind is clearly not afraid to take the gloves off if the going gets rough. When Vinoly started describing Libeskind's design as 'the Wailing Wall', Libeskind called Vinoly's design 'two skeletons in the sky', and suggested that for Vinoly to name it 'the World Cultural Center' smacked of the Stalinist Palace of Culture in Warsaw.

The troubling issue for Libeskind now is whether he is an architect, in the widest sense, or one who has focused entirely on the idea of commemorating tragedy in one form or another. After Berlin, he was once asked if he could design another Jewish museum. He turned it down: 'I can't be a professional Jewish museum builder,' he replied. But then he went on to accept a commission to build a Holocaust museum in San Francisco, and has also designed the UK's Imperial War Museum North. The question really should not be which Libeskind is the real one, the intellectual or the populist, but is his project right for New York?

In the months that followed the competition, an increasingly bitter dialogue between Libeskind and David Childs ended with Childs taking control of the so-called Freedom Tower and a series of other architects, including Norman Foster and Jean Nouvel, being appointed to take on other parts of the project. The big tower retained that height of 1,776 feet – the tallest in the world – but otherwise it is all SOM's work, architecturally, though one Yale student sued Childs claiming he had stolen his twisted-skyscraper idea.

Something remarkable happened to the global balance of cultural power in February 1996. Competing teams of Korean and Japanese contractors, working continuously by sweltering tropical day and arc-lit night for three years, finally topped out the twin towers of the Petronas Centre in Kuala Lumpur. With their Bangladeshi workforce earning just a few dollars a day, collapsing exhausted to sleep in site-hut beds newly vacated by the next shift, and directed by Australian foremen and German engineers, they had done it at last.

For the first time since the Gothic cathedrals were built, the world's tallest structure is no longer in the West. From the centre of what was once a torpid colonial city, the towers erupt skyward, like fireworks, leaving a trail eighty-five floors high that dominates every view of the horizon from Kuala Lumpur's elevated highways as well as its twisting lanes, where rain storms still leave cars ankle deep in red mud. With heavy nods to Islamic geometry, it looks uncomfortably like a couple of giant extruded pineapples, tempered by a spidery bridge at the forty-first floor that seems to come straight from a sword and sorcery epic.

The design is the work of Cesar Pelli, the Argentine-born American architect who built Britain's tallest tower at Canary Wharf, as well as Manhattan's World Financial Center and, more recently, the tallest tower in Hong Kong. But this is not primarily an exercise in architecture. It is an assertion of political will in steel, marble and glass. The Petronas Centre eclipsed Chicago's Sears Tower, previously the world's tallest building, for the express purpose of demonstrating the determination of Mohammed Mahathir, the Malaysian Prime Minister at the time, to be taken seriously as a figure on the world stage.

In the process, the development swallowed up a colonial-era race-course at the heart of a city that is frantically reconfiguring itself as a metropolis. It also provoked serious worries among international bankers that Mahathir's buildings would signal that Malaysia's decade-long boom was turning to bust. Exactly who was going to occupy all those millions of square feet of office space? For America, which invented the art of skyscraper building, the prospect of Malaysian hubris is little compensation for being overtaken by an upstart Asian nation of just 23 million people.

The Americans alone had the secret of building high. They had the sense of conviction to make towers that look like more than giant refrigerators. By comparison, most European attempts at building high are as unconvincing as East German efforts to copy American consumer goods.

The whole exercise began shrouded in deceptive vagueness. In an attempt not to alert any of the dozen or more competitors around the world when the designs were first published, Pelli would only say that the towers were going to be big, but would never spell out exactly how big. Something very similar had happened in New York back in the 1930s, when William Van Alen did not reveal the full truth about his design for the Chrysler Building until its nearest competitor for the title of New York's tallest skyscraper was safely completed. Then he had the spire that forms its final flourish assembled inside the tower and installed overnight in a stunning conjuring trick to shoot effortlessly past its rival.

There is of course something ludicrously childish about the irrational urge to build high, simply for the sake of being the world's highest. But the idea of extreme height shows no sign of relaxing its grip on the world's imagination. The kind of people who present themselves as hard-headed, rational, infinitely cautious businessmen rush headlong into attempts to build ever taller structures. And yet, despite its transparently childish ambition, the twin towers are so readily identifiable that Kuala Lumpur is no longer just another anonymous Asian city.

With so much at stake, a curiously elaborate set of rules has been drawn up to measure and compare the height of skyscrapers to deal with the possibility of cheating. The tallest inhabited floor, the tallest enclosed space, and the tallest projection are all recorded and documented with the zealousness of schoolboy enthusiasts collecting aircraft registration numbers to ensure that like is compared with like. But it seems scarcely possible that the Tall Buildings Council, which records all this data, has actually been out there to measure and independently verify the claims that building owners make. These are, moreover, structures that make dubious economic sense. Extreme height inevitably carries cost penalties and creates buildings that are hard to use efficiently. You cannot let out a single square foot until they are entirely finished, so large sections remain empty, earning no revenue. And extreme height means that a much larger percentage of each floor is being devoted to lifts and structure than in more modest buildings. But that doesn't stop people doing it. Before he was exposed as a crook, Robert Maxwell claimed to be serious about buying the Sears Tower in Chicago, but only if the purchase price included the right to rename it the Maxwell Tower. The Prince of Wales once asked Cesar Pelli why Canary Wharf had to be so tall. The answer that Pelli was too polite to give was that the docklands development needed a skyscraper as its centrepiece for the entirely irrational and yet essential purpose of impressing the sceptics. It made nowhere suddenly into somewhere.

The tallest towers in the world are now being built in cities that few in the West could place on the map. Pusan in South Korea, Tianjin and Guanzhou in China. Within seven years they had caught up with the Petronas towers. The 101 Tower, a ninety-one-storey skyscraper in Taipei, a good 100 feet taller than the Petronas, eclipsed Kuala Lumpur in 2004. And in Shanghai, Kohn Pedersen Fox's World Financial Center with ninety-four floors, topped by a Ferris wheel, will turn out to be even taller. Mori and KPF are responsible for the Roppongi Hills tower in Tokyo, which, ugly and misshapen though it looks, has successfully introduced a new element into the usual mix of accommodation for tall buildings – the Mori Art Museum, which claimed an astonishing 750,000 visitors for its first exhibition, on the penultimate two floors.

The trouble with skyscrapers is that we cannot make up our minds about them. We lurch from celebrating them as the primitive signals of virile economic health to deploring their brutal impact on the fragile skyline of historic cities. Norman Foster's striking new tower in the City of London – on the site of the Baltic Exchange, devastated by an IRA bomb in 1992 – is a representation of that duality. It's huge but seems to insinuate itself into the landscape by stealth. We are not even meant to call it the Swiss Re tower. That would smack too much of a cult of personality for its careful insurance company owners.

According to the agents struggling to let the empty upper half of its forty floors, the gherkin, as it has been nicknamed, is actually 30 St Mary Axe, the kind of blandly discreet name that could suggest almost anything – a Georgian rectory perhaps, or a dignified stone-faced banking hall. Anything, in fact, except what it really is: the most conspicuous eruption on London's skyline in a quarter of a century; a single building that is as big as a small town, with 500,000 square feet of space able to accommodate 4,000 people with ease. Whatever it's called, this is the tower that ignited London's current preoccupation with the skyscraper. It broke the 600-feet barrier in the Square Mile for the first time since 1979, when Tower 42 – Richard Seifert's brash, steel-lined rolling pin, originally the home of the NatWest bank – opened the field to the rush of tall buildings that followed.

Most towers have all the charisma of an upended loaf of sliced white bread. We are expected to get excited about skyscrapers simply on the basis of their height, an attribute that is supposed to make us overlook the fact that everything else about them is banal and exceptionally uninteresting. A slick skin – if you are lucky – a marble-lined lift lobby with a couple of black leather-and-chrome chairs, followed by a stack of identical floors, one on top of the other. The architecture, if there is any, is confined to a foot-deep zone around the outer wall. Norman Foster's tower is not like that. Despite its obvious phallic shape, it is more than the one-liner you might initially expect.

Foster has always been interested in subverting the conventional filing-cabinet repetitiveness of the office building. In the case of the Hong Kong and Shanghai Bank, with its exoskeleton structure and a hollowed-out interior atrium that allowed the public to swarm all over the ground beneath, he succeeded to an extent that has never been equalled. But that was a one-off, a handmade Bugatti. Swiss Re is more like a suave, polished, factory-engineered BMW. The structure is a muscular steel basket sheathed in a smooth glass skin. At the pavement, it emerges from the diamond-pattern glass to create an arcade of shops at street level. The argument against the tower during the controversy over its planning application was that it would look too dominant on the skyline. Not only would it be excessively tall, the circular plan and shape would make it even more prominent. In fact, although the gherkin is visible from long distances, it can't be seen from everywhere. As you move around the City, it slips in and out of view. Clearly this is an effect that is beyond the control of the architect. But Foster has been careful to create a civilized dialogue between the tower and its nearest neighbours. The result is an intimate new plaza, where the sun casts reflections of the diamond pattern of Foster's building over its neighbours, like tattoos or the logos on Louis Vuitton luggage. Close up, it's impossible to see the top of the tower, which curves out of sight like a balloon. Further away, especially from the east, the tower erupts over the City's fringes like a colossus, a King Kong, which, thanks to the diamond-shaped windows, looks as if it is wearing giant argyle socks. The pattern even suggests an affinity with a Tudor casement window.

As important as the layered exterior, with its dual skins of glass and opening windows designed to minimize the energy load, is the fact that the tower is not conceived as a single monolith but has been designed to function as a stack of grouped floors. Cloyingly, the architects call them villages. Each group of six floors is linked by a spiralling open atrium that twists around the building, opening up the structure and offering a sense of belonging to a wider entity than merely the floor on which you happen to be sitting. The result is a disruption of the oppressive flat ceiling that is the most universal and negative aspect of deep-plan, aircraft hangar-sized office floors.

Once, when you went up one of the few isolated towers, you were alone in the clouds. Now you find yourself up on the thirtieth floor, eyeball to eyeball with people looking back at you from the thirtieth floor on the other side of the road. The fabric of the city is being squeezed upwards, into the sky. The Swiss Re's pièce de résistance is the last two floors in the nose cone of the tower, what Foster calls 'the mountain top', and you can see what he means. The peak is a glass bubble, with 360-degree, uninterrupted views. This is, for once, an interior that justifies the word sensational. There is nothing to get in the way of an awesomely dramatic outlook. You have left the solid, dependable pavements of the City of London and climbed into the stratosphere to look down on the capital as if you were a mountaineer. Emerge from the lift doors and you are suddenly transported into Doctor Evil's lair. The view, from Windsor to the Thames estuary, is magnificent, fit for a master of the universe; the place radiates a sense of power over the human ants below. All this is too much for a Swiss insurance company so dedicated to egalitarianism that it has not a single corporate parking place in the basement. Even senior executives are expected to travel by public transport (a taxi is still a form of public transport). There is no way that the chairman of such an organization could possibly have his desk up here. As a result, this is a communal dining facility, somewhere for tenants to take their guests for a corporate lunch, to look down over Europe's financial heart – and get a glimpse of the jets taking off from Heathrow, twenty miles away, the glinting river wrapping itself around the Tate Modern, the Tower of London and Canary Wharf in a series of tight serpentine coils. And it's also a place to reflect on the paradox of a structure that seems so ordinary at street level, and so out of the ordinary up here in the clouds.

14

An Incurable Condition

Enough empires have collapsed immediately after their rulers have finished building a sumptuous capital city, ostensibly for the national good but more likely to personify and glorify their regimes, to suggest that architecture is not always a particularly effective political tool. Haussmann's brand new boulevards did not stop the Parisian mob from burning down the Tuileries in 1870 after Napoleon III's ignominious end, or the bloodshed of the Commune and the appalling violence of its suppression that followed. The Prussians may have been impressed by the splendours of Paris, yet the trappings of a superior urban civilization were not enough to deter them from their invasion of France. But without Haussmann, France would have been a different place, and a poorer and less commanding state. And the fact that Hitler did his best to have Paris destroyed in 1944 would suggest that architectural symbolism did indeed have an essential part to play in Great Power conflict.

The British left New Delhi just twenty years after Lutyens and Baker completed an imperial capital intended to last for centuries. The city looked and felt authoritative enough for India to adopt it for its own use, but evidently was not a sufficiently convincing demonstration of the superiority of European civilization to dissuade Indians from demanding their independence from the power that built it.

As demonstrated by the Shah of Iran's ill-fated attempt to rebuild Tehran as a modern Western city, and Ferdinand and Imelda Marcos's compulsion for dropping monumental concrete cubes all over Manila, architecture has on occasion actually speeded up the process of regime change. Such projects have seemed more like the follies of the advanced stages of monomania than rational development. But just because it is not always effective does not mean that the will to build is unconnected with statecraft. Military force seldom achieves its objectives either, but no historian would suggest that its disposition is irrelevant to the fate of nations, or that it is possible fully to understand history without exploring the nature of its use.

Buildings last a long time, but their political role may only be relevant at the moment of their initial creation. It is a moment of relevance that may come again in quite a different context. Britain's House of Commons meant one thing when it was built, something very different when it was destroyed by enemy action in the Second World War, and something different again in the daily grind of political life. Germany's Reichstag became the symbol of Nazi Germany's defeat when the Red Army occupied it in 1945, even though it had played no part in Hitler's regime. Half a century later, the Bonn Parliament's decision to move the seat of the reunited Germany to Berlin, and then to commission a British architect to restore the Reichstag for its new purpose, was an explicit use of architecture with a political purpose on a number of different levels. It was expressing a newfound sense of national identity. At the same time, choosing Norman Foster was a conciliatory gesture to demonstrate the continuing change in the German identity since the totalitarian years and its rejection of narrow nationalism. Foster's glass-domed roof, with its spiralling ramp open to the public, allowing the German electorate the freedom to wander over the heads of their representatives, is another deliberate signal of the regime's intentions. It is as much of a rhetorical statement about its progressive values as Foster's provision of an air-conditioning system for the parliament that does not depend on fossil fuels.

Building is not just about the practical provision of shelter, or the construction of the modern infrastructure of a state. Though it may appear to be rooted in pragmatism, it is a powerful and extraordinarily revealing expression of human psychology. It has a significance both at the largest scale and at the most personal. It is a means for inflating the individual ego to the scale of a landscape, a city, or even a nation.

It reflects the ambitions and insecurities and motivations of those who build and, because of that, it offers a faithful reflection of the nature of power, its strategies, its consolations and its impact on those who wield it.

What architecture does – as no other cultural form can – is to glorify and magnify the individual autocrat and suppress the individual into the mass. It can be seen as the first, and still one of the most powerful, forms of mass communication. That is why it has flourished under so many autocratic political systems. And it is why it has a way of appealing to powerful individuals looking to make their mark. It has both an intellectual and a material impact.

It's hardly possible to find a single twentieth-century autocrat who achieved power who didn't embark on a campaign of building – from Hitler and Mussolini, to Stalin, Mao, Saddam Hussein and Kim Il Sung. Indeed it has been argued that, for Hitler, architecture was not simply a tool for the creation of the Nazi regime, but that he saw things the other way around. For Hitler, establishing the Nazi regime was as much a means for realizing his architectural ambitions.

That closeness between totalitarianism and architecture is what gives monumental building the sinister undertone that George Orwell was thinking of in the essay that he wrote about politics and culture shortly before his death. Orwell suggested that, while poetry might survive in a totalitarian age and that 'certain arts or half arts, such as architecture might even find tyranny beneficial', the prose writer 'would have no choice between silence and death'. It is the sardonic observation of one of the keenest literary intelligences that Britain has produced. From the first, Orwell had understood the nature of Stalinism, its determination to co-opt cultural life as an essential part of its strategy for maintaining its grip on power, and its corruption of everything and everyone it touched. The cultural elite, provided they played their parts as expected in the apparatus of the State, were loaded with honours and privileges. And even the dissidents were persecuted rather than ignored, a situation that the intelligentsia of the West has always quietly envied.

Orwell had seen the images of Stalin's buildings, and had understood the monuments of Hitler's Germany for what they actually were. Despite the lordly disdain of the prose writer for the architect, his was an acidly perceptive view, and one that should shape an understanding of architecture as it is practised – not just by the hacks ready to blow with any political wind, or the reactionary and the deluded, but also what might be called the practitioners of high architecture. Le Corbusier and Mies van der Rohe, or Rem Koolhaas or Renzo Piano, Wallace Harrison or Frank Gehry, are not free agents. Their work depends on their engagement with the political context of the world. And in that world the totalitarians and the egotists and the monomaniacs have, on past form, suggested that they will offer architects, whatever their personal political views, more opportunities for work than the liberal democracies. It has been strongly centralized states, such as Mitterrand's France, or outright dictatorships such as the Shah's Iran, that have been a more typical model of architectural patronage than the liberal regimes with their typical policies of benign neglect. Post-Franco Barcelona and the Netherlands of the 1990s can be seen as atypical exceptions, following in the tradition of small states that have used modernism as an architectural language to demonstrate their visibility, or to make a break with an unhappy past.

On one level, architecture never changes. Despite the veneer of the contemporary, architecture is intimately concerned with the primal issues confronting us in our attempts to come to terms with who we are, and where we are, and what life is. Architecture is constantly about the same things: power, glory, spectacle, memory, identity. And yet it always changes. The processes, the materials, the timescales that shape building have shifted. No one can co-opt a particular architectural language for ever.

Architects have given up trying to persuade us that buildings have the power to make our lives better or worse. Of course architecture can do that, in the sense that leaking roofs make us wet, and weathertight ones keep us warm, but that is not what interests most architects. And perhaps that is why architects are now so keen to pose as artists, liberating themselves from the alibi of function. Architecture does trigger emotional responses at a personal level, as well as for a society at large. It reflects our vanities and our aspirations, our weaknesses and our ambitions, and our complexes.

An understanding of what it is that motivates us to build, and the nature of the elusive relationship between architecture and power, is a key insight into our existence and can allow us to free ourselves from its most pernicious aspects.

Architecture exerts an abiding fascination on the most egotistical of individuals, desperate to use it to glorify themselves – the billionaire museum trustees, the skyscraper builders and the mansion owners. Equally, it can be put to work by reforming mayors looking to transform their cities for the better. Whatever the architect's intentions, in the end they find themselves being defined not by their own rhetoric, but by the impulses that have driven the rich and the powerful to employ architects, and to seek to shape the world.

Sources

Dawn Ades, Tim Benton, David Elliott and Iain Boyd Whyte: *Art and Power: Europe under the Dictators 1930–45*, London, 1996

Michael Thad Allen: *The Business of Genocide: The SS, Slave Labour and the Concentration Camps*, New York, 2002

Anders Aman: *Architecture and Ideology in Eastern Europe during the Stalin Era: An Aspect of Cold War History*, Cambridge and London, 1992

Berthet Pochy: *Interior Design*, London, 1994

Richard Bosworth: *Mussolini*, London, 2002

Gordon Bunshaft: interview for Chicago Oral History Project, April 1989, online at www.artic.edu/aic/libraries/caohp/bunshaft

Robert Caro: *The Power Broker: Robert Moses and the Fall of New York*, New York, 1975

Jean Louis Cohen: *Le Corbusier and the Mystique of the USSR: Theories and Projects for Moscow 1928–36*, Princeton, 1992

Timothy J. Colton: *Moscow: Governing the Socialist Metropolis*, Cambridge and London, 1995

Eric Darton: *Divided We Stand: A Biography of New York's World Trade Center*, New York, 1999

Philip Davies: *Splendours of the Raj: British India 1660–1947*, London 1985

Nicholas Farrell: *Mussolini: A New Life*, London 2003

Joachim Fest: *Speer: The Final Verdict*, New York, 2002

Robert Fitch: *The Assassination of New York*, New York, 1993

Valerie Fraser: *Building the New World: Studies in the Modern Architecture of Latin America*, London, 2000

Paul Goldberger: *Up from Zero: Politics, Architecture and the Rebuilding of New York*, New York, 2004

Thomas S. Hines: *Richard Neutra and the Search for Modern Architecture*, Oxford, 1982

Adolf Hitler: *Mein Kampf* (trans. Ralph Manhein), New York, 1999

Eric Hobsbawm and Terence Ranger (eds.): *The Invention of Tradition*, Cambridge, 1983

Elaine S. Hochman: *Architects of Fortune: Mies van der Rohe and the Third Reich*, New York, 1990

Elaine S. Hochman: *Bauhaus: Crucible of Modernism*, New York, 1997

Robert Hughes: 'Of Gods and Monsters', *Guardian*, 1 February 2003

Charles Jencks: *Le Corbusier and the Tragic View of Architecture*, London, 1973

Lindsay Jones: *The Hermeneutics of Sacred Architecture*, Cambridge, 2000

Patrick Kinross: *Ataturk: The Rebirth of a Nation*, London, 1993

Brian Ladd: *The Ghosts of Berlin: Confronting German History in the Urban Landscape*, London and Chicago, 1998

Barbara Lane: *Architecture and Politics in Germany 1918–45*, Cambridge, 1985

Lars Olof Larsson: *Albert Speer: Le Plan de Berlin 1937–1943*, Brussels, 1983

Mark Leonard: interview with Rem Koolhaas, *Financial Times*, 6 March 2004

Simon Leys: *Broken Images: Essays on Chinese Culture and Politics*, London, 1979

Simon Leys: *The Emperor's New Clothes: Mao and the Cultural Revolution*, London, 1977

Kanan Makiya: *The Monument: Art and Vulgarity in Saddam Hussein's Iraq*, New York, 2002

Simon Sebag Montefiore: *Stalin: The Court of the Red Tsar*, London, 2004

Victoria Newhouse: *Wallace K. Harrison, Architect*, New York, 1989

Philip Nobel: *Sixteen Acres: The Rebuilding of the World Trade Center Site*, London, 2005

Farah Pahlavi: *An Enduring Love: My Life with the Shah*, New York, 2004

J. Fiona Ragheb (ed.): *Frank Gehry, Architect*, New York, 2001

Jane Ridley: *The Architect and His Wife: A life of Edwin Lutyens*, London, 2002

Peter G. Rowe: *Seng Kuan: Architectural Encounters with Essence and Form in Modern China*, London, 2002

Antonella Russo: *Il Fascismo in mostra*, Rome, 1992

Harrison Salisbury: *The New Emperors: Mao and Deng, a Dual Biography*, London 1992

Sandro Scarrocchia: *Albert Speer e Marcello Piacentini: L'Architettura del totalitarismo negli anni trenta*, Milan, 1999

Matthias Schmidt: *Albert Speer: The End of a Myth*, New York, 1984

Robert H. Schuller: *My Journey*, New York, 2001

Franz Schulze: *Philip Johnson: Life and Work*, New York, 1996

Franz Schulze: *Mies: A Critical Biography*, Chicago and London, 1985

Alex Scoobie: *Hitler's State Architecture: The Impact of Classical Antiquity*, London, 1990

Gitta Sereny: *Albert Speer: His Battle with Truth*, London, 1995

William L. Shirer: *Berlin Diaries, 1934–41*, New York, 1941

Philip Short: *Mao: A Life*, London, 1990

David Spaeth: *Mies van der Rohe*, New York, 1985

Albert Speer: *Inside the Third Reich*, New York, 1970

Frederic Spotts: *Hitler and the Power of Aesthetics*, London, 2003

Deyan Sudjic and Helen Jones: *Architecture and Democracy*, Glasgow, 1999

Robert R. Taylor: *The Word in Stone: The Role of Architecture in the National Socialist Ideology*, Berkeley and London, 1974

Lawrence Vale: *Architecture, Power and National Identity*, New Haven, 1992

Michael Z. Wise: *Capital Dilemma*, New York, 1998

Carter Wiseman: *The Architecture of I. M. Pei*, London, 1990

Minoru Yamasaki: *A Life in Architecture*, New York, 1979

Index